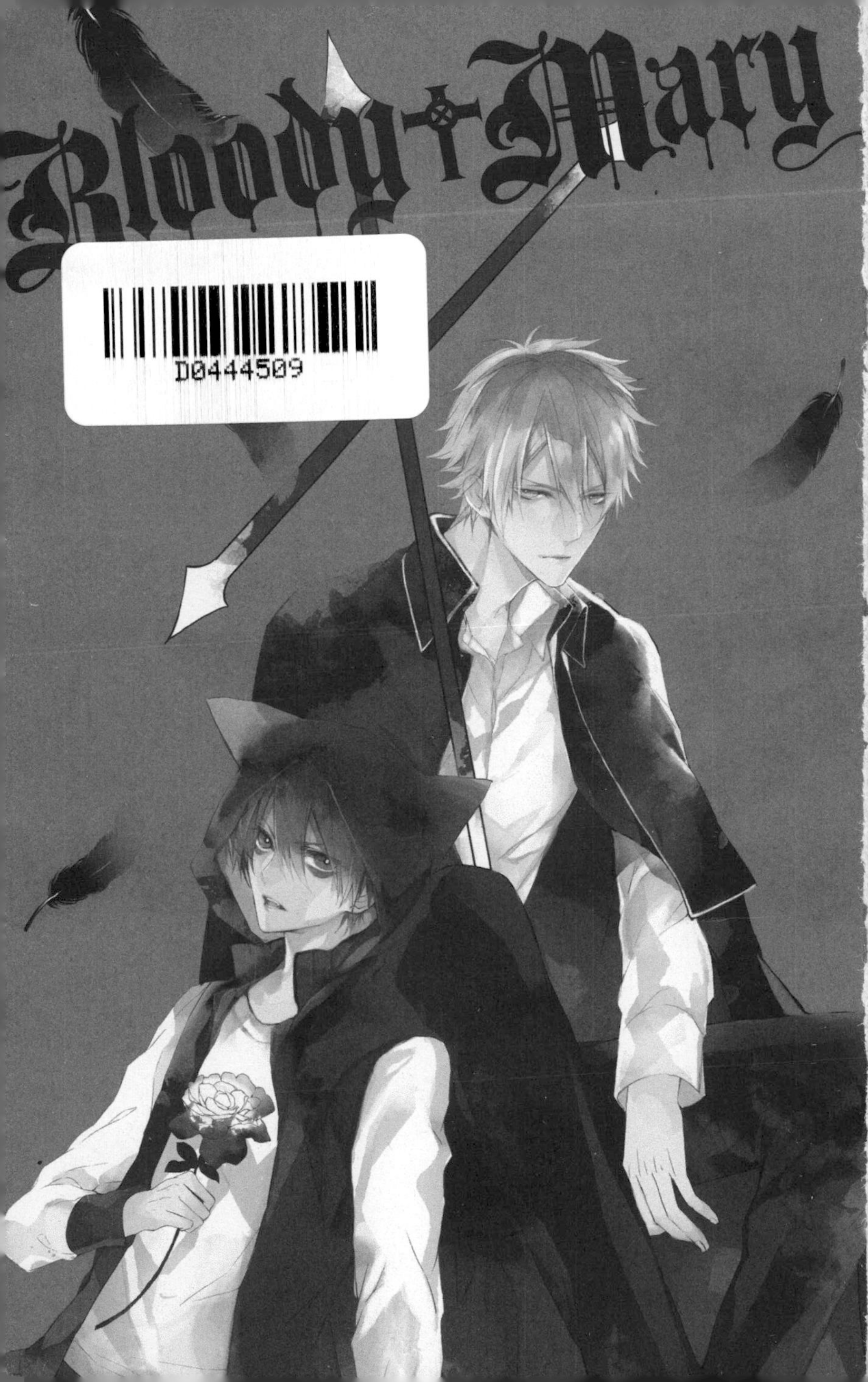
Bloody+Mary

Bloody † Mary

② contents

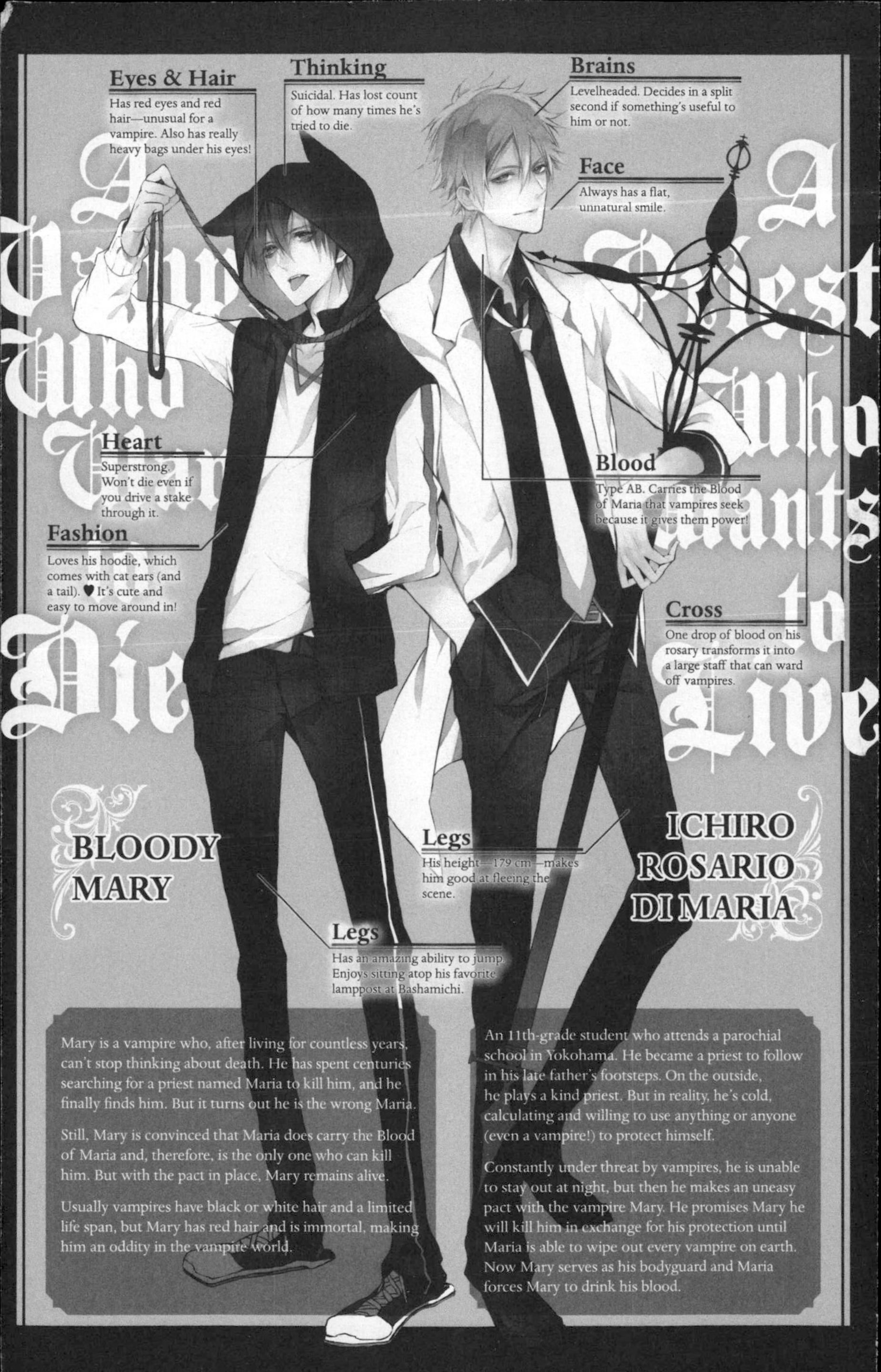
Eyes & Hair
Has red eyes and red hair—unusual for a vampire. Also has really heavy bags under his eyes!
Thinking
Suicidal. Has lost count of how many times he's tried to die.
Brains
Levelheaded. Decides in a split second if something's useful to him or not.
Face
Always has a flat, unnatural smile.
Heart
Superstrong. Won't die even if you drive a stake through it.
Blood
Type AB. Carries the Blood of Maria that vampires seek because it gives them power!
Fashion
Loves his hoodie, which comes with cat ears (and a tail). ♥ It's cute and easy to move around in!
Cross
One drop of blood on his rosary transforms it into a large staff that can ward off vampires.
BLOODY MARY
Legs
His height—179 cm—makes him good at fleeing the scene.
ICHIRO ROSARIO DI MARIA
Legs
Has an amazing ability to jump. Enjoys sitting atop his favorite lamppost at Bashamichi.
Mary is a vampire who, after living for countless years, can't stop thinking about death. He has spent centuries searching for a priest named Maria to kill him, and he finally finds him. But it turns out he is the wrong Maria.
Still, Mary is convinced that Maria does carry the Blood of Maria and, therefore, is the only one who can kill him. But with the pact in place, Mary remains alive.
Usually vampires have black or white hair and a limited life span, but Mary has red hair and is immortal, making him an oddity in the vampire world.
An 11th-grade student who attends a parochial school in Yokohama. He became a priest to follow in his late father's footsteps. On the outside, he plays a kind priest. But in reality, he's cold, calculating and willing to use anything or anyone (even a vampire!) to protect himself.
Constantly under threat by vampires, he is unable to stay out at night, but then he makes an uneasy pact with the vampire Mary. He promises Mary he will kill him in exchange for his protection until Maria is able to wipe out every vampire on earth. Now Mary serves as his bodyguard and Maria forces Mary to drink his blood.

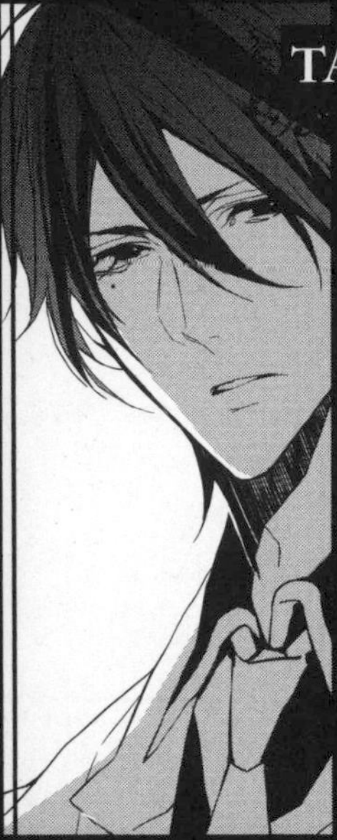

TAKUMI SAKURABA

The student council president of the school that Maria attends. The Sakuraba family is an extremely influential family that controls much of Japan from behind the scenes and has conducted vampire research for generations. The di Maria family has fringe connections with the Sakurabas.

He grew up with Maria and thinks of him as his little brother.

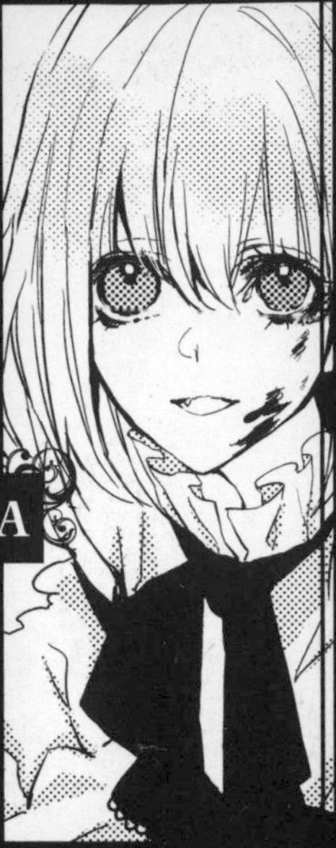

HYDRA

A young-looking female vampire (who's actually older than Mary) who appears at Maria's church steps. She seems to be an acquaintance of Mary, but he has no recollection of her. She also carries a grudge against Mary.

Story of Bloody Mary

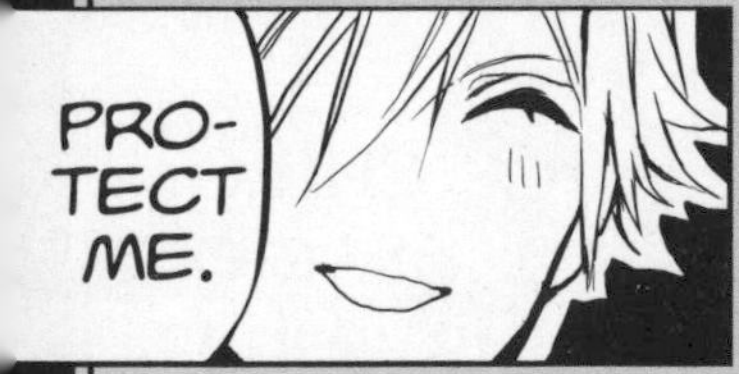
PRO-
TECT
ME.

Mary, an immortal vampire who wants to die, has been searching for hundreds of years for an exorcist who carries the Blood of Maria, which gives the exorcist the ability to kill vampires. After thinking he's finally found him, it turns out that it's the wrong Maria! However, Maria does carry the Blood of Maria, which is made evident by the nonstop vampire assaults. Mary wants nothing more than for Maria to kill him, but Maria puts into place a pact wherein he will only kill Mary in exchange for Mary's protection until the threat of vampires is extinguished.

\+ +

Now Mary lives at the church with Maria, despite a protective barrier that usually prevents vampires from entering the church. Mary's unusual ability to penetrate the barrier leads Maria to do some research on him, and he learns that Mary is an anomaly among vampires.

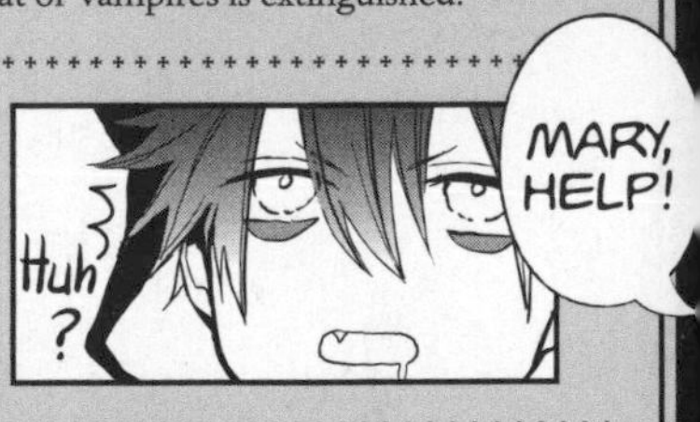
MARY,
HELP!
Huh
?

\+ +

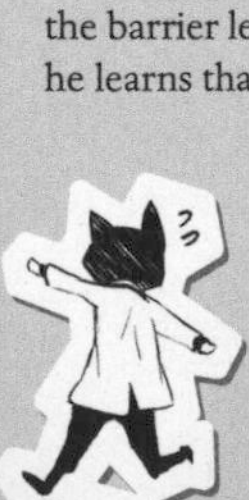

And although Maria already knew that he had the ability to use his rosary to ward off vampires, it turns out the Sakuraba family was purposefully hiding that fact.

Meanwhile, Takumi ventures deep into the Sakuraba estate and meets a man who looks exactly like Maria...

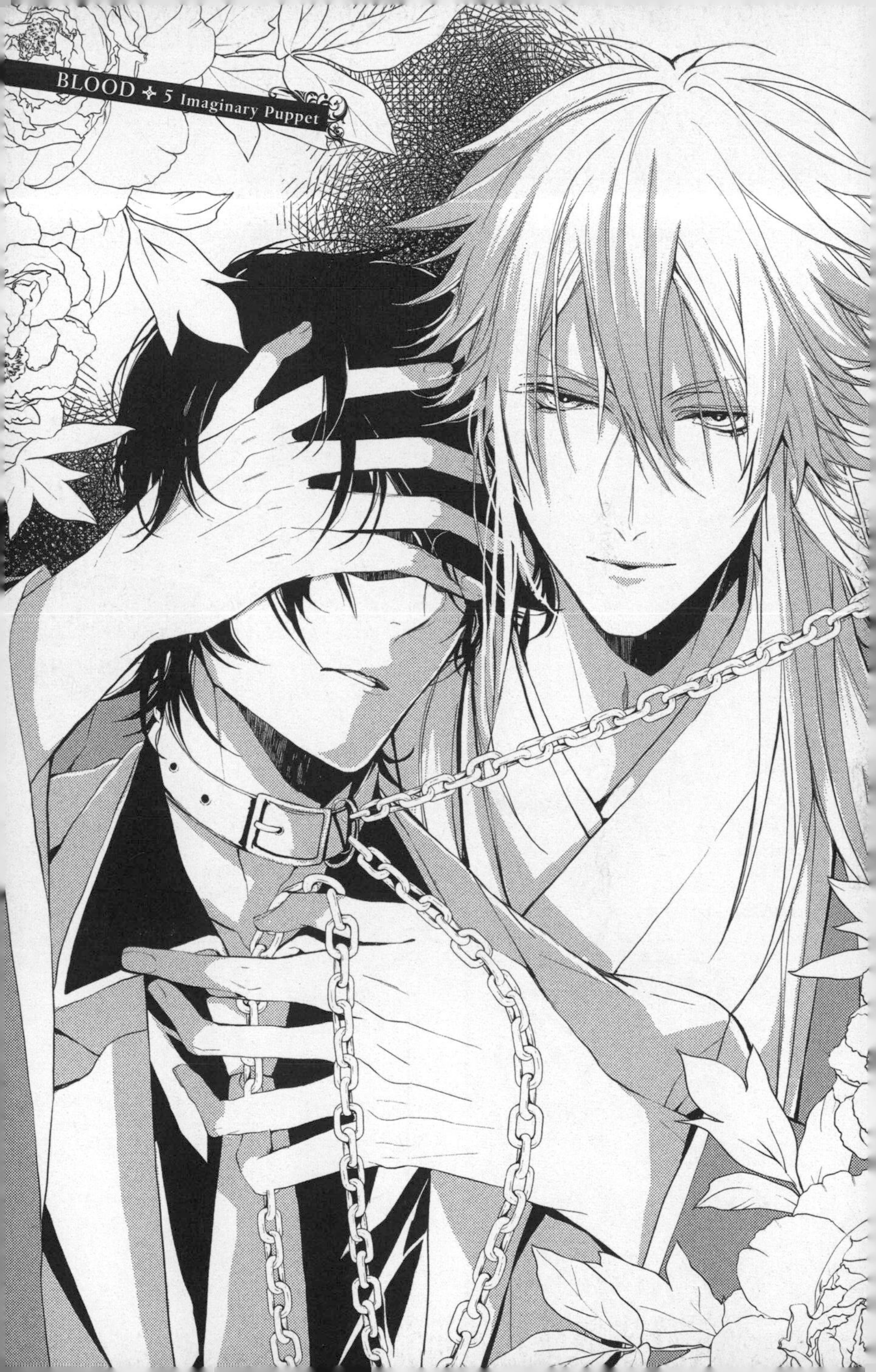
BLOOD ✦ 5 Imaginary Puppet

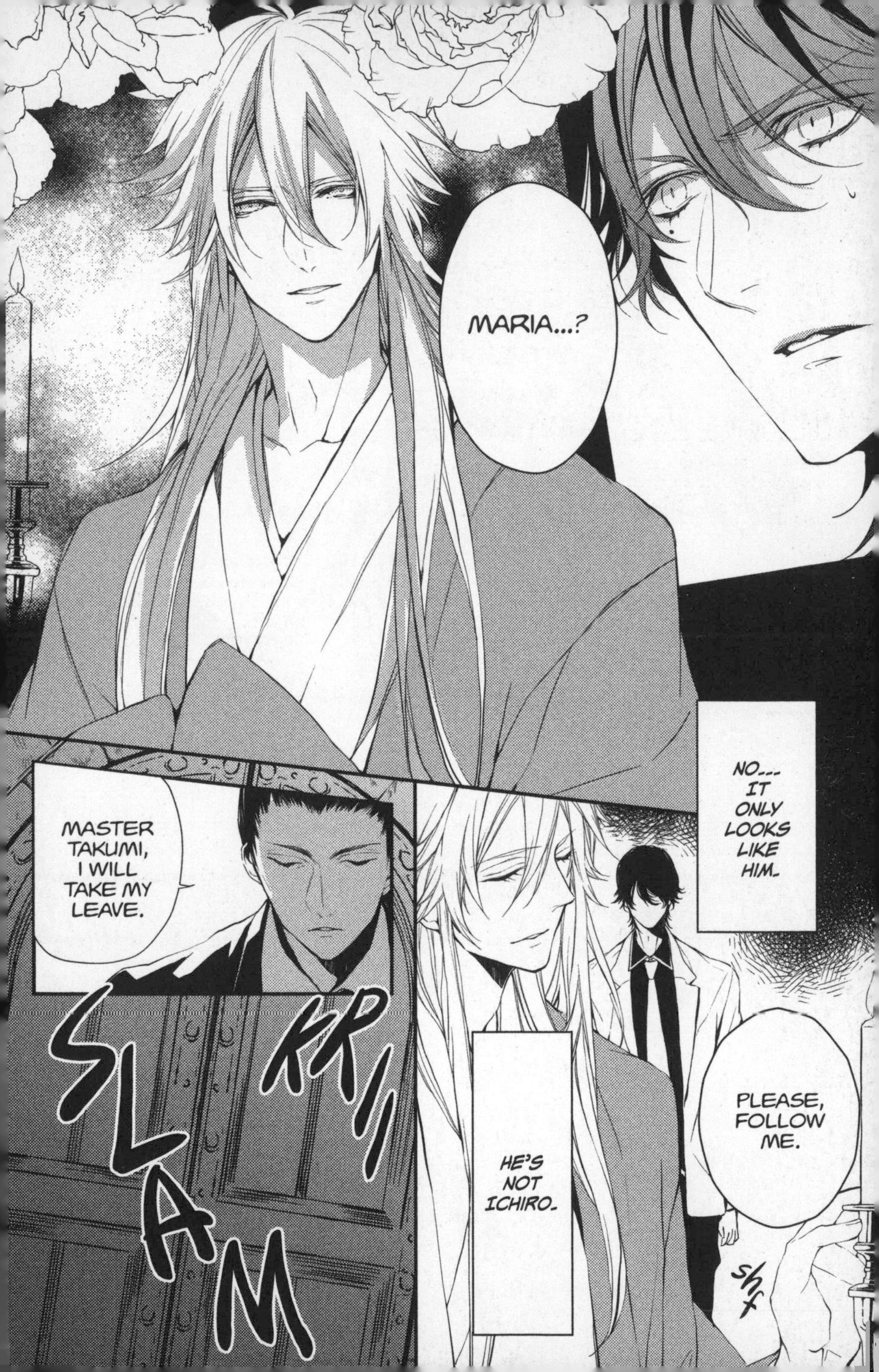
MARIA...?
NO... IT ONLY LOOKS LIKE HIM.
PLEASE, FOLLOW ME.
HE'S NOT ICHIRO.
shf
MASTER TAKUMI, I WILL TAKE MY LEAVE.
KRII
SLAM

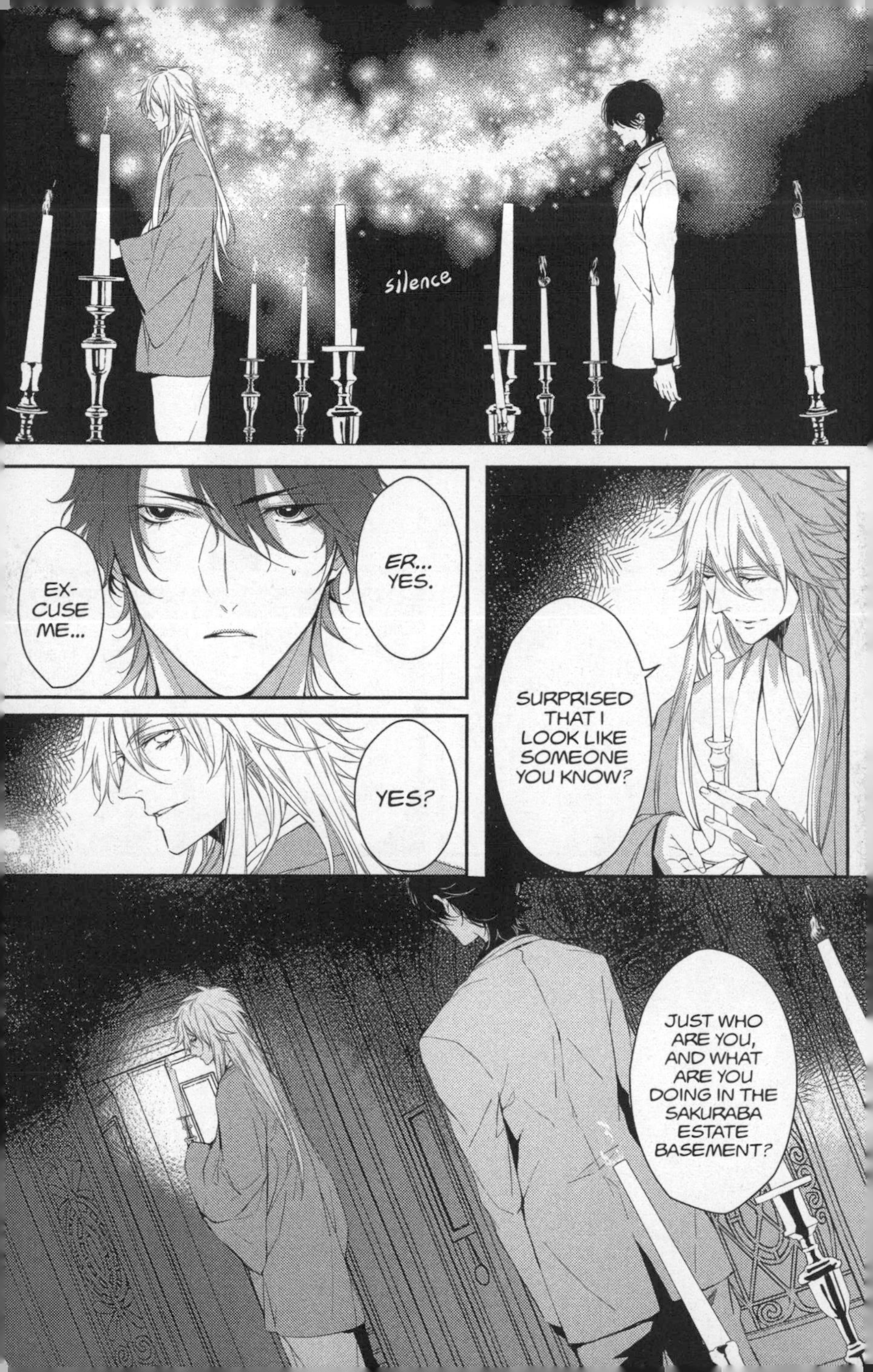
silence
SURPRISED THAT I LOOK LIKE SOMEONE YOU KNOW?
ER... YES.
EX-CUSE ME...
YES?
JUST WHO ARE YOU, AND WHAT ARE YOU DOING IN THE SAKURABA ESTATE BASEMENT?

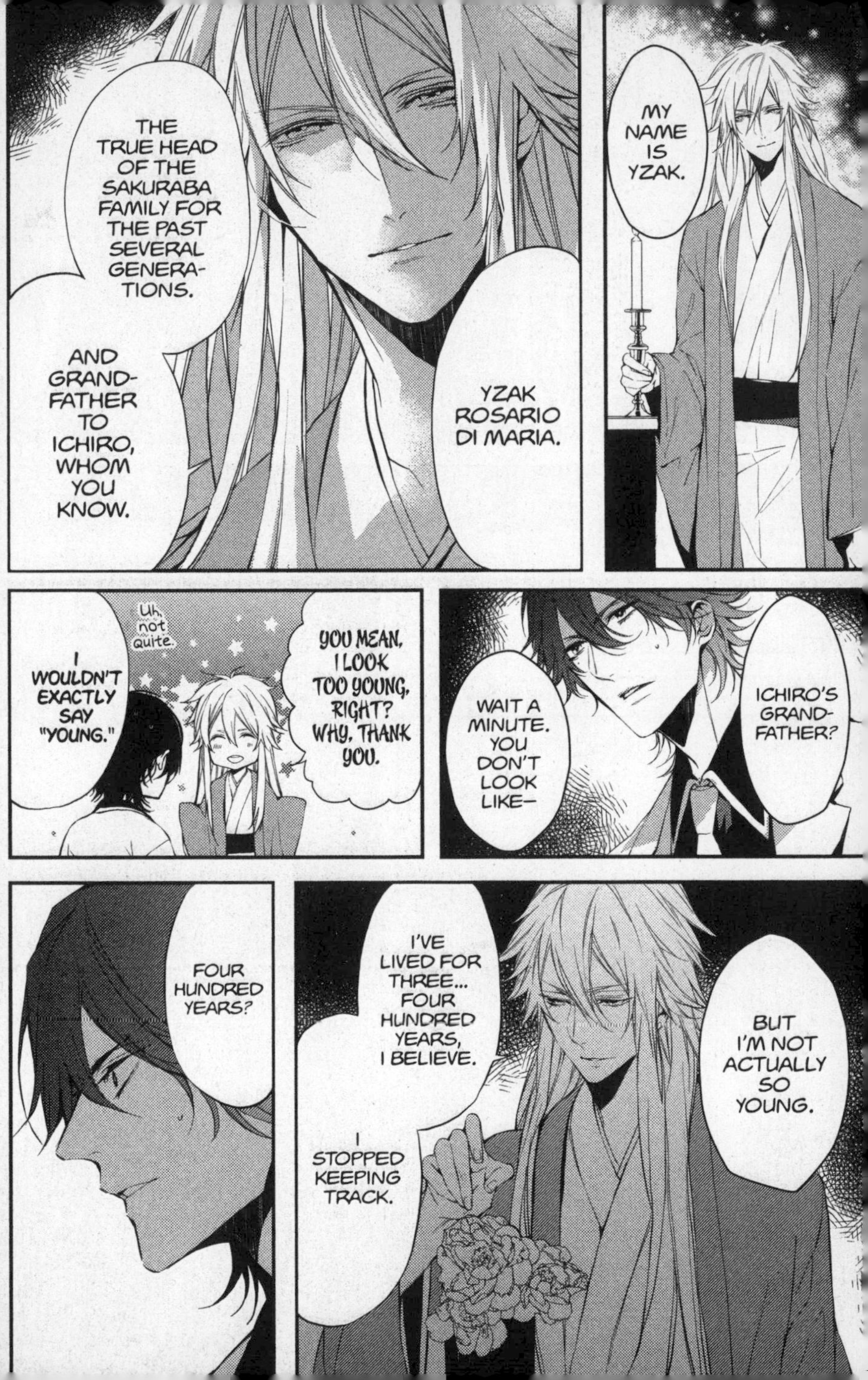
MY NAME IS YZAK.
YZAK ROSARIO DI MARIA.
THE TRUE HEAD OF THE SAKURABA FAMILY FOR THE PAST SEVERAL GENERATIONS.
AND GRANDFATHER TO ICHIRO, WHOM YOU KNOW.
ICHIRO'S GRANDFATHER?
WAIT A MINUTE. YOU DON'T LOOK LIKE—
YOU MEAN, I LOOK TOO YOUNG, RIGHT? WHY, THANK YOU.
Uh, not quite.
I WOULDN'T EXACTLY SAY "YOUNG."
BUT I'M NOT ACTUALLY SO YOUNG.
I'VE LIVED FOR THREE... FOUR HUNDRED YEARS, I BELIEVE.
I STOPPED KEEPING TRACK.
FOUR HUNDRED YEARS?

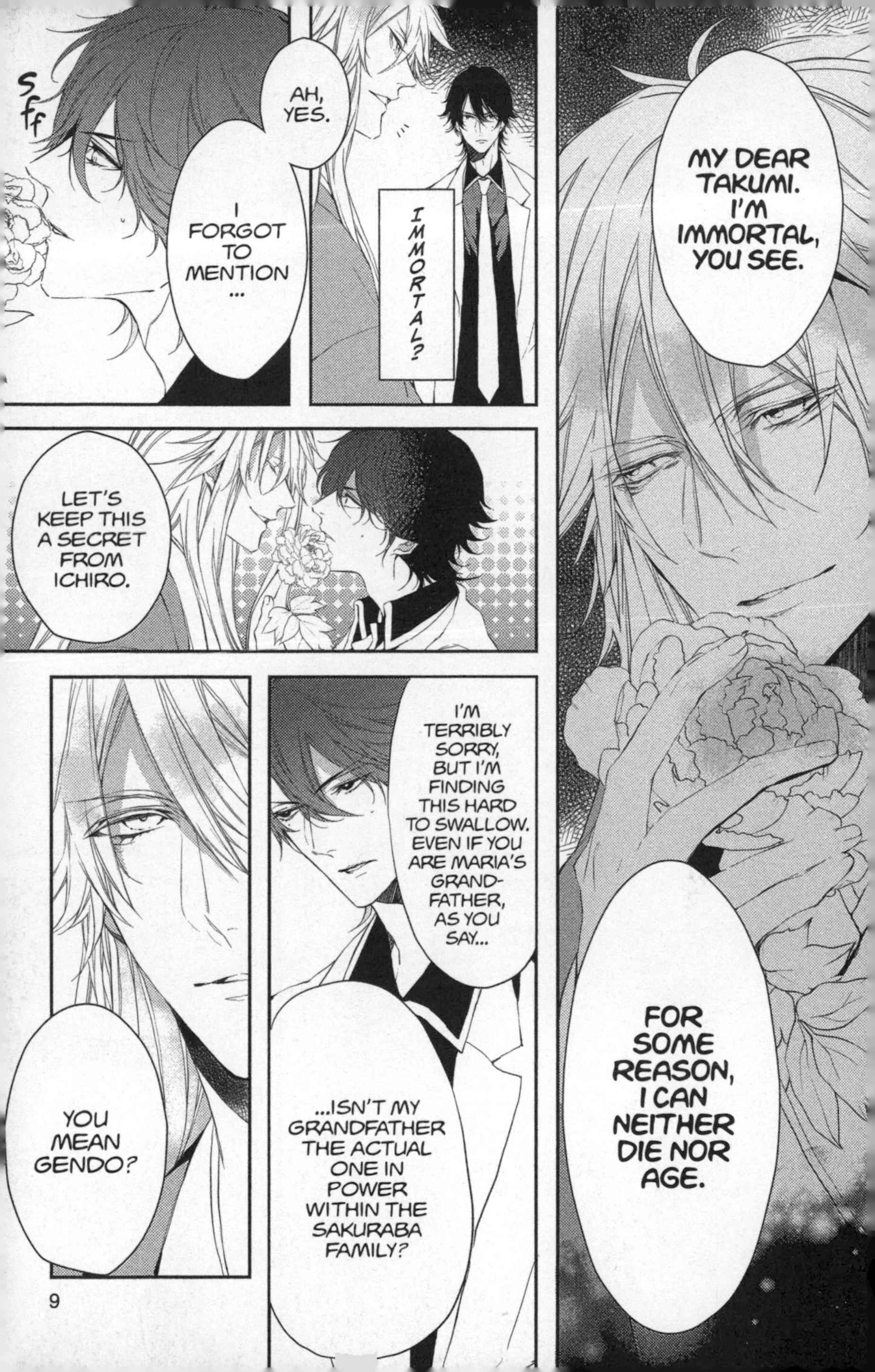
MY DEAR TAKUMI. I'M IMMORTAL, YOU SEE.
FOR SOME REASON, I CAN NEITHER DIE NOR AGE.
IMMORTAL?
AH, YES.
I FORGOT TO MENTION...
Sff
LET'S KEEP THIS A SECRET FROM ICHIRO.
I'M TERRIBLY SORRY, BUT I'M FINDING THIS HARD TO SWALLOW. EVEN IF YOU ARE MARIA'S GRANDFATHER, AS YOU SAY...
...ISN'T MY GRANDFATHER THE ACTUAL ONE IN POWER WITHIN THE SAKURABA FAMILY?
YOU MEAN GENDO?

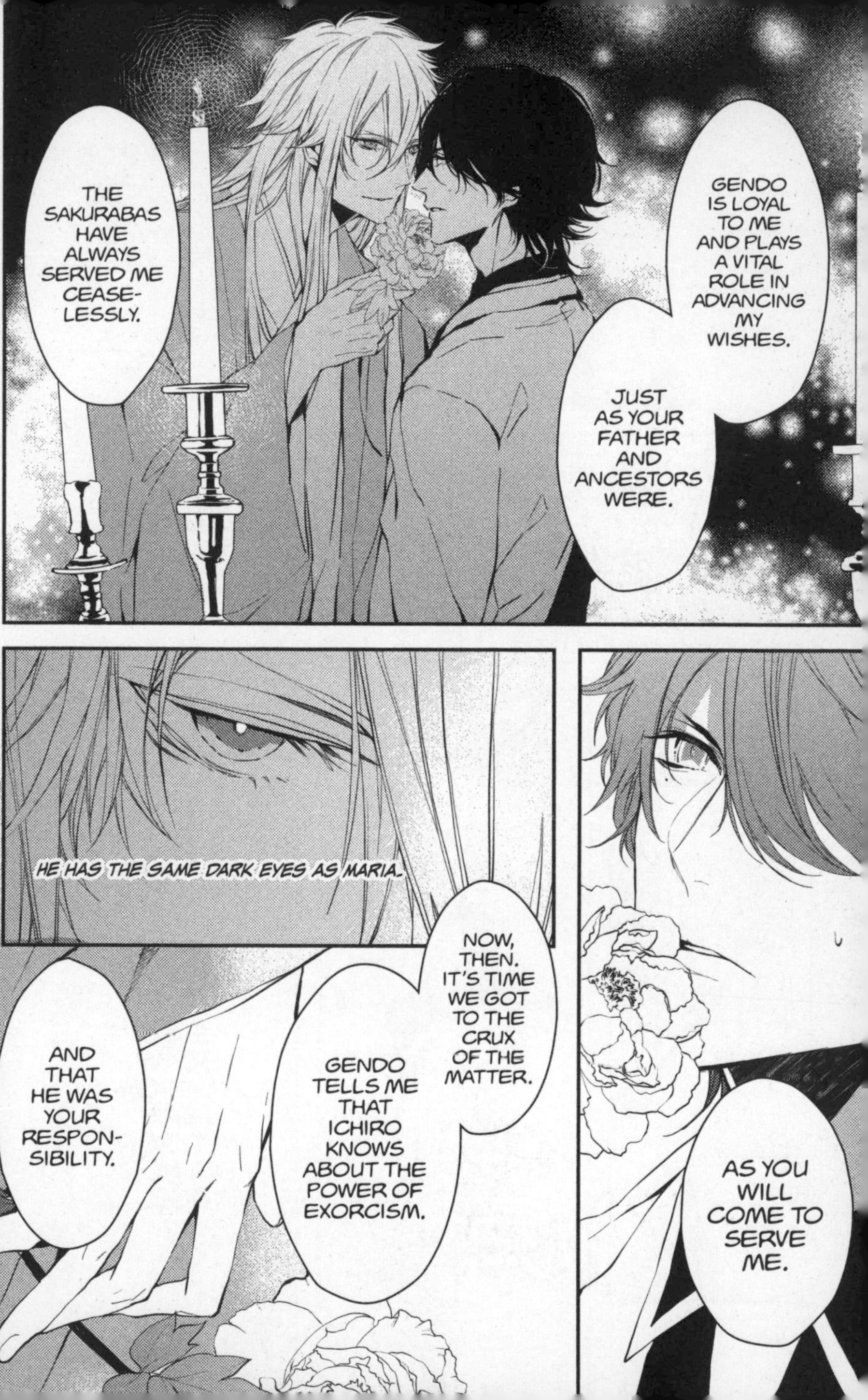
GENDO IS LOYAL TO ME AND PLAYS A VITAL ROLE IN ADVANCING MY WISHES.
JUST AS YOUR FATHER AND ANCESTORS WERE.
THE SAKURABAS HAVE ALWAYS SERVED ME CEASE-LESSLY.
AS YOU WILL COME TO SERVE ME.
HE HAS THE SAME DARK EYES AS MARIA.
NOW, THEN. IT'S TIME WE GOT TO THE CRUX OF THE MATTER.
GENDO TELLS ME THAT ICHIRO KNOWS ABOUT THE POWER OF EXORCISM.
AND THAT HE WAS YOUR RESPON-SIBILITY.

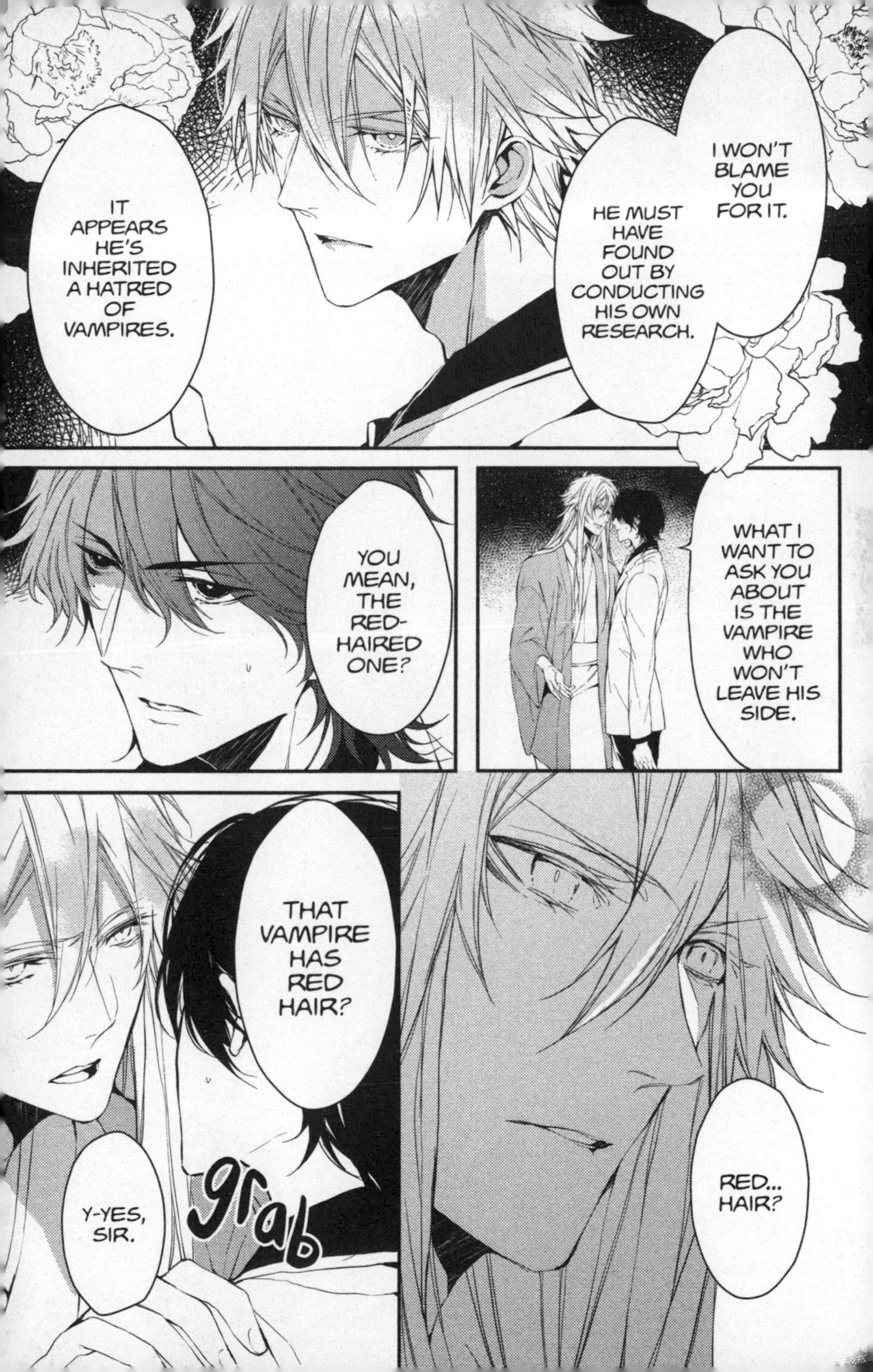
I WON'T BLAME YOU FOR IT.
HE MUST HAVE FOUND OUT BY CONDUCTING HIS OWN RESEARCH.
IT APPEARS HE'S INHERITED A HATRED OF VAMPIRES.
WHAT I WANT TO ASK YOU ABOUT IS THE VAMPIRE WHO WON'T LEAVE HIS SIDE.
YOU MEAN, THE RED-HAIRED ONE?
RED... HAIR?
THAT VAMPIRE HAS RED HAIR?
grab
Y-YES, SIR.

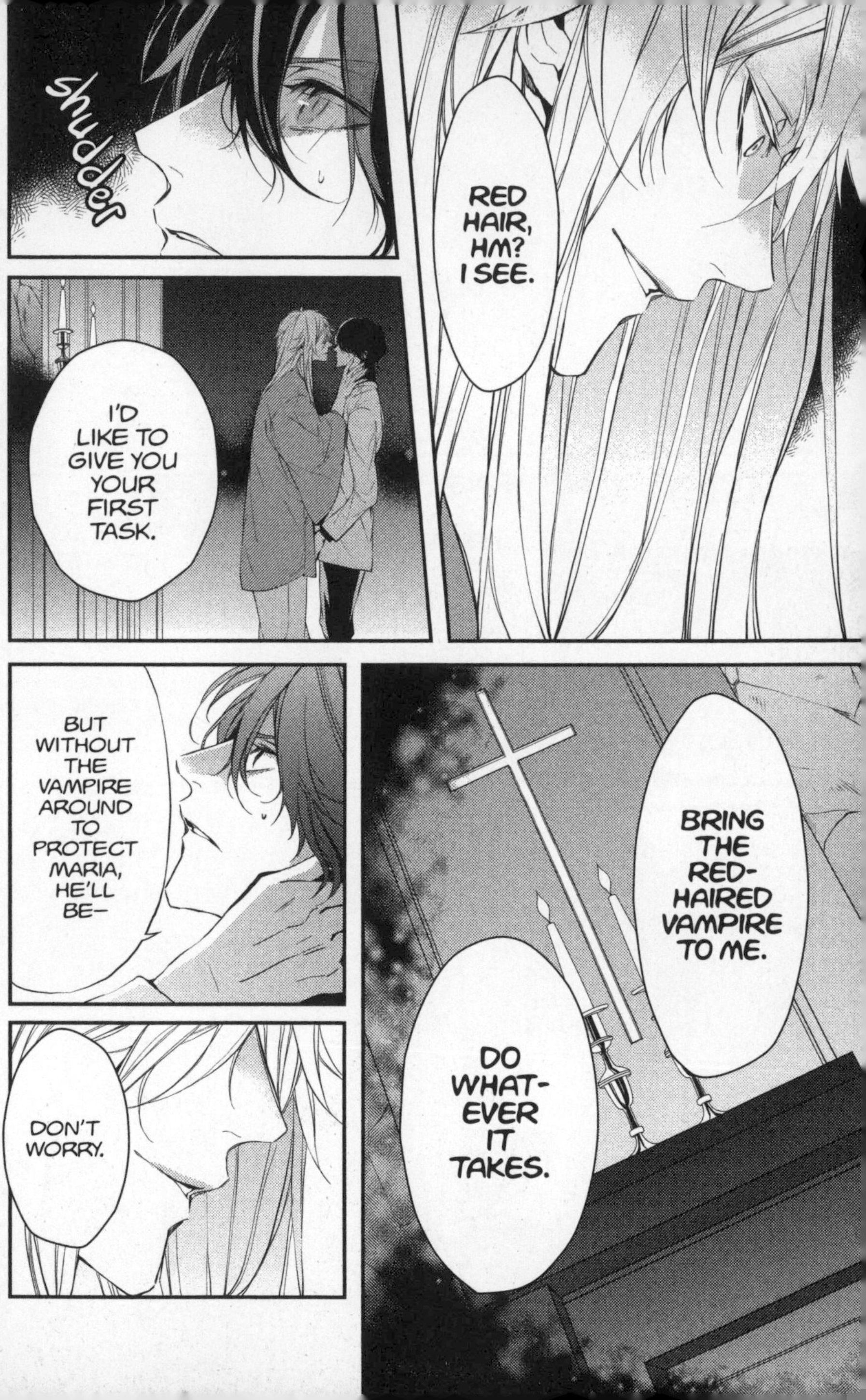
RED HAIR, HM? I SEE.
shudder
I'D LIKE TO GIVE YOU YOUR FIRST TASK.
BRING THE RED-HAIRED VAMPIRE TO ME.
DO WHATEVER IT TAKES.
BUT WITHOUT THE VAMPIRE AROUND TO PROTECT MARIA, HE'LL BE—
DON'T WORRY.

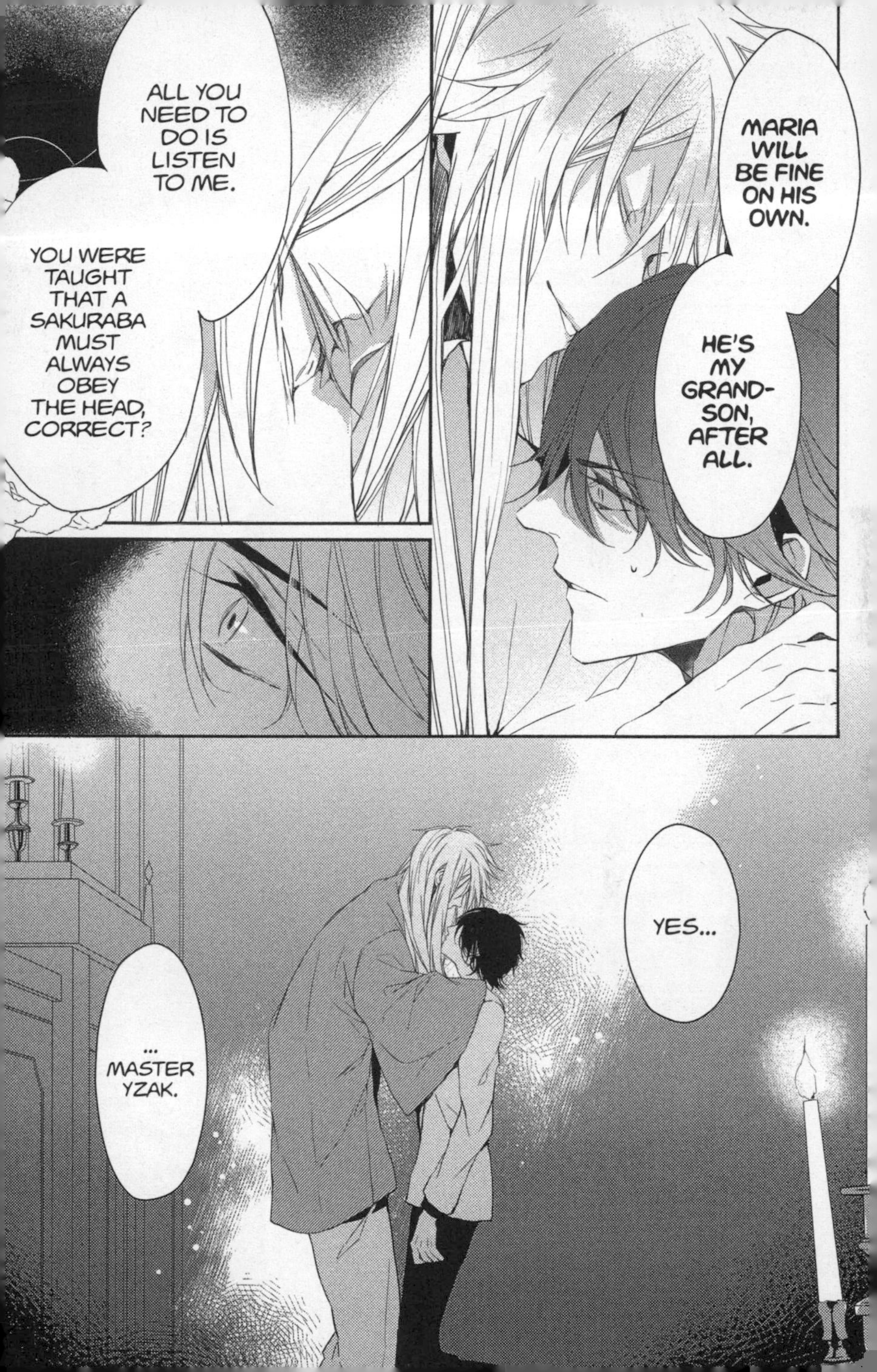
MARIA WILL BE FINE ON HIS OWN.
HE'S MY GRANDSON, AFTER ALL.
ALL YOU NEED TO DO IS LISTEN TO ME.
YOU WERE TAUGHT THAT A SAKURABA MUST ALWAYS OBEY THE HEAD, CORRECT?
YES...
... MASTER YZAK.

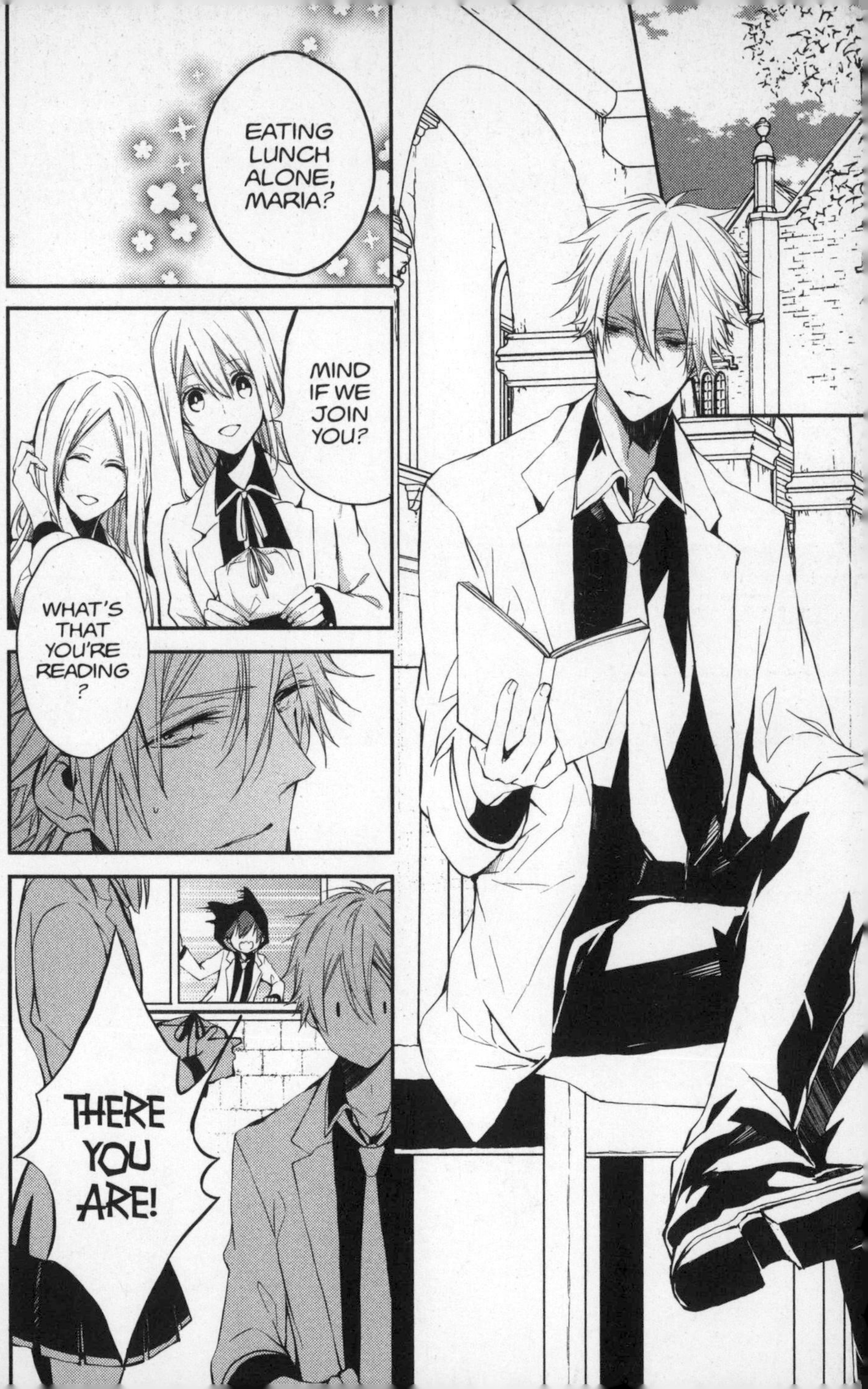
EATING LUNCH ALONE, MARIA?
MIND IF WE JOIN YOU?
WHAT'S THAT YOU'RE READING?
THERE YOU ARE!

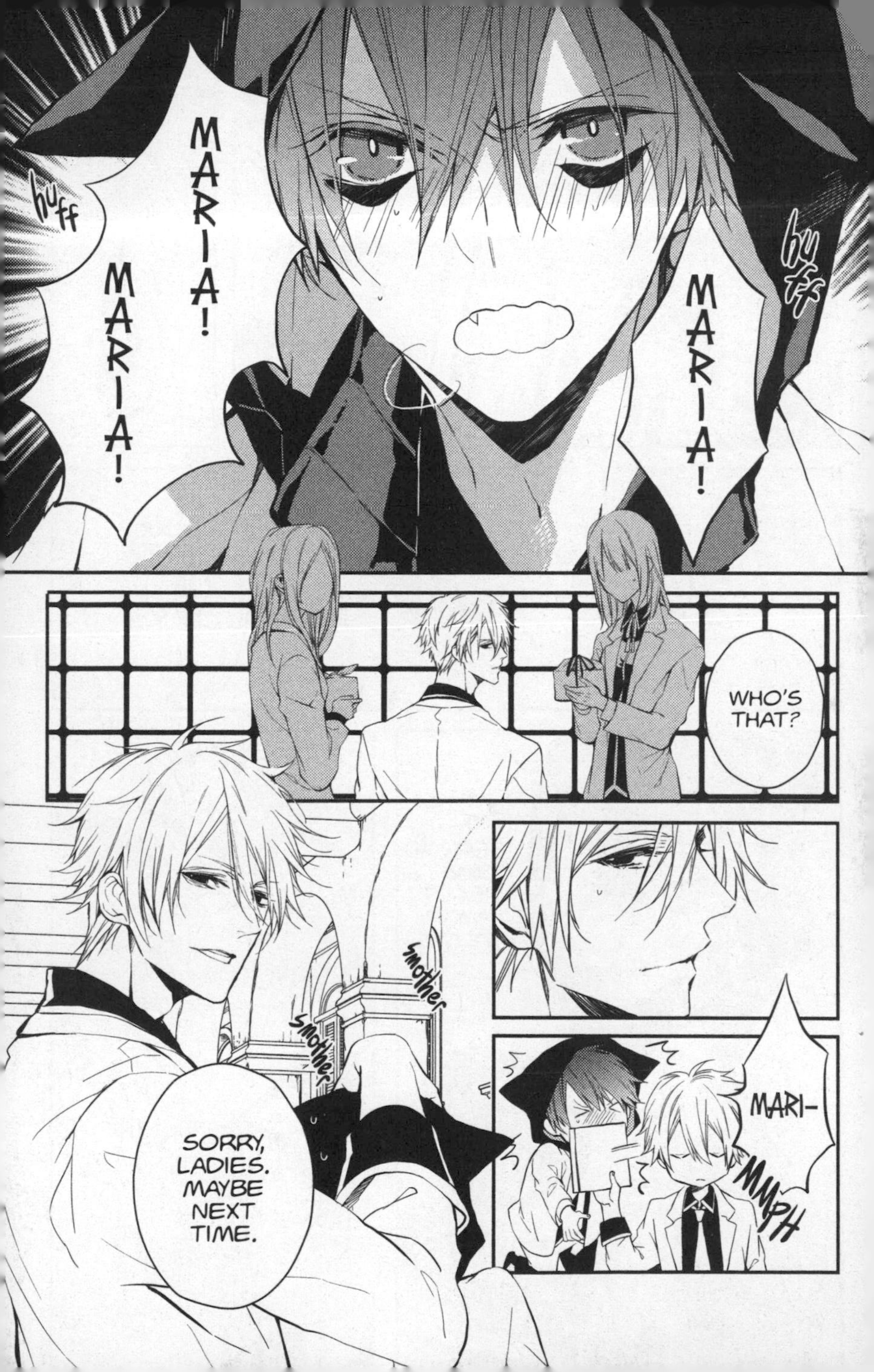
huff
MARIA!
MARIA! MARIA!
huff
WHO'S THAT?
MARI-
MMPH
smother
smother
SORRY, LADIES. MAYBE NEXT TIME.

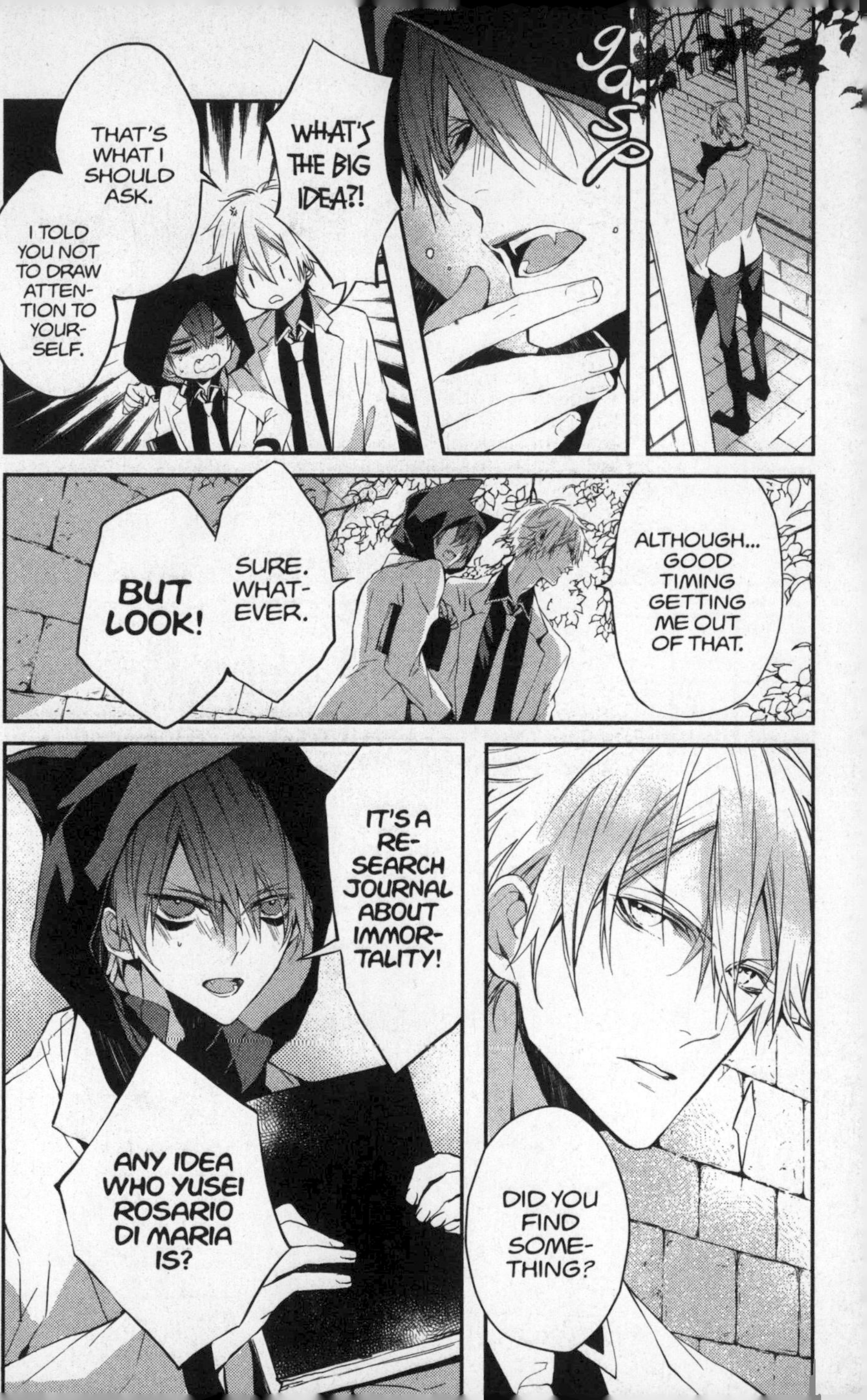
gasp
WHAT'S THE BIG IDEA?!
THAT'S WHAT I SHOULD ASK.
I TOLD YOU NOT TO DRAW ATTENTION TO YOURSELF.
ALTHOUGH... GOOD TIMING GETTING ME OUT OF THAT.
SURE. WHATEVER.
BUT LOOK!
DID YOU FIND SOMETHING?
IT'S A RESEARCH JOURNAL ABOUT IMMORTALITY!
ANY IDEA WHO YUSEI ROSARIO DI MARIA IS?

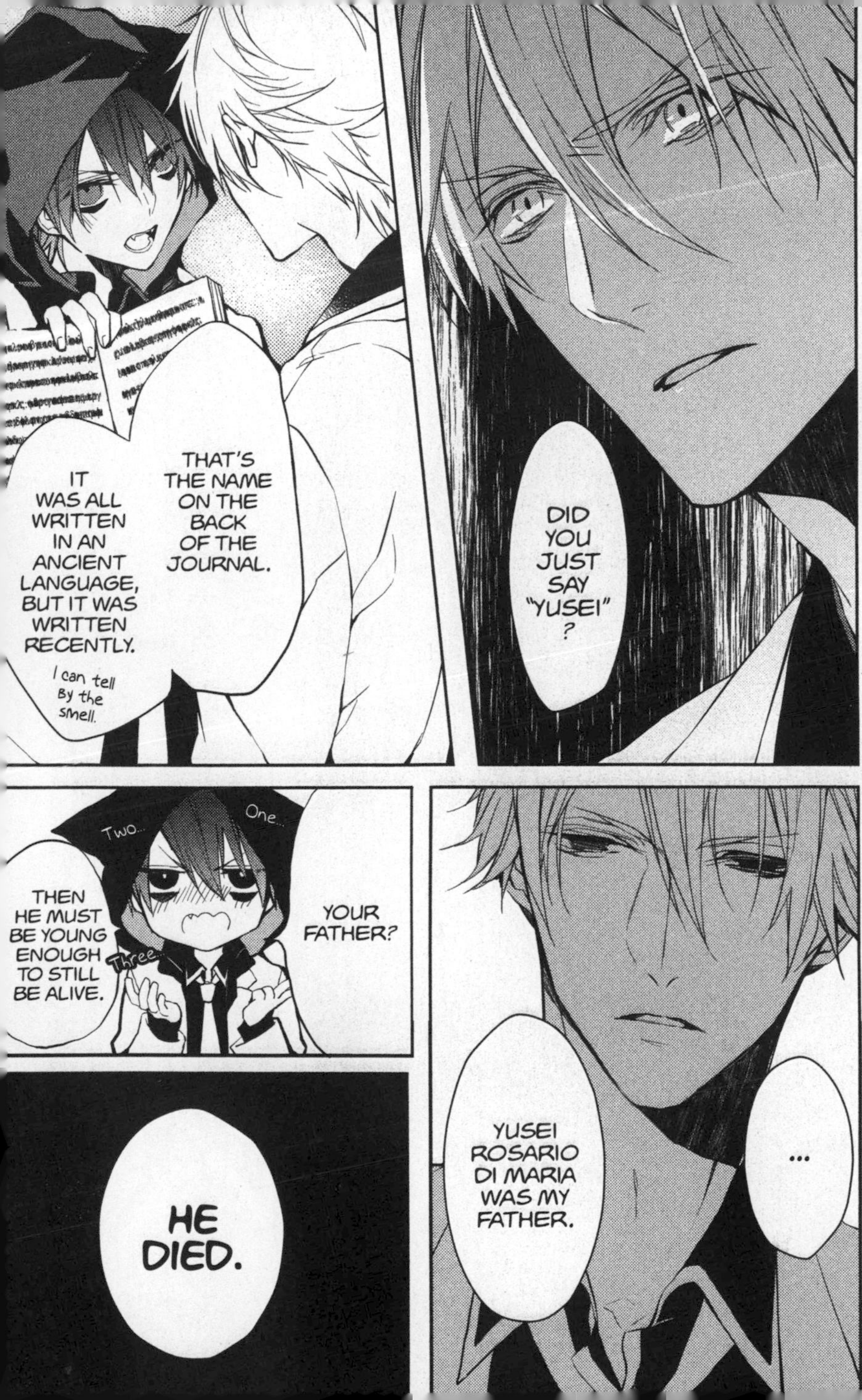
DID YOU JUST SAY "YUSEI"?
THAT'S THE NAME ON THE BACK OF THE JOURNAL.
IT WAS ALL WRITTEN IN AN ANCIENT LANGUAGE, BUT IT WAS WRITTEN RECENTLY.
I can tell by the smell.
...
YUSEI ROSARIO DI MARIA WAS MY FATHER.
One...
Two...
YOUR FATHER?
THEN HE MUST BE YOUNG ENOUGH TO STILL BE ALIVE.
Three...
HE DIED.

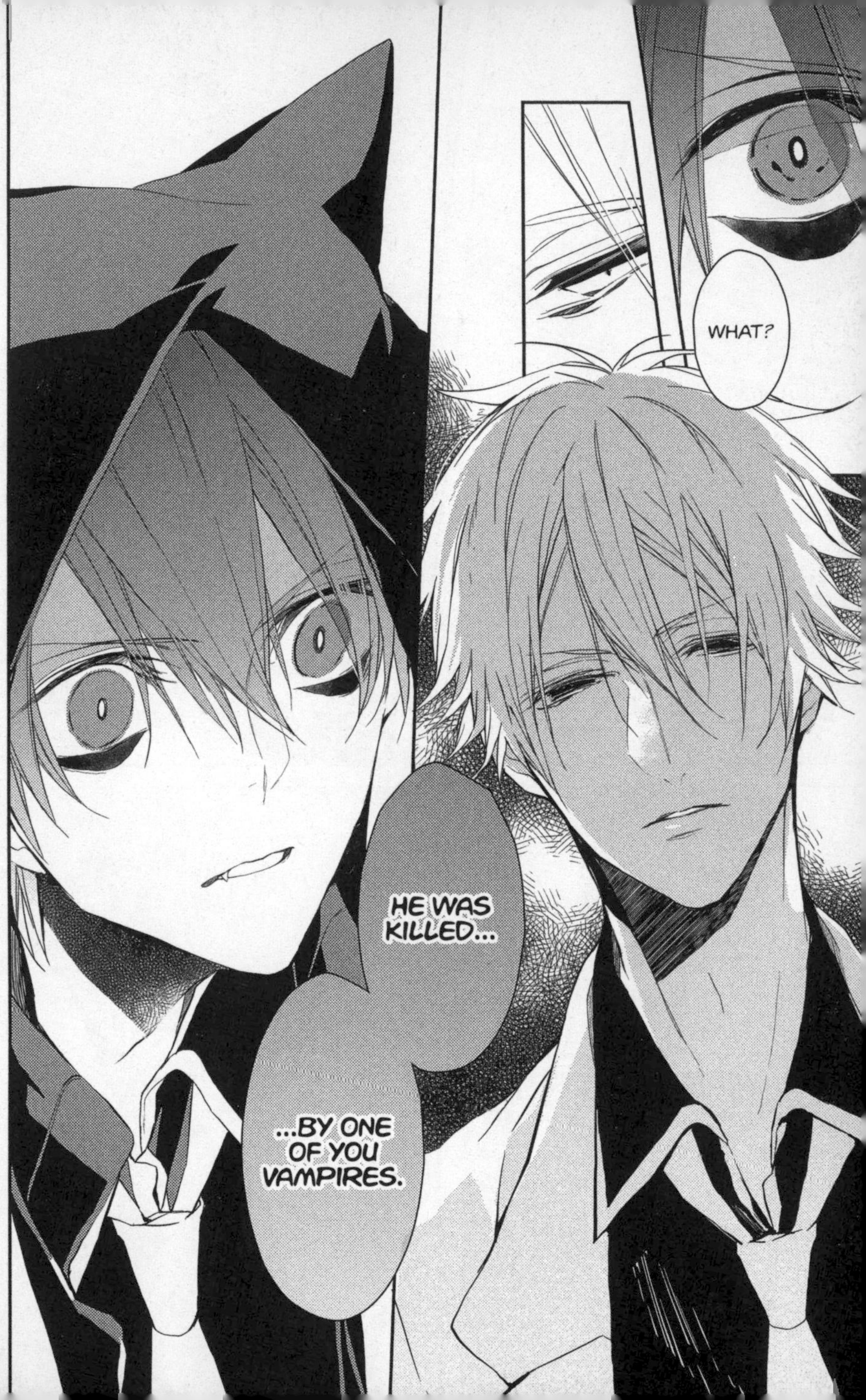
WHAT?
HE WAS KILLED...
...BY ONE OF YOU VAMPIRES.

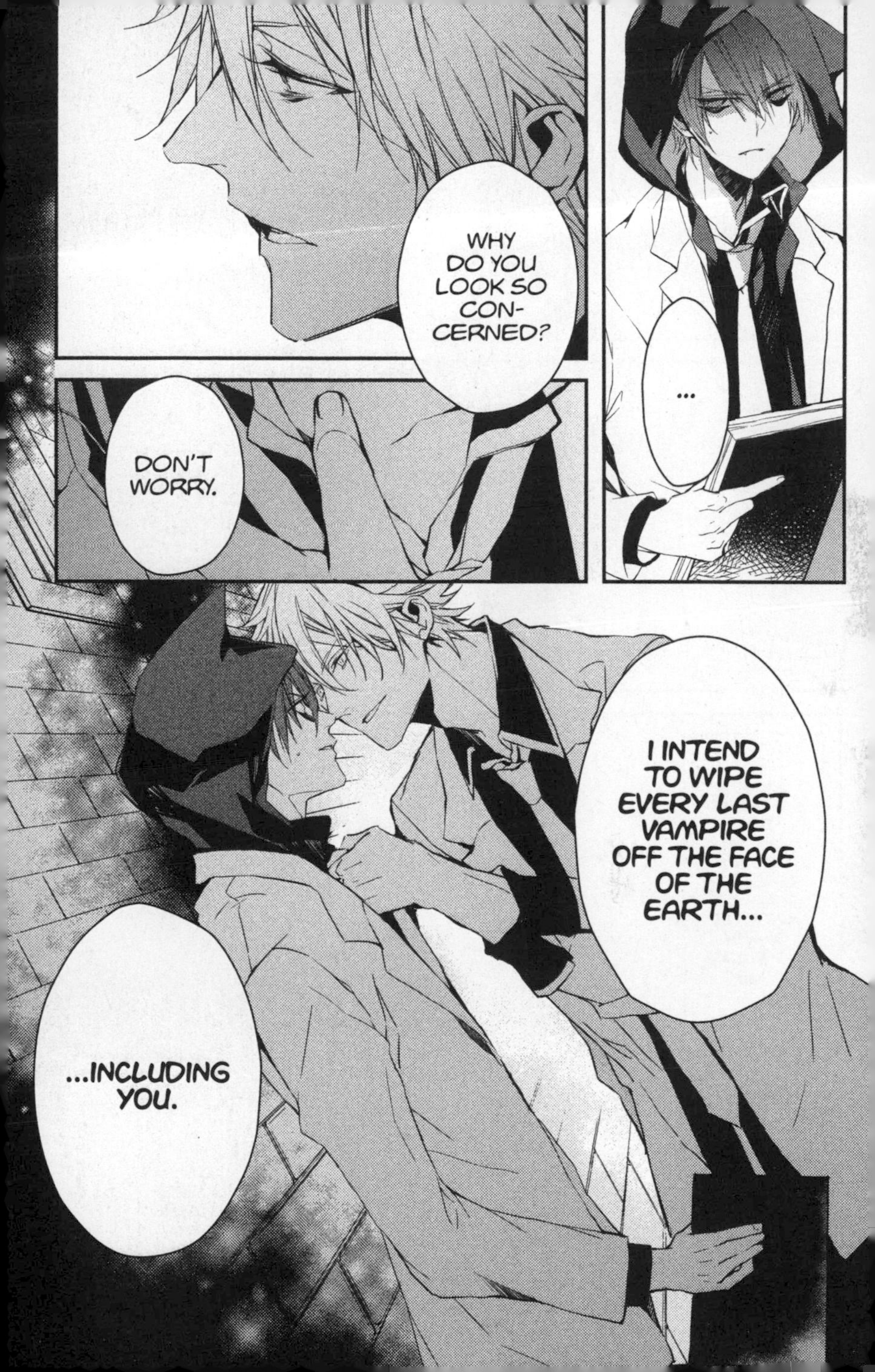
...
WHY DO YOU LOOK SO CON-CERNED?
DON'T WORRY.
I INTEND TO WIPE EVERY LAST VAMPIRE OFF THE FACE OF THE EARTH...
...INCLUDING YOU.

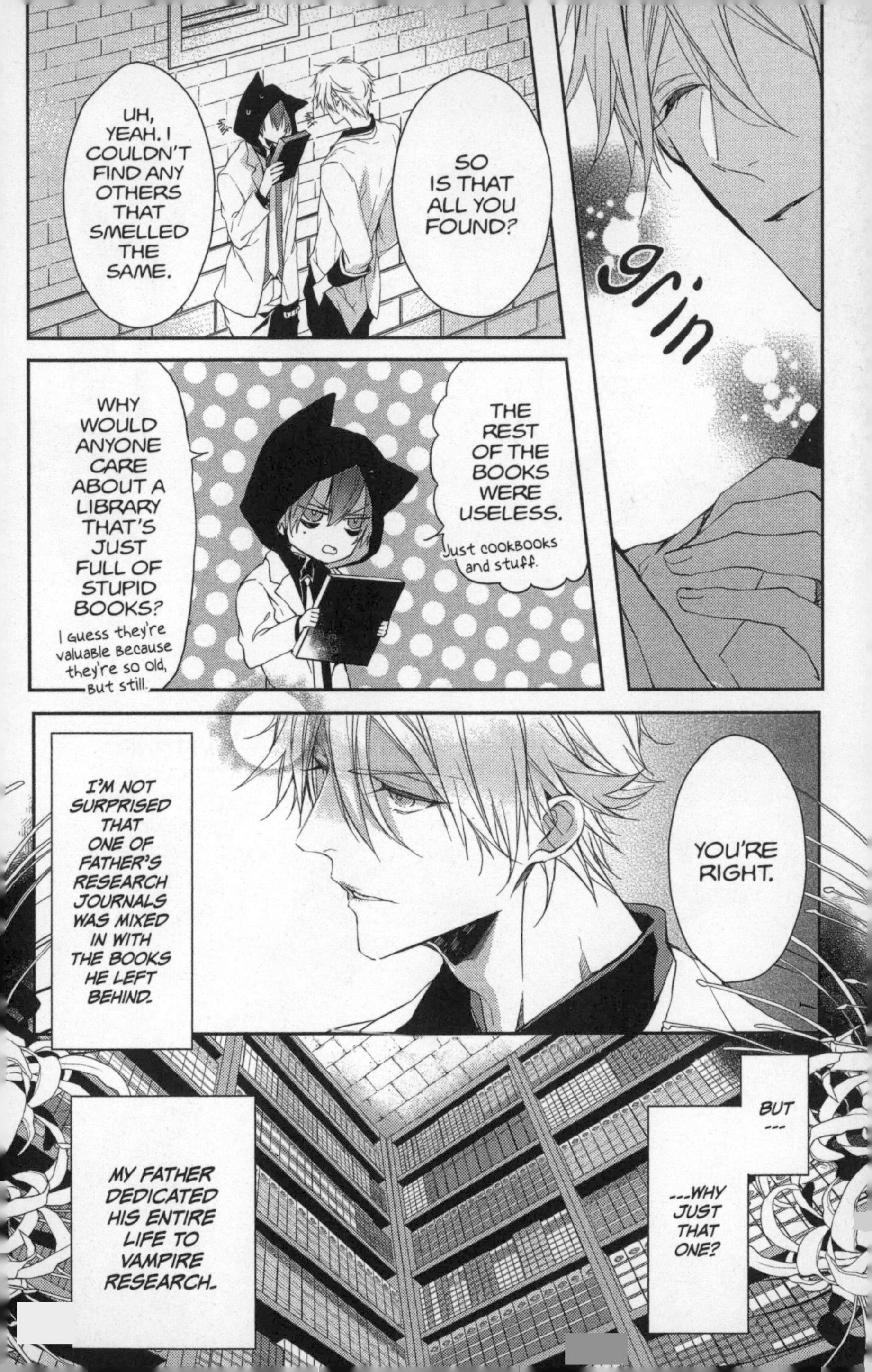
grin
SO IS THAT ALL YOU FOUND?
UH, YEAH. I COULDN'T FIND ANY OTHERS THAT SMELLED THE SAME.
THE REST OF THE BOOKS WERE USELESS.
Just cookbooks and stuff.
WHY WOULD ANYONE CARE ABOUT A LIBRARY THAT'S JUST FULL OF STUPID BOOKS?
I guess they're valuable because they're so old, but still.
YOU'RE RIGHT.
I'M NOT SURPRISED THAT ONE OF FATHER'S RESEARCH JOURNALS WAS MIXED IN WITH THE BOOKS HE LEFT BEHIND.
BUT---
---WHY JUST THAT ONE?
MY FATHER DEDICATED HIS ENTIRE LIFE TO VAMPIRE RESEARCH.

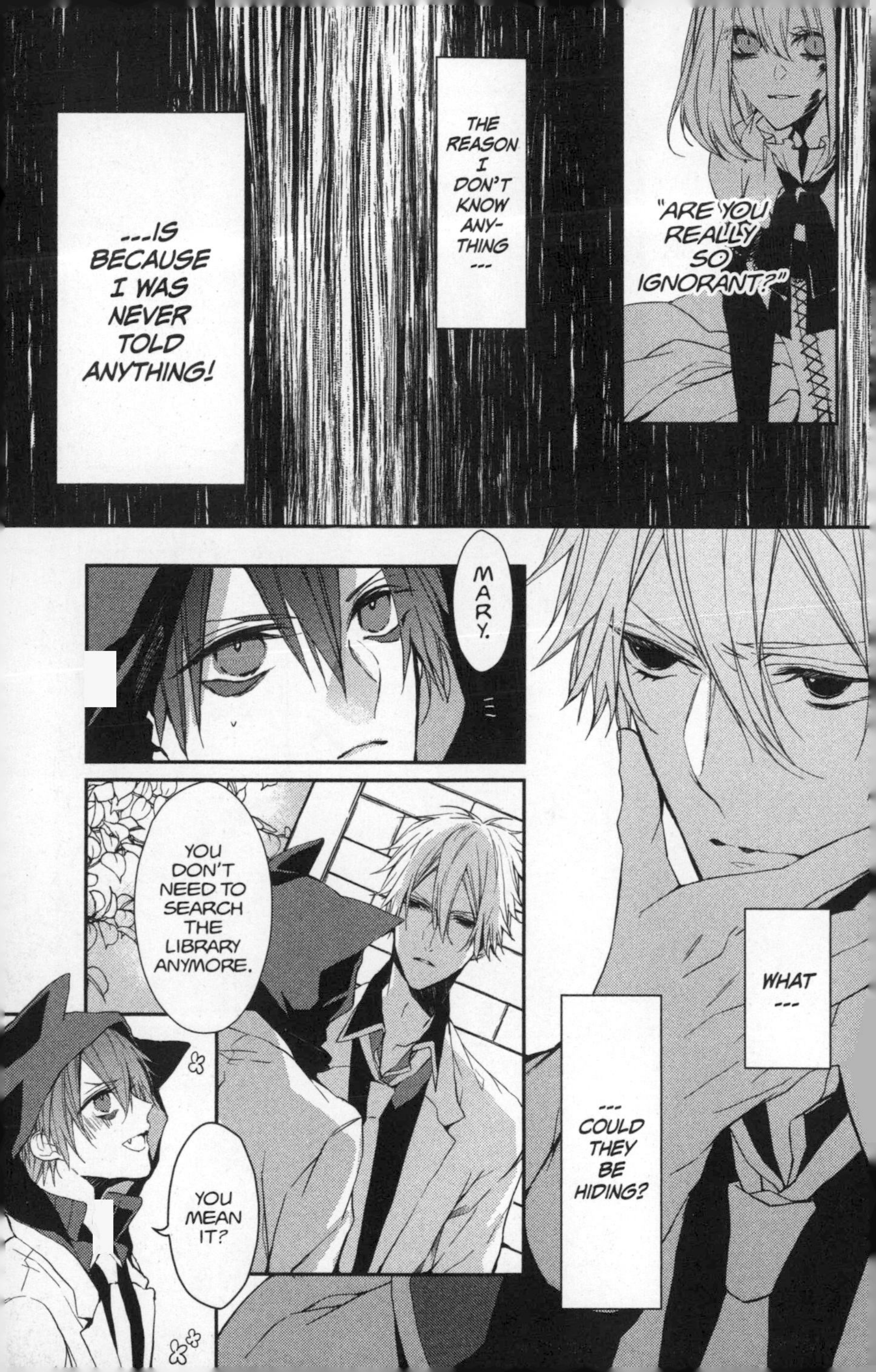
"ARE YOU REALLY SO IGNORANT?"
THE REASON I DON'T KNOW ANY-THING ---
---IS BECAUSE I WAS NEVER TOLD ANYTHING!
WHAT ---
---COULD THEY BE HIDING?
MARY.
YOU DON'T NEED TO SEARCH THE LIBRARY ANYMORE.
YOU MEAN IT?

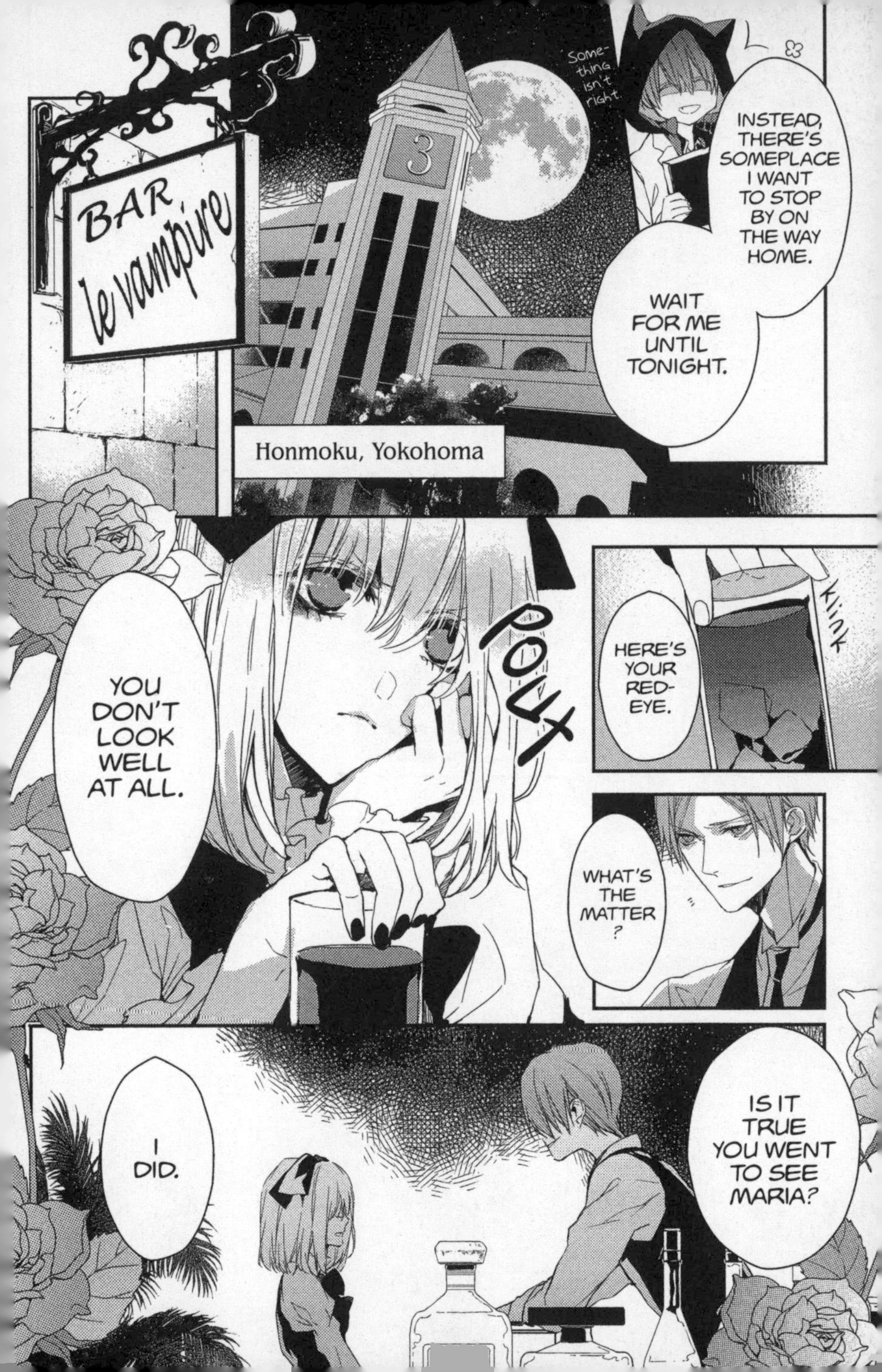
INSTEAD, THERE'S SOMEPLACE I WANT TO STOP BY ON THE WAY HOME.
Something isn't right.
WAIT FOR ME UNTIL TONIGHT.
BAR le vampire
3
Honmoku, Yokohoma
klink
HERE'S YOUR RED-EYE.
WHAT'S THE MATTER?
POUT
YOU DON'T LOOK WELL AT ALL.
IS IT TRUE YOU WENT TO SEE MARIA?
I DID.

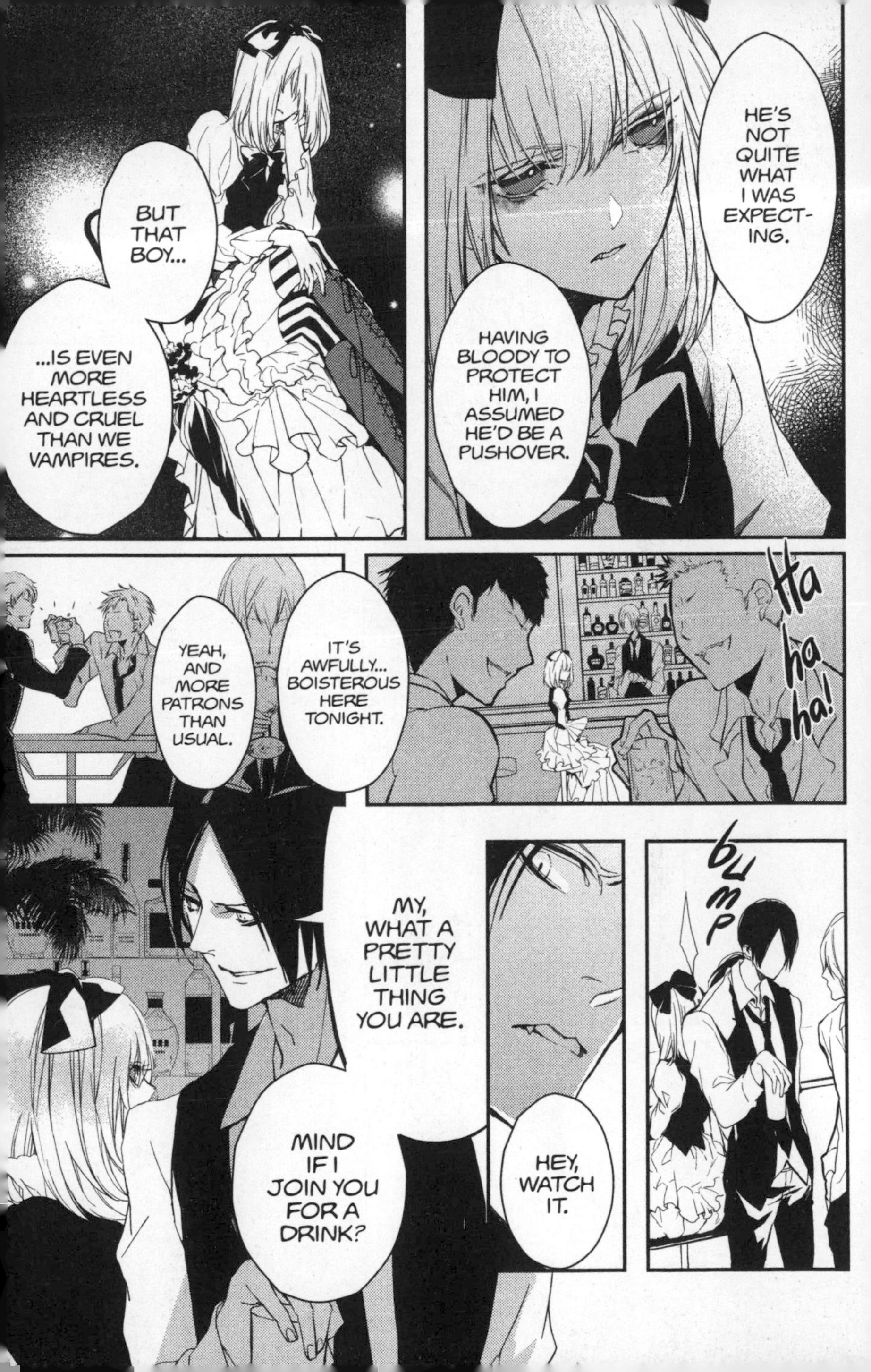
HE'S NOT QUITE WHAT I WAS EXPECT-ING.
HAVING BLOODY TO PROTECT HIM, I ASSUMED HE'D BE A PUSHOVER.
BUT THAT BOY...
...IS EVEN MORE HEARTLESS AND CRUEL THAN WE VAMPIRES.
Ha ha ha!
IT'S AWFULLY... BOISTEROUS HERE TONIGHT.
YEAH, AND MORE PATRONS THAN USUAL.
bump
HEY, WATCH IT.
MY, WHAT A PRETTY LITTLE THING YOU ARE.
MIND IF I JOIN YOU FOR A DRINK?

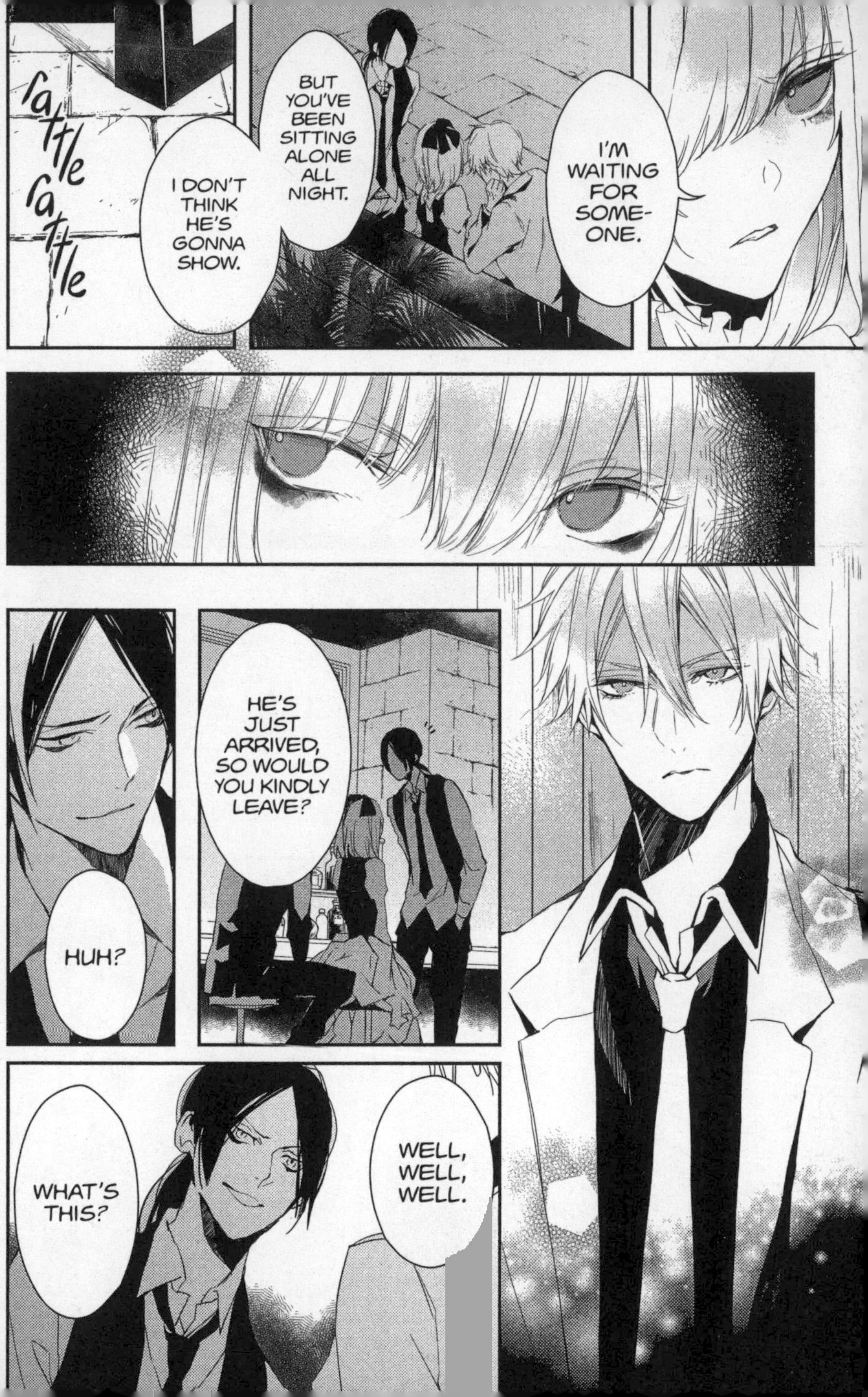
I'M WAITING FOR SOME-ONE.
BUT YOU'VE BEEN SITTING ALONE ALL NIGHT.
I DON'T THINK HE'S GONNA SHOW.
rattle rattle rattle
HE'S JUST ARRIVED, SO WOULD YOU KINDLY LEAVE?
HUH?
WELL, WELL, WELL.
WHAT'S THIS?

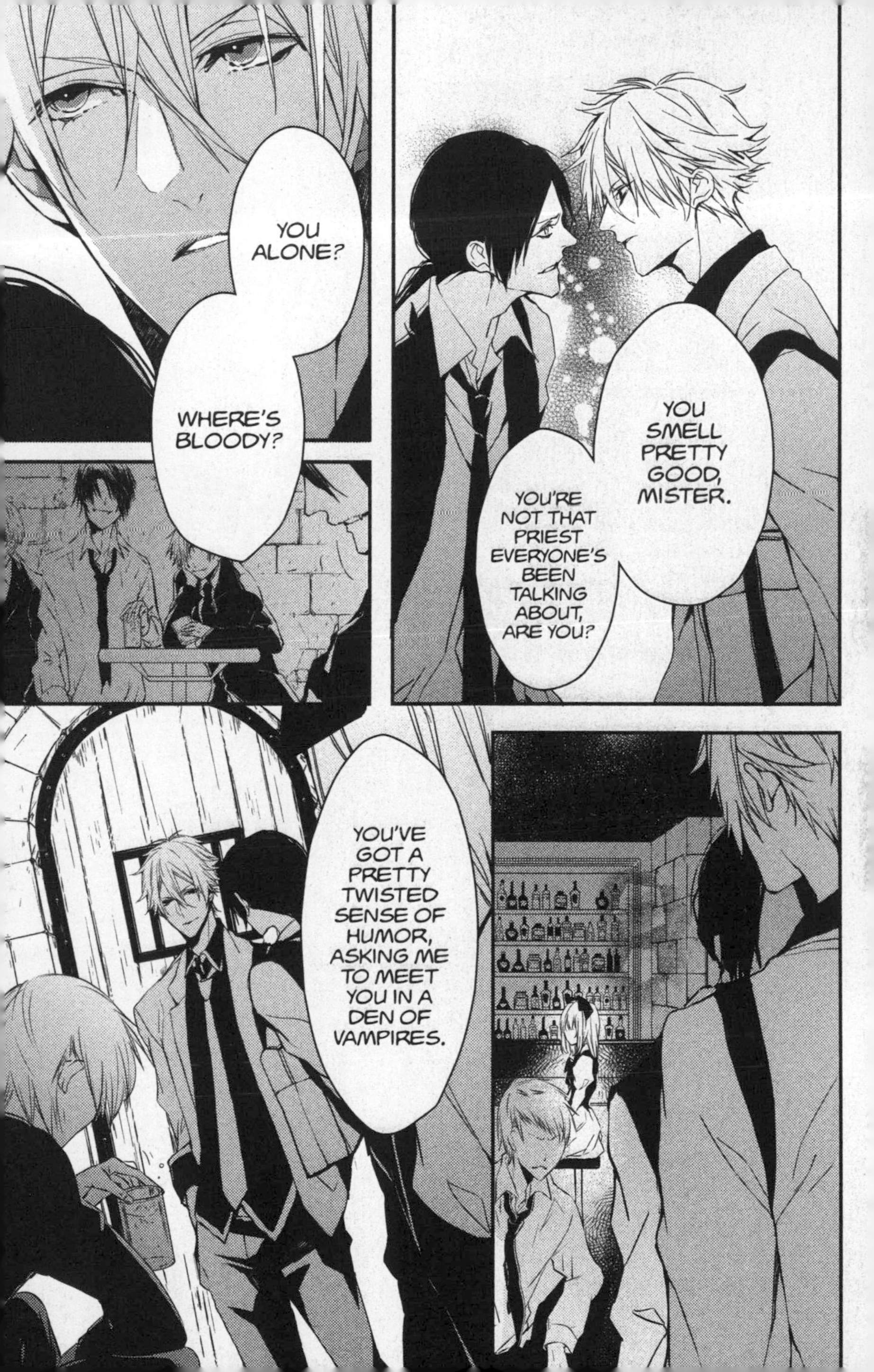
YOU SMELL PRETTY GOOD, MISTER.
YOU'RE NOT THAT PRIEST EVERYONE'S BEEN TALKING ABOUT, ARE YOU?
YOU ALONE?
WHERE'S BLOODY?
YOU'VE GOT A PRETTY TWISTED SENSE OF HUMOR, ASKING ME TO MEET YOU IN A DEN OF VAMPIRES.

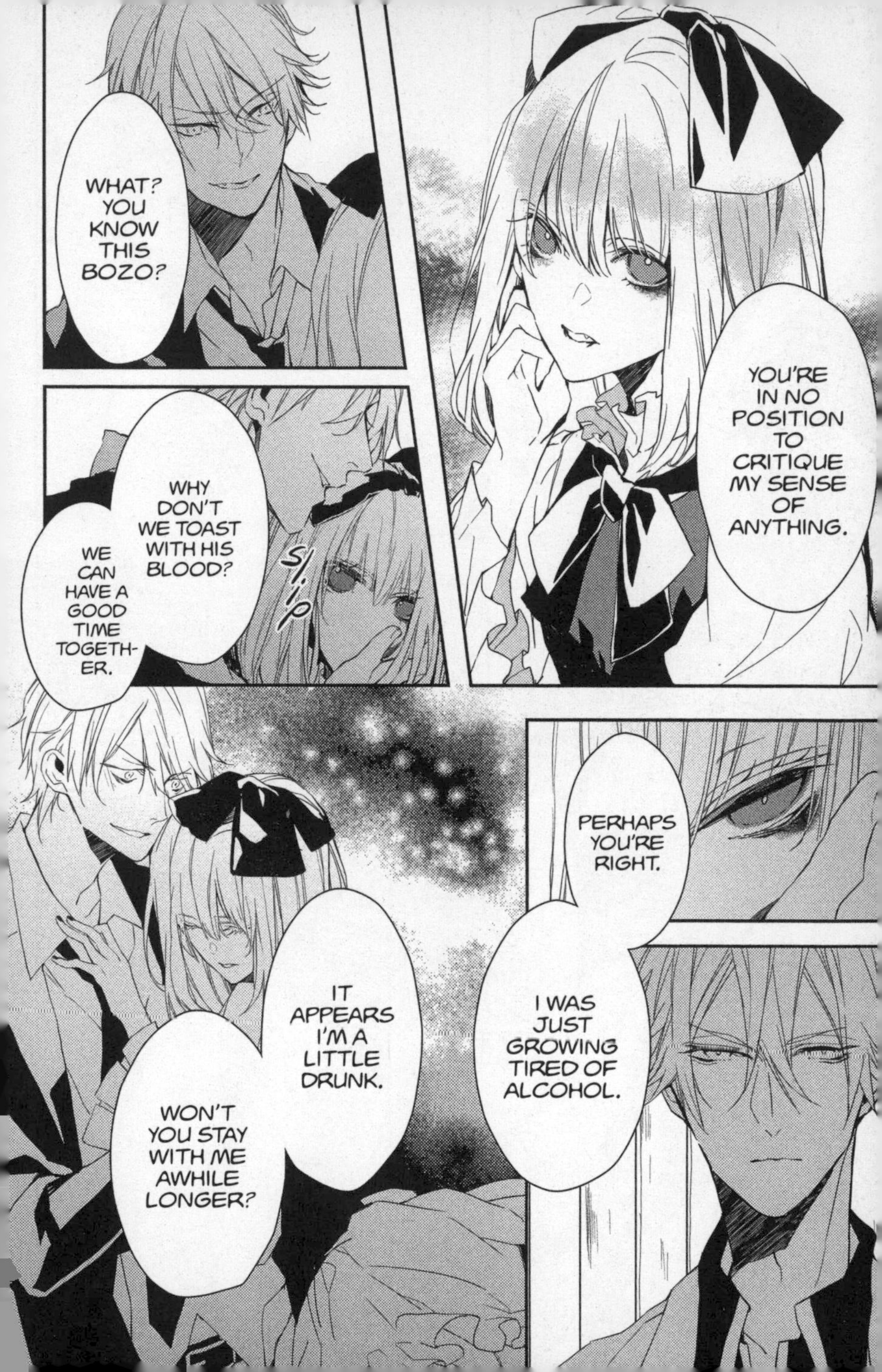
YOU'RE IN NO POSITION TO CRITIQUE MY SENSE OF ANYTHING.
WHAT? YOU KNOW THIS BOZO?
WHY DON'T WE TOAST WITH HIS BLOOD?
WE CAN HAVE A GOOD TIME TOGETH-ER.
SLIP
PERHAPS YOU'RE RIGHT.
I WAS JUST GROWING TIRED OF ALCOHOL.
IT APPEARS I'M A LITTLE DRUNK.
WON'T YOU STAY WITH ME AWHILE LONGER?

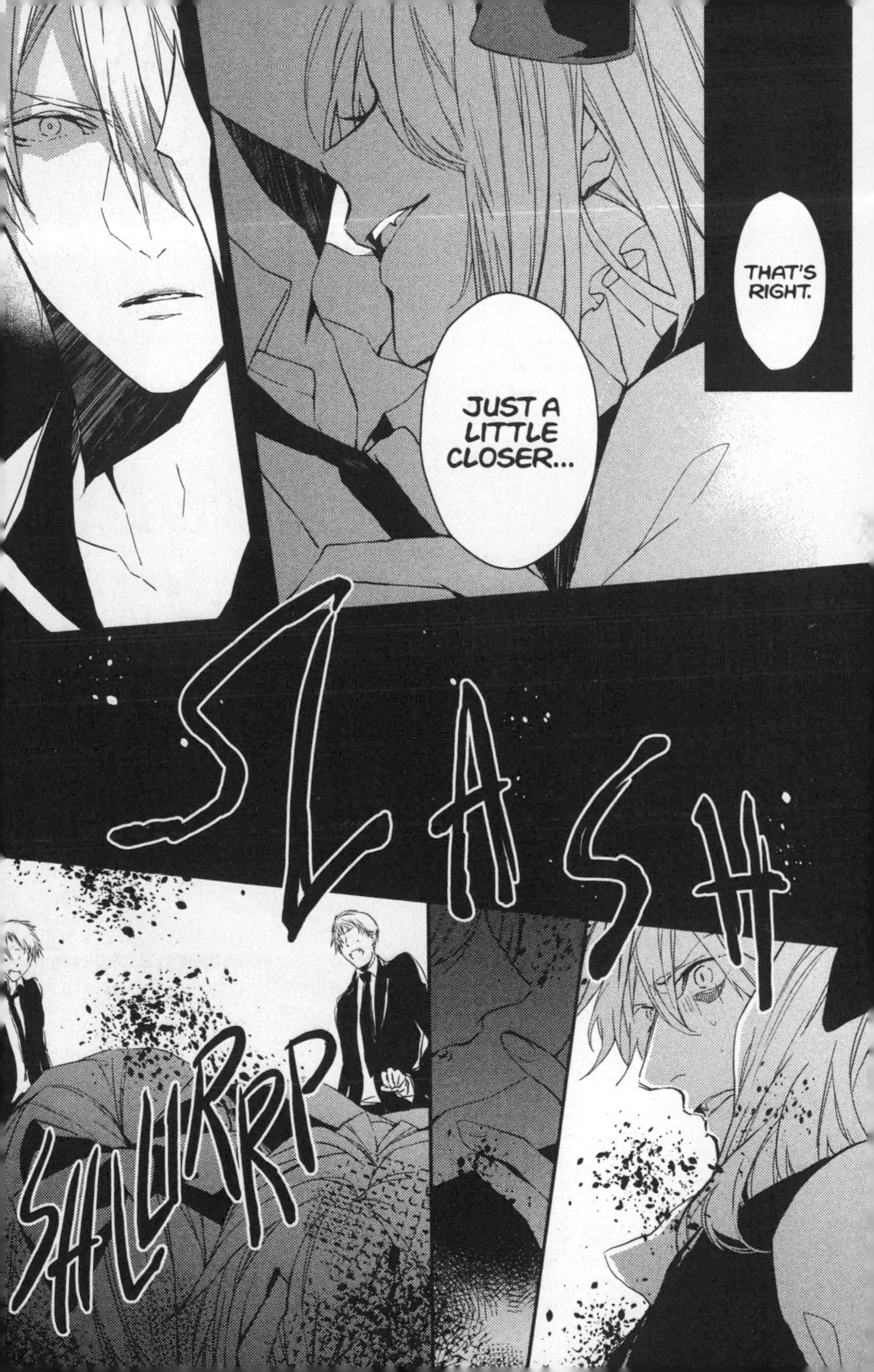
THAT'S RIGHT.
JUST A LITTLE CLOSER...
SLASH
SHLURRP

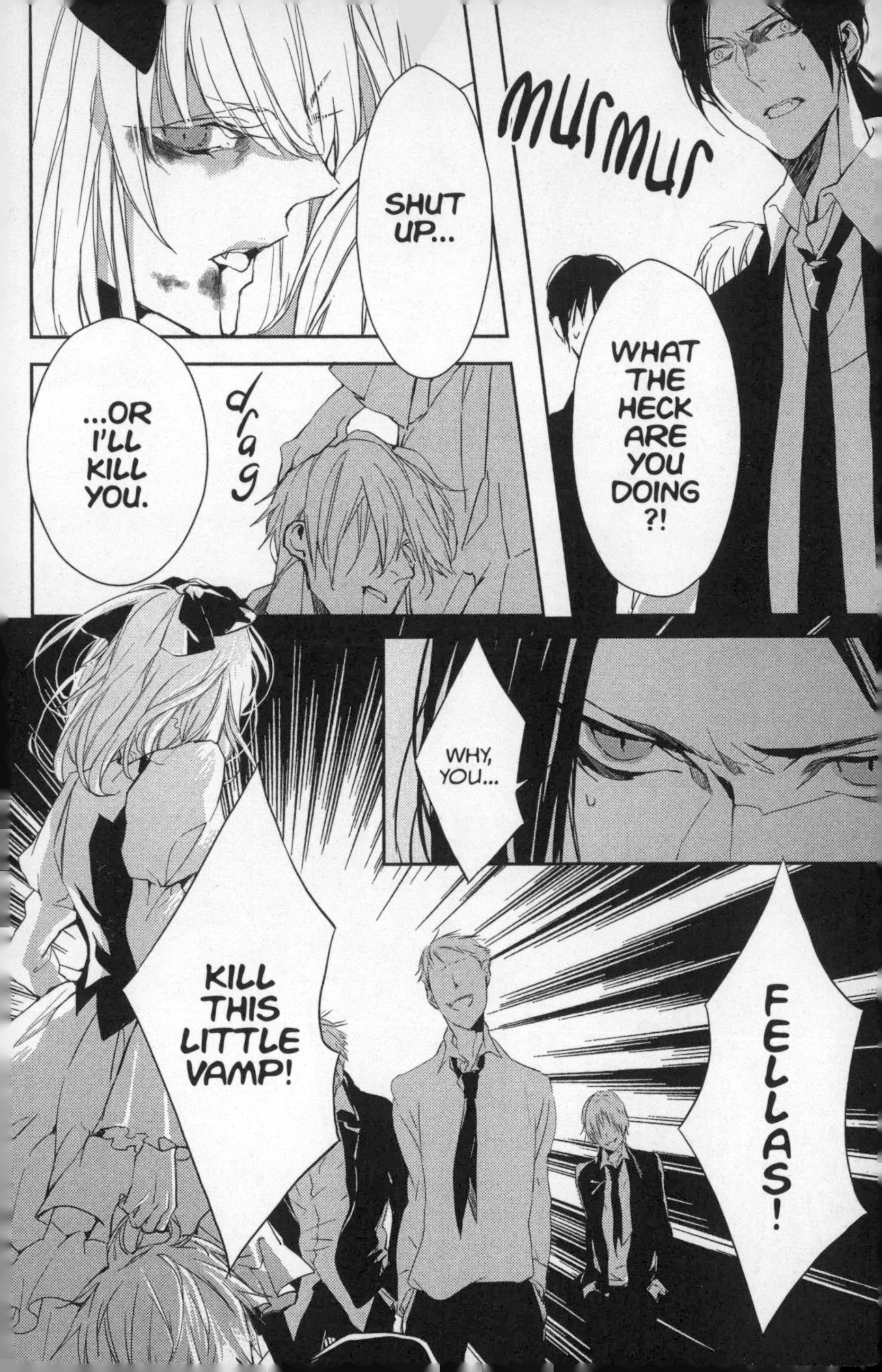
MUSMUS
WHAT THE HECK ARE YOU DOING ?!
SHUT UP...
drag
...OR I'LL KILL YOU.
WHY, YOU...
FELLAS!
KILL THIS LITTLE VAMP!

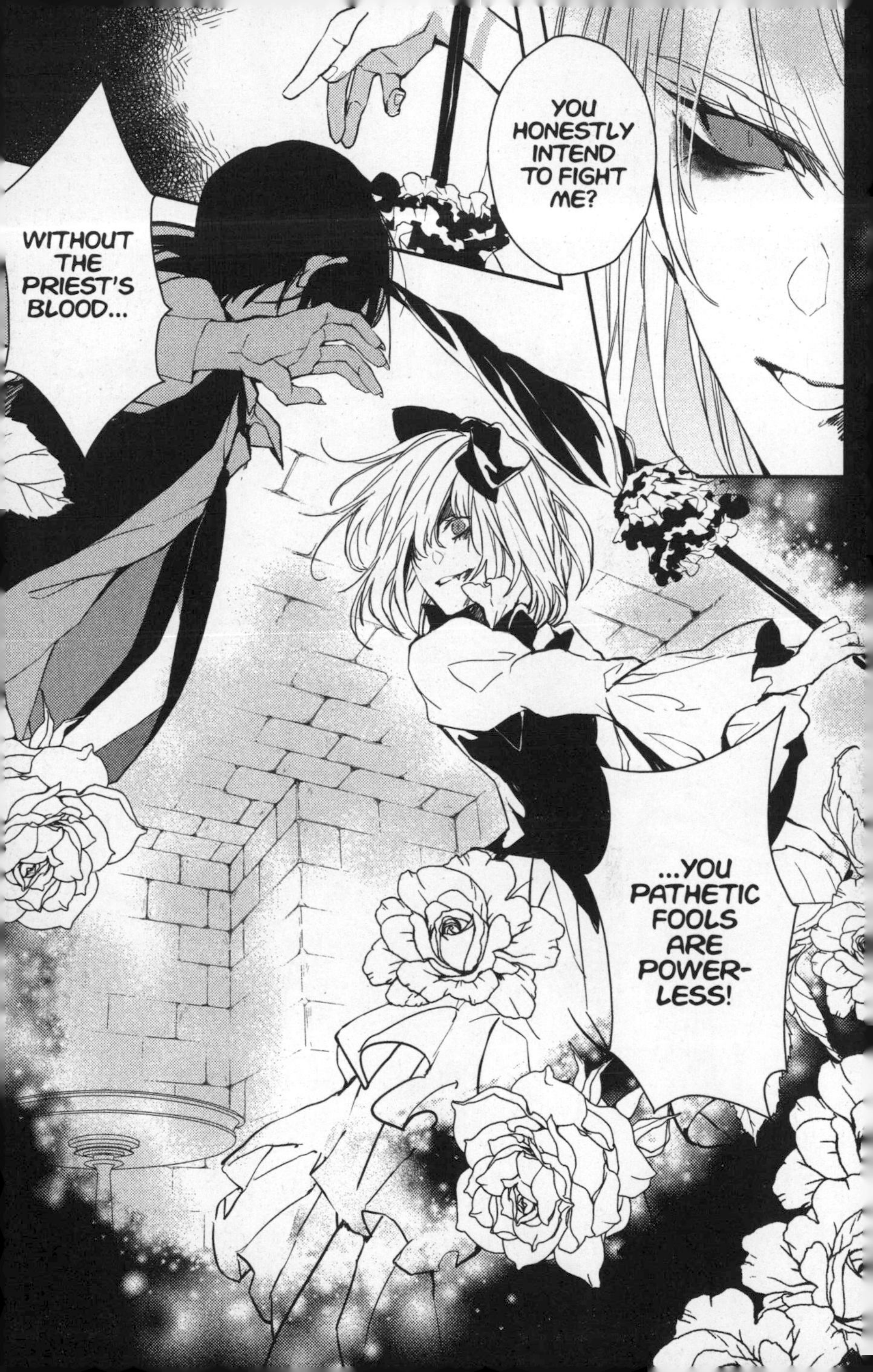
YOU HONESTLY INTEND TO FIGHT ME?
WITHOUT THE PRIEST'S BLOOD...
...YOU PATHETIC FOOLS ARE POWER-LESS!

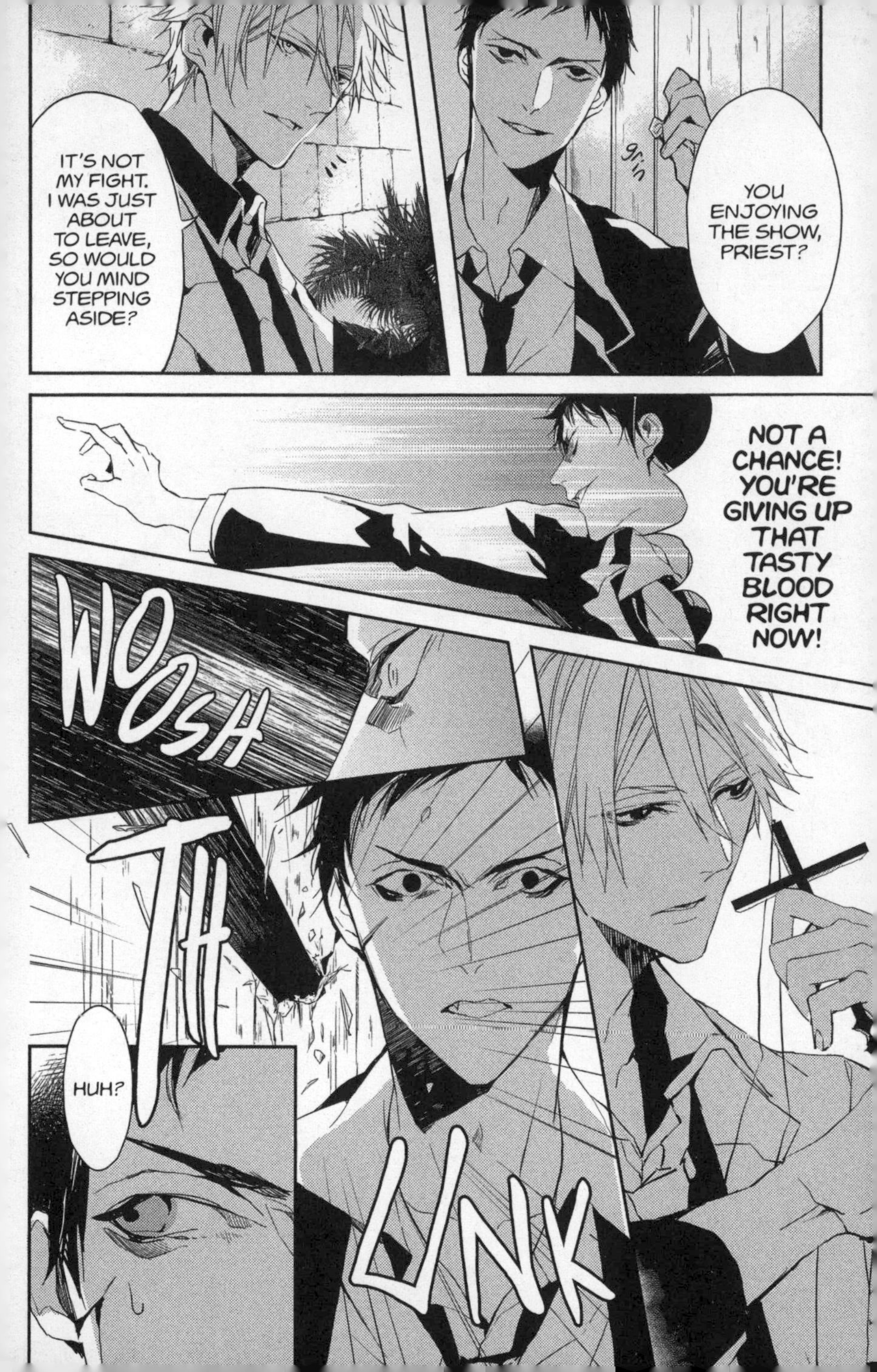
grin
YOU ENJOYING THE SHOW, PRIEST?
IT'S NOT MY FIGHT. I WAS JUST ABOUT TO LEAVE, SO WOULD YOU MIND STEPPING ASIDE?
NOT A CHANCE! YOU'RE GIVING UP THAT TASTY BLOOD RIGHT NOW!
WOOSH
THUNK
HUH?

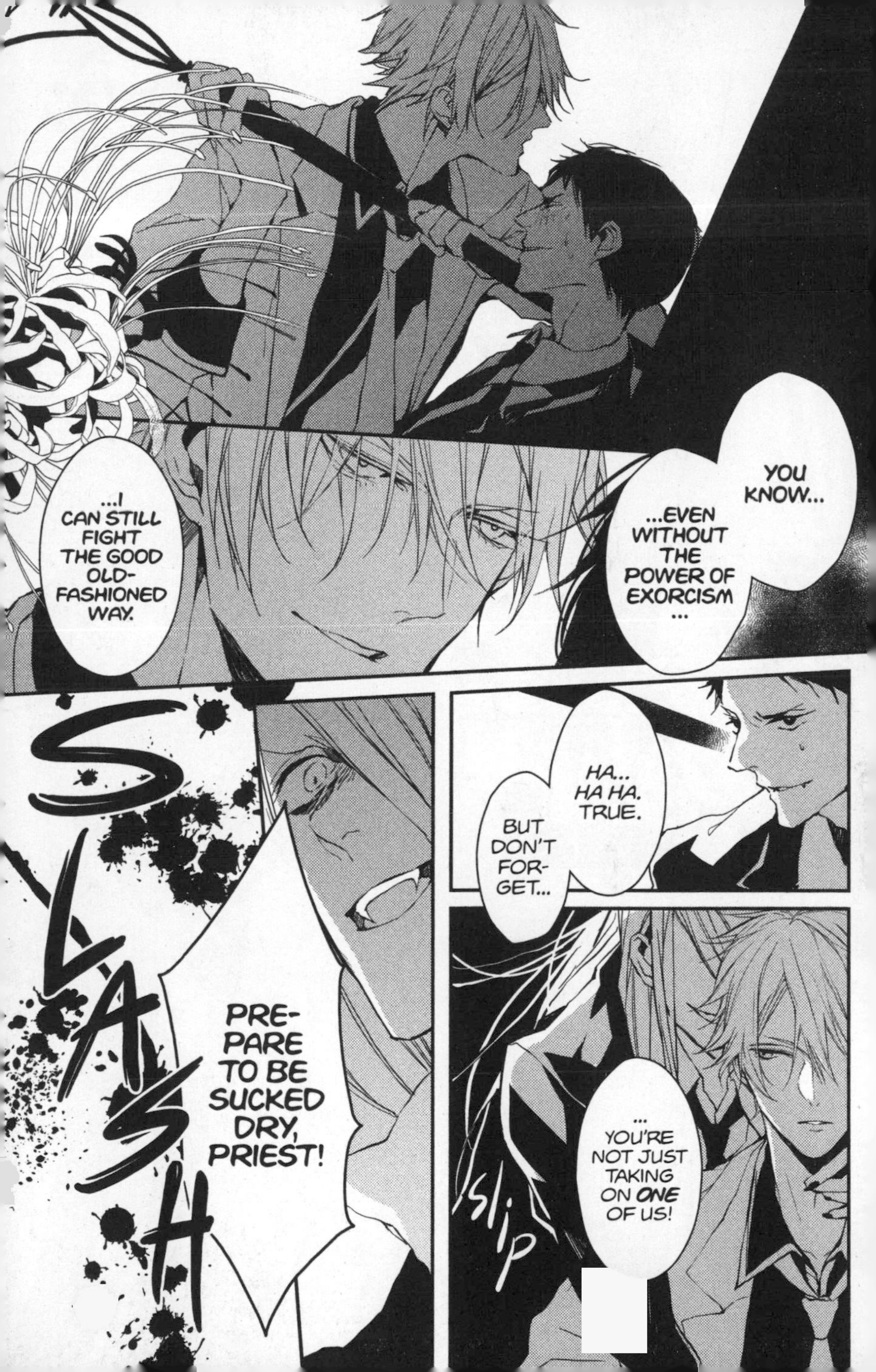
YOU KNOW...
...EVEN WITHOUT THE POWER OF EXORCISM...
...I CAN STILL FIGHT THE GOOD OLD-FASHIONED WAY.
HA... HA HA. TRUE.
BUT DON'T FOR-GET...
slip
...YOU'RE NOT JUST TAKING ON *ONE* OF US!
SLASH
PRE-PARE TO BE SUCKED DRY, PRIEST!

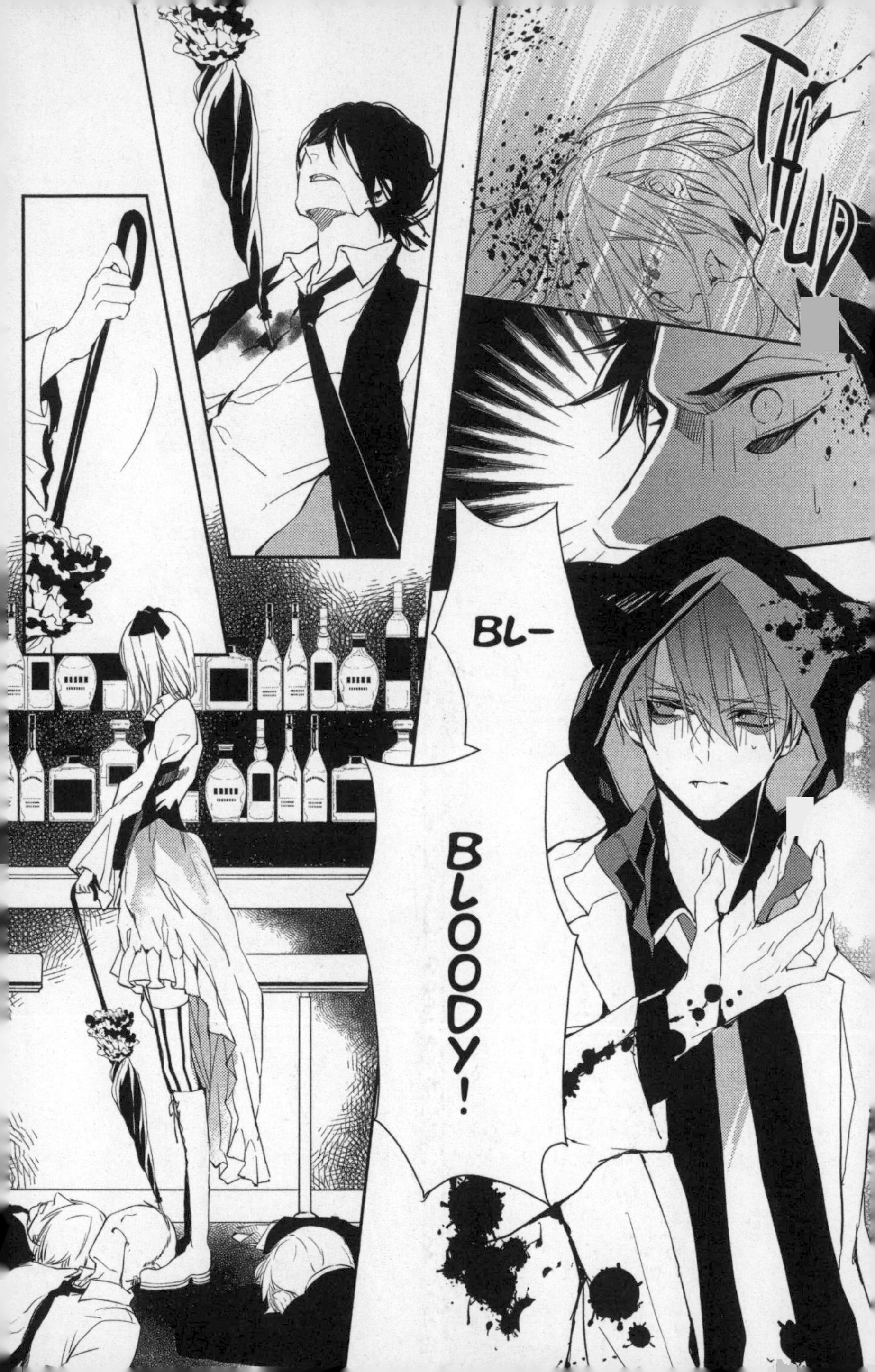
THUD
BL-
BLOOODY!

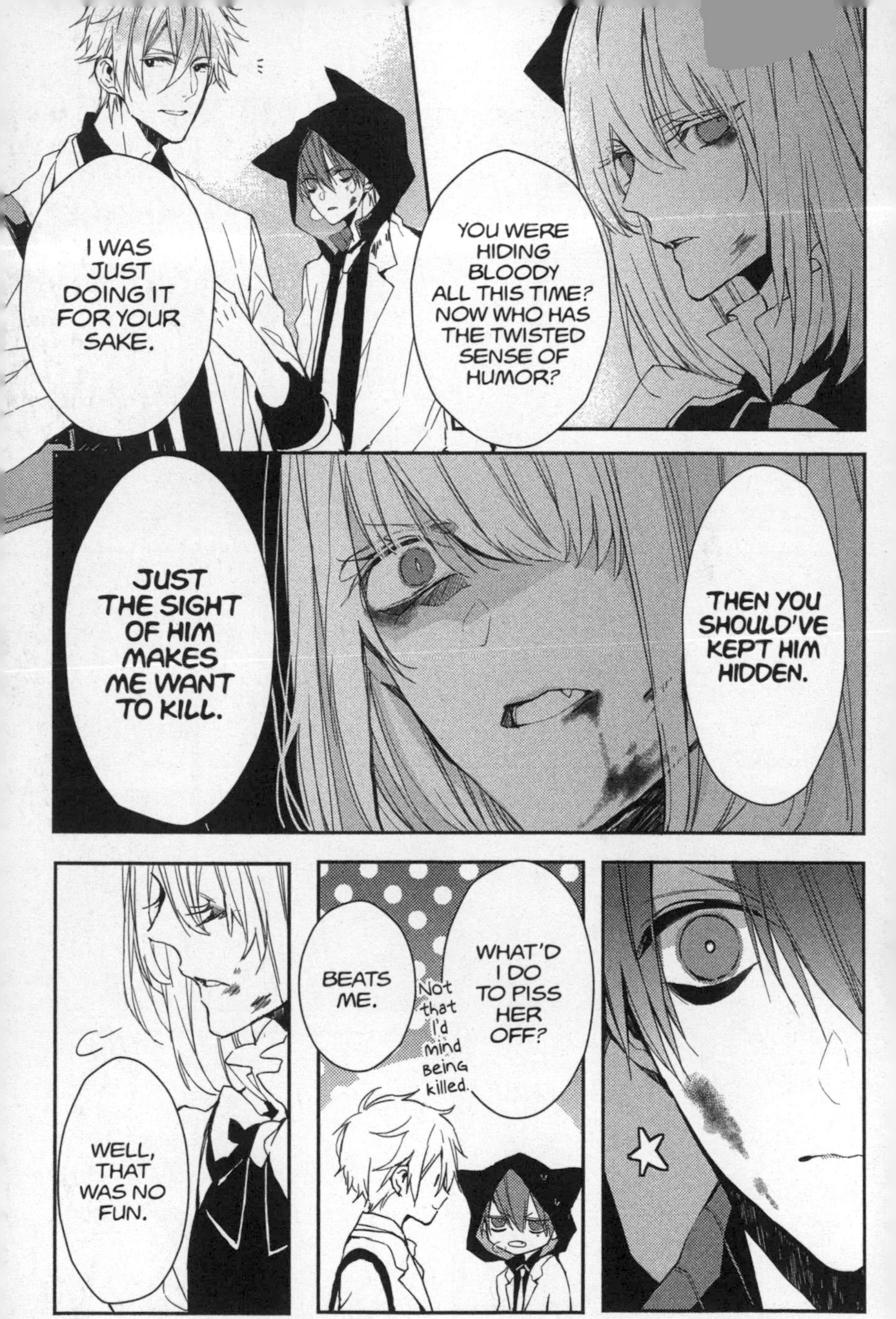
YOU WERE HIDING BLOODY ALL THIS TIME? NOW WHO HAS THE TWISTED SENSE OF HUMOR?
I WAS JUST DOING IT FOR YOUR SAKE.
THEN YOU SHOULD'VE KEPT HIM HIDDEN.
JUST THE SIGHT OF HIM MAKES ME WANT TO KILL.
WHAT'D I DO TO PISS HER OFF?
Not that I'd mind being killed.
BEATS ME.
WELL, THAT WAS NO FUN.

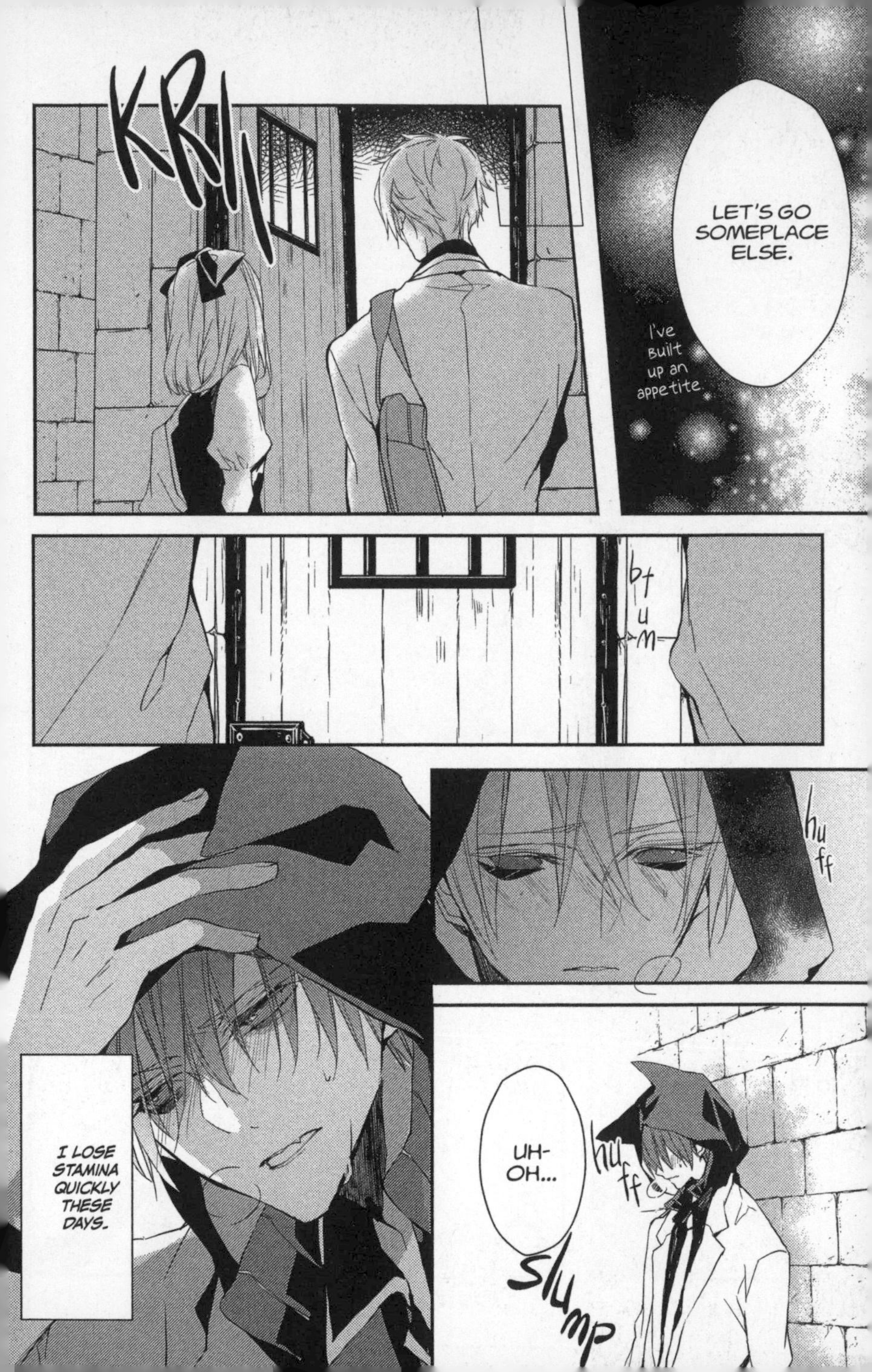
LET'S GO SOMEPLACE ELSE.
I've built up an appetite.
KRII
btum
huff
UH-OH...
huff
slump
I LOSE STAMINA QUICKLY THESE DAYS.

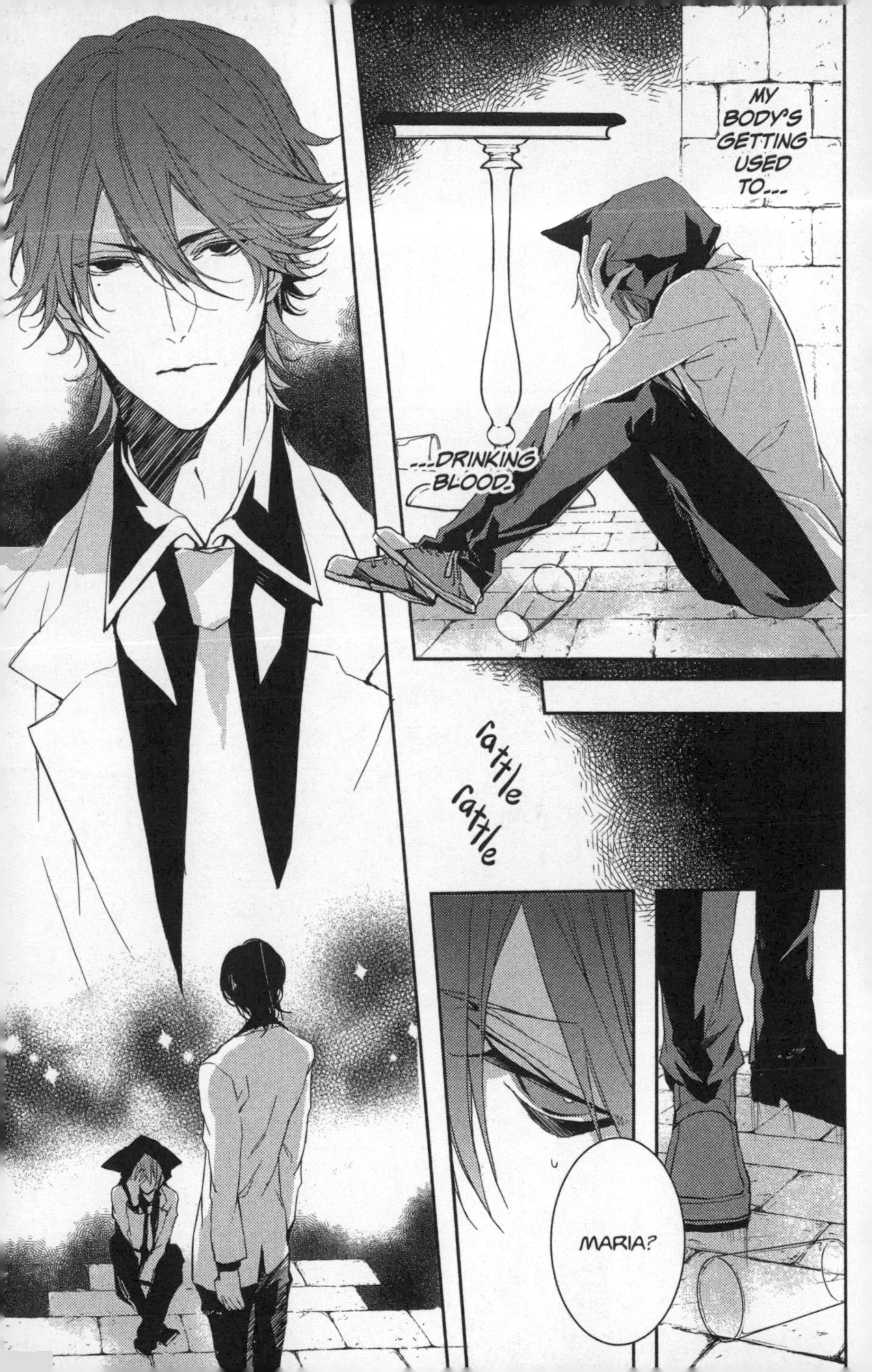
MY BODY'S GETTING USED TO...
...DRINKING BLOOD.
rattle rattle
MARIA?

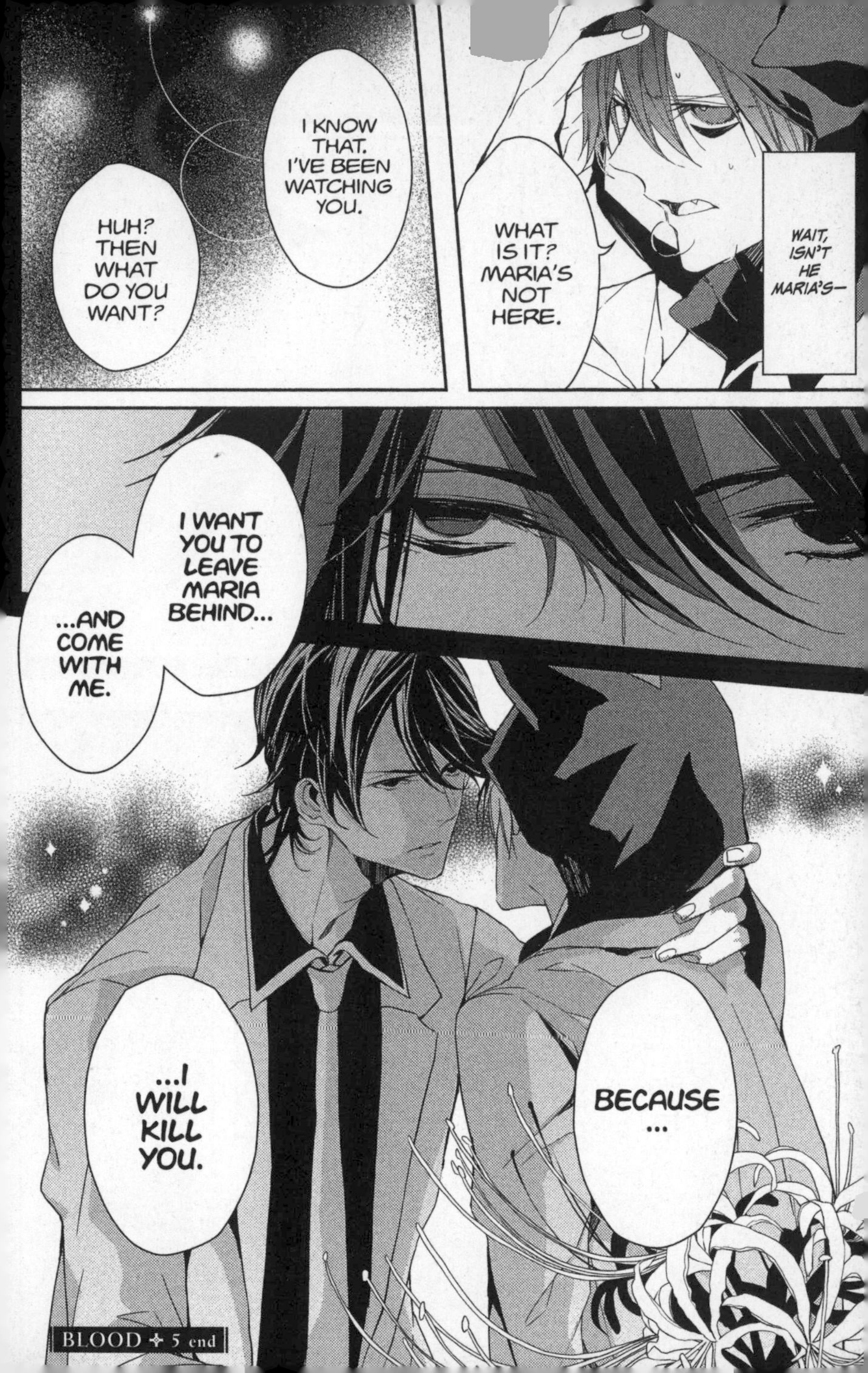
WAIT, ISN'T HE MARIA'S—
WHAT IS IT? MARIA'S NOT HERE.
I KNOW THAT. I'VE BEEN WATCHING YOU.
HUH? THEN WHAT DO YOU WANT?
I WANT YOU TO LEAVE MARIA BEHIND...
...AND COME WITH ME.
BECAUSE...
...I WILL KILL YOU.

BLOOD ✦ 5 end

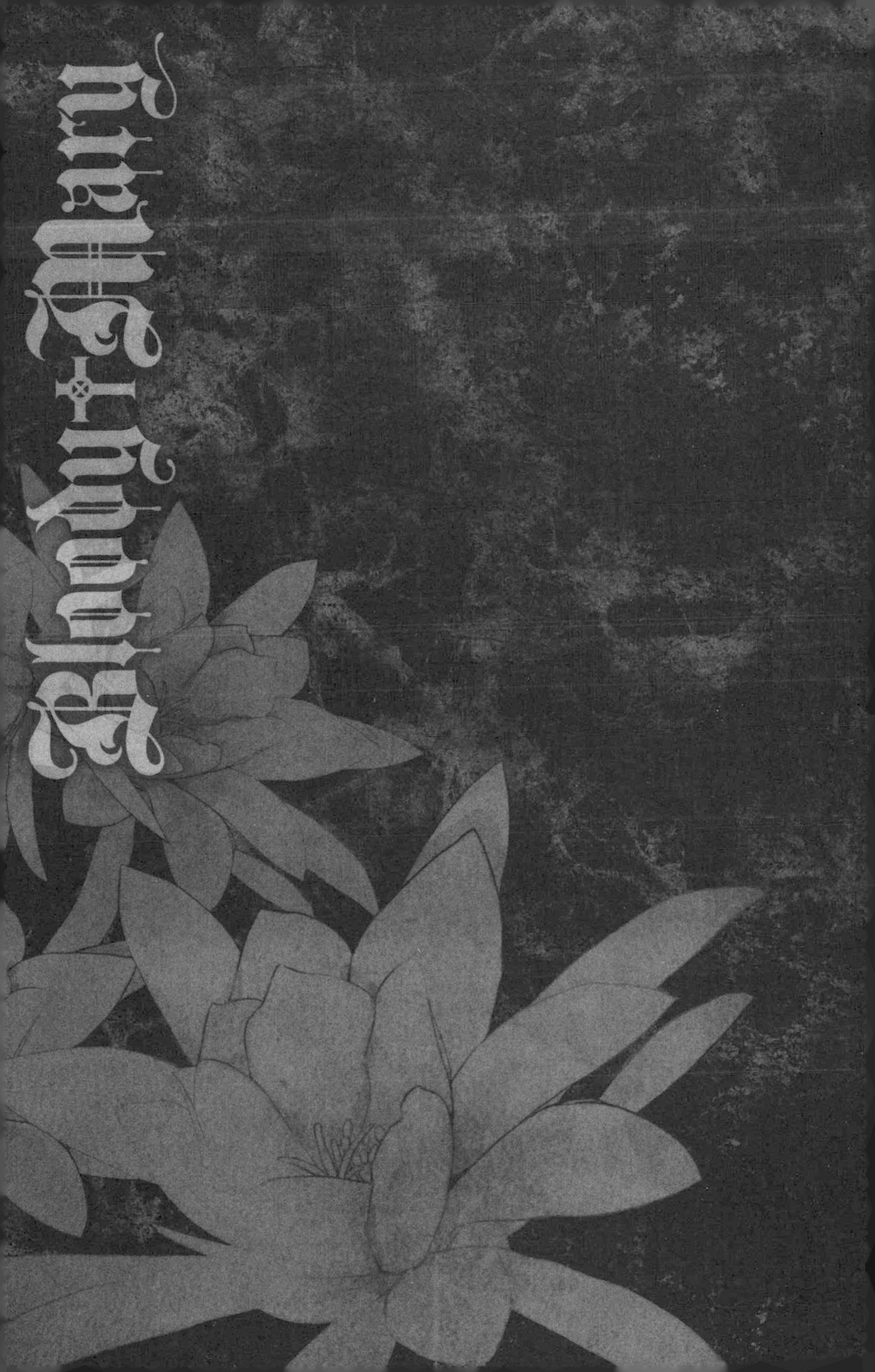
Bloody+Mary

Bloody✝Mary

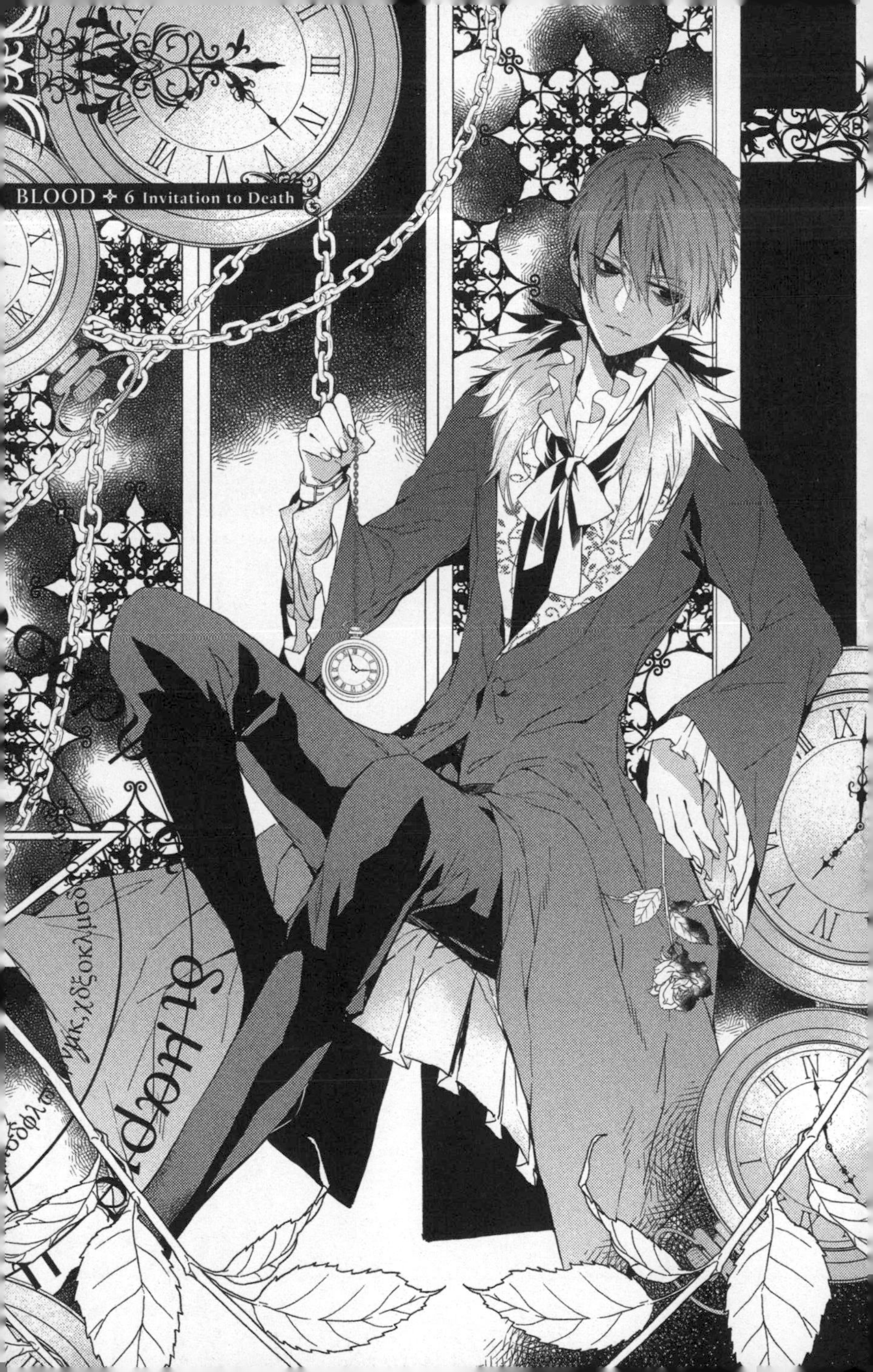
BLOOD ✣ 6 Invitation to Death

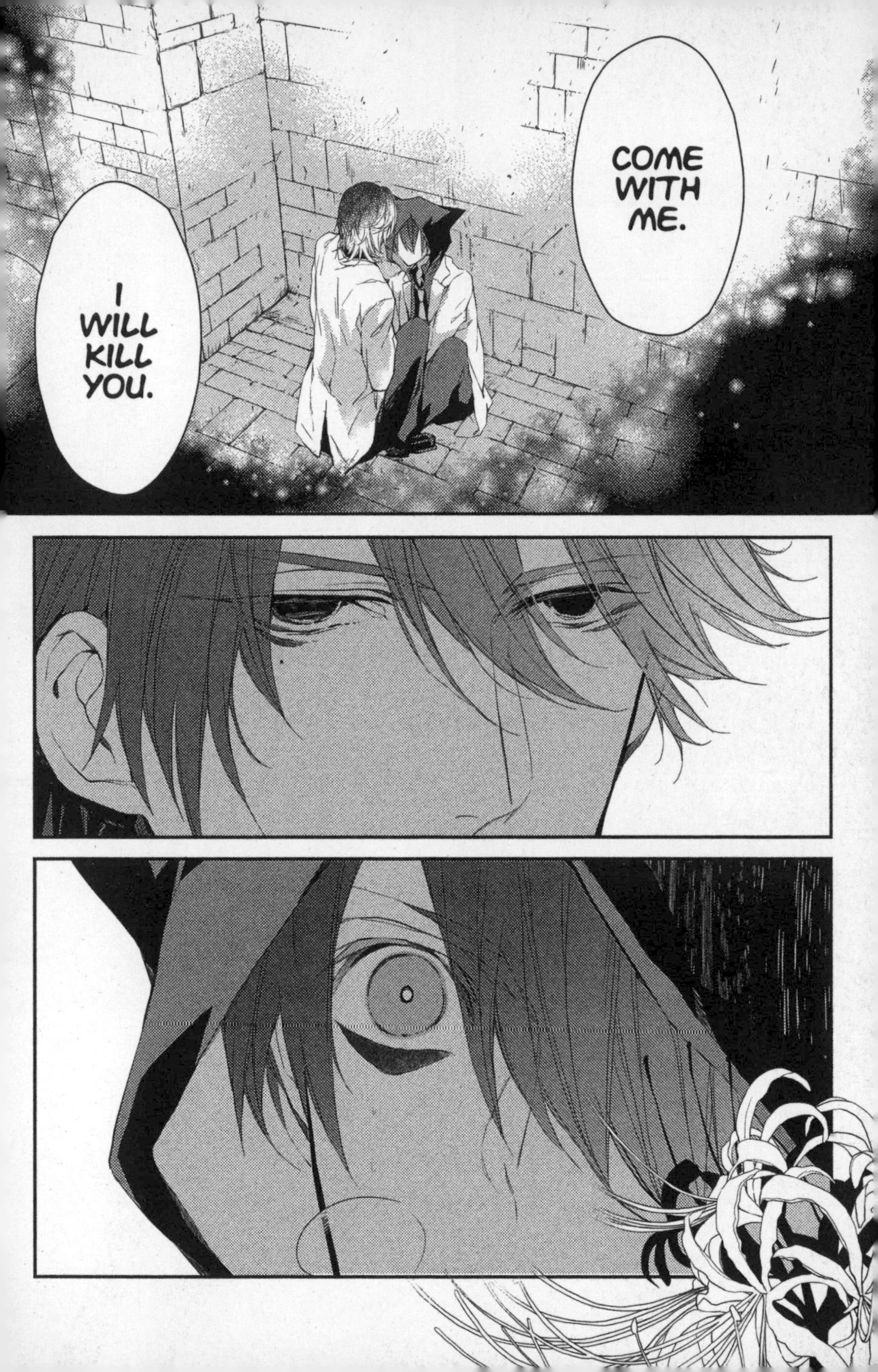
COME WITH ME.
I WILL KILL YOU.

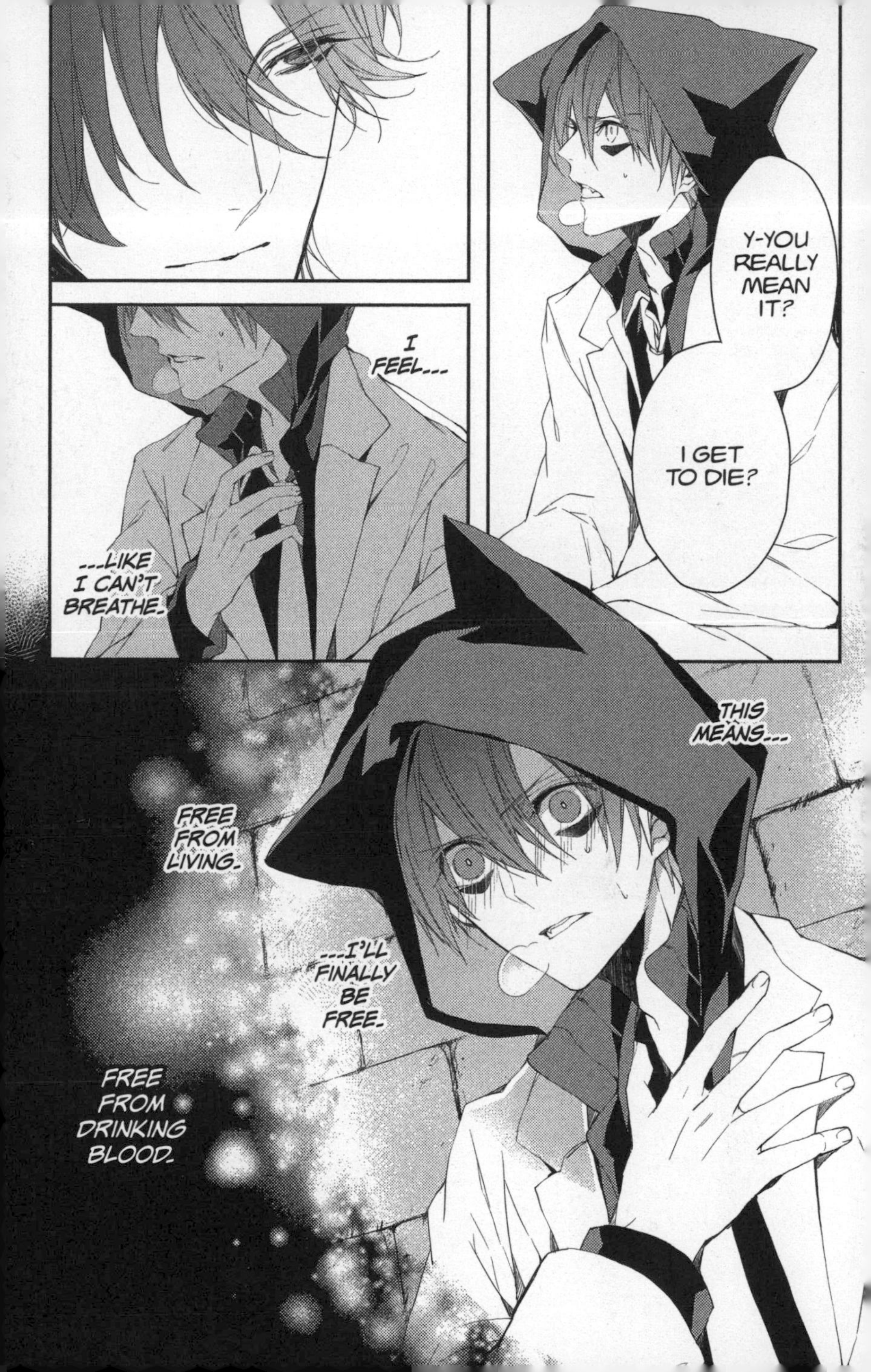

Y-YOU REALLY MEAN IT?
I GET TO DIE?
I FEEL...
...LIKE I CAN'T BREATHE.
THIS MEANS...
...I'LL FINALLY BE FREE.
FREE FROM LIVING.
FREE FROM DRINKING BLOOD.

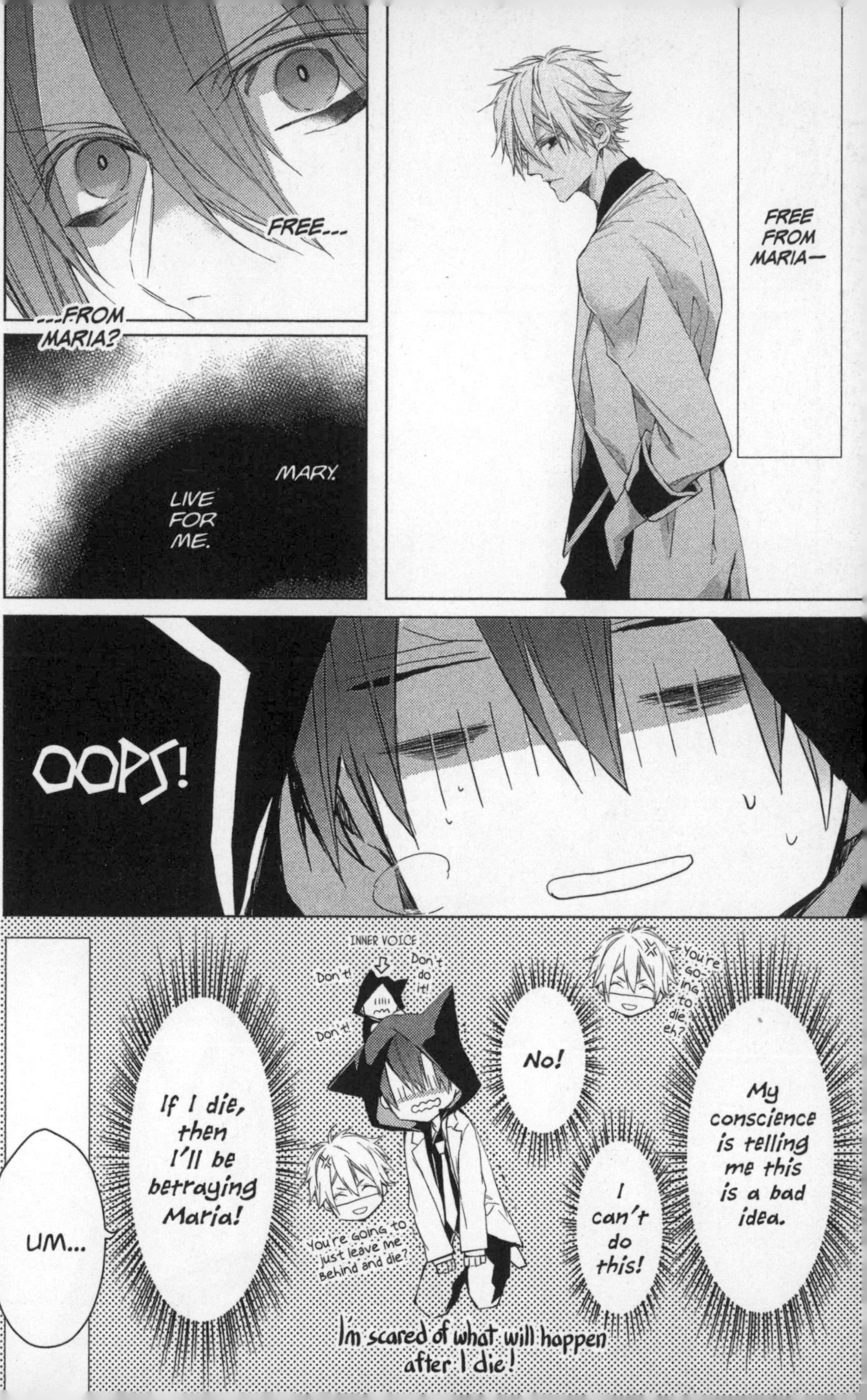
FREE FROM MARIA—
FREE...
...FROM MARIA?
MARY.
LIVE FOR ME.
OOPS!
You're going to die, eh?
My conscience is telling me this is a bad idea.
No!
I can't do this!
INNER VOICE
Don't do it!
Don't!
Don't!
If I die, then I'll be betraying Maria!
You're going to just leave me behind and die?
I'm scared of what will happen after I die!
UM...

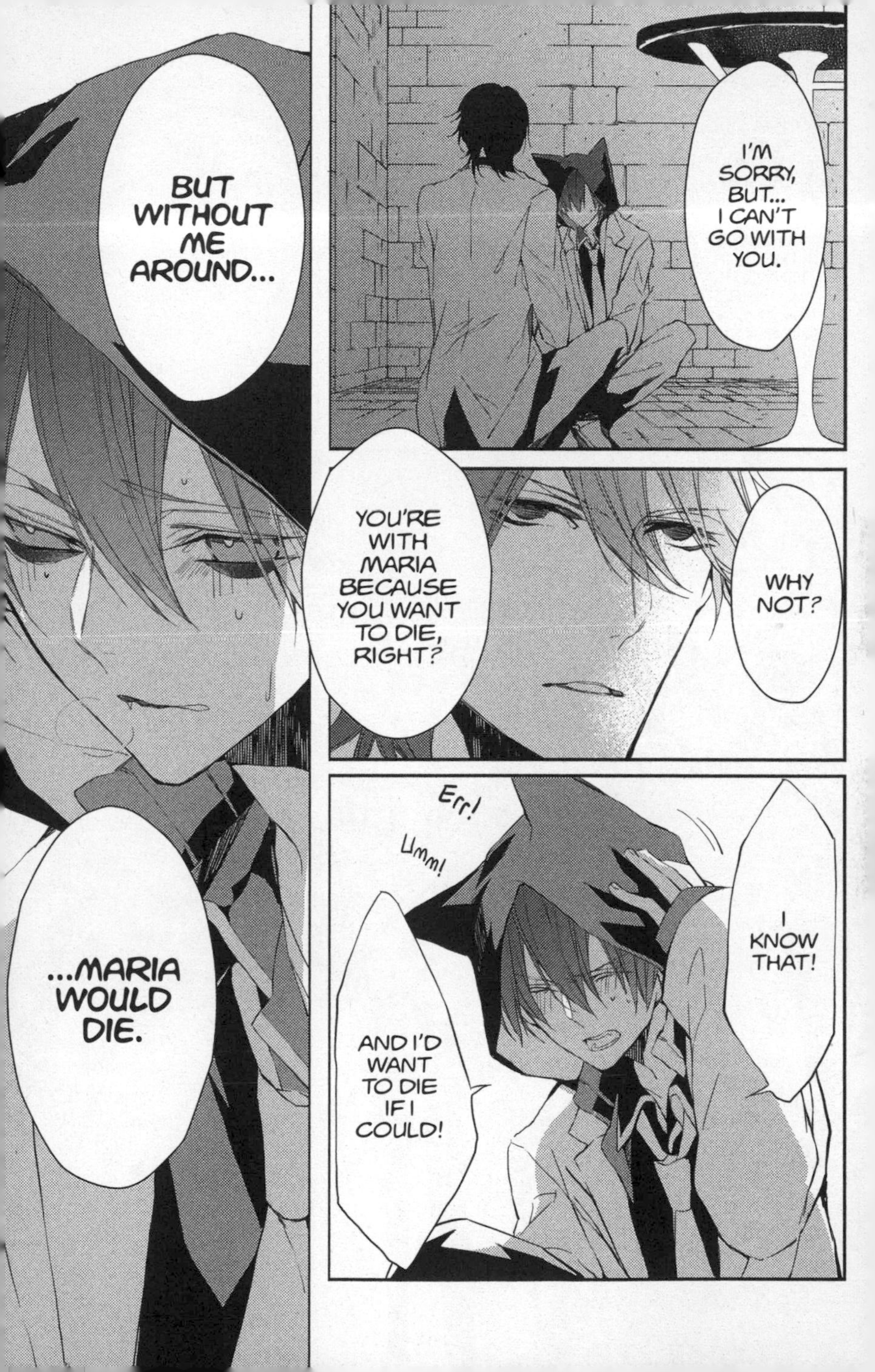
I'M SORRY, BUT... I CAN'T GO WITH YOU.
WHY NOT?
YOU'RE WITH MARIA BECAUSE YOU WANT TO DIE, RIGHT?
I KNOW THAT!
Err!
Umm!
AND I'D WANT TO DIE IF I COULD!
BUT WITHOUT ME AROUND...
...MARIA WOULD DIE.

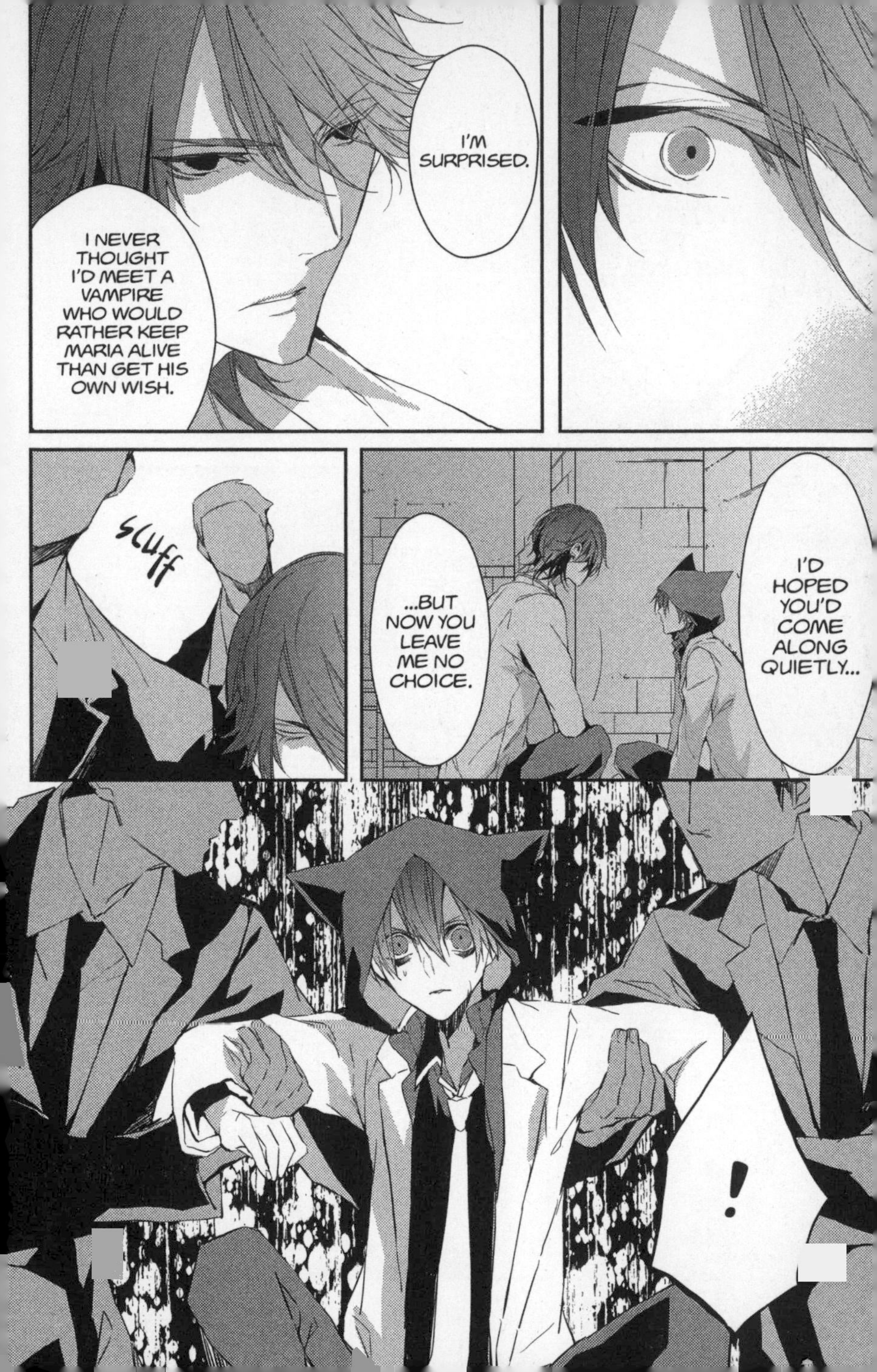
I'M SURPRISED.
I NEVER THOUGHT I'D MEET A VAMPIRE WHO WOULD RATHER KEEP MARIA ALIVE THAN GET HIS OWN WISH.
I'D HOPED YOU'D COME ALONG QUIETLY...
...BUT NOW YOU LEAVE ME NO CHOICE.
scuff
!

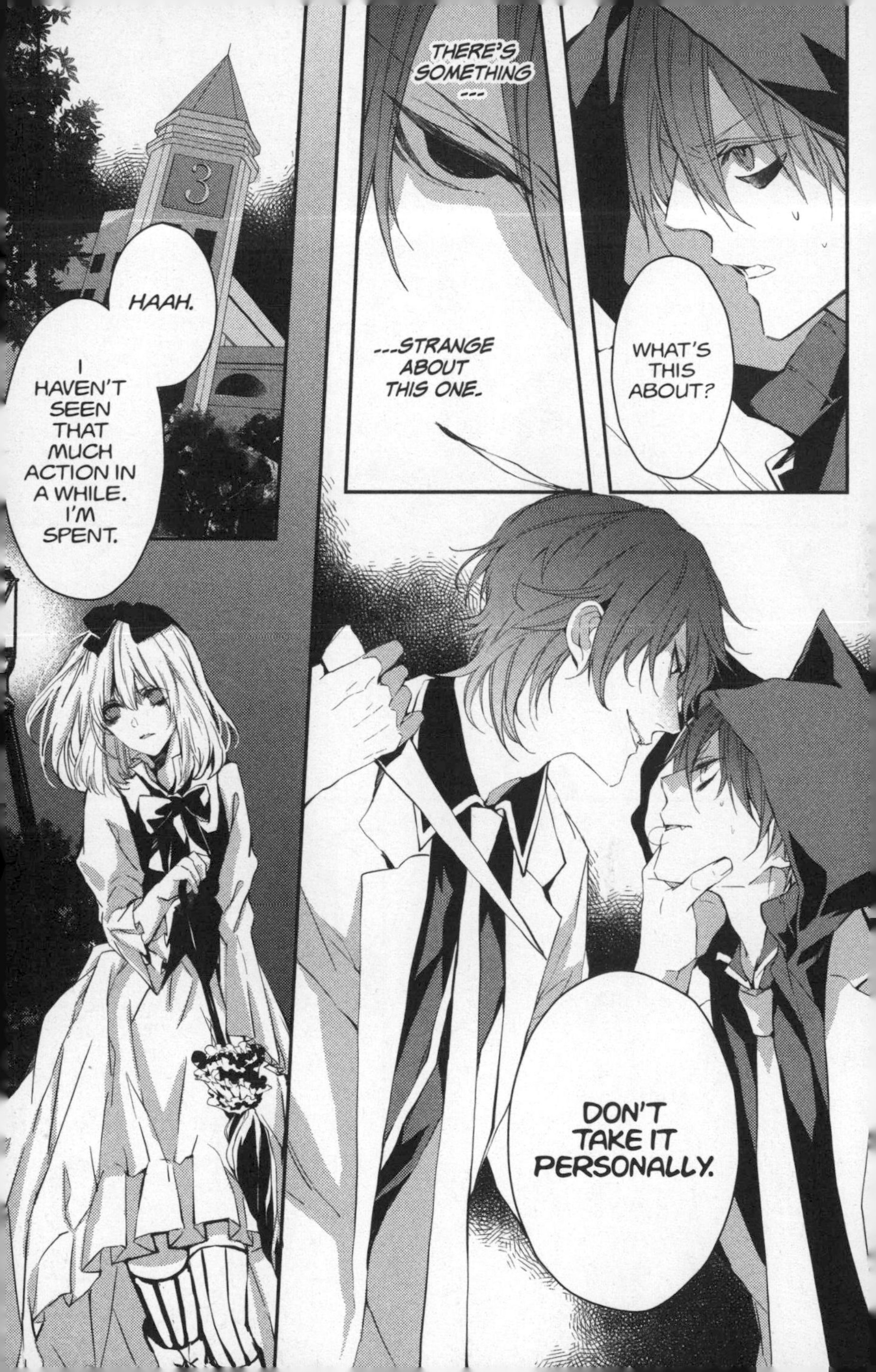
WHAT'S THIS ABOUT?
THERE'S SOMETHING ---
---STRANGE ABOUT THIS ONE.
DON'T TAKE IT PERSONALLY.
HAAH.
I HAVEN'T SEEN THAT MUCH ACTION IN A WHILE. I'M SPENT.

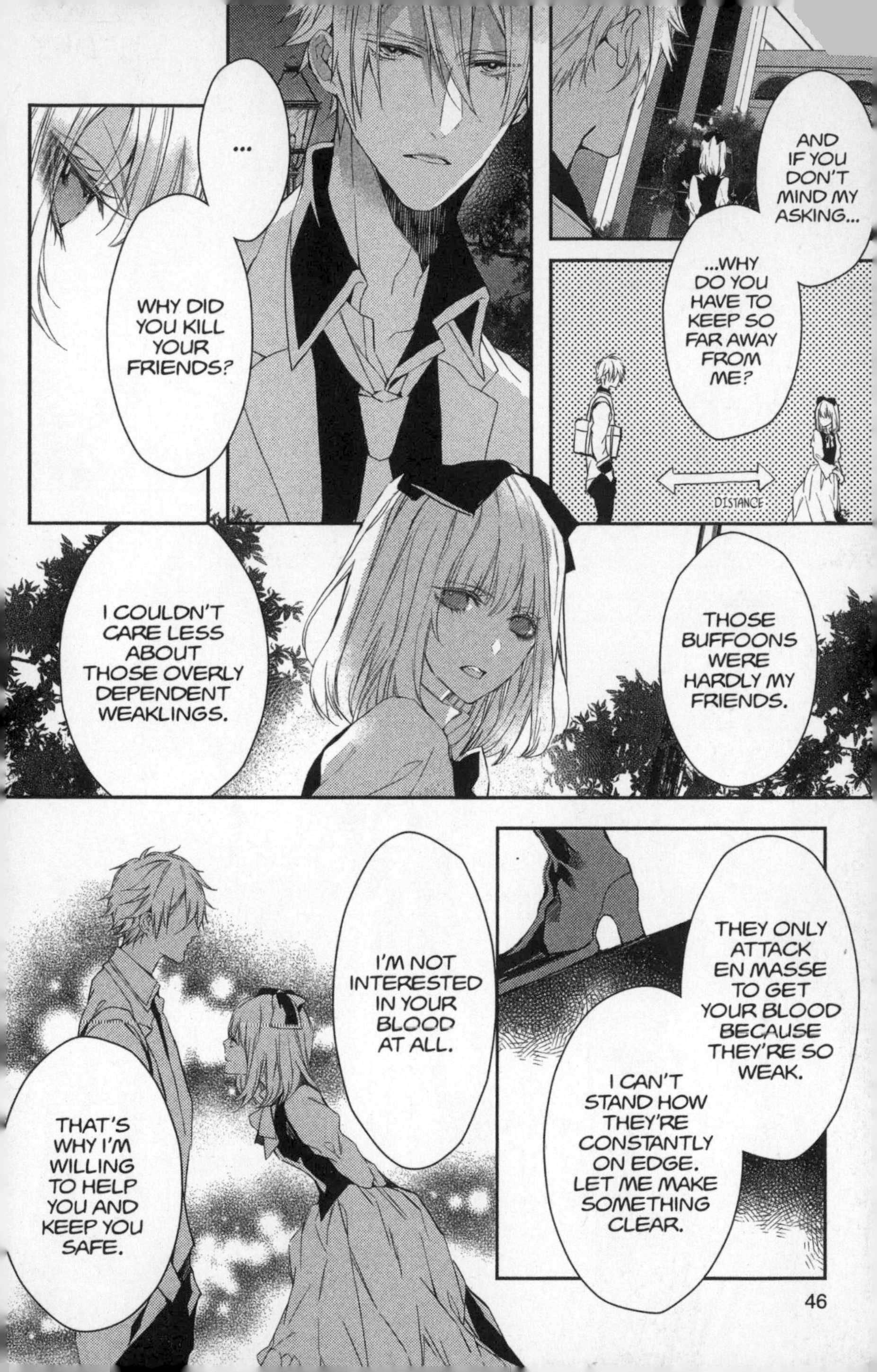
AND IF YOU DON'T MIND MY ASKING...
...WHY DO YOU HAVE TO KEEP SO FAR AWAY FROM ME?
DISTANCE
...
WHY DID YOU KILL YOUR FRIENDS?
THOSE BUFFOONS WERE HARDLY MY FRIENDS.
I COULDN'T CARE LESS ABOUT THOSE OVERLY DEPENDENT WEAKLINGS.
THEY ONLY ATTACK EN MASSE TO GET YOUR BLOOD BECAUSE THEY'RE SO WEAK.
I CAN'T STAND HOW THEY'RE CONSTANTLY ON EDGE. LET ME MAKE SOMETHING CLEAR.
I'M NOT INTERESTED IN YOUR BLOOD AT ALL.
THAT'S WHY I'M WILLING TO HELP YOU AND KEEP YOU SAFE.

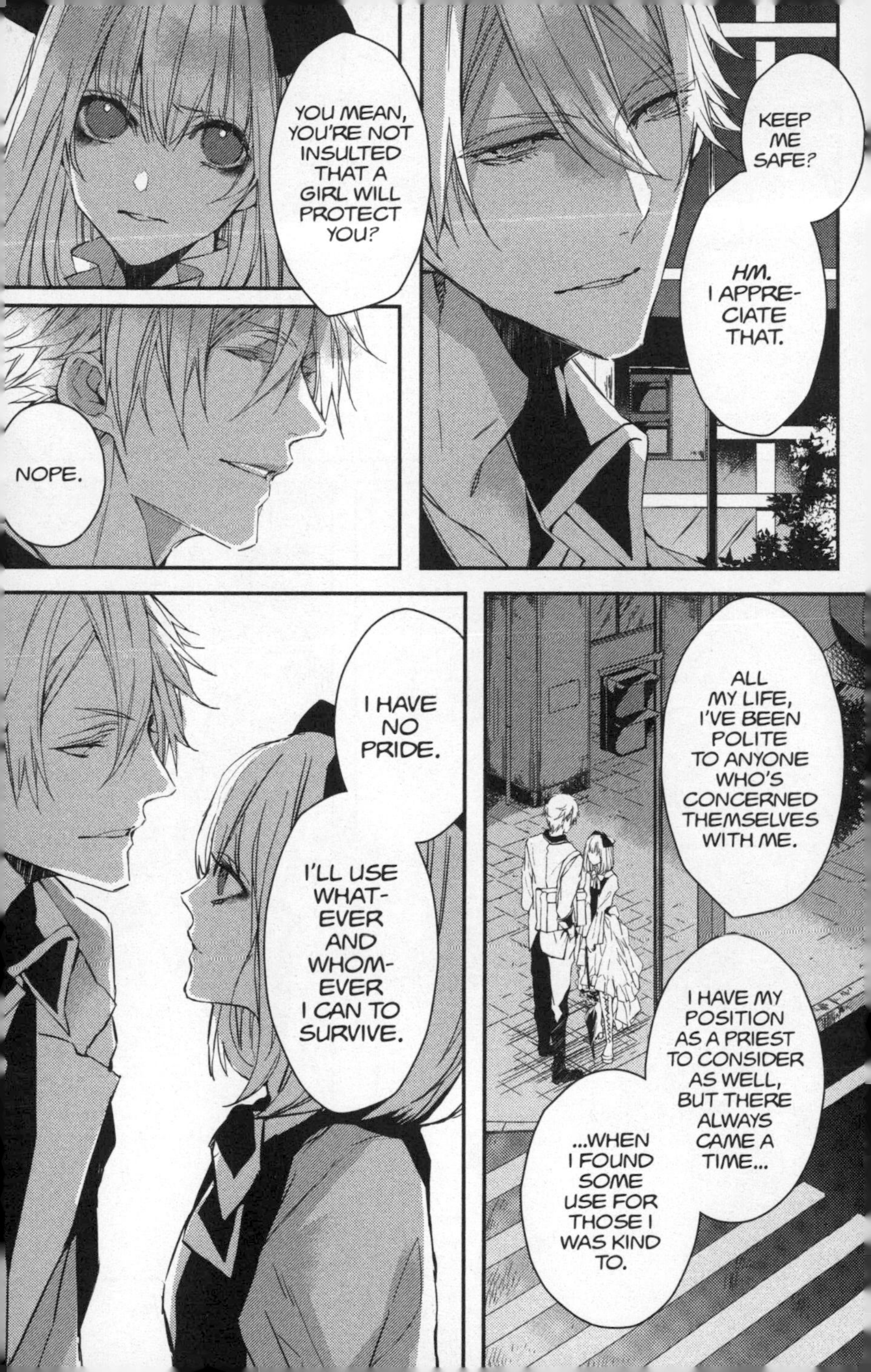
KEEP ME SAFE?
HM. I APPRE-CIATE THAT.
YOU MEAN, YOU'RE NOT INSULTED THAT A GIRL WILL PROTECT YOU?
NOPE.
ALL MY LIFE, I'VE BEEN POLITE TO ANYONE WHO'S CONCERNED THEMSELVES WITH ME.
I HAVE MY POSITION AS A PRIEST TO CONSIDER AS WELL, BUT THERE ALWAYS CAME A TIME...
...WHEN I FOUND SOME USE FOR THOSE I WAS KIND TO.
I HAVE NO PRIDE.
I'LL USE WHAT-EVER AND WHOM-EVER I CAN TO SURVIVE.

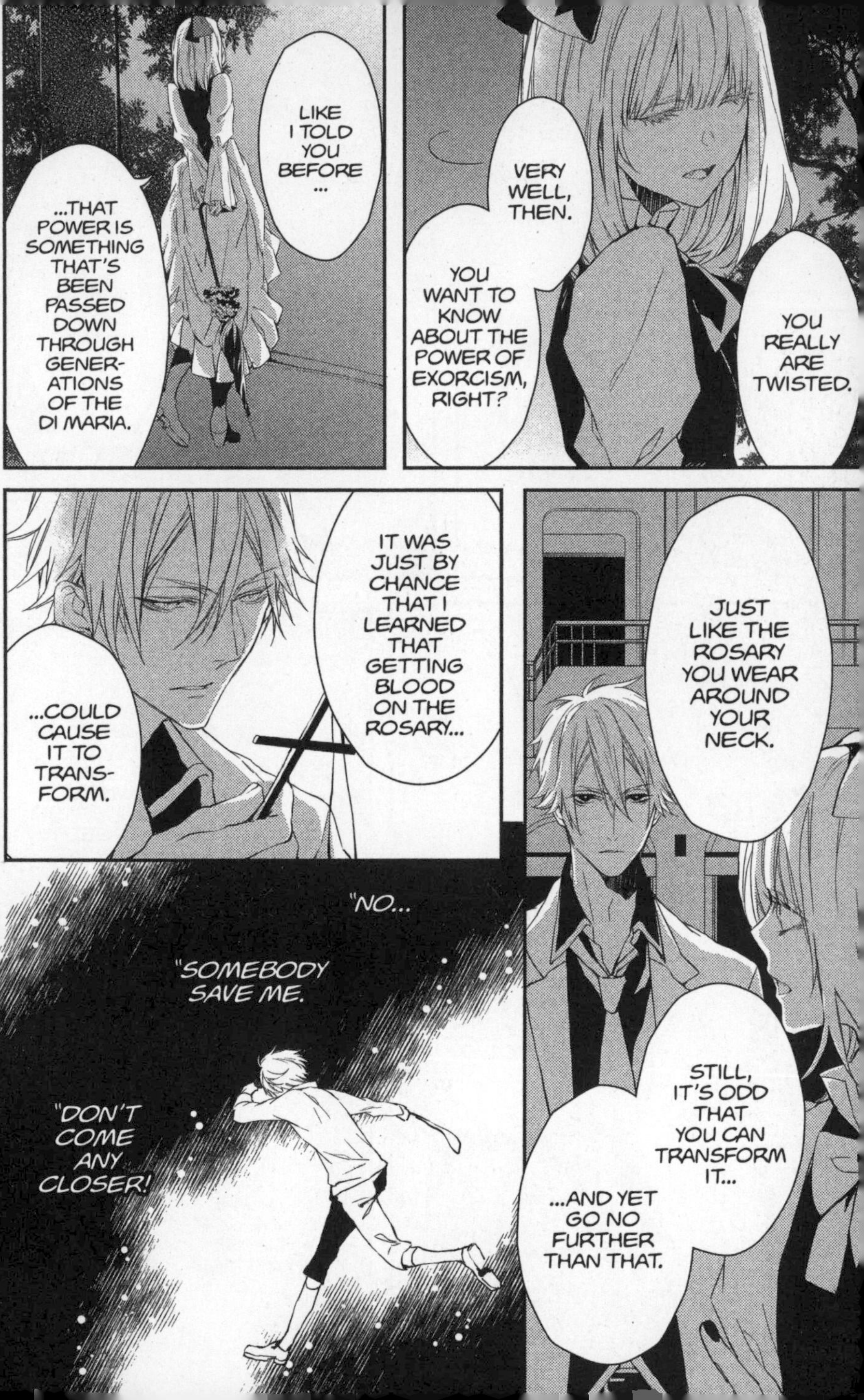
YOU REALLY ARE TWISTED.
VERY WELL, THEN.
YOU WANT TO KNOW ABOUT THE POWER OF EXORCISM, RIGHT?
LIKE I TOLD YOU BEFORE ...
...THAT POWER IS SOMETHING THAT'S BEEN PASSED DOWN THROUGH GENER-ATIONS OF THE DI MARIA.
JUST LIKE THE ROSARY YOU WEAR AROUND YOUR NECK.
STILL, IT'S ODD THAT YOU CAN TRANSFORM IT...
...AND YET GO NO FURTHER THAN THAT.
IT WAS JUST BY CHANCE THAT I LEARNED THAT GETTING BLOOD ON THE ROSARY...
...COULD CAUSE IT TO TRANS-FORM.
"NO...
"SOMEBODY SAVE ME.
"DON'T COME ANY CLOSER!

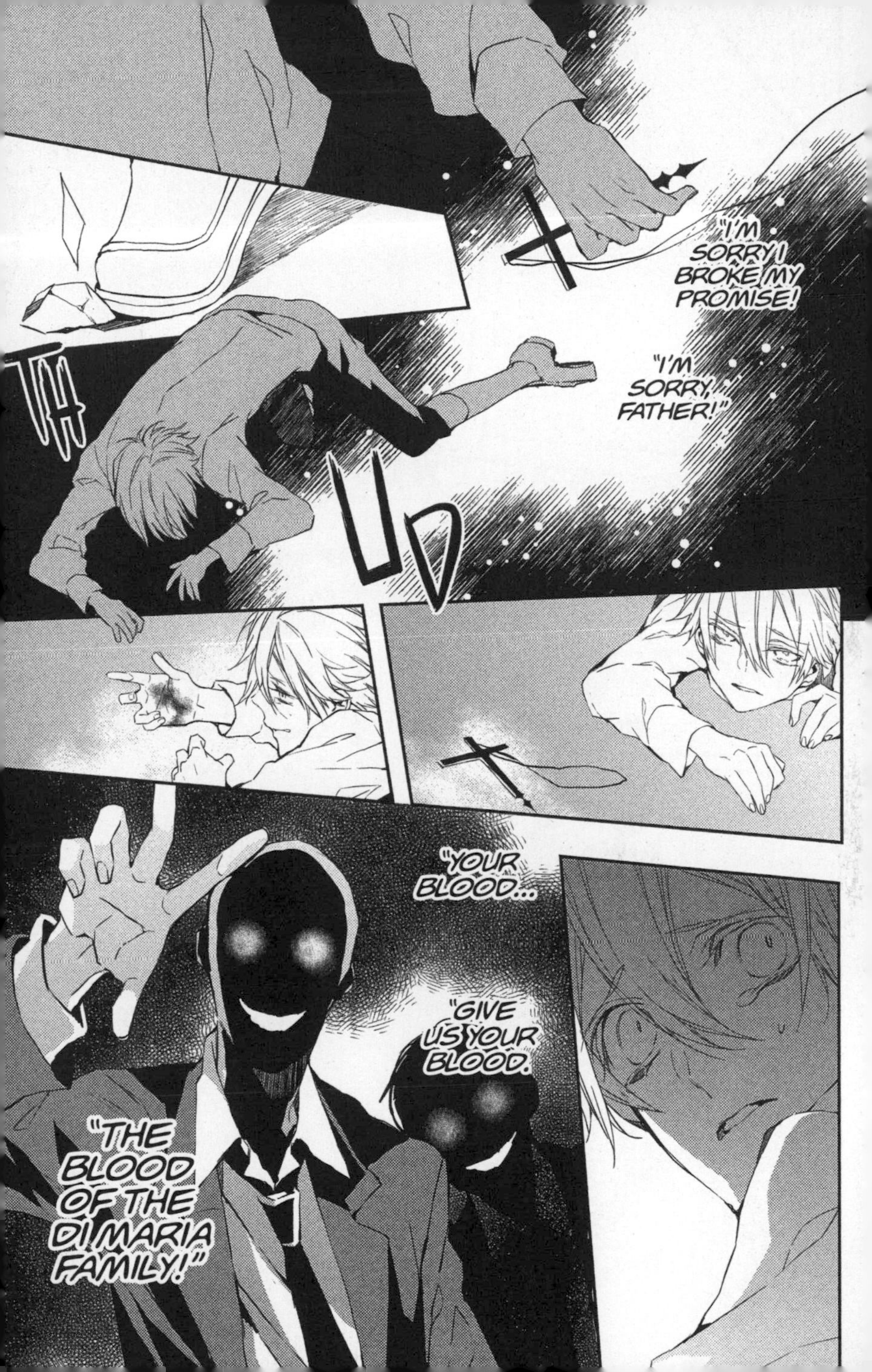
"I'M SORRY I BROKE MY PROMISE!
"I'M SORRY, FATHER!"
THUD
"YOUR BLOOD...
"GIVE US YOUR BLOOD.
"THE BLOOD OF THE DI MARIA FAMILY!"

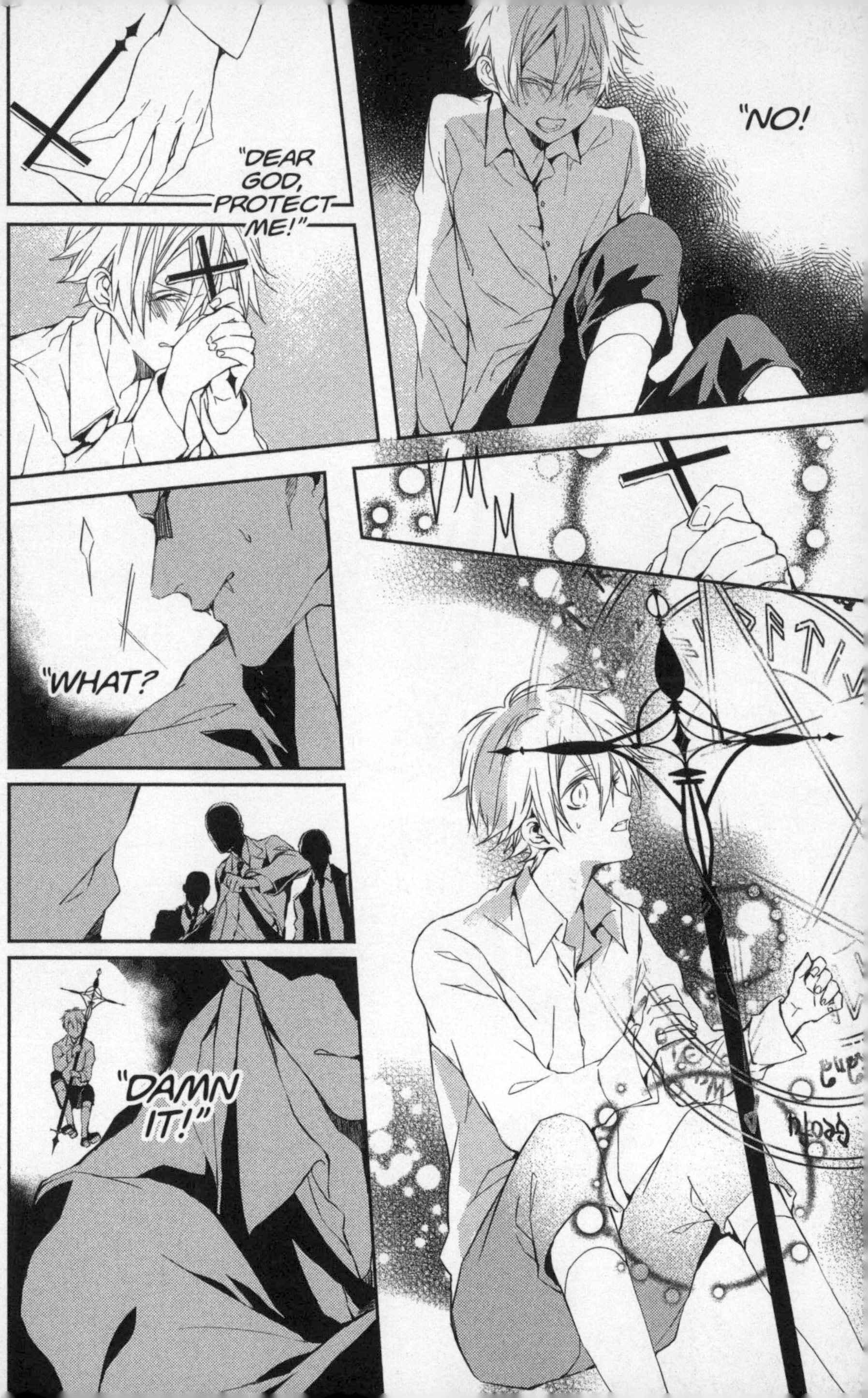
"NO!
"DEAR GOD, PROTECT ME!"
"WHAT?
"DAMN IT!"

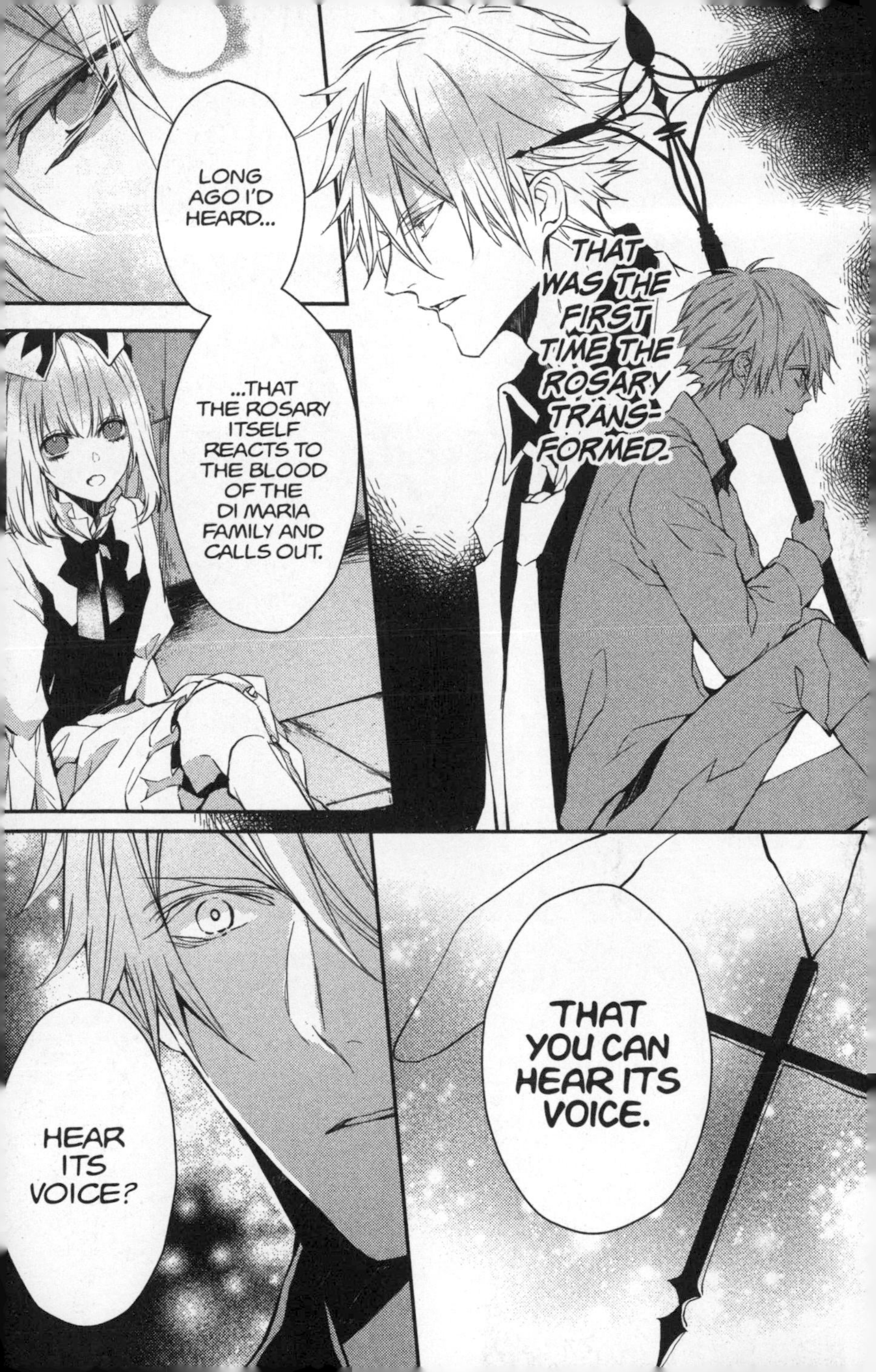
THAT WAS THE FIRST TIME THE ROSARY TRANS-FORMED.
LONG AGO I'D HEARD...
...THAT THE ROSARY ITSELF REACTS TO THE BLOOD OF THE DI MARIA FAMILY AND CALLS OUT.
THAT YOU CAN HEAR ITS VOICE.
HEAR ITS VOICE?

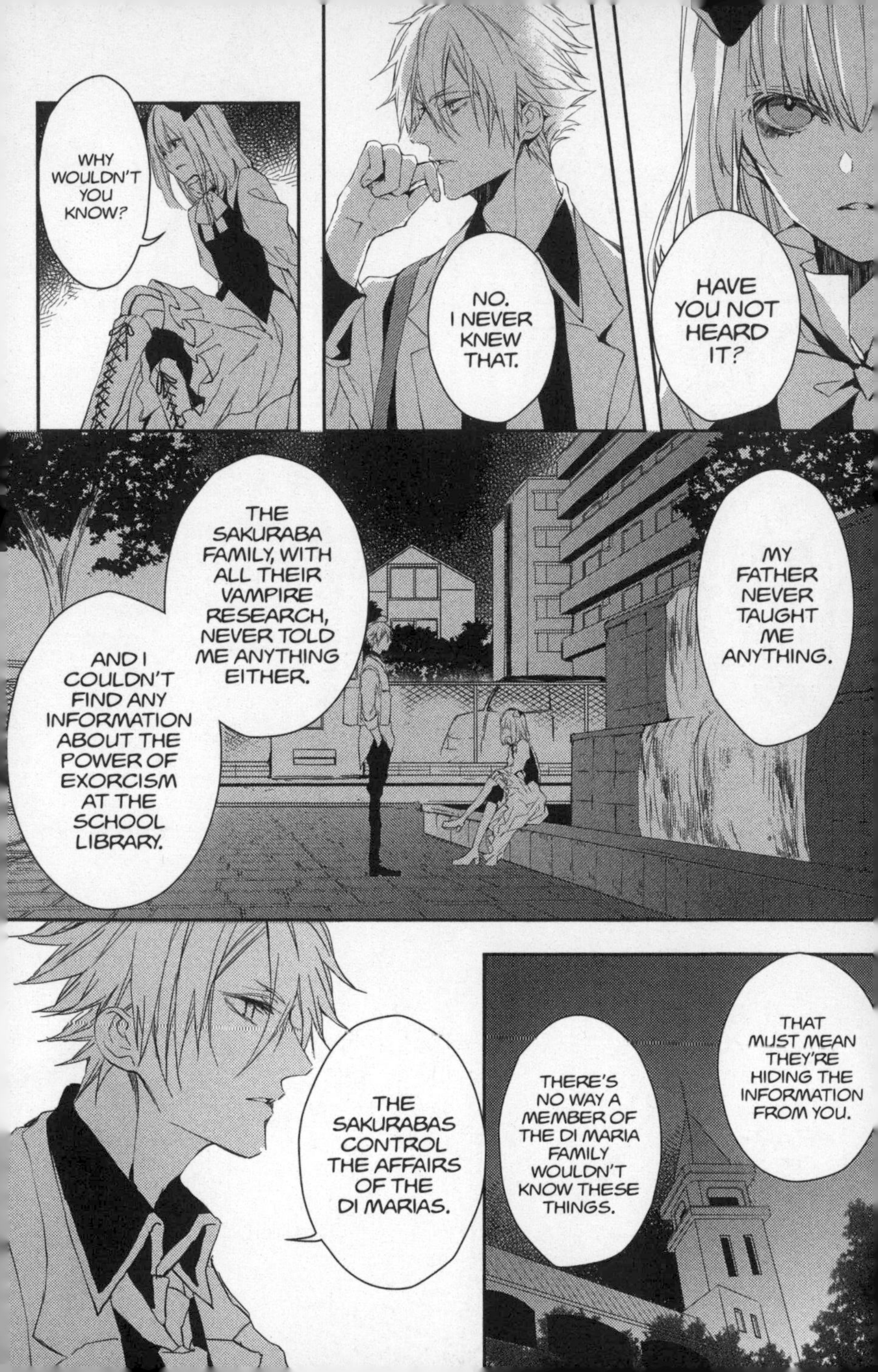
HAVE YOU NOT HEARD IT?
NO. I NEVER KNEW THAT.
WHY WOULDN'T YOU KNOW?
MY FATHER NEVER TAUGHT ME ANYTHING.
THE SAKURABA FAMILY, WITH ALL THEIR VAMPIRE RESEARCH, NEVER TOLD ME ANYTHING EITHER.
AND I COULDN'T FIND ANY INFORMATION ABOUT THE POWER OF EXORCISM AT THE SCHOOL LIBRARY.
THAT MUST MEAN THEY'RE HIDING THE INFORMATION FROM YOU.
THERE'S NO WAY A MEMBER OF THE DI MARIA FAMILY WOULDN'T KNOW THESE THINGS.
THE SAKURABAS CONTROL THE AFFAIRS OF THE DI MARIAS.

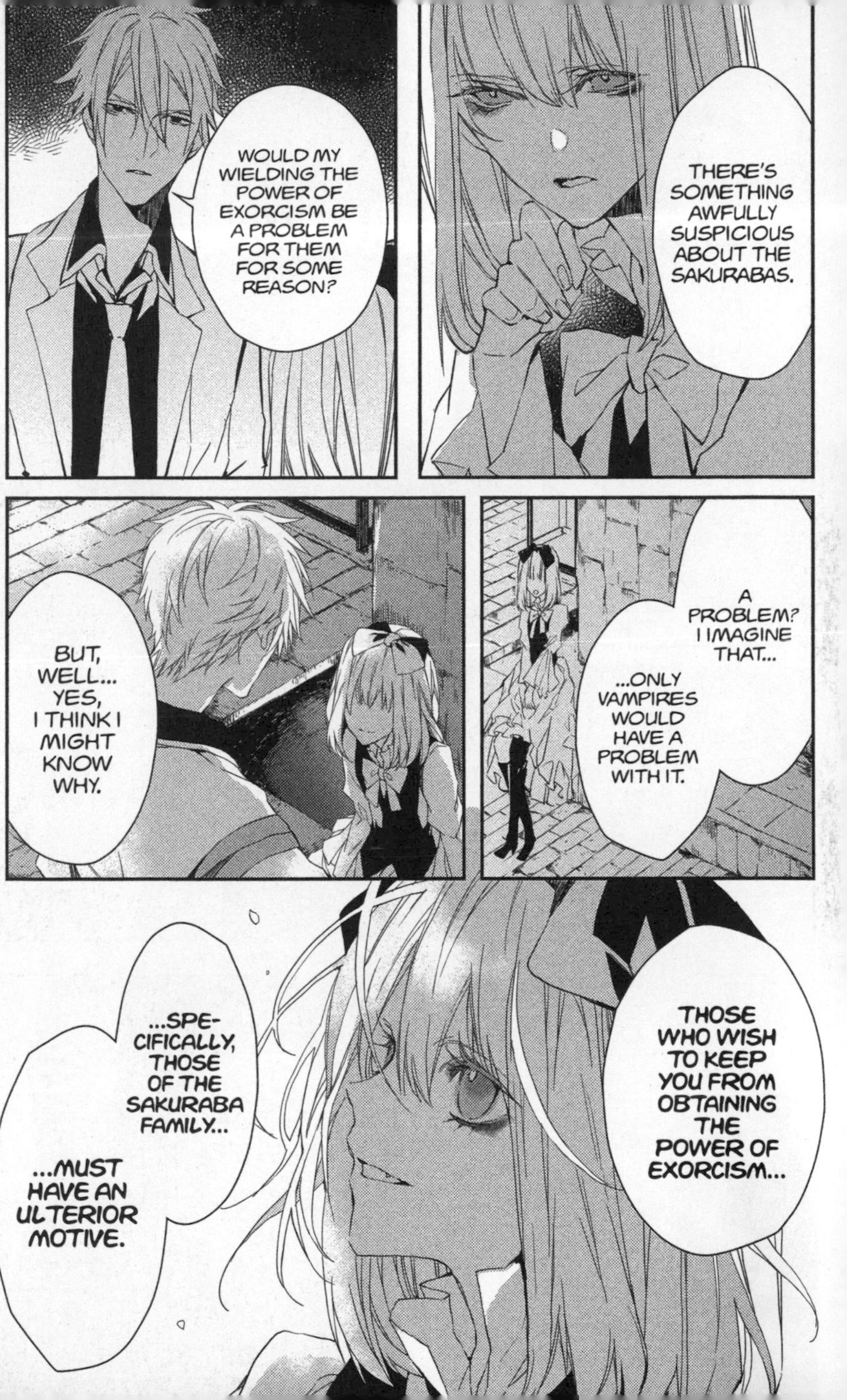
THERE'S SOMETHING AWFULLY SUSPICIOUS ABOUT THE SAKURABAS.
WOULD MY WIELDING THE POWER OF EXORCISM BE A PROBLEM FOR THEM FOR SOME REASON?
A PROBLEM? I IMAGINE THAT...
...ONLY VAMPIRES WOULD HAVE A PROBLEM WITH IT.
BUT, WELL... YES, I THINK I MIGHT KNOW WHY.
THOSE WHO WISH TO KEEP YOU FROM OBTAINING THE POWER OF EXORCISM...
...SPE-CIFICALLY, THOSE OF THE SAKURABA FAMILY...
...MUST HAVE AN ULTERIOR MOTIVE.

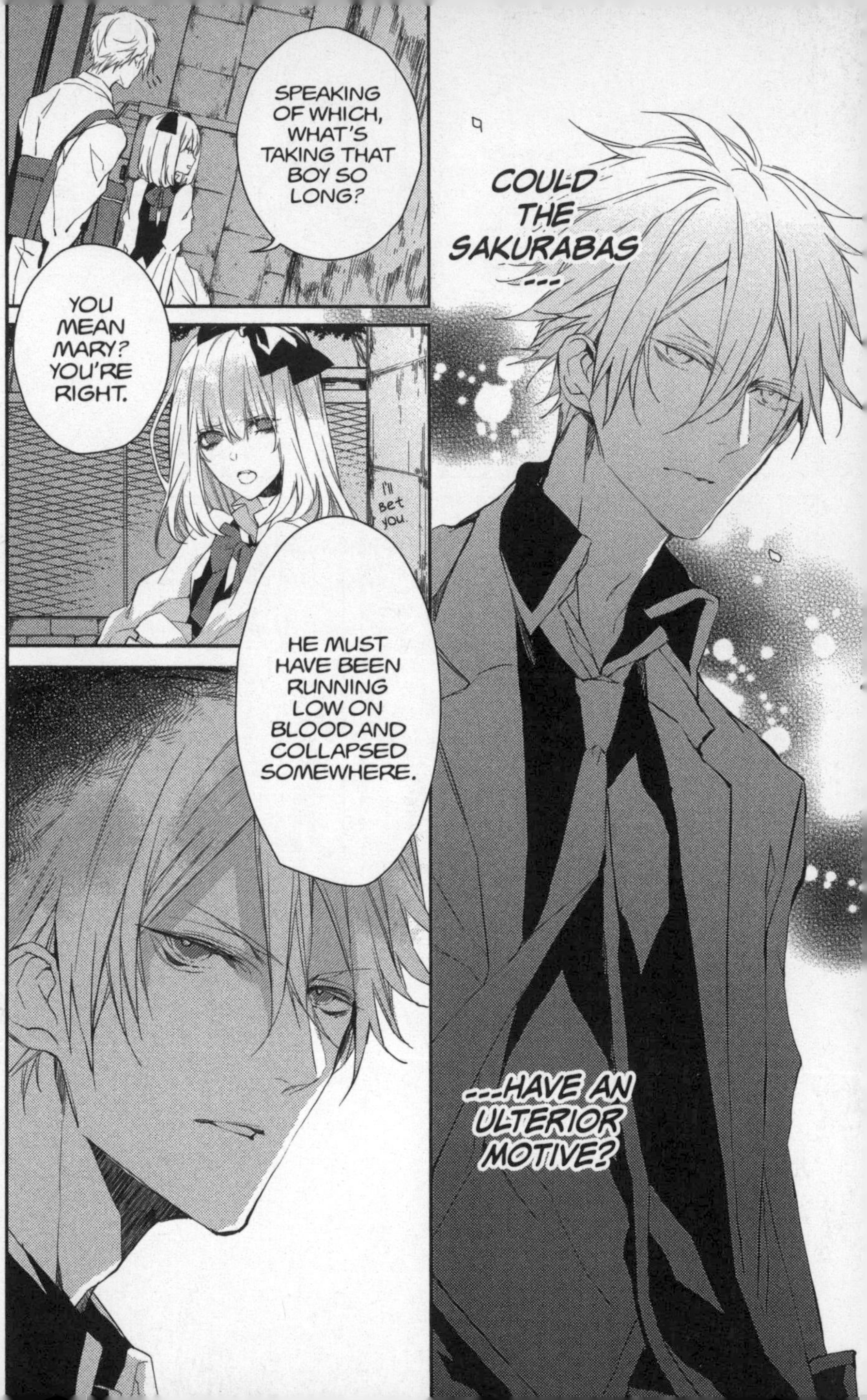
COULD THE SAKURABAS---
---HAVE AN ULTERIOR MOTIVE?
SPEAKING OF WHICH, WHAT'S TAKING THAT BOY SO LONG?
YOU MEAN MARY? YOU'RE RIGHT.
I'll bet you.
HE MUST HAVE BEEN RUNNING LOW ON BLOOD AND COLLAPSED SOMEWHERE.

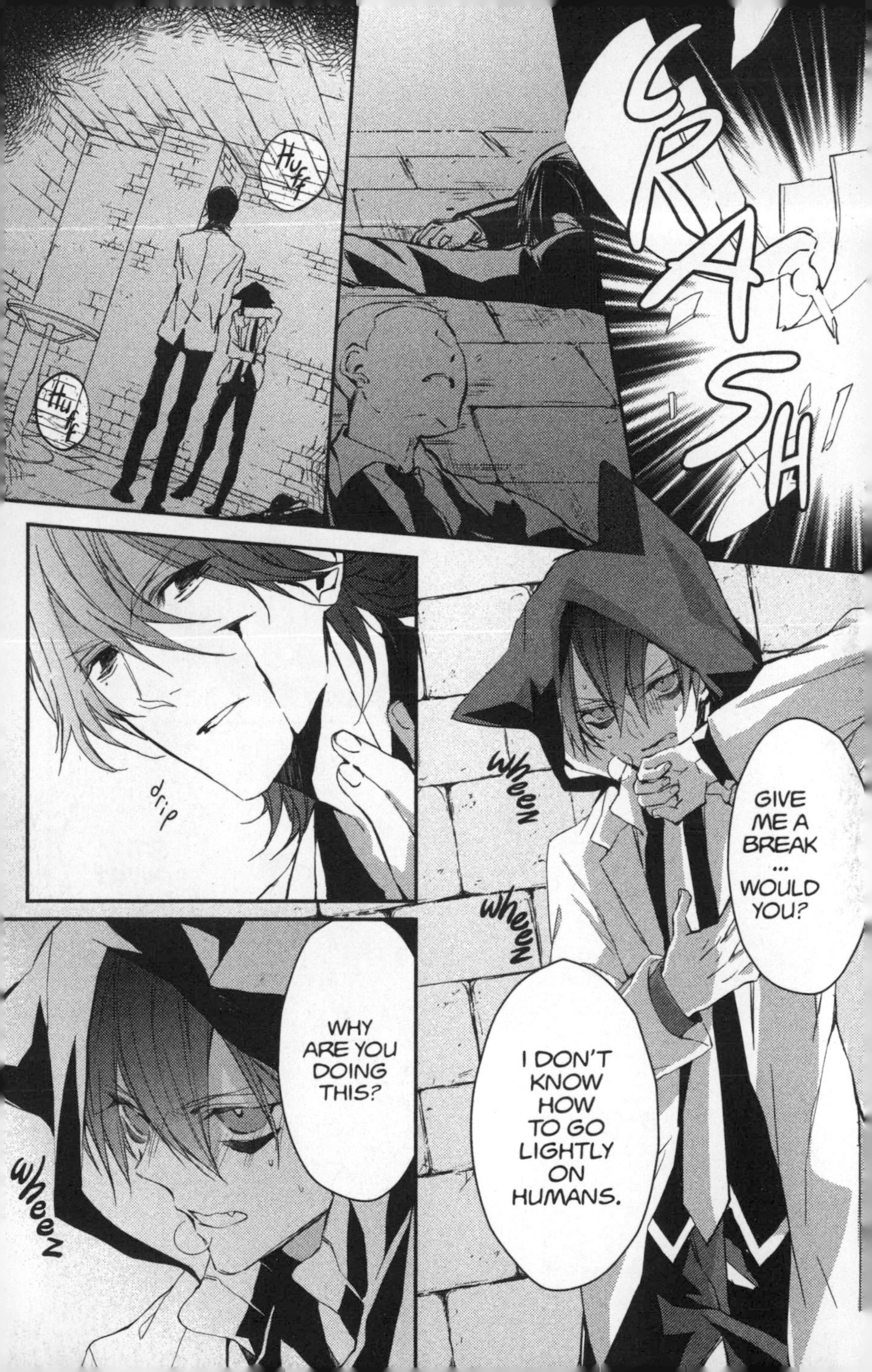
CRASH!
Huff
Huff
GIVE ME A BREAK ... WOULD YOU?
wheez
wheez
I DON'T KNOW HOW TO GO LIGHTLY ON HUMANS.
drip
WHY ARE YOU DOING THIS?
wheez

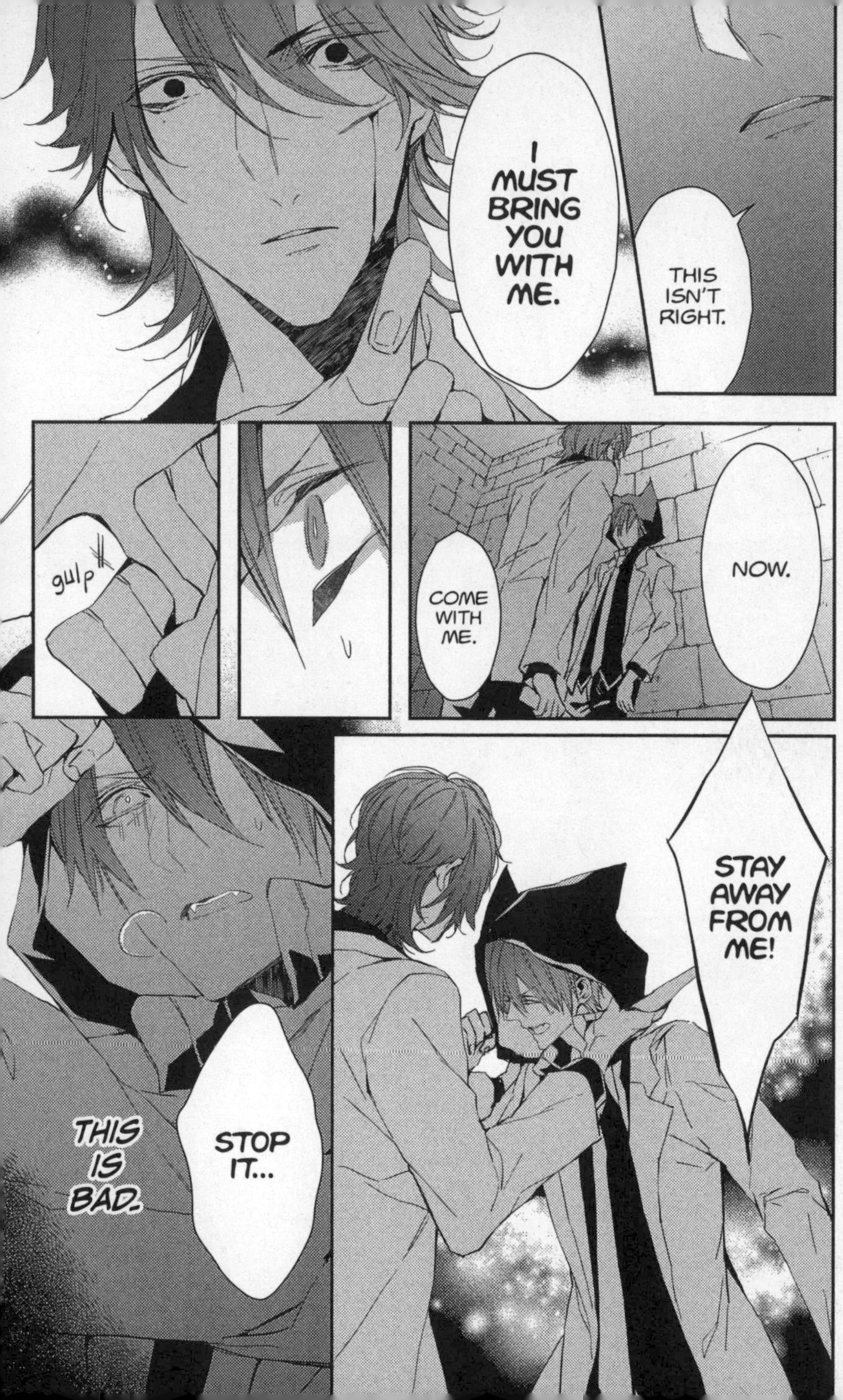
THIS ISN'T RIGHT.
I MUST BRING YOU WITH ME.
NOW.
COME WITH ME.
gulp
STAY AWAY FROM ME!
STOP IT...
THIS IS BAD.

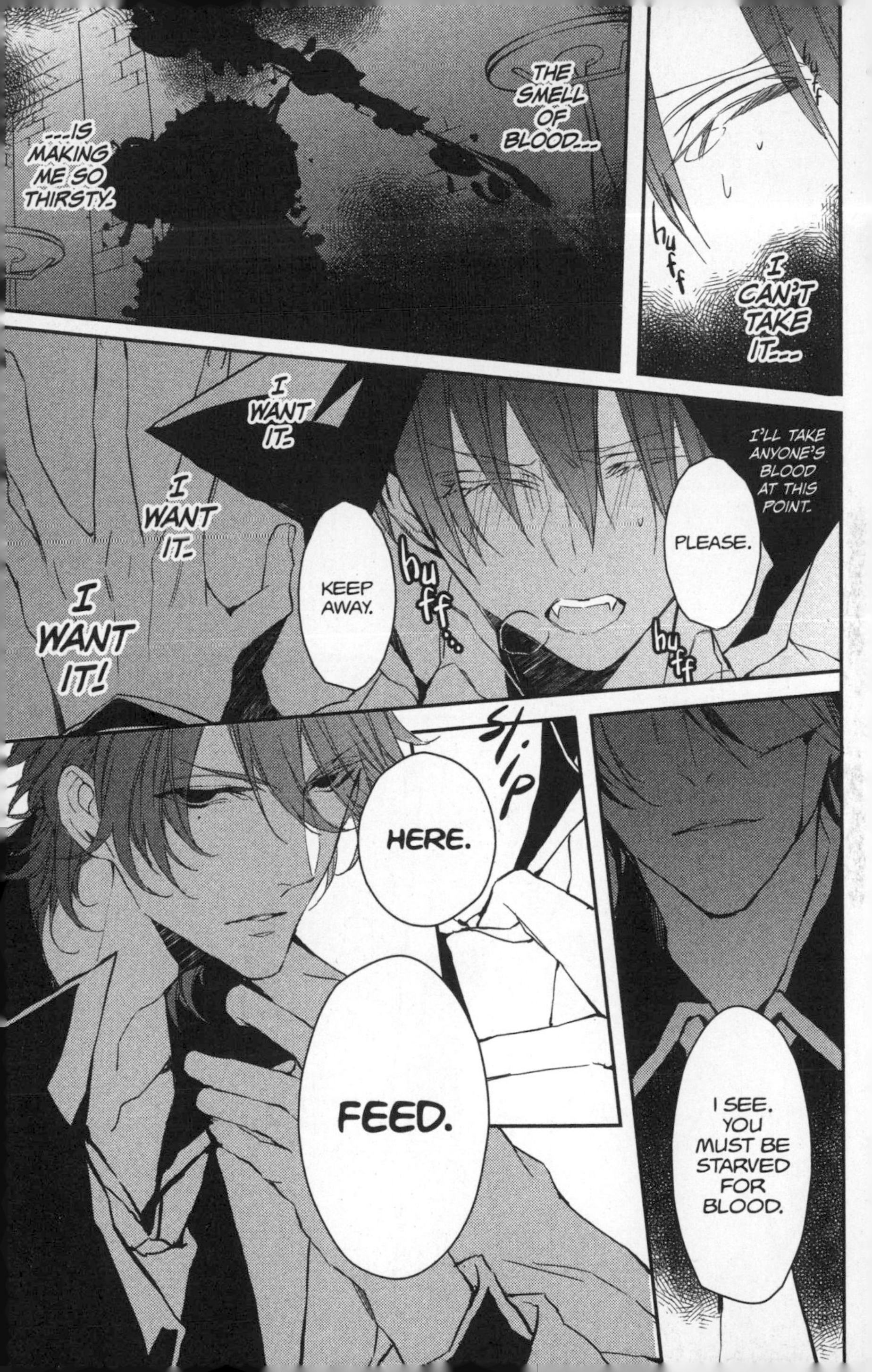
huff
huff
I CAN'T TAKE IT...
THE SMELL OF BLOOD...
...IS MAKING ME SO THIRSTY.
I'LL TAKE ANYONE'S BLOOD AT THIS POINT.
PLEASE.
huff
KEEP AWAY.
huff...
I WANT IT.
I WANT IT.
I WANT IT!
I SEE. YOU MUST BE STARVED FOR BLOOD.
slip
HERE.
FEED.

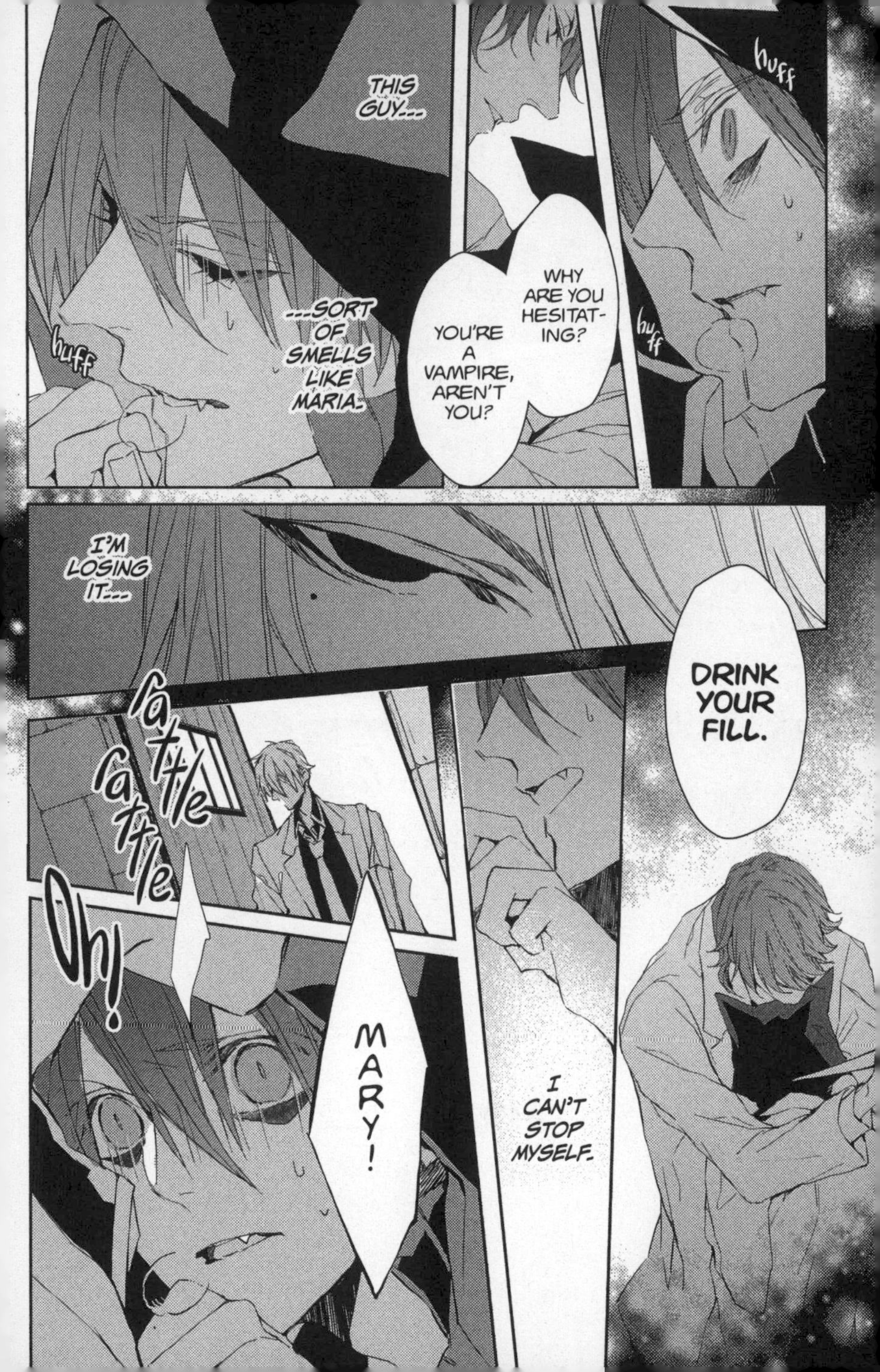
huff
huff
WHY ARE YOU HESITATING?
YOU'RE A VAMPIRE, AREN'T YOU?
THIS GUY...
...SORT OF SMELLS LIKE MARIA.
huff
I'M LOSING IT...
DRINK YOUR FILL.
I CAN'T STOP MYSELF.
rattle rattle
Oh!
MARY!

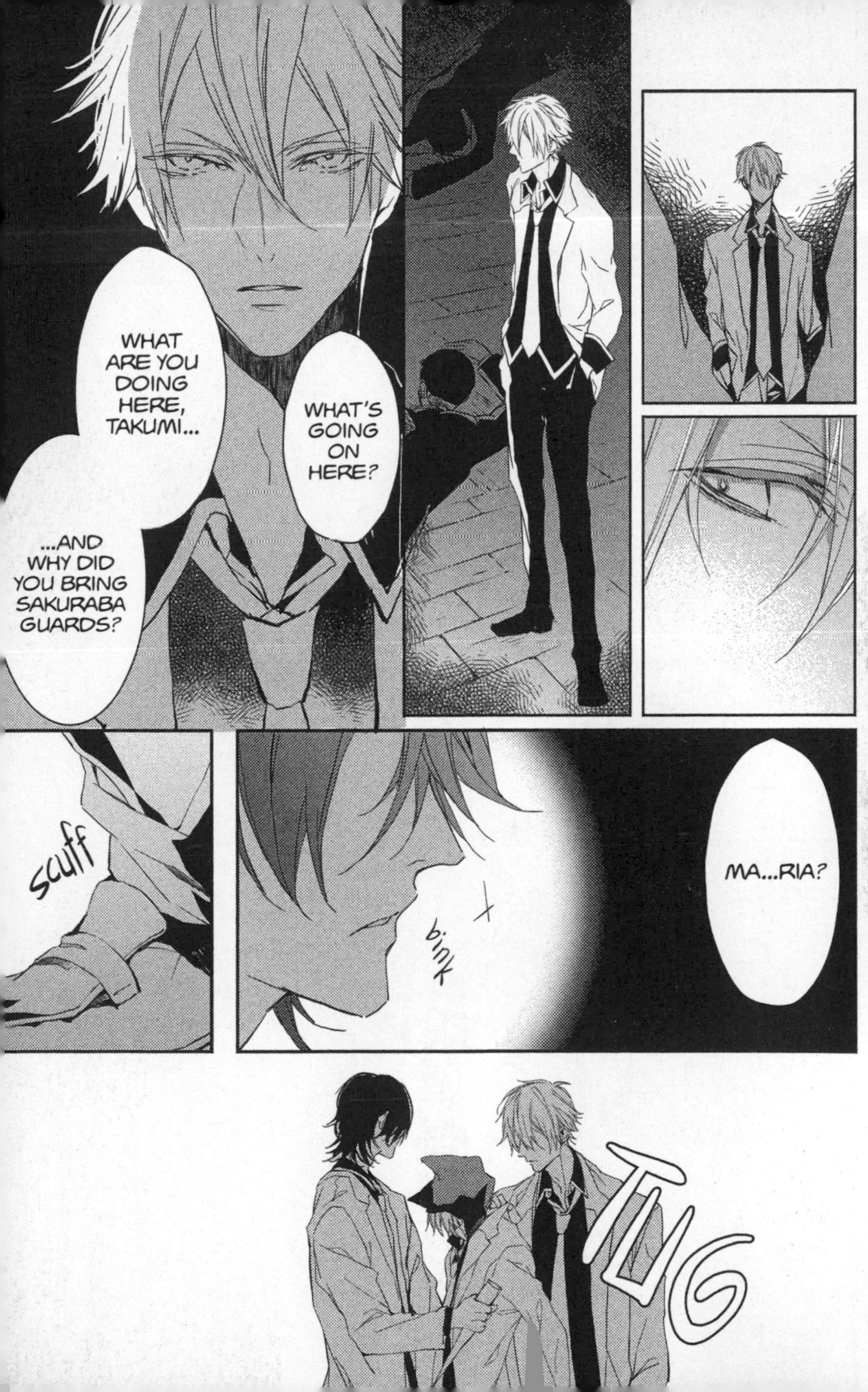
WHAT'S GOING ON HERE?
WHAT ARE YOU DOING HERE, TAKUMI...
...AND WHY DID YOU BRING SAKURABA GUARDS?
MA...RIA?
blink
scuff
TUG

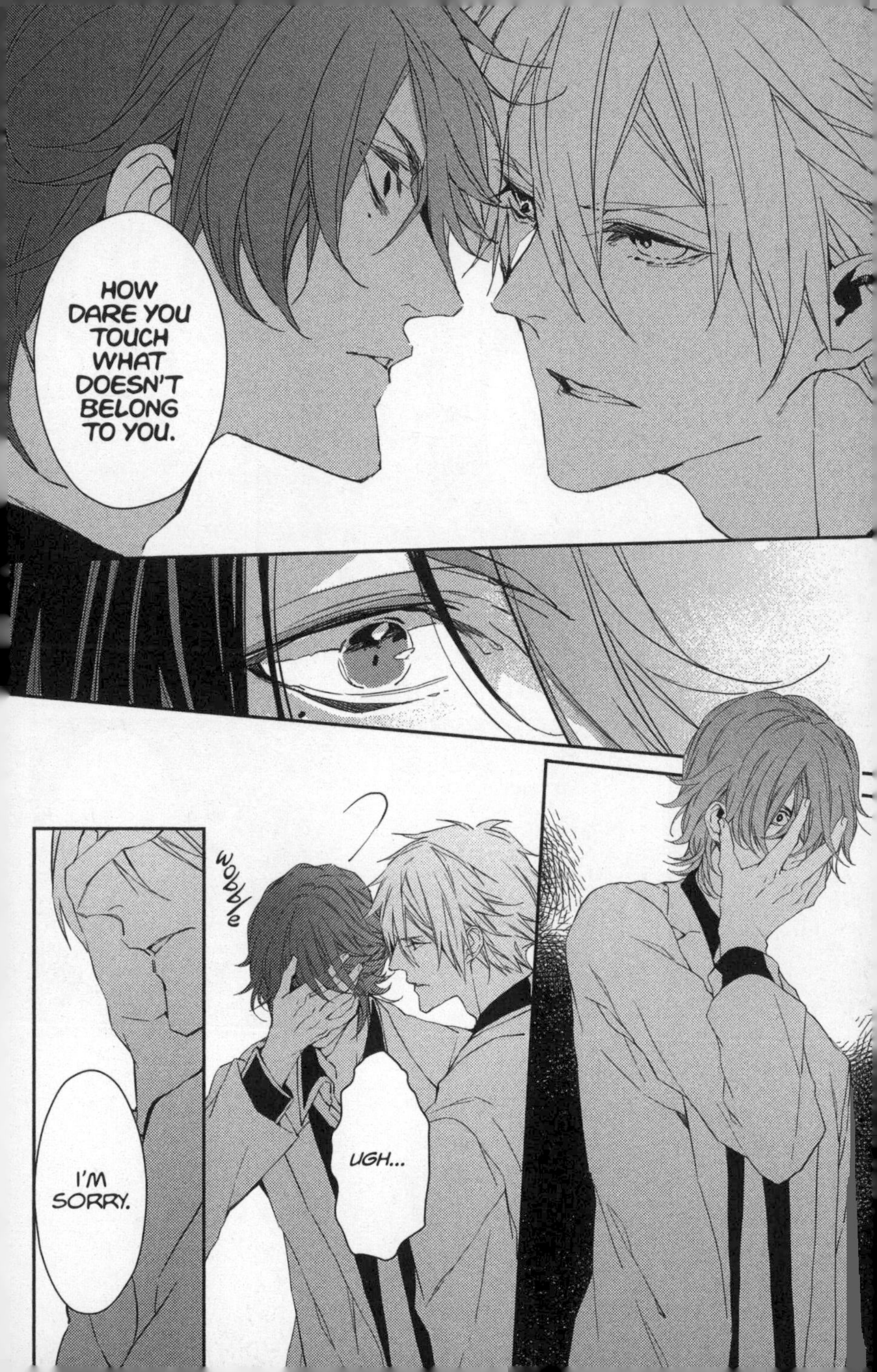
HOW DARE YOU TOUCH WHAT DOESN'T BELONG TO YOU.
wobble
UGH...
I'M SORRY.

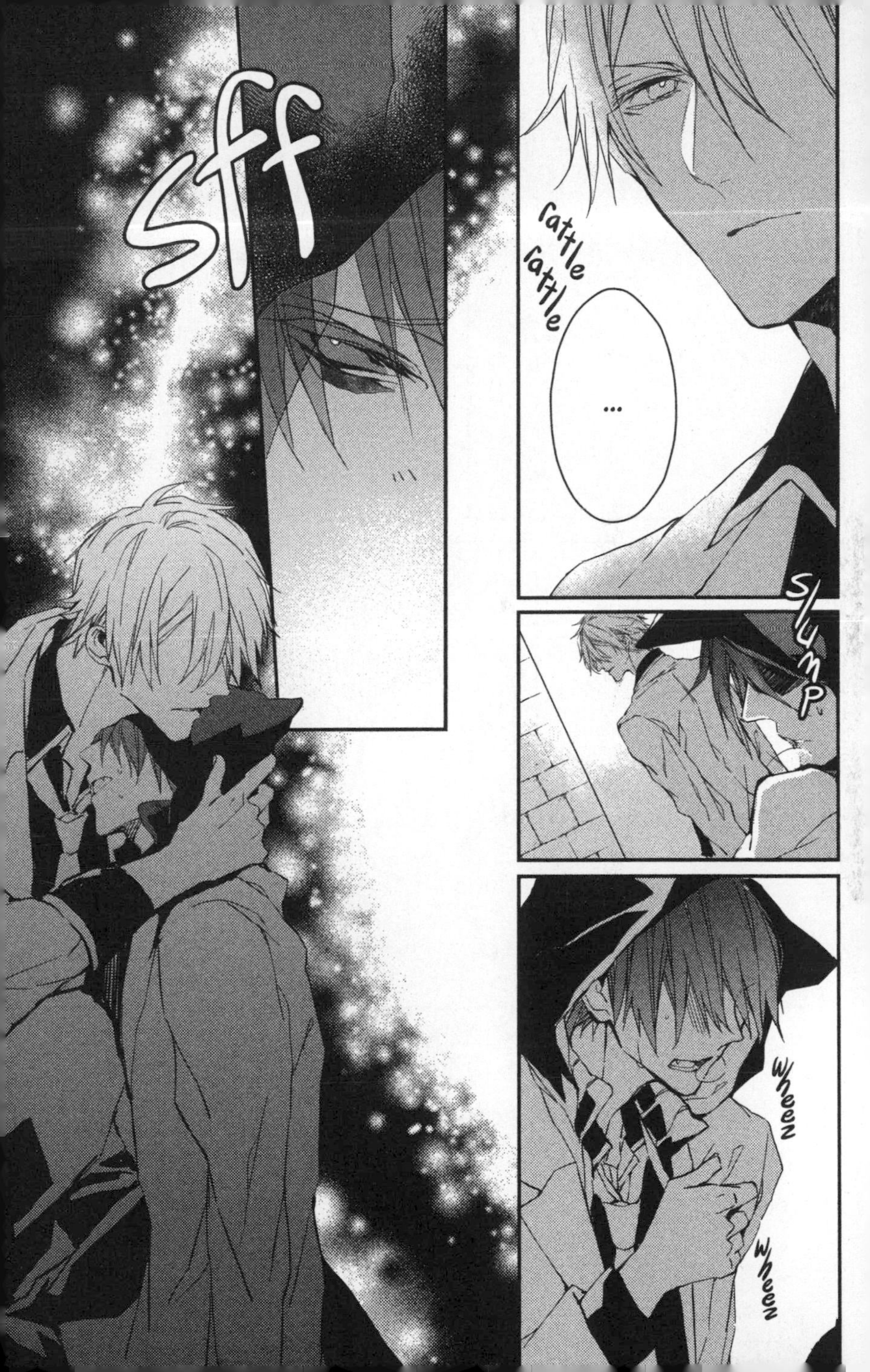
rattle rattle
...
slump
wheeze
wheeze
sff

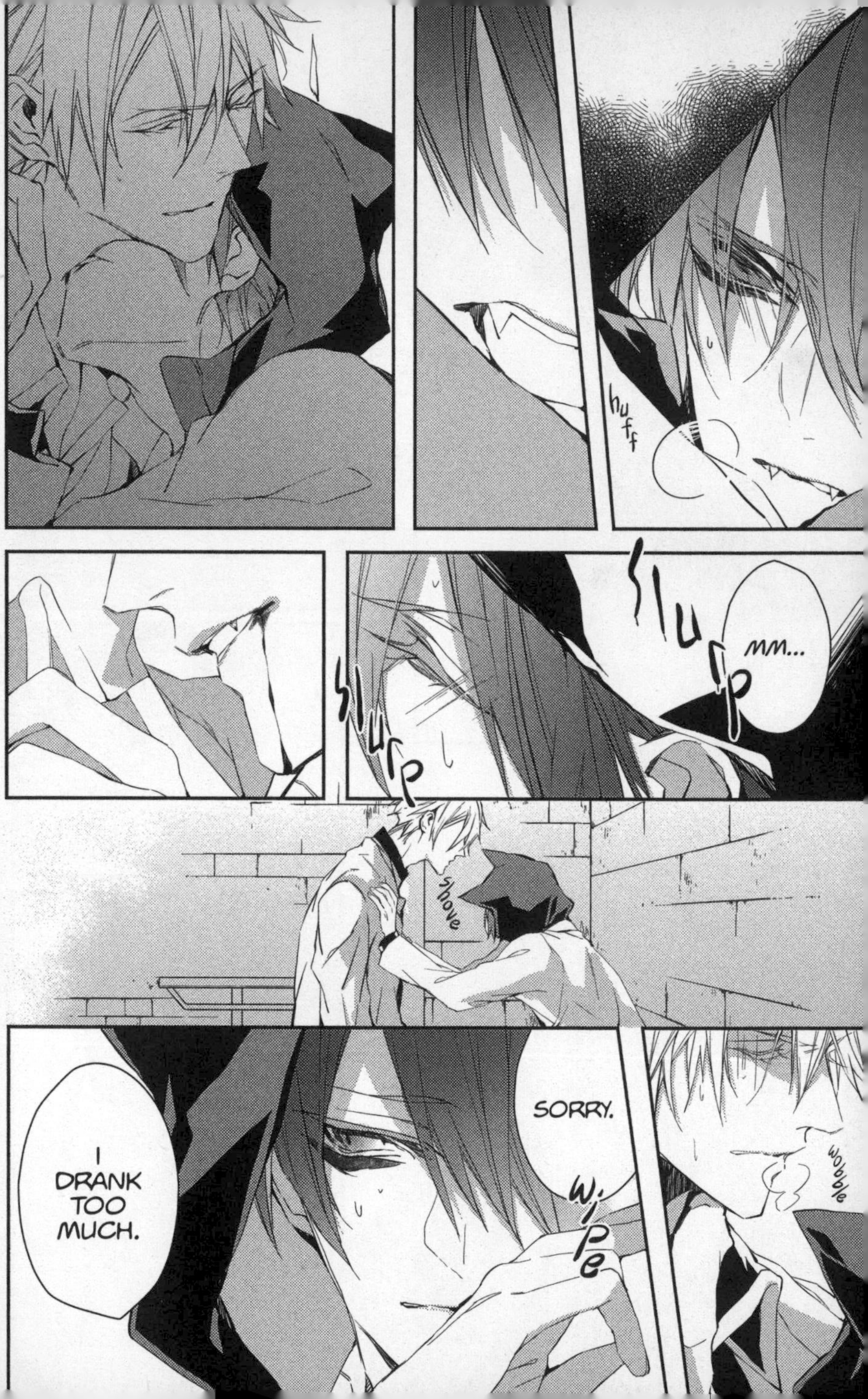
huff
slurp
mm...
slurp
shove
wobble
SORRY.
wipe
I DRANK TOO MUCH.

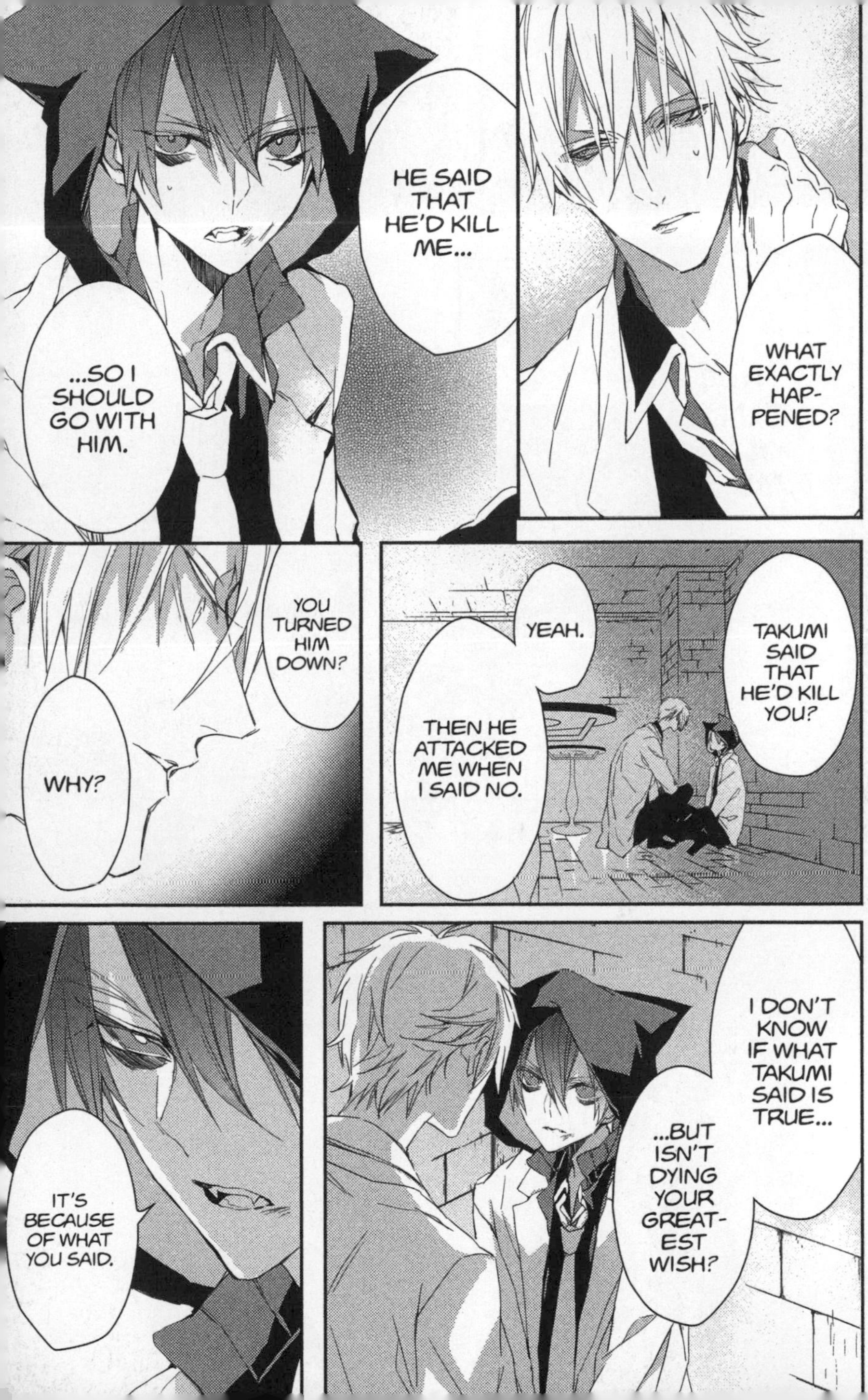
WHAT EXACTLY HAP-PENED?
HE SAID THAT HE'D KILL ME...
...SO I SHOULD GO WITH HIM.
TAKUMI SAID THAT HE'D KILL YOU?
YEAH.
THEN HE ATTACKED ME WHEN I SAID NO.
YOU TURNED HIM DOWN?
WHY?
I DON'T KNOW IF WHAT TAKUMI SAID IS TRUE...
...BUT ISN'T DYING YOUR GREAT-EST WISH?
IT'S BECAUSE OF WHAT YOU SAID.

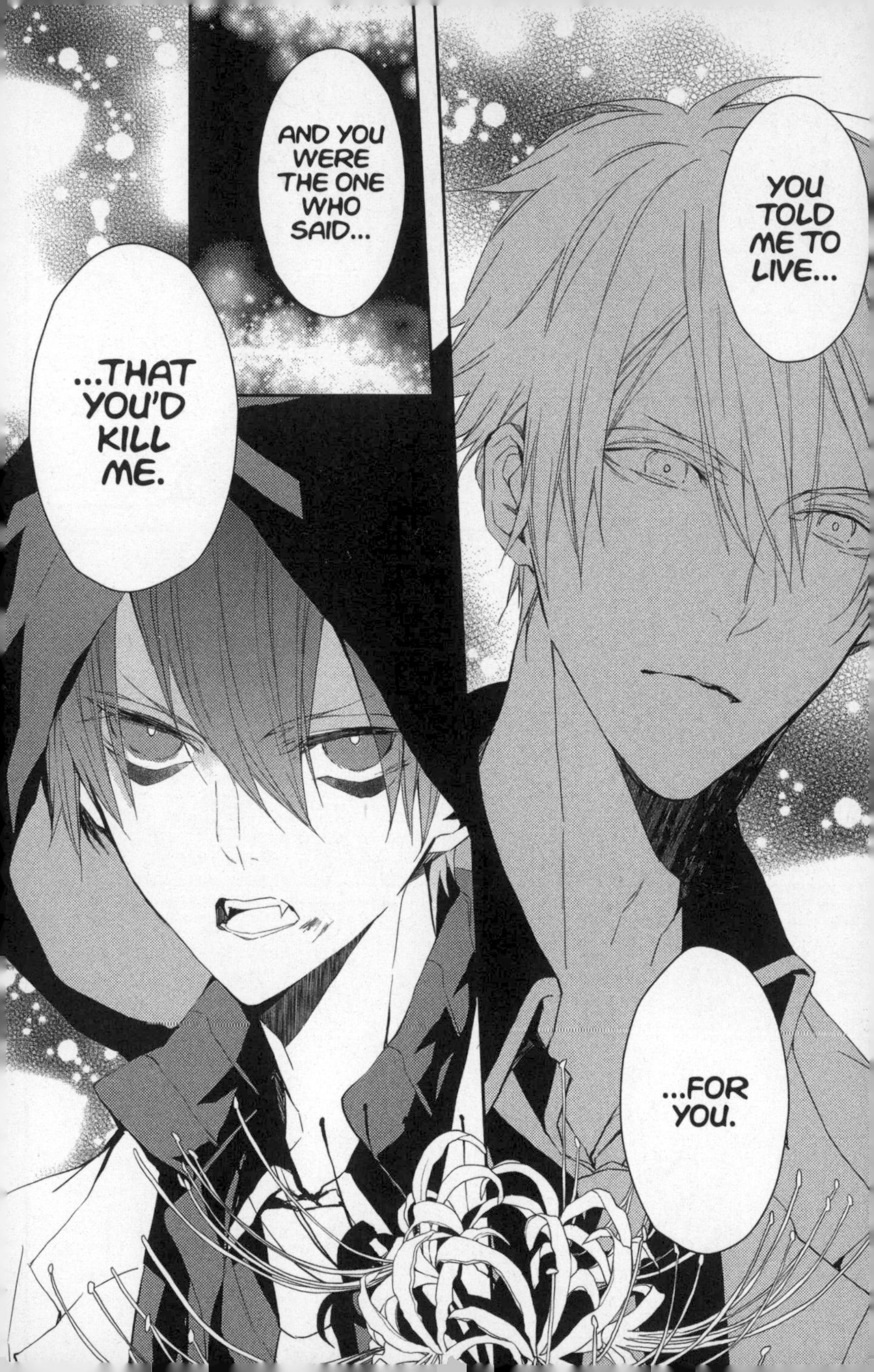
YOU TOLD ME TO LIVE...
...FOR YOU.
AND YOU WERE THE ONE WHO SAID...
...THAT YOU'D KILL ME.

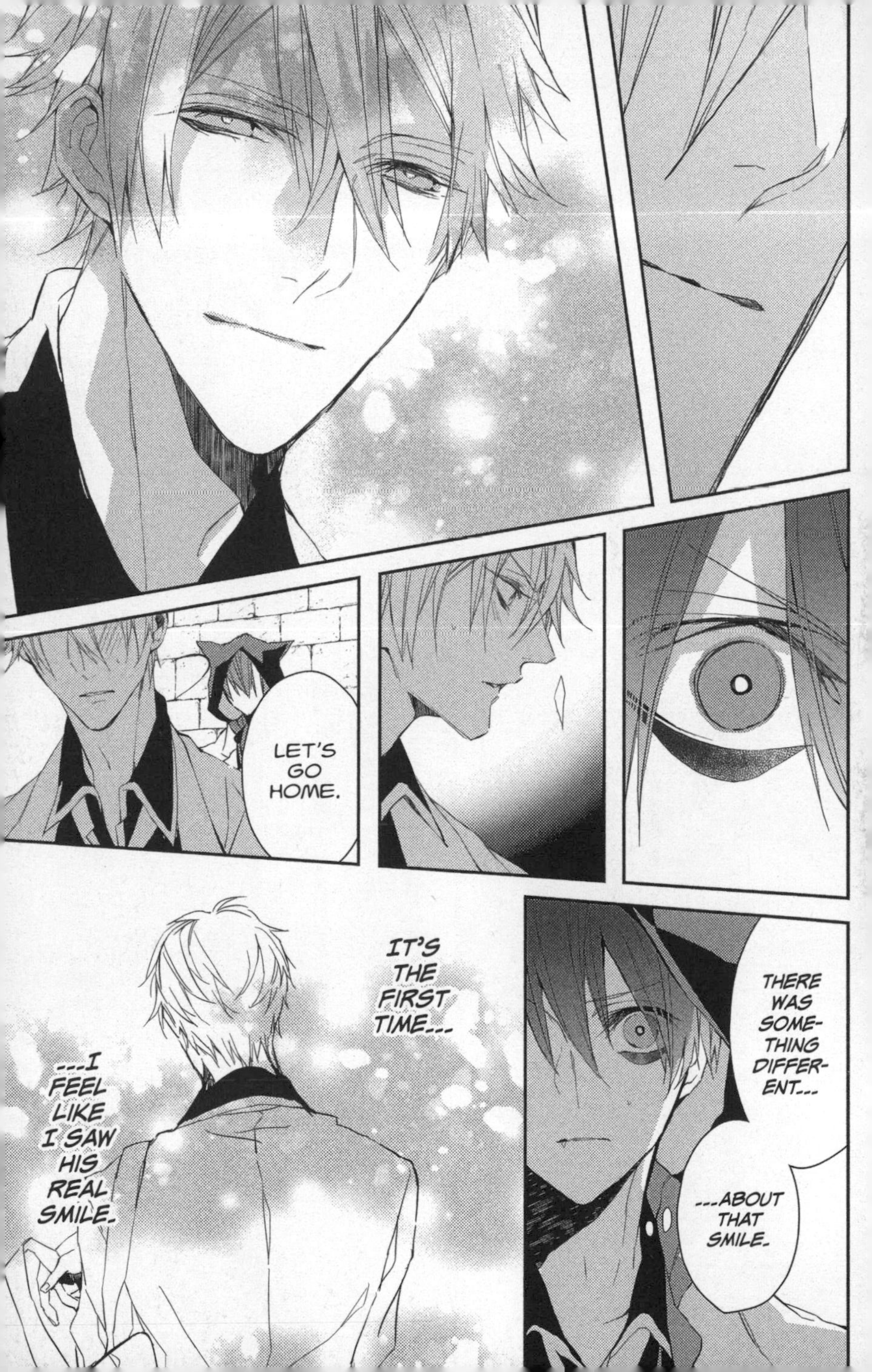
LET'S GO HOME.
THERE WAS SOME-THING DIFFER-ENT...
...ABOUT THAT SMILE.
IT'S THE FIRST TIME...
...I FEEL LIKE I SAW HIS REAL SMILE.

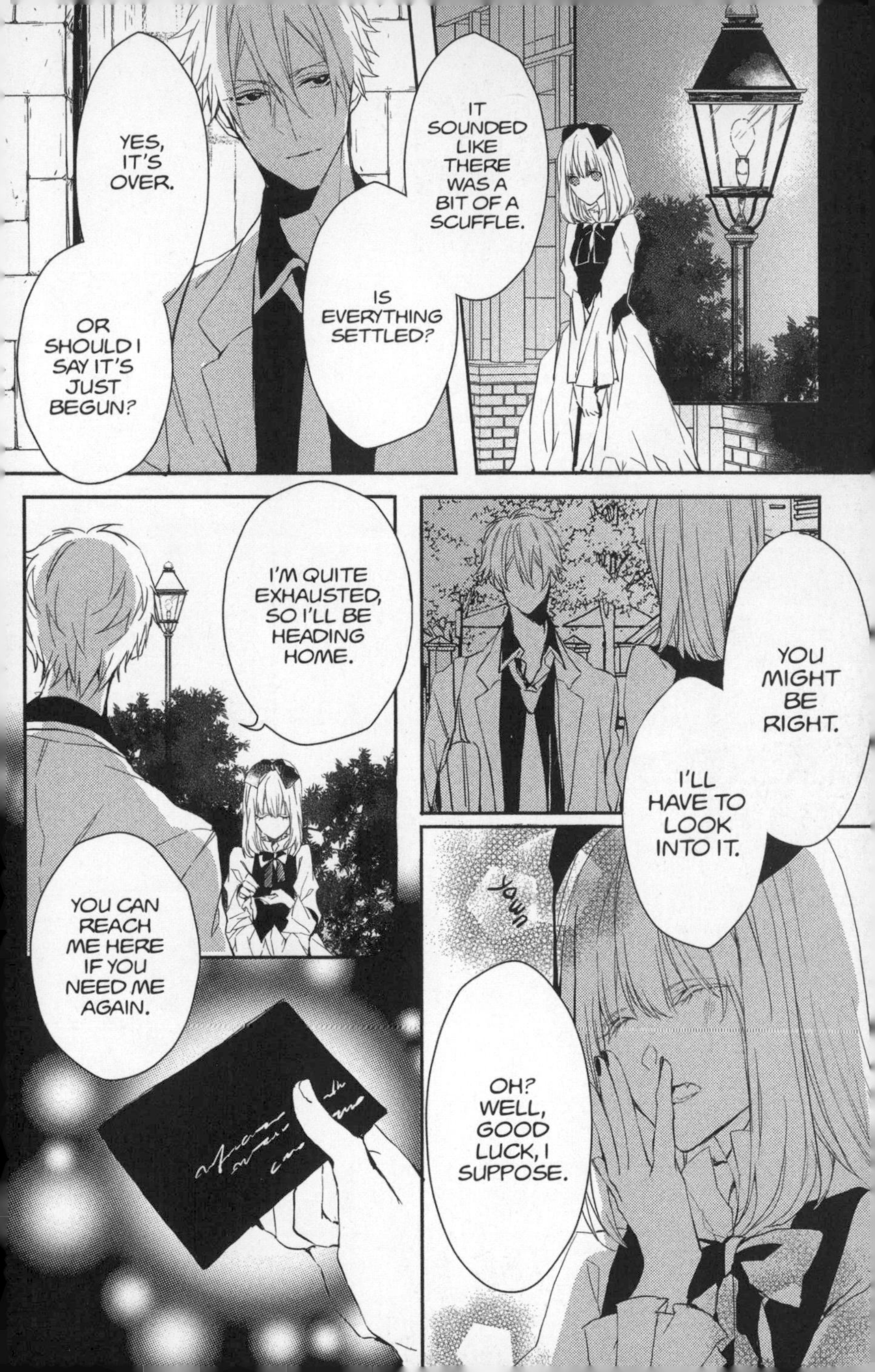
IT SOUNDED LIKE THERE WAS A BIT OF A SCUFFLE.
IS EVERYTHING SETTLED?
YES, IT'S OVER.
OR SHOULD I SAY IT'S JUST BEGUN?
YOU MIGHT BE RIGHT.
I'LL HAVE TO LOOK INTO IT.
YAWN
OH? WELL, GOOD LUCK, I SUPPOSE.
I'M QUITE EXHAUSTED, SO I'LL BE HEADING HOME.
YOU CAN REACH ME HERE IF YOU NEED ME AGAIN.

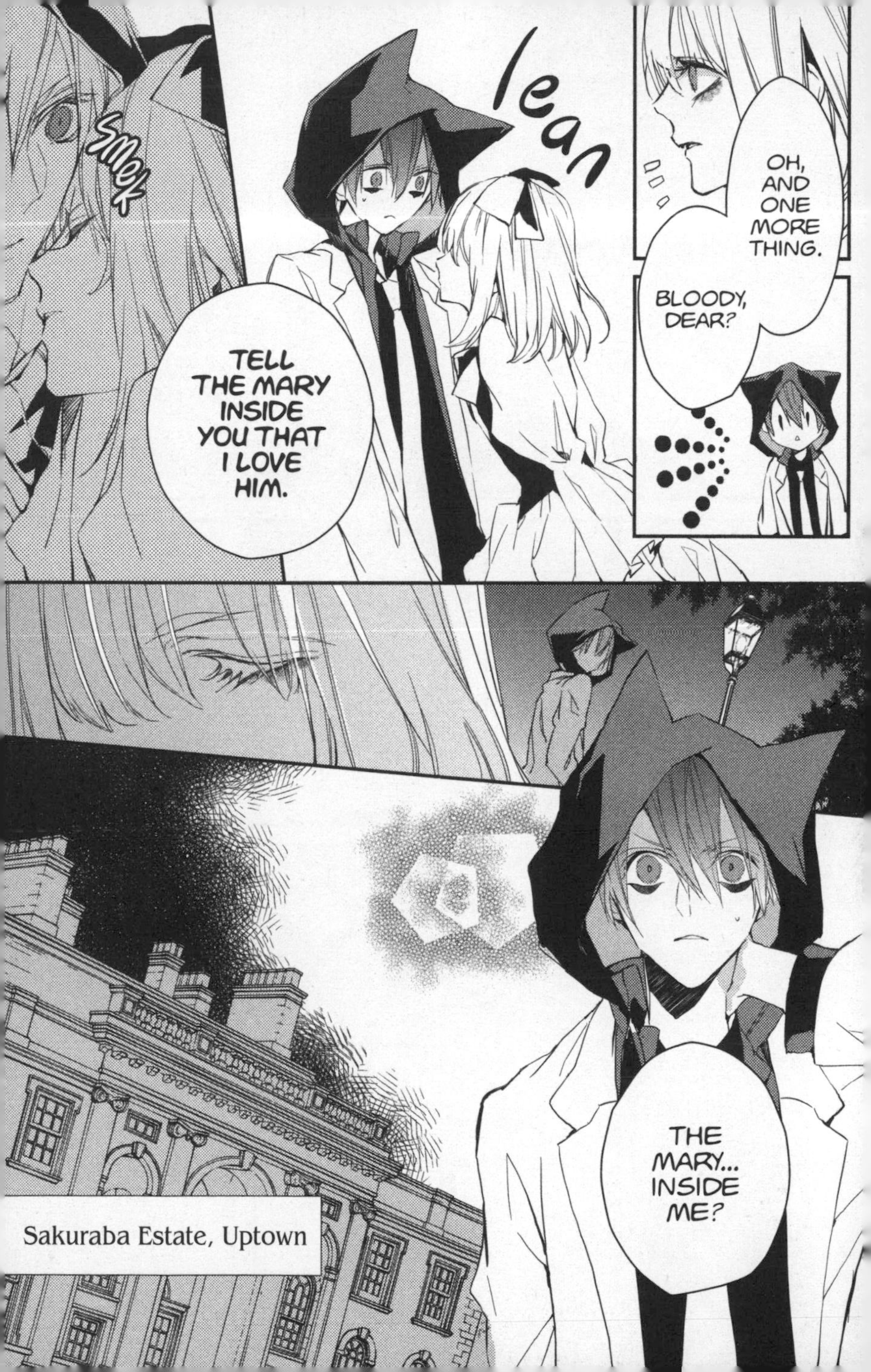
OH, AND ONE MORE THING.
BLOODY, DEAR?
lean
TELL THE MARY INSIDE YOU THAT I LOVE HIM.
SMEK
THE MARY... INSIDE ME?
Sakuraba Estate, Uptown

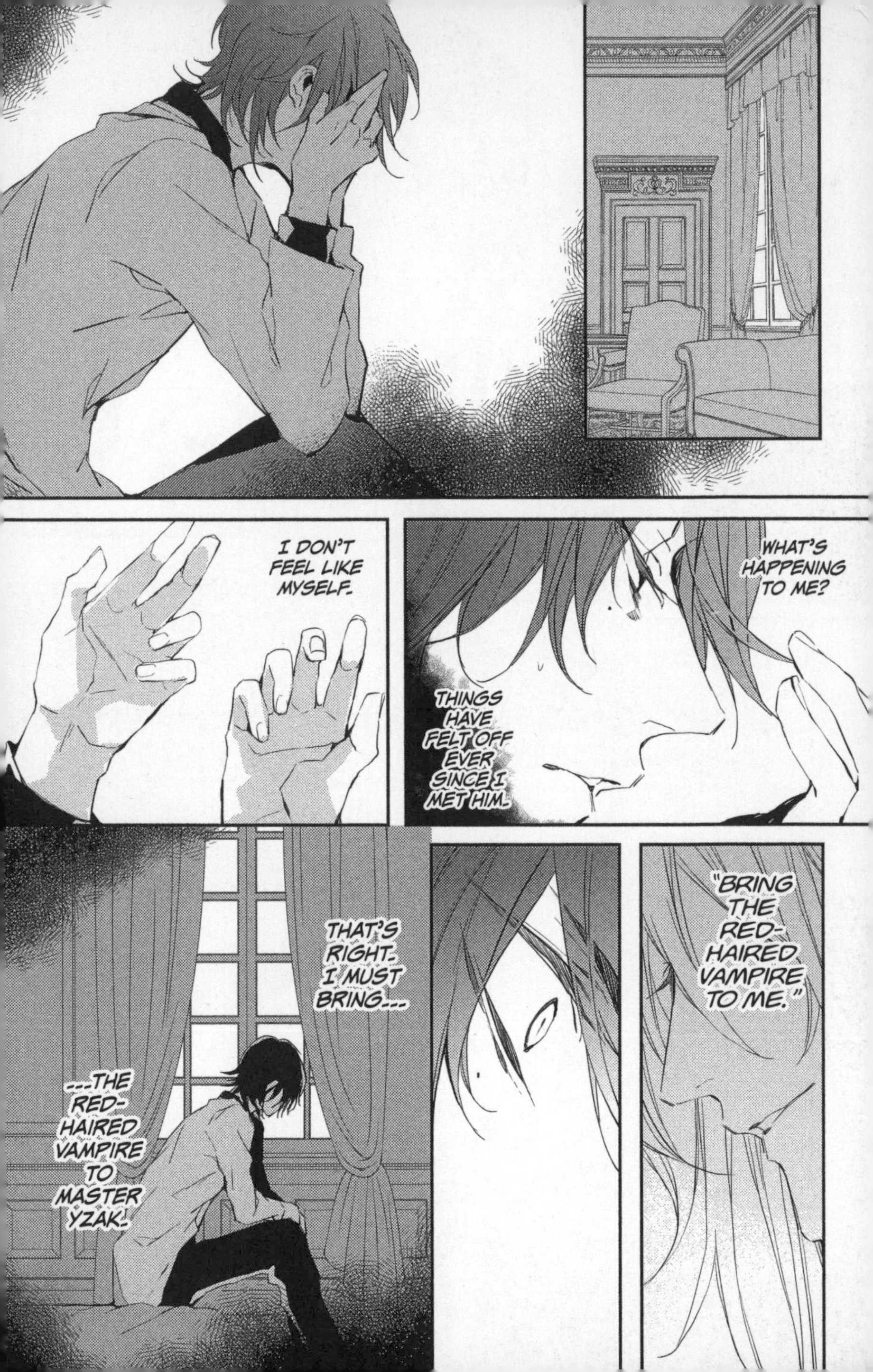
WHAT'S HAPPENING TO ME?
THINGS HAVE FELT OFF EVER SINCE I MET HIM.
I DON'T FEEL LIKE MYSELF.
"BRING THE RED-HAIRED VAMPIRE TO ME."
THAT'S RIGHT. I MUST BRING...
...THE RED-HAIRED VAMPIRE TO MASTER YZAK.

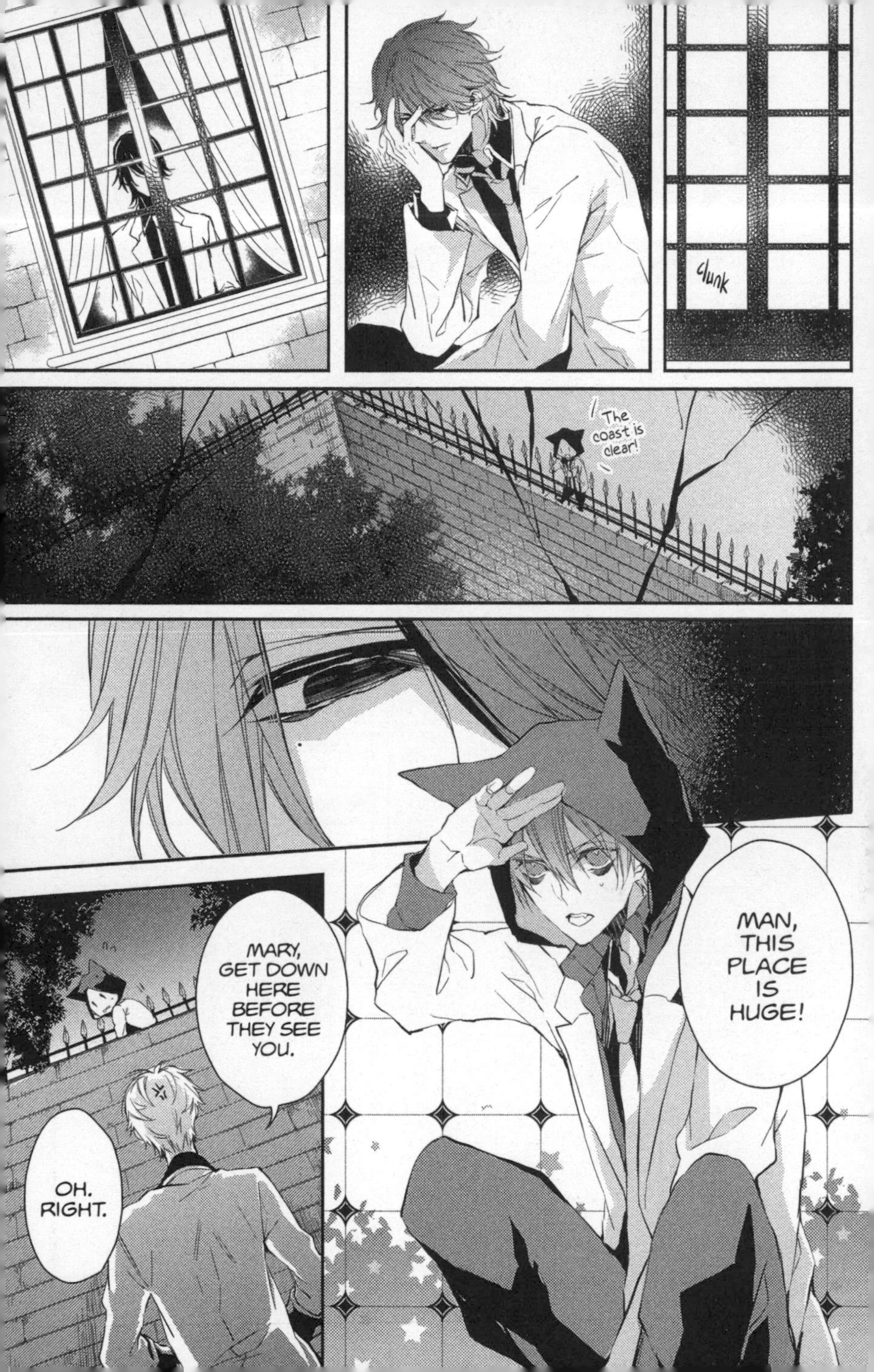
clunk
The coast is clear!
MAN, THIS PLACE IS HUGE!
MARY, GET DOWN HERE BEFORE THEY SEE YOU.
OH. RIGHT.

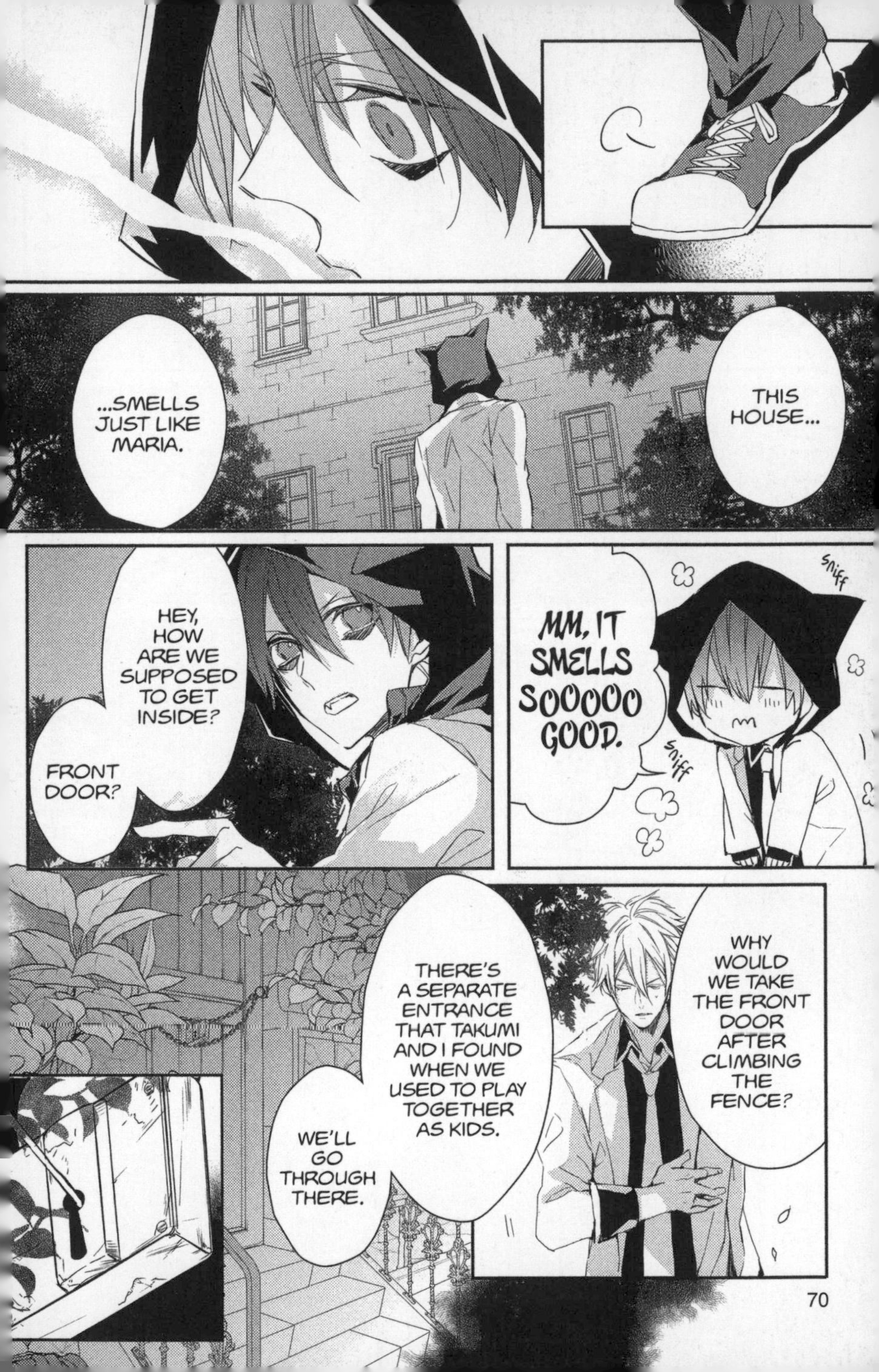
THIS HOUSE...
...SMELLS JUST LIKE MARIA.
MM, IT SMELLS SOOOOO GOOD.
SNIFF
SNIFF
HEY, HOW ARE WE SUPPOSED TO GET INSIDE?
FRONT DOOR?
WHY WOULD WE TAKE THE FRONT DOOR AFTER CLIMBING THE FENCE?
THERE'S A SEPARATE ENTRANCE THAT TAKUMI AND I FOUND WHEN WE USED TO PLAY TOGETHER AS KIDS.
WE'LL GO THROUGH THERE.

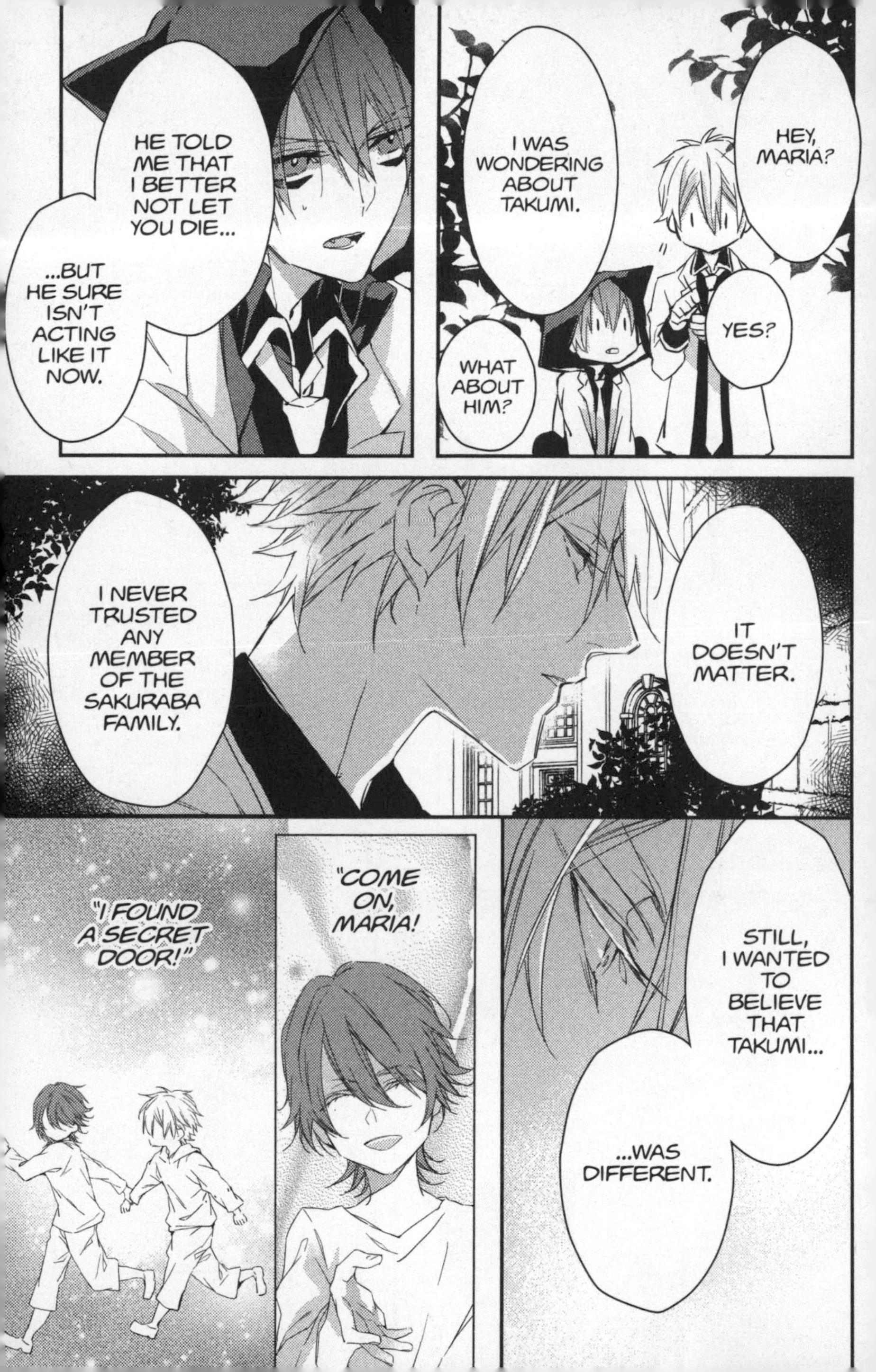
HEY, MARIA?
I WAS WONDERING ABOUT TAKUMI.
YES?
WHAT ABOUT HIM?
HE TOLD ME THAT I BETTER NOT LET YOU DIE...
...BUT HE SURE ISN'T ACTING LIKE IT NOW.
IT DOESN'T MATTER.
I NEVER TRUSTED ANY MEMBER OF THE SAKURABA FAMILY.
STILL, I WANTED TO BELIEVE THAT TAKUMI...
...WAS DIFFERENT.
"COME ON, MARIA!
"I FOUND A SECRET DOOR!"

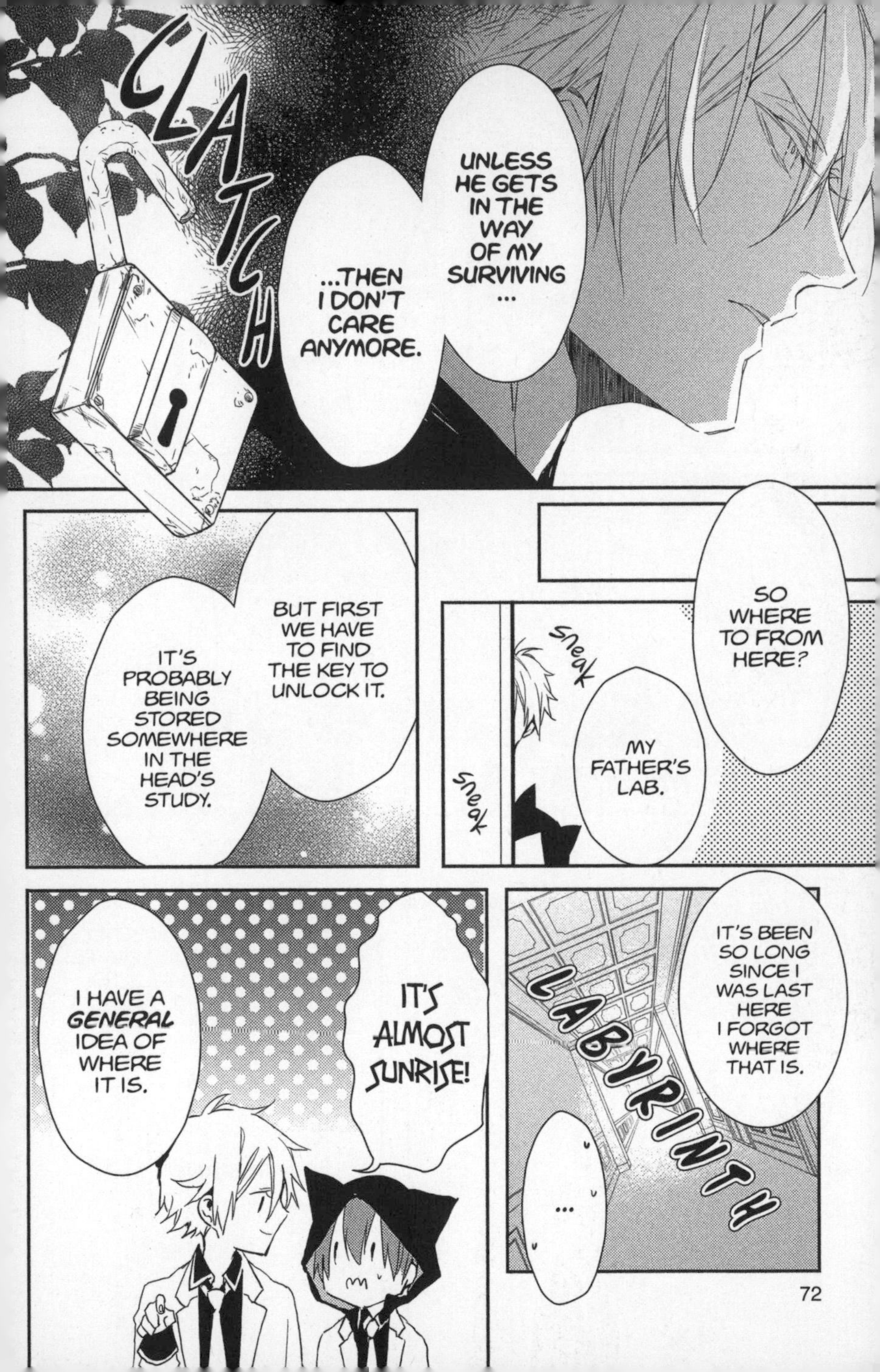
UNLESS HE GETS IN THE WAY OF MY SURVIVING ...
...THEN I DON'T CARE ANYMORE.
CLATCH
SO WHERE TO FROM HERE?
sneak
sneak
MY FATHER'S LAB.
BUT FIRST WE HAVE TO FIND THE KEY TO UNLOCK IT.
IT'S PROBABLY BEING STORED SOMEWHERE IN THE HEAD'S STUDY.
IT'S BEEN SO LONG SINCE I WAS LAST HERE I FORGOT WHERE THAT IS.
LABYRINTH
...
IT'S ALMOST SUNRISE!
I HAVE A GENERAL IDEA OF WHERE IT IS.

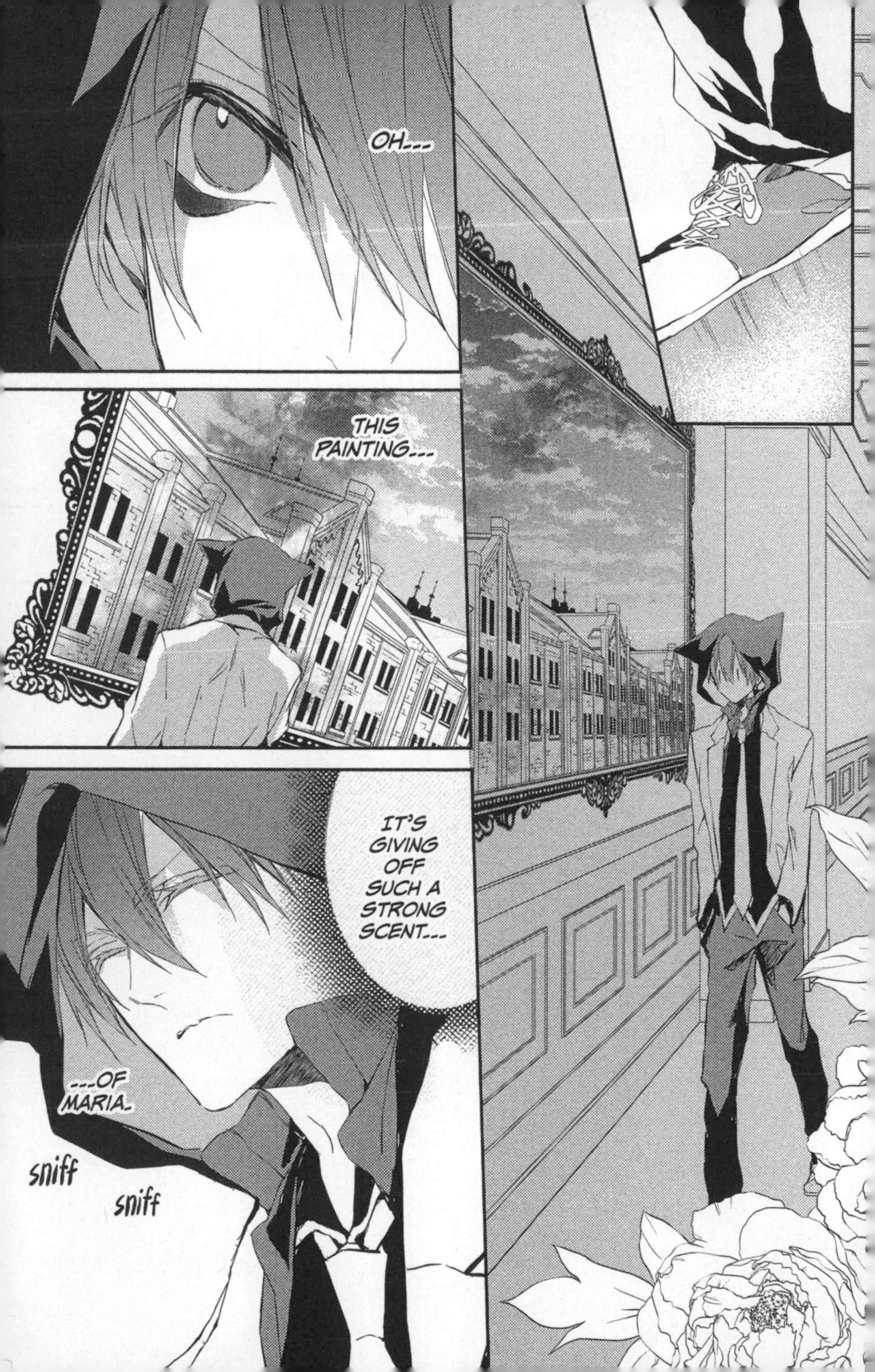
OH...
THIS PAINTING...
IT'S GIVING OFF SUCH A STRONG SCENT...
...OF MARIA.
sniff
sniff

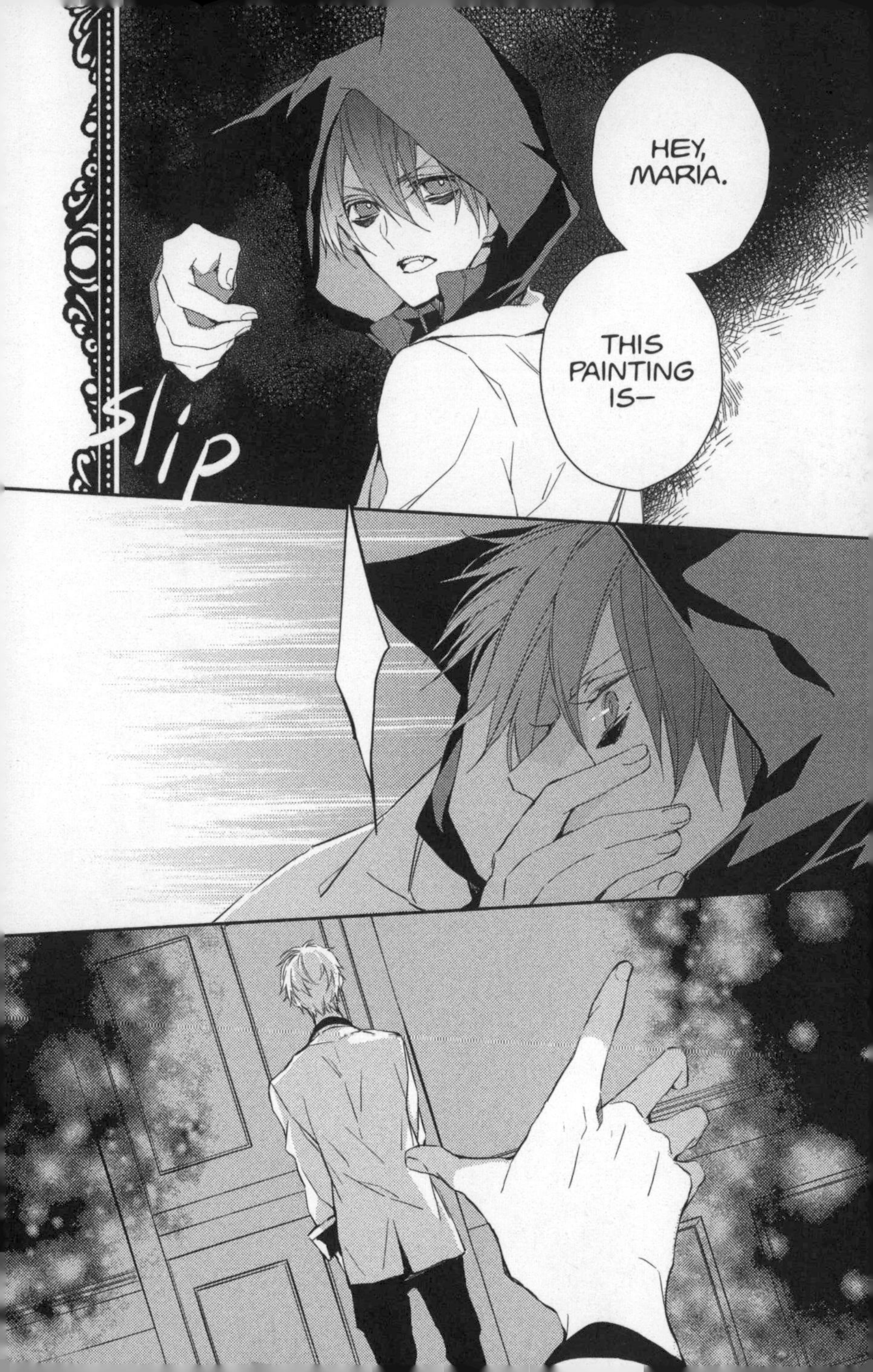
HEY, MARIA.
THIS PAINTING IS—
slip

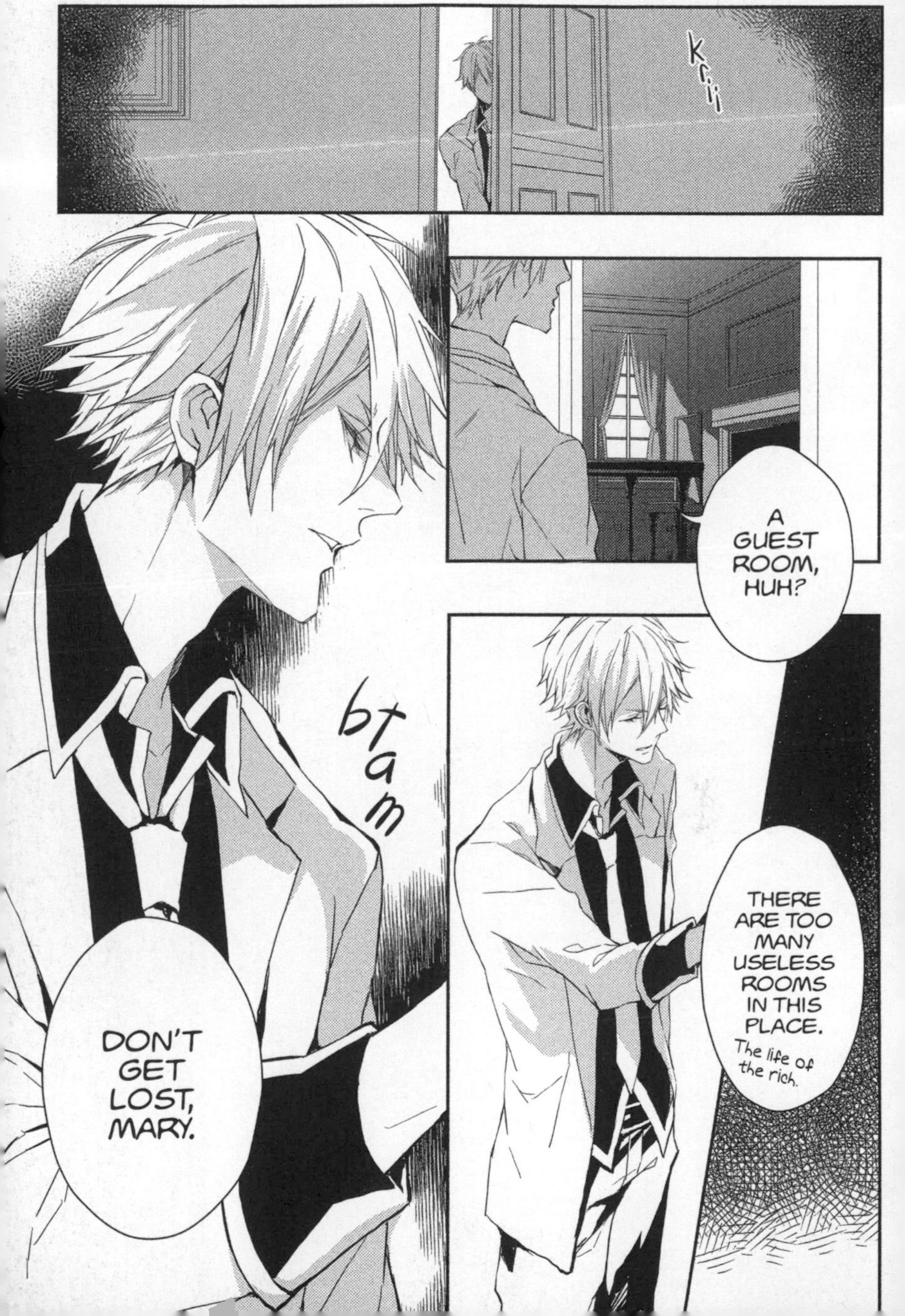
Kriii
A GUEST ROOM, HUH?
THERE ARE TOO MANY USELESS ROOMS IN THIS PLACE.
The life of the rich.
btam
DON'T GET LOST, MARY.

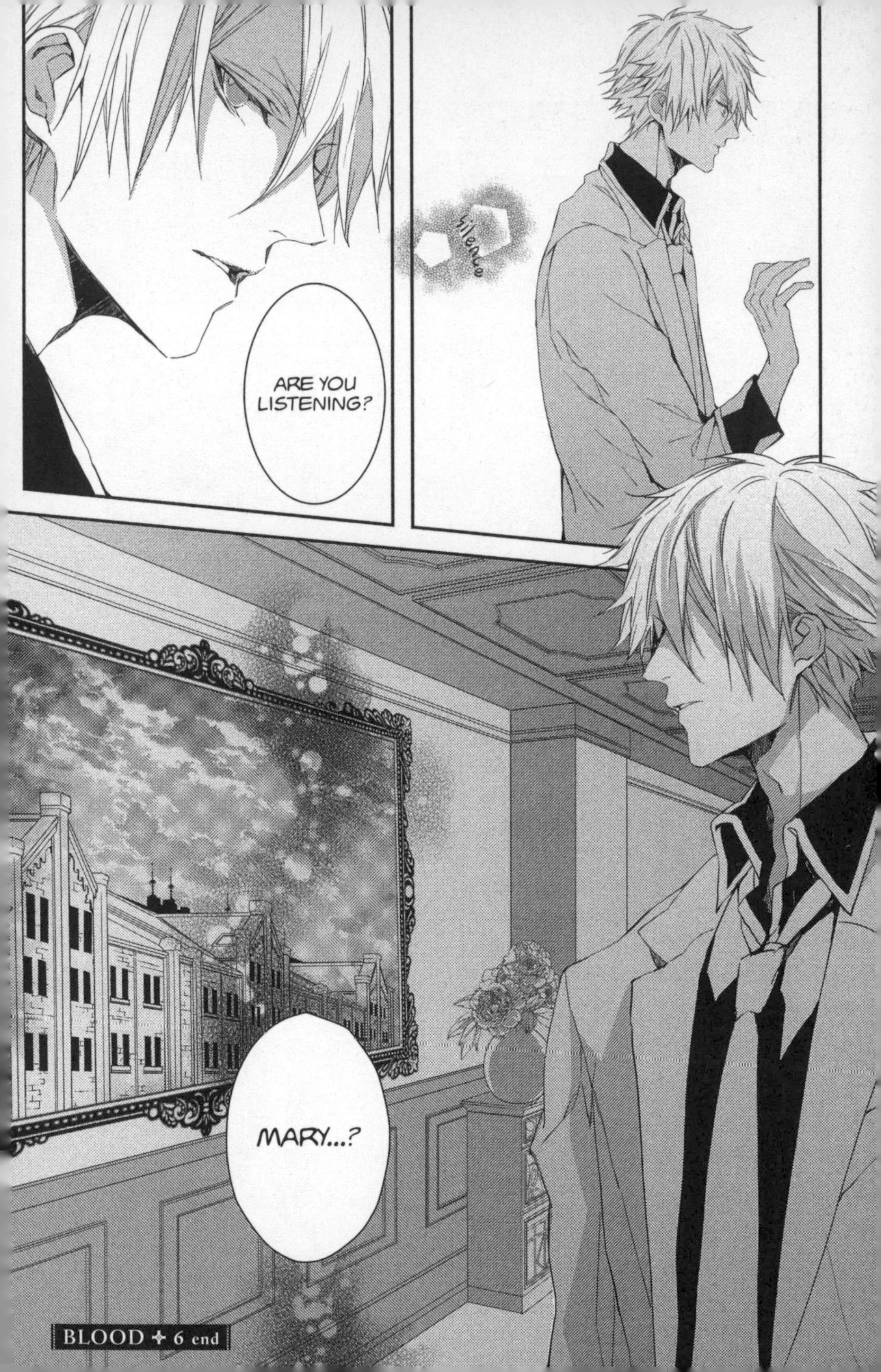
silence
ARE YOU LISTENING?
MARY...?

Bloody✝Mary

Plunk

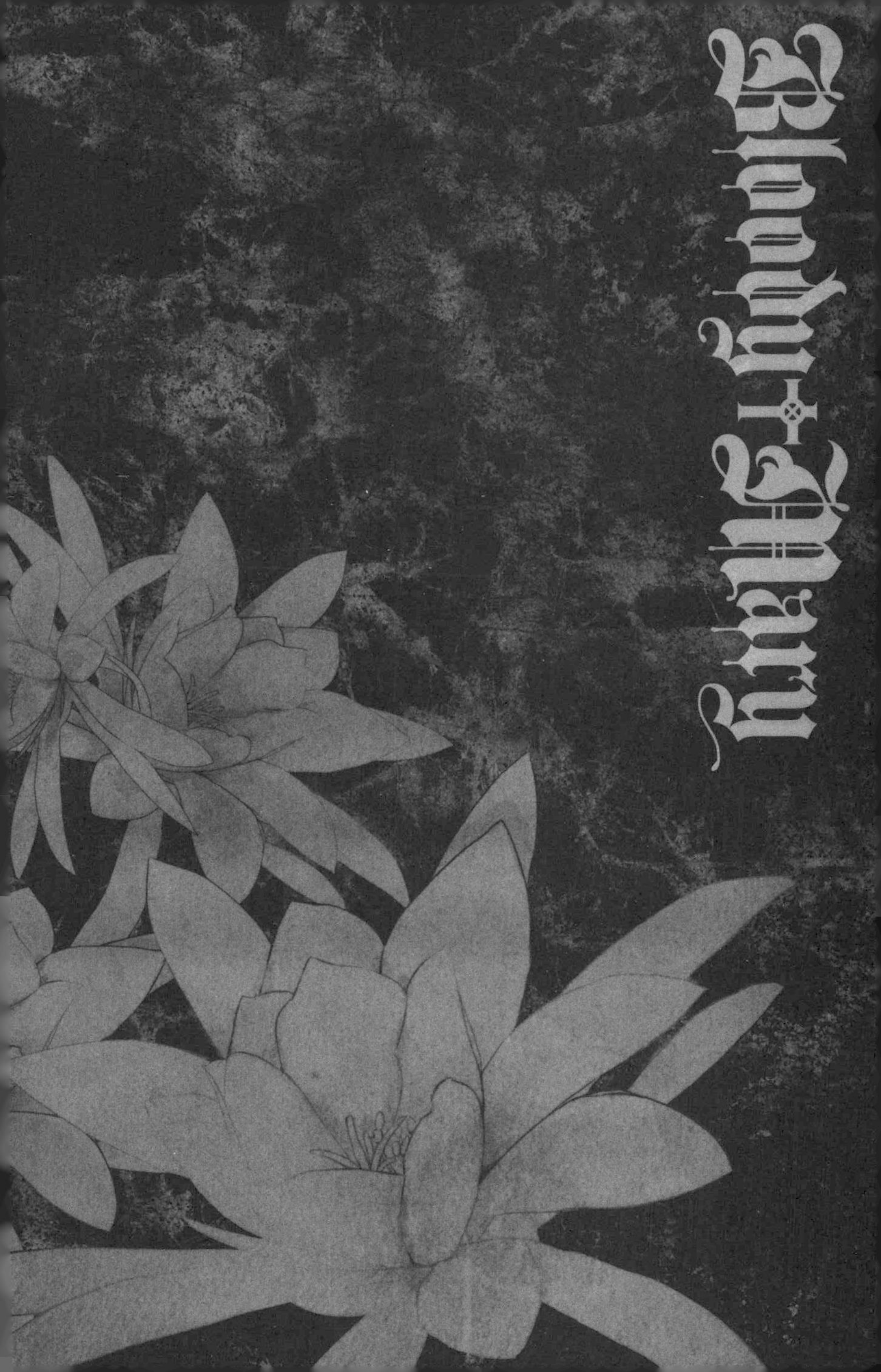
Bloody+Mary

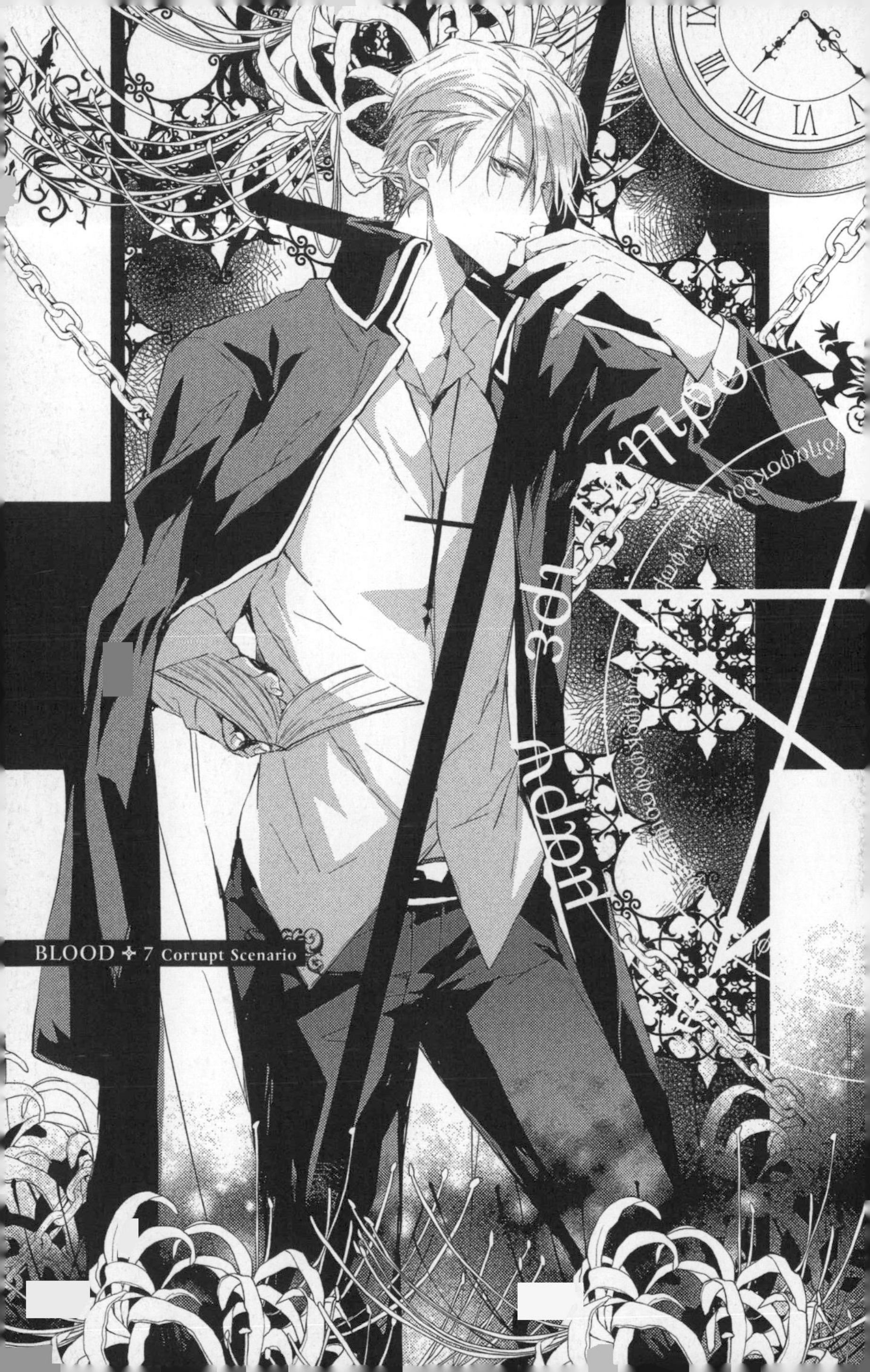
BLOOD ✣ 7 Corrupt Scenario

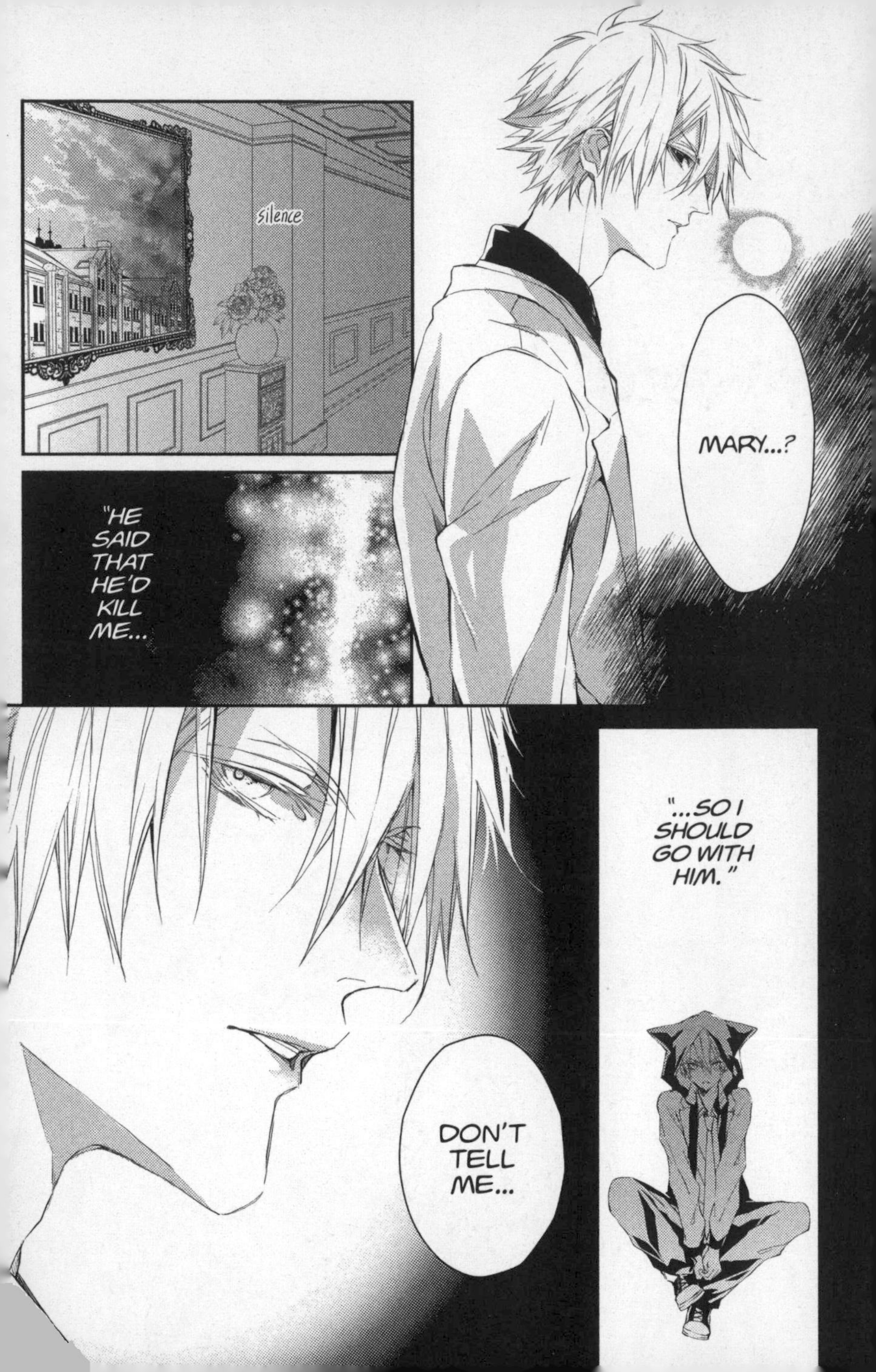
MARY...?
silence
"HE SAID THAT HE'D KILL ME...
"...SO I SHOULD GO WITH HIM."
DON'T TELL ME...

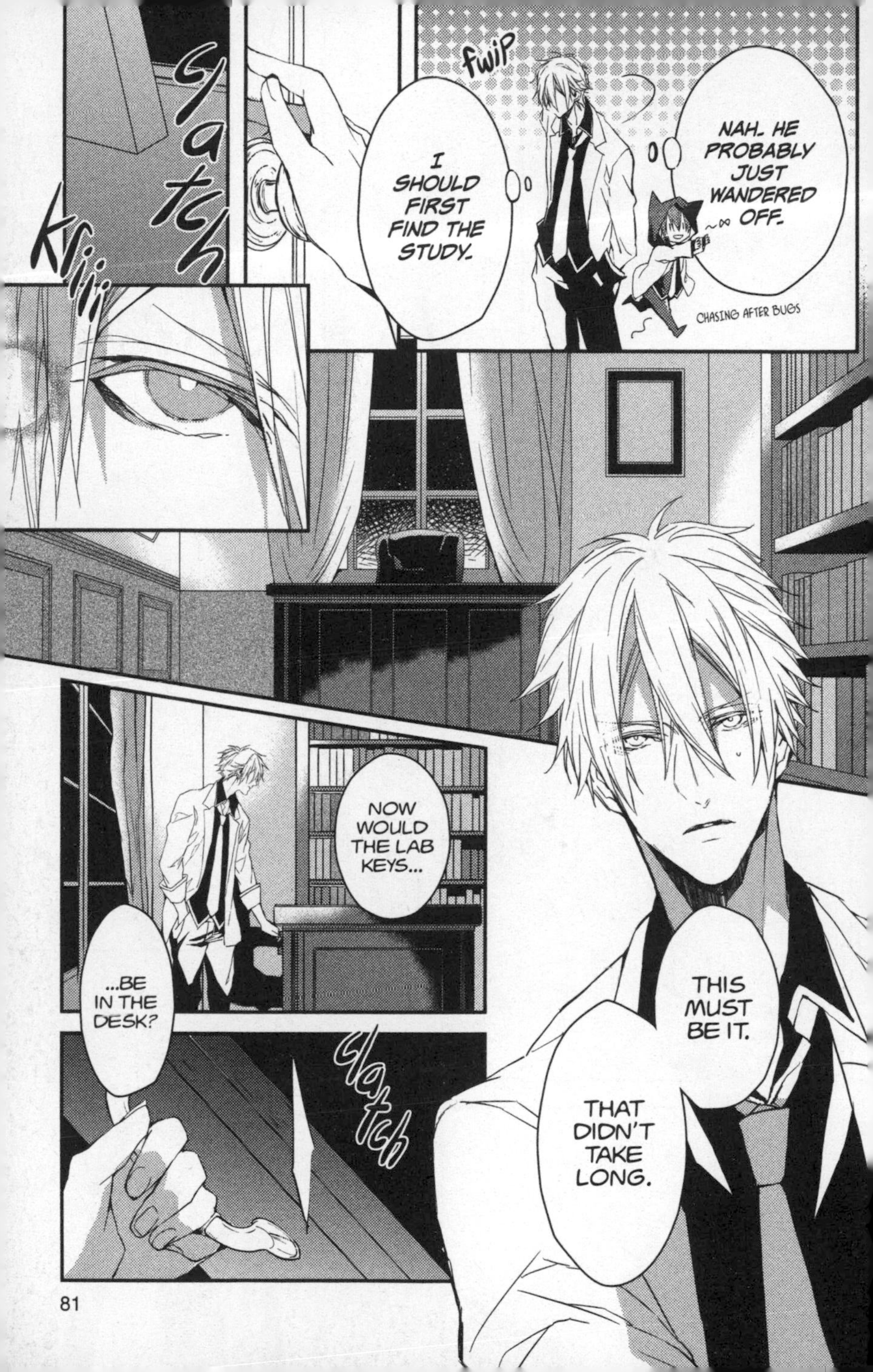
NAH. HE PROBABLY JUST WANDERED ~∞ OFF.
CHASING AFTER BUGS
FWIP
I SHOULD FIRST FIND THE STUDY.
CLATCH
KRIIII
THIS MUST BE IT.
THAT DIDN'T TAKE LONG.
NOW WOULD THE LAB KEYS...
...BE IN THE DESK?
CLATCH

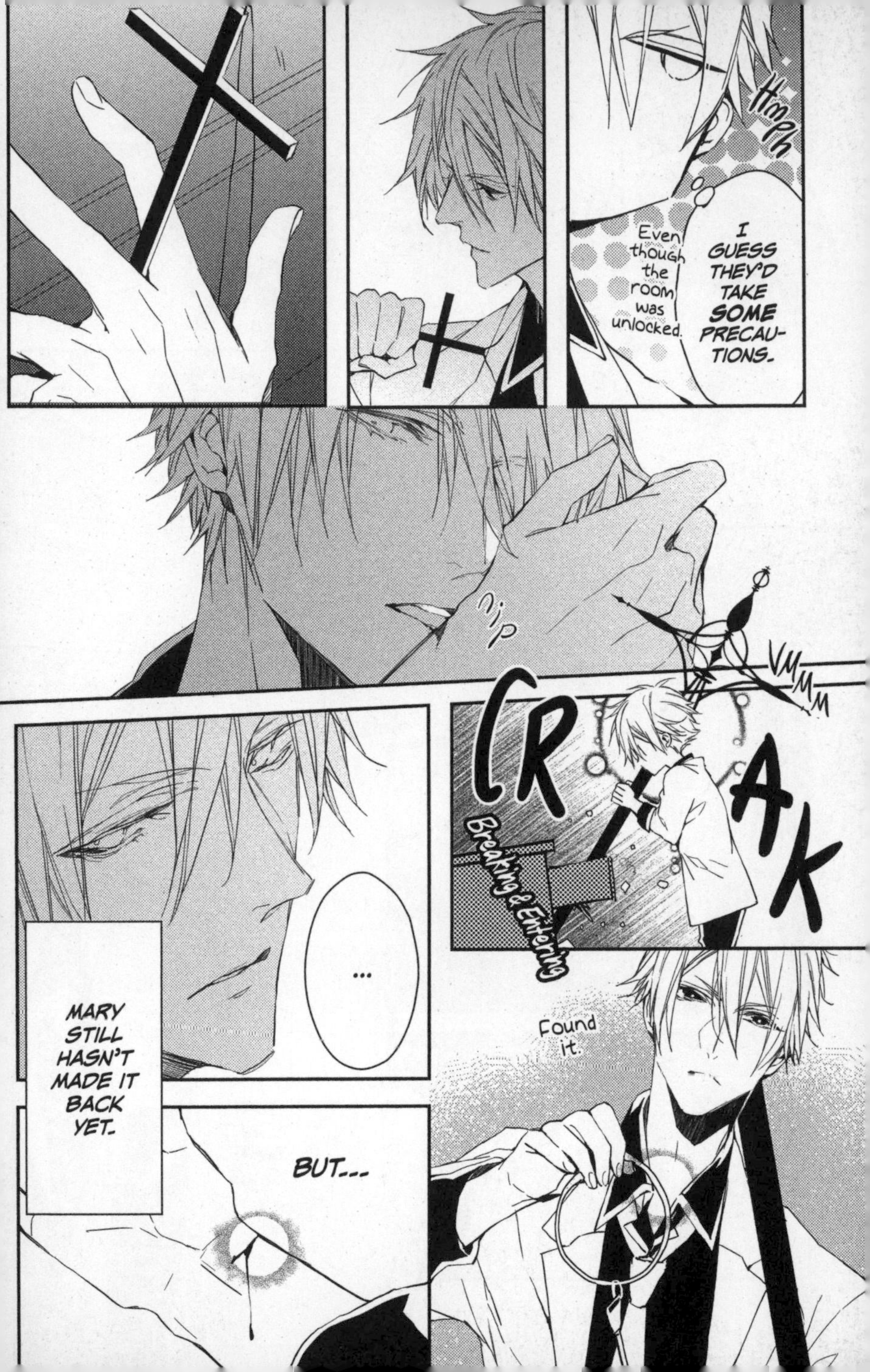
Hmph
I GUESS THEY'D TAKE SOME PRECAUTIONS.
Even though the room was unlocked.
nip
VMMMM
CRAK
Breaking & Entering
...
Found it.
MARY STILL HASN'T MADE IT BACK YET.
BUT...

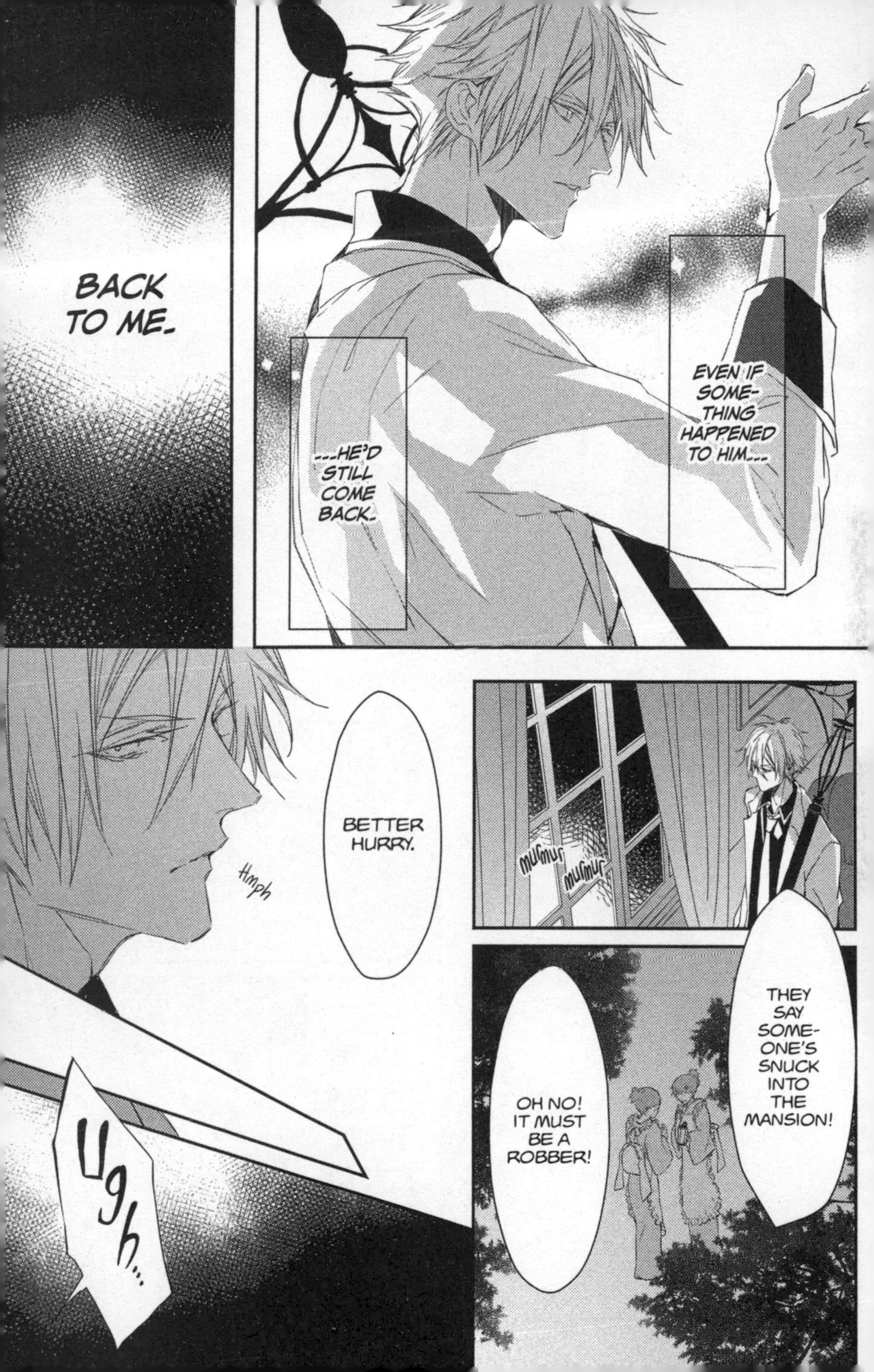
EVEN IF SOME-THING HAPPENED TO HIM...
...HE'D STILL COME BACK.
BACK TO ME.
MURMUR MURMUR
THEY SAY SOME-ONE'S SNUCK INTO THE MANSION!
OH NO! IT MUST BE A ROBBER!
BETTER HURRY.
Hmph
Ugh...

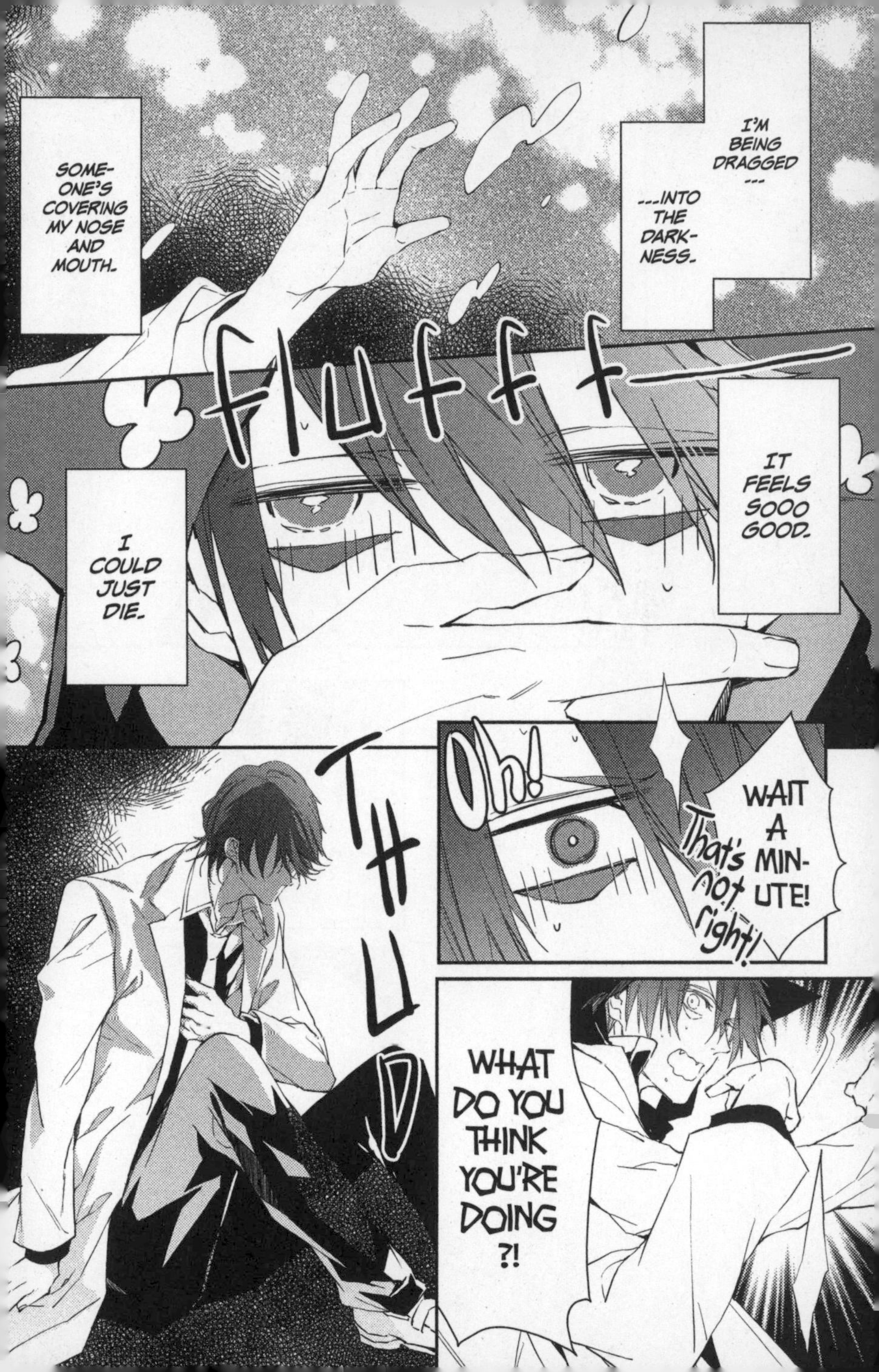
I'M BEING DRAGGED ---
---INTO THE DARKNESS.
SOMEONE'S COVERING MY NOSE AND MOUTH.
fluffff
IT FEELS SOOO GOOD.
I COULD JUST DIE.
Oh!
WAIT A MINUTE!
That's not right!
WHAT DO YOU THINK YOU'RE DOING ?!
THUD

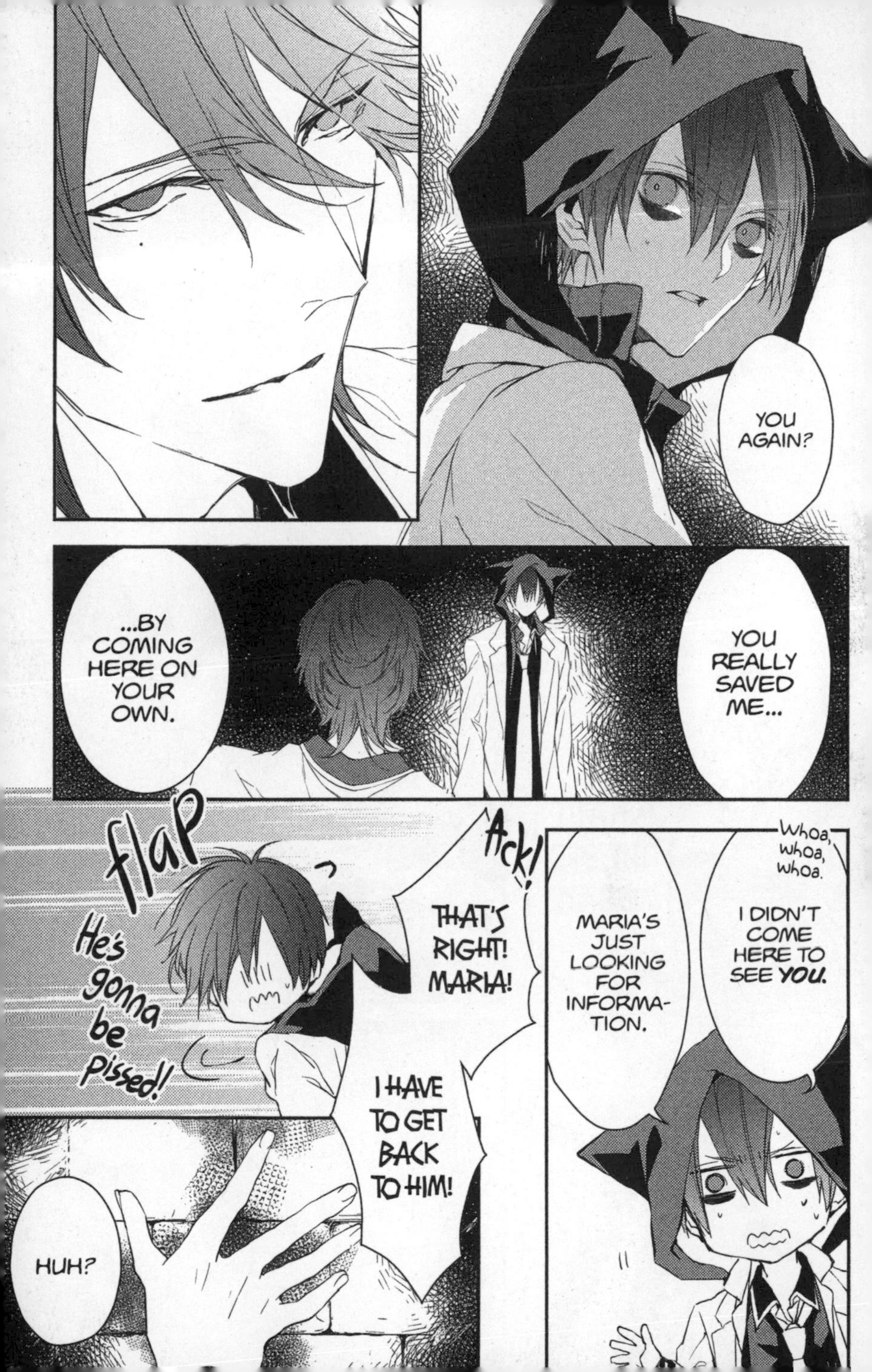
YOU AGAIN?
YOU REALLY SAVED ME...
...BY COMING HERE ON YOUR OWN.
Whoa, whoa, whoa.
I DIDN'T COME HERE TO SEE YOU.
MARIA'S JUST LOOKING FOR INFORMATION.
Ack!
THAT'S RIGHT! MARIA!
flap
He's gonna be pissed!
I HAVE TO GET BACK TO HIM!
HUH?

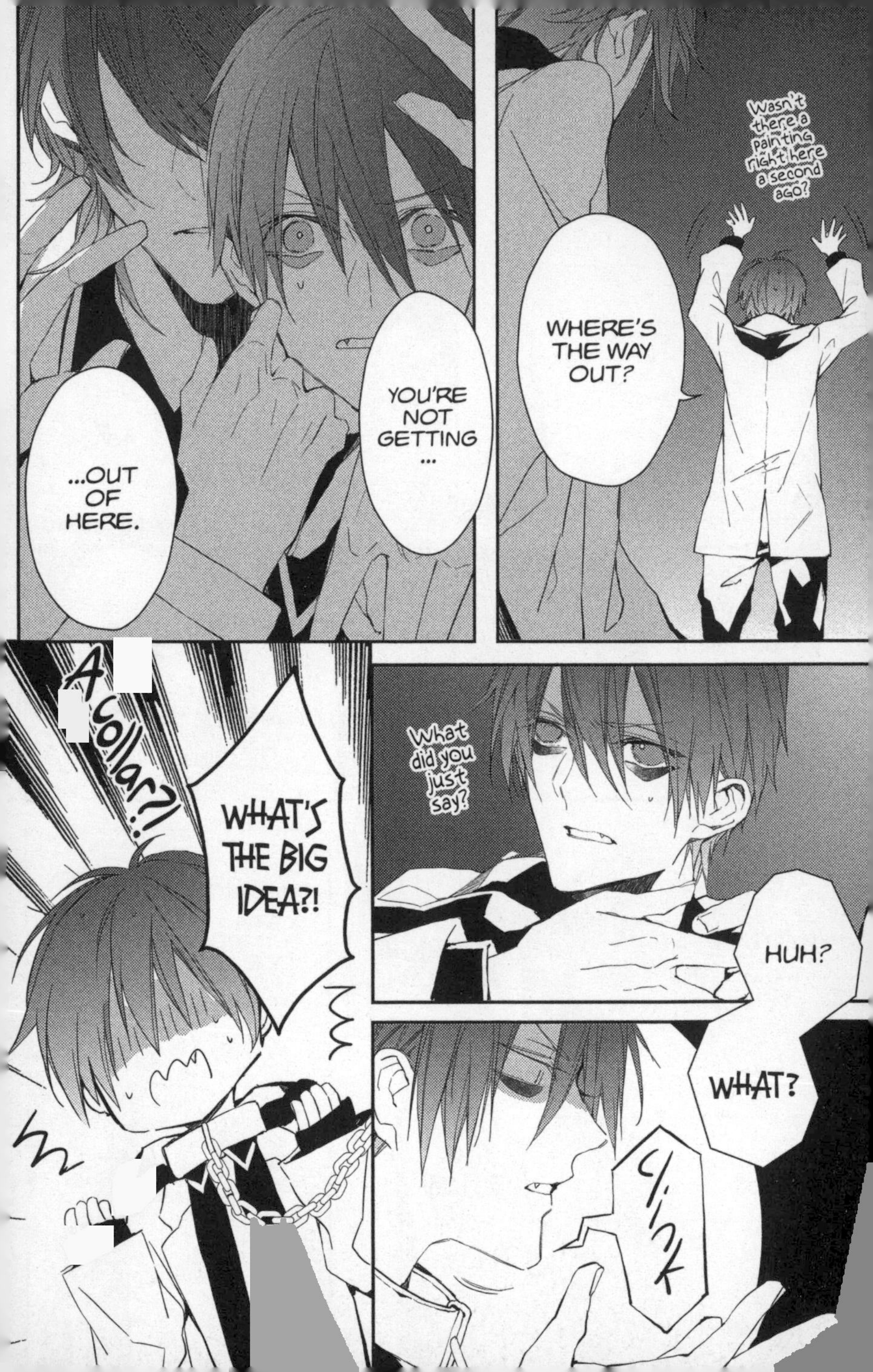
Wasn't there a painting right here a second ago?
WHERE'S THE WAY OUT?
YOU'RE NOT GETTING ...
...OUT OF HERE.
What did you just say?
HUH?
WHAT?
clink
A collar?!
WHAT'S THE BIG IDEA?!

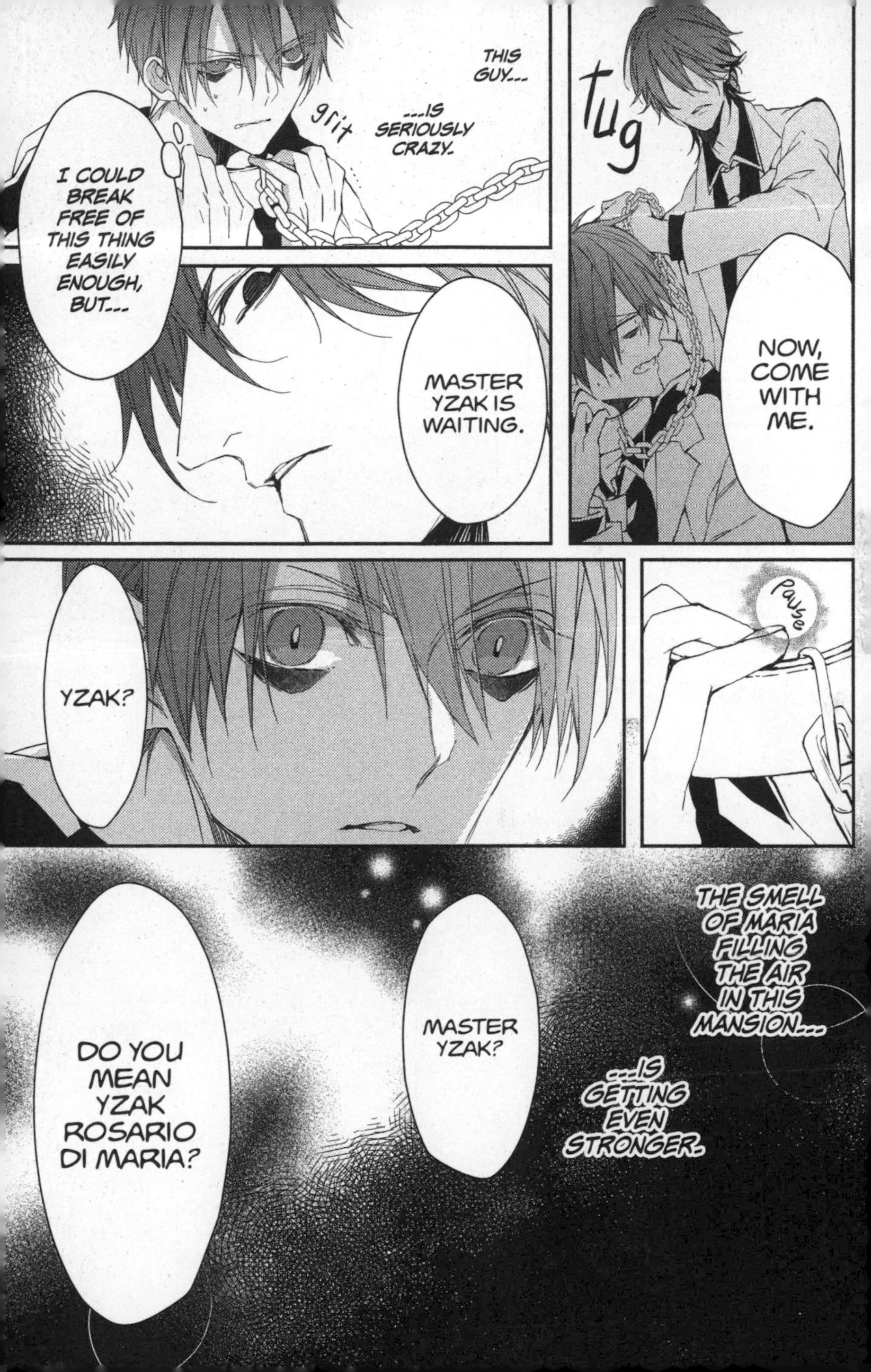
tug
NOW, COME WITH ME.
THIS GUY...
...IS SERIOUSLY CRAZY.
grit
I COULD BREAK FREE OF THIS THING EASILY ENOUGH, BUT...
MASTER YZAK IS WAITING.
pause
YZAK?
THE SMELL OF MARIA FILLING THE AIR IN THIS MANSION...
...IS GETTING EVEN STRONGER.
MASTER YZAK?
DO YOU MEAN YZAK ROSARIO DI MARIA?

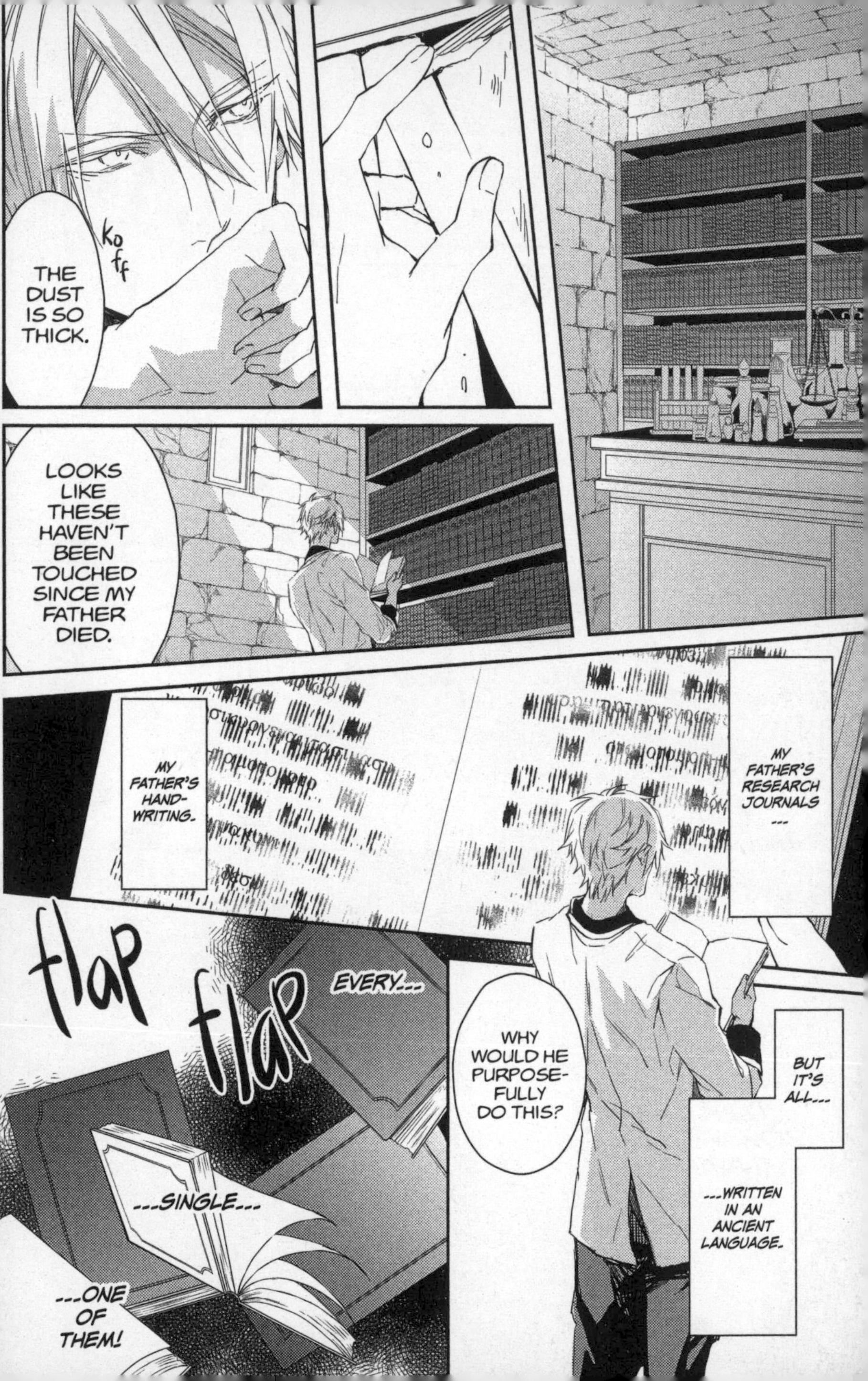
koff
THE DUST IS SO THICK.
LOOKS LIKE THESE HAVEN'T BEEN TOUCHED SINCE MY FATHER DIED.
MY FATHER'S RESEARCH JOURNALS...
MY FATHER'S HAND-WRITING.
BUT IT'S ALL...
...WRITTEN IN AN ANCIENT LANGUAGE.
WHY WOULD HE PURPOSE-FULLY DO THIS?
flap
flap
EVERY...
...SINGLE...
...ONE OF THEM!

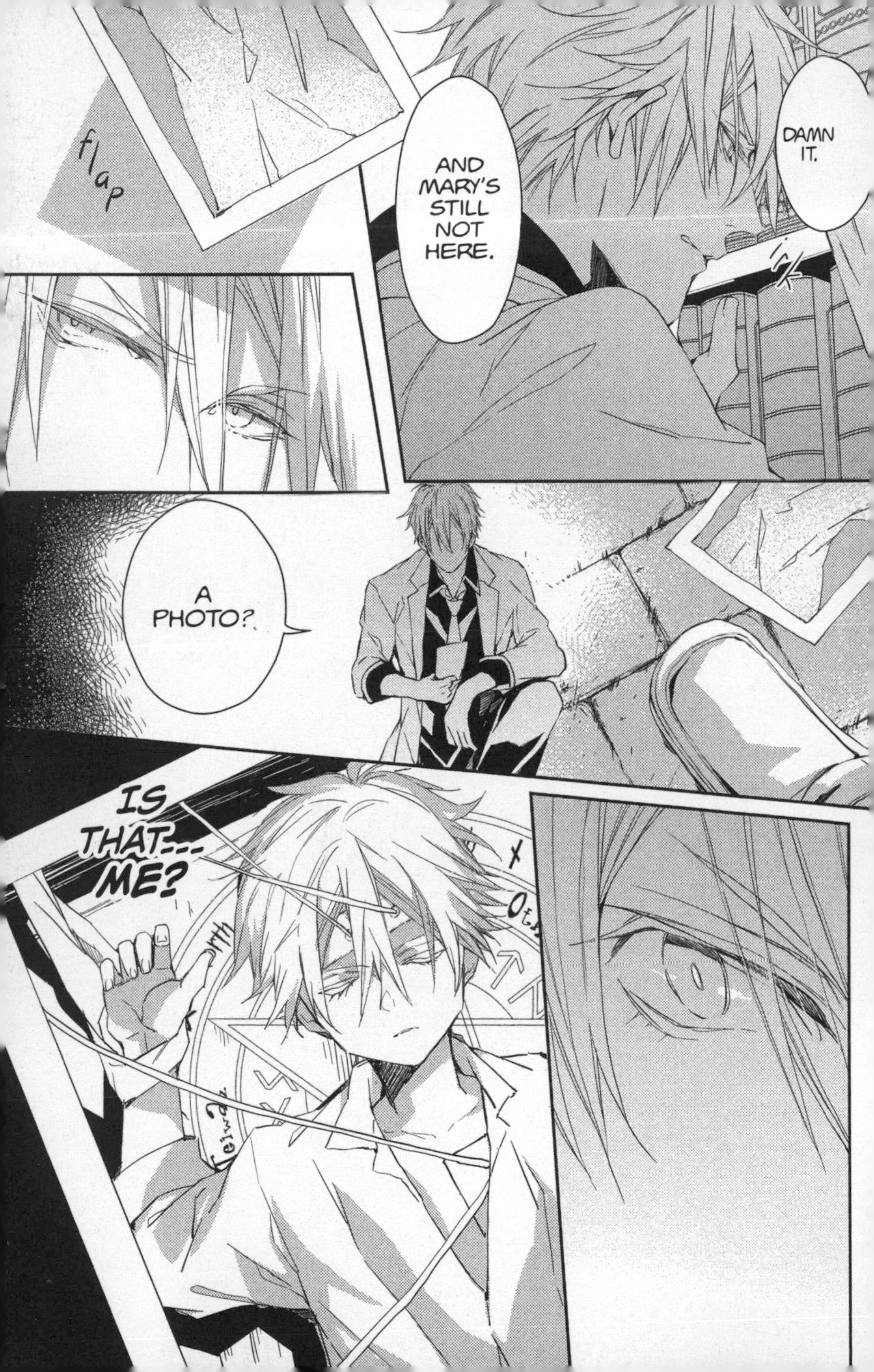
DAMN IT.
AND MARY'S STILL NOT HERE.
flap
A PHOTO?
IS THAT... ME?

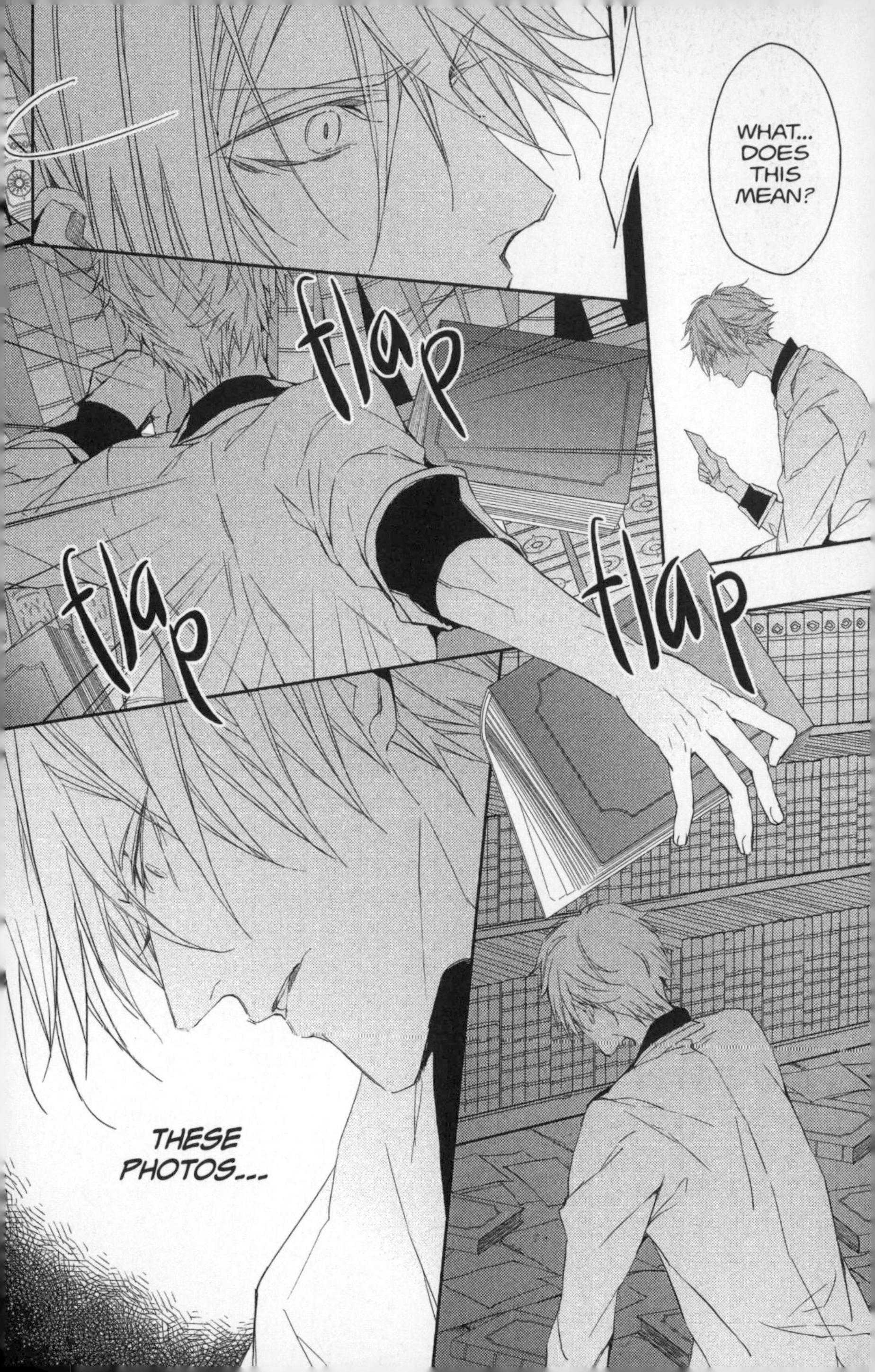
WHAT... DOES THIS MEAN?
flap
flap
flap
THESE PHOTOS...

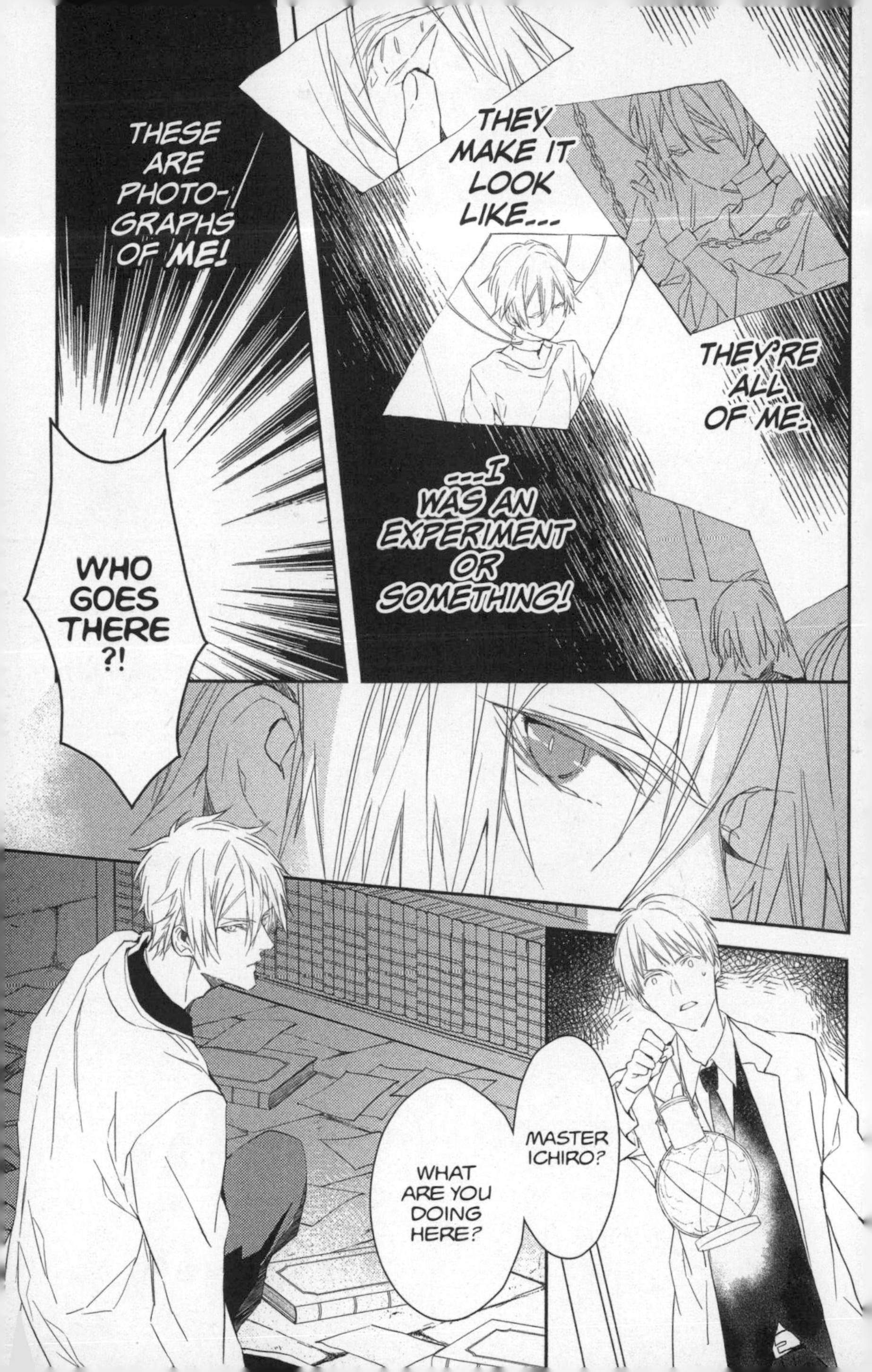
THEY'RE ALL OF ME.
THEY MAKE IT LOOK LIKE...
...I WAS AN EXPERIMENT OR SOMETHING!
THESE ARE PHOTOGRAPHS OF ME!
WHO GOES THERE?!
MASTER ICHIRO?
WHAT ARE YOU DOING HERE?

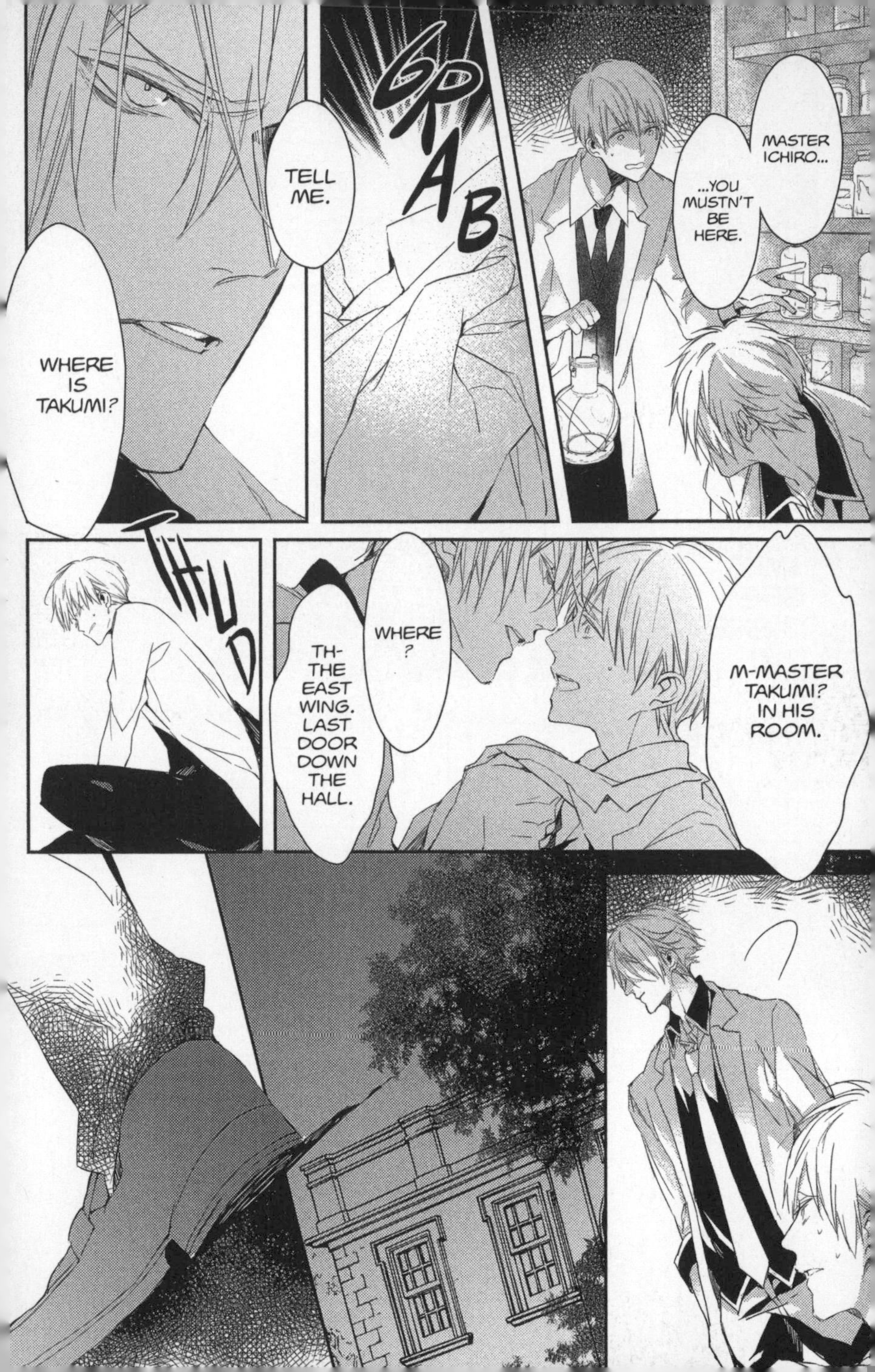
MASTER ICHIRO...
...YOU MUSTN'T BE HERE.
GRAB
TELL ME.
WHERE IS TAKUMI?
M-MASTER TAKUMI? IN HIS ROOM.
WHERE?
TH-THE EAST WING. LAST DOOR DOWN THE HALL.
THUD

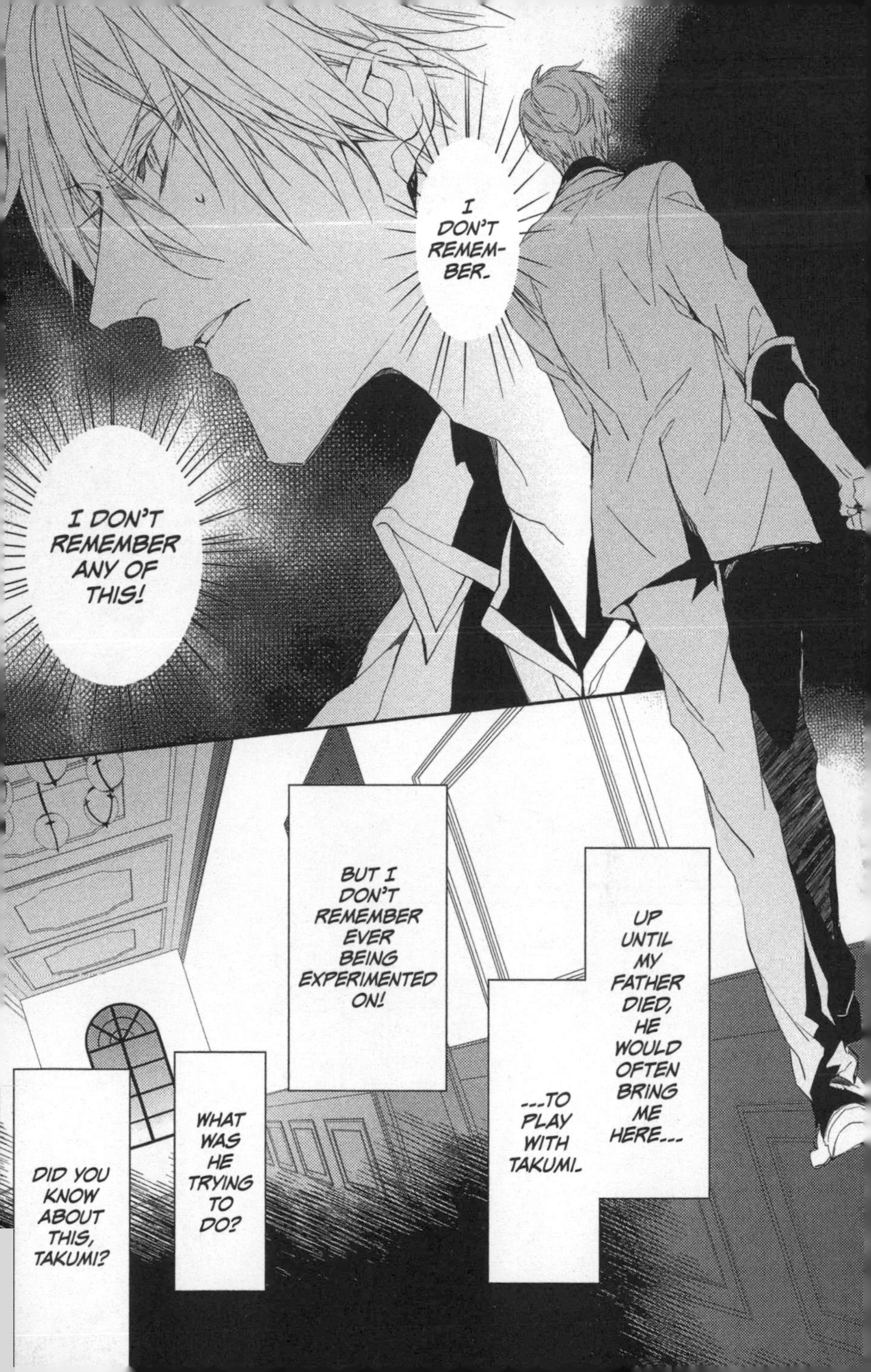
I DON'T REMEMBER.
I DON'T REMEMBER ANY OF THIS!
UP UNTIL MY FATHER DIED, HE WOULD OFTEN BRING ME HERE...
...TO PLAY WITH TAKUMI.
BUT I DON'T REMEMBER EVER BEING EXPERIMENTED ON!
WHAT WAS HE TRYING TO DO?
DID YOU KNOW ABOUT THIS, TAKUMI?

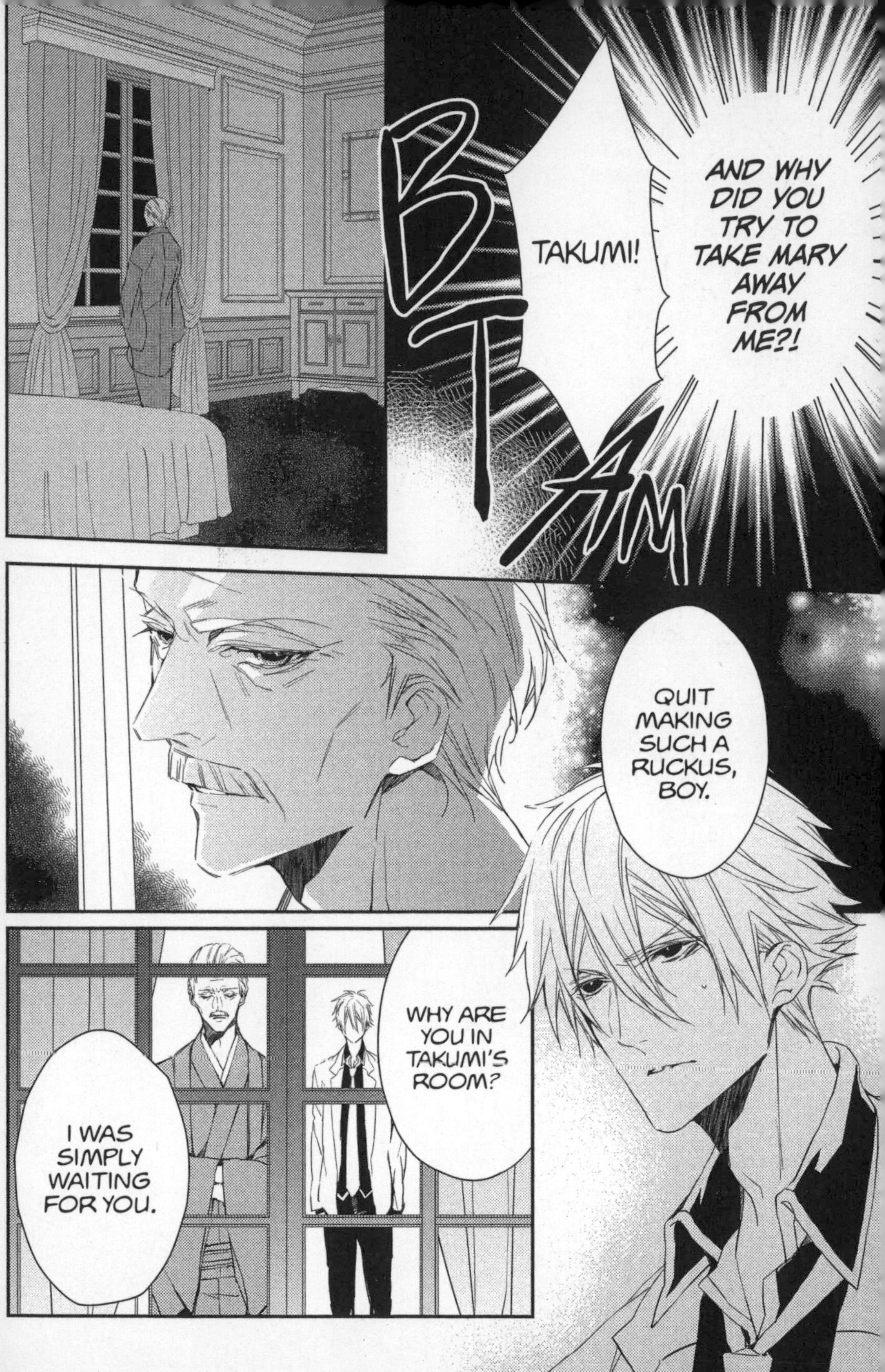
BLAM
TAKUMI!
AND WHY DID YOU TRY TO TAKE MARY AWAY FROM ME?!
QUIT MAKING SUCH A RUCKUS, BOY.
WHY ARE YOU IN TAKUMI'S ROOM?
I WAS SIMPLY WAITING FOR YOU.

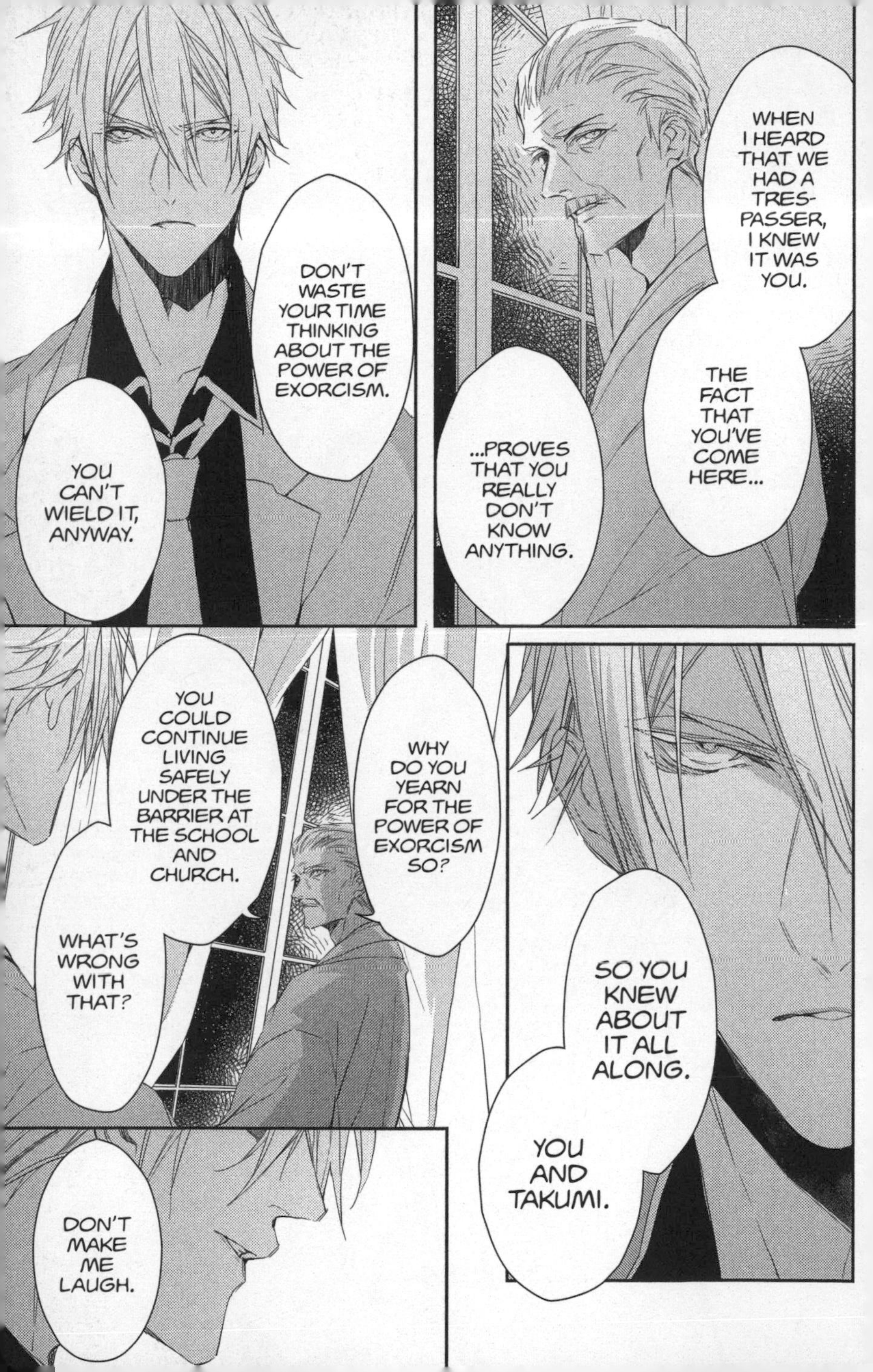
WHEN I HEARD THAT WE HAD A TRES-PASSER, I KNEW IT WAS YOU.
THE FACT THAT YOU'VE COME HERE...
...PROVES THAT YOU REALLY DON'T KNOW ANYTHING.
DON'T WASTE YOUR TIME THINKING ABOUT THE POWER OF EXORCISM.
YOU CAN'T WIELD IT, ANYWAY.
SO YOU KNEW ABOUT IT ALL ALONG.
YOU AND TAKUMI.
WHY DO YOU YEARN FOR THE POWER OF EXORCISM SO?
YOU COULD CONTINUE LIVING SAFELY UNDER THE BARRIER AT THE SCHOOL AND CHURCH.
WHAT'S WRONG WITH THAT?
DON'T MAKE ME LAUGH.

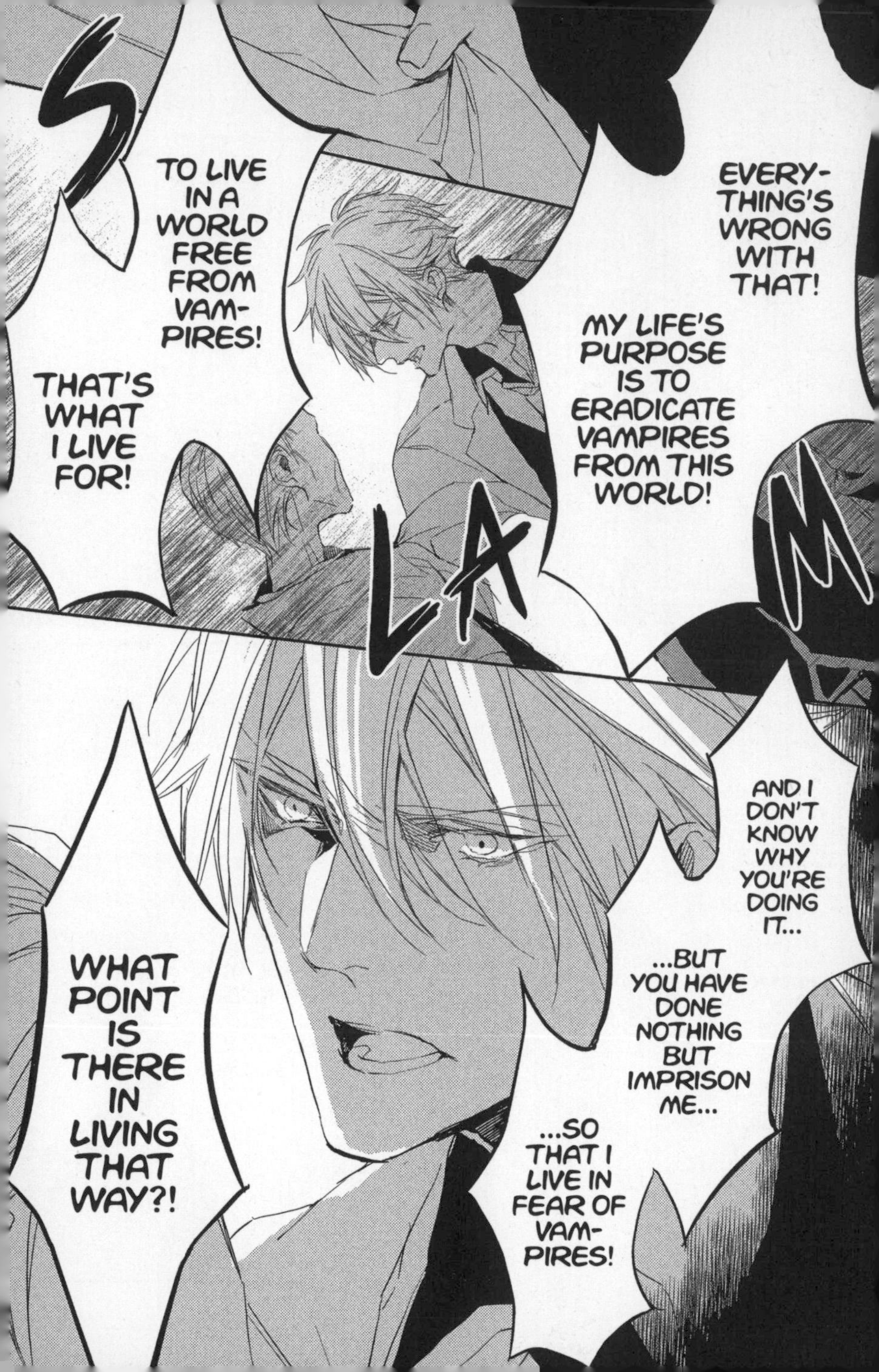
MY LIFE'S PURPOSE IS TO ERADICATE VAMPIRES FROM THIS WORLD!
TO LIVE IN A WORLD FREE FROM VAMPIRES!
THAT'S WHAT I LIVE FOR!
EVERYTHING'S WRONG WITH THAT!
SLAM
AND I DON'T KNOW WHY YOU'RE DOING IT...
...BUT YOU HAVE DONE NOTHING BUT IMPRISON ME...
...SO THAT I LIVE IN FEAR OF VAMPIRES!
WHAT POINT IS THERE IN LIVING THAT WAY?!

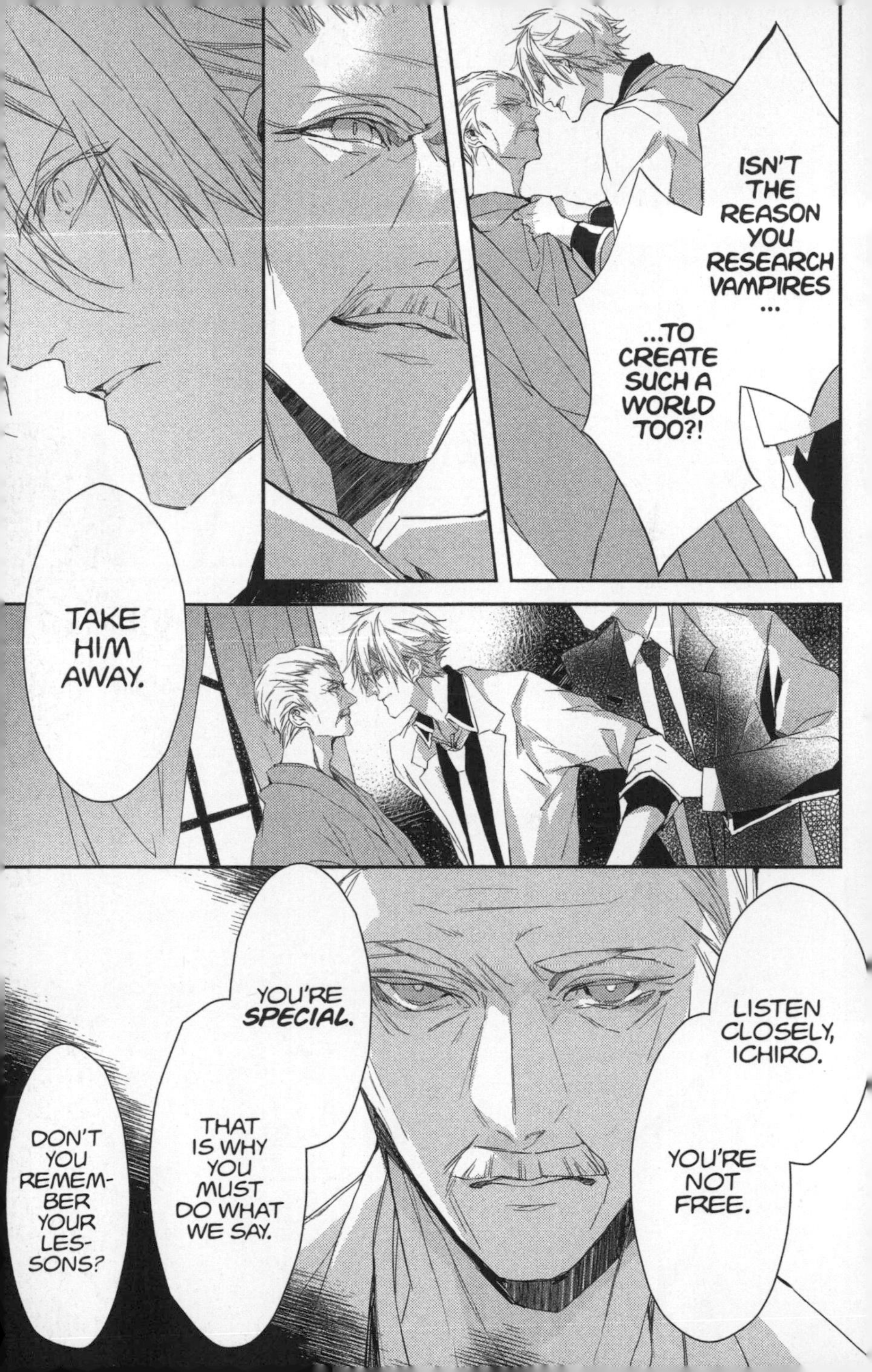
ISN'T THE REASON YOU RESEARCH VAMPIRES...
...TO CREATE SUCH A WORLD TOO?!
TAKE HIM AWAY.
LISTEN CLOSELY, ICHIRO.
YOU'RE NOT FREE.
YOU'RE *SPECIAL*.
THAT IS WHY YOU MUST DO WHAT WE SAY.
DON'T YOU REMEMBER YOUR LESSONS?

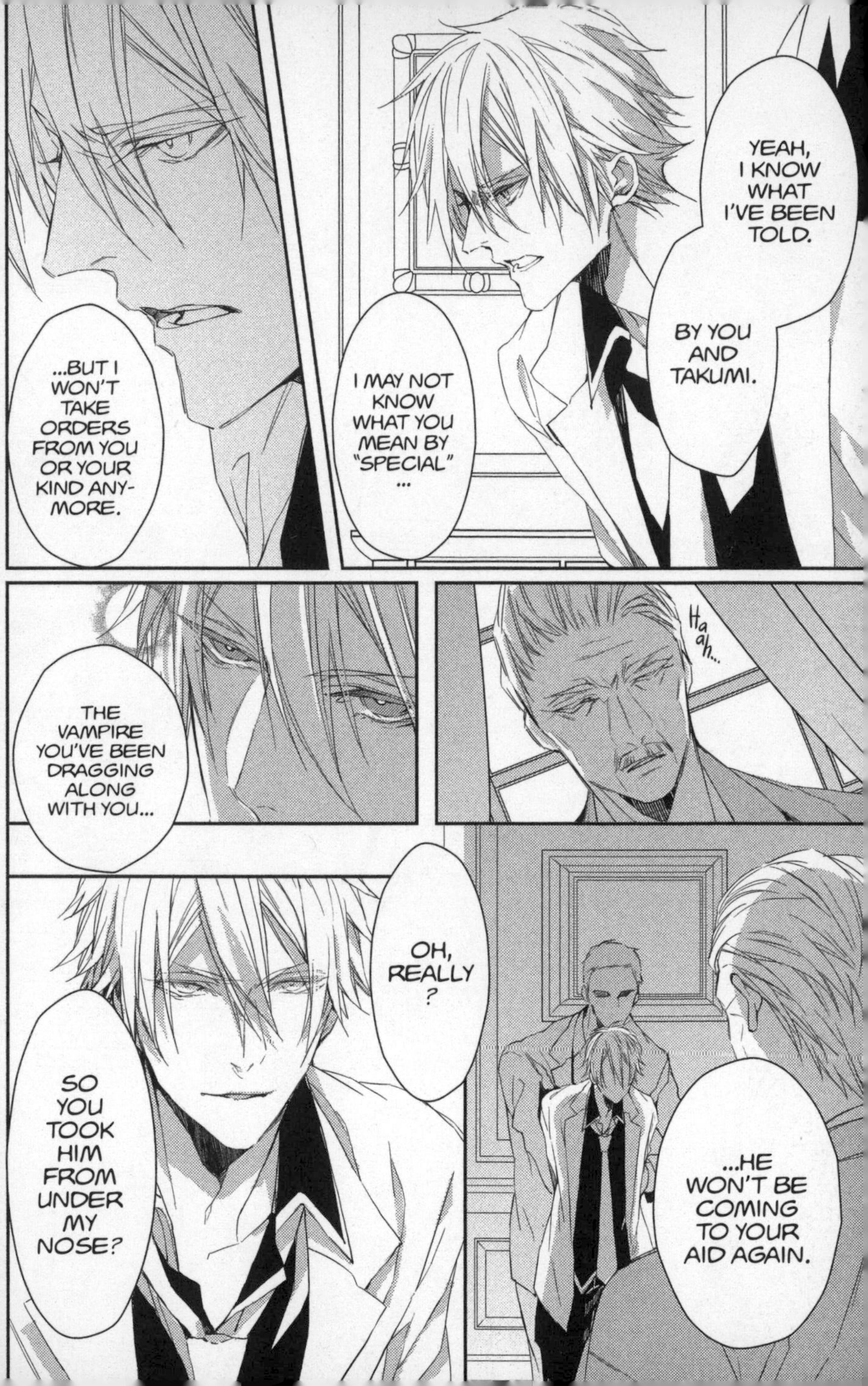
YEAH, I KNOW WHAT I'VE BEEN TOLD.
BY YOU AND TAKUMI.
I MAY NOT KNOW WHAT YOU MEAN BY "SPECIAL" ...
...BUT I WON'T TAKE ORDERS FROM YOU OR YOUR KIND ANY-MORE.
Haah...
THE VAMPIRE YOU'VE BEEN DRAGGING ALONG WITH YOU...
...HE WON'T BE COMING TO YOUR AID AGAIN.
OH, REALLY?
SO YOU TOOK HIM FROM UNDER MY NOSE?

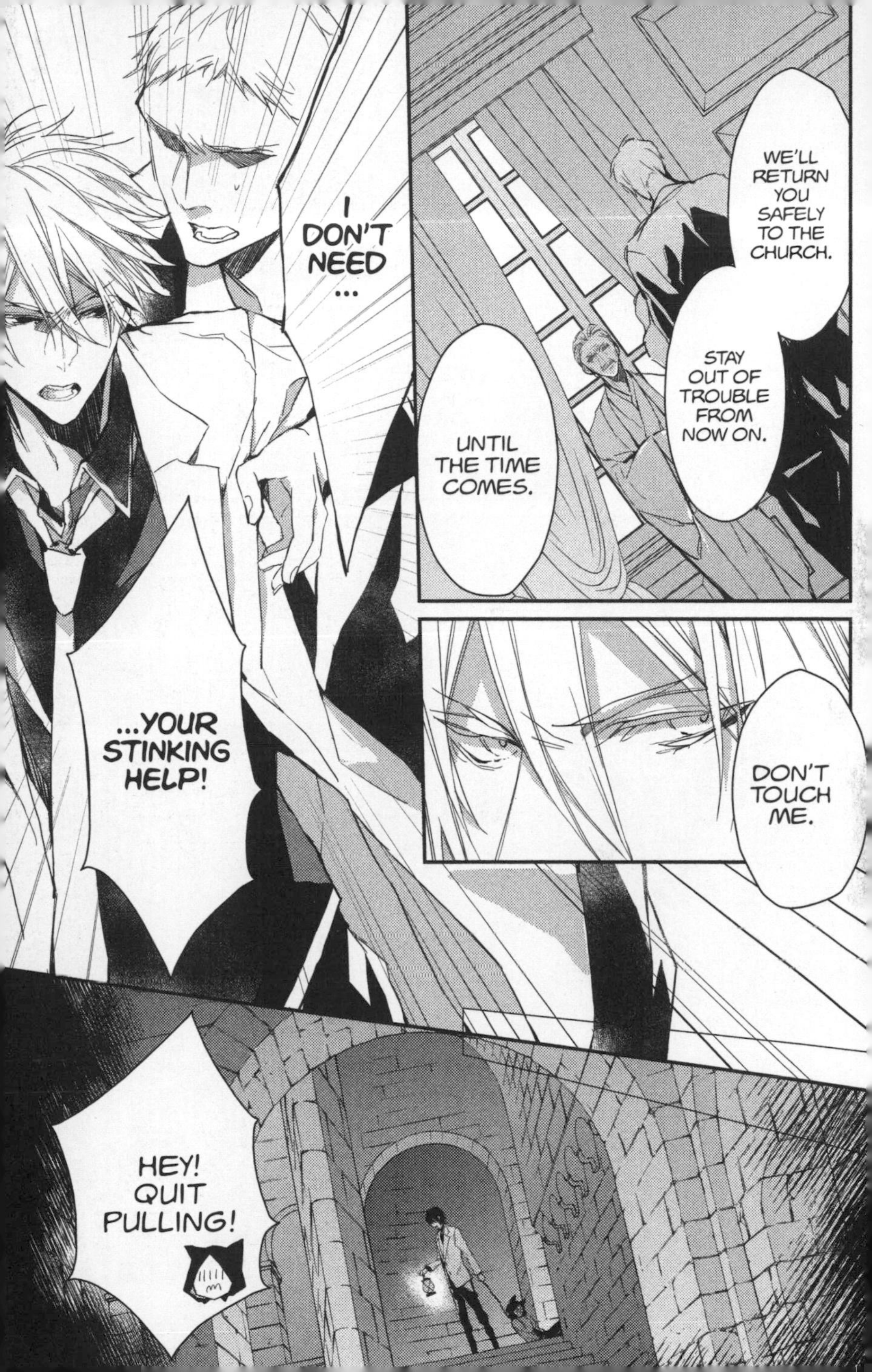
WE'LL RETURN YOU SAFELY TO THE CHURCH.
STAY OUT OF TROUBLE FROM NOW ON.
UNTIL THE TIME COMES.
DON'T TOUCH ME.
I DON'T NEED ...
...YOUR STINKING HELP!
HEY! QUIT PULLING!

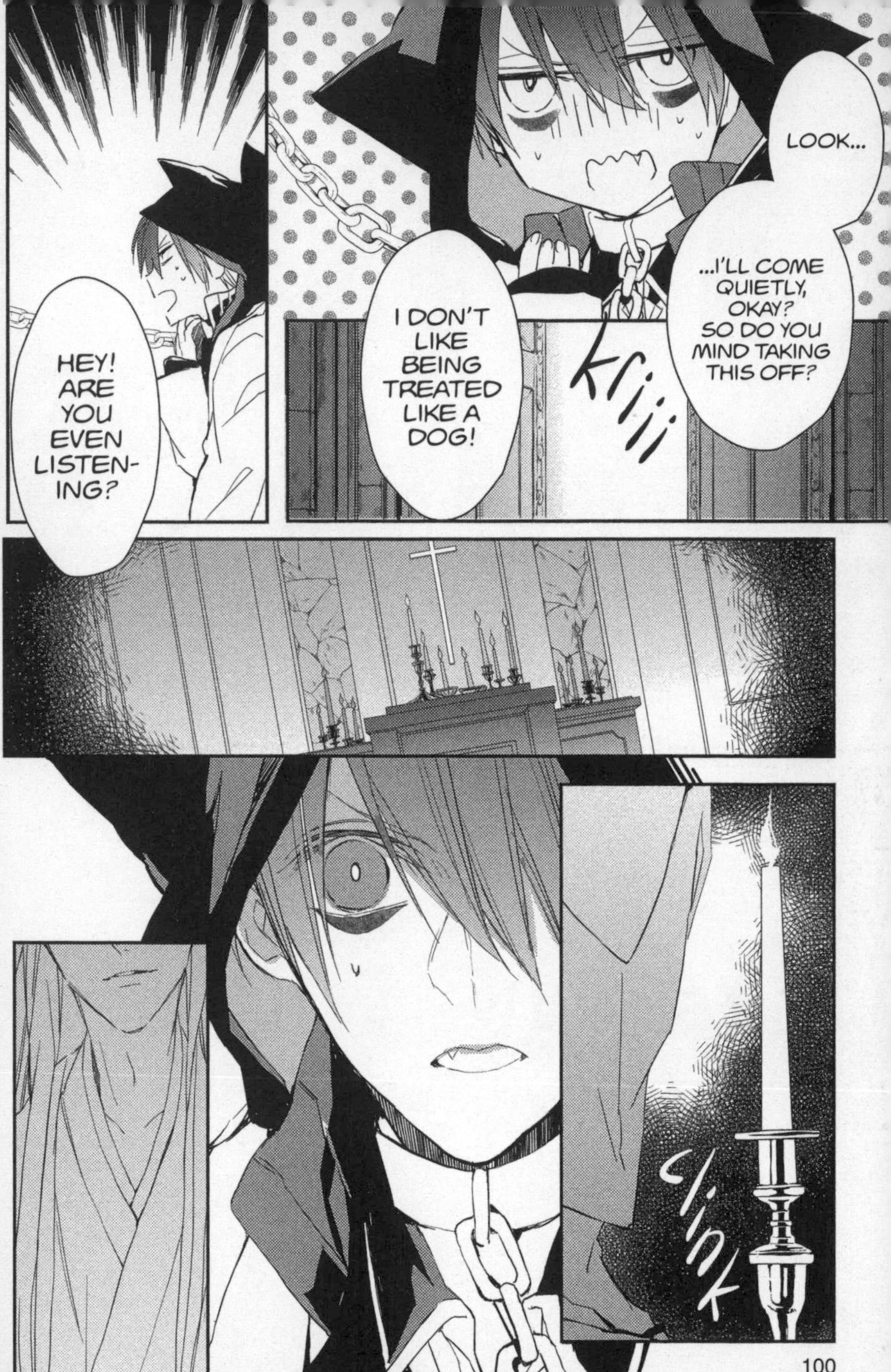
LOOK...
...I'LL COME QUIETLY, OKAY? SO DO YOU MIND TAKING THIS OFF?
I DON'T LIKE BEING TREATED LIKE A DOG!
kriiii
HEY! ARE YOU EVEN LISTEN-ING?
clink

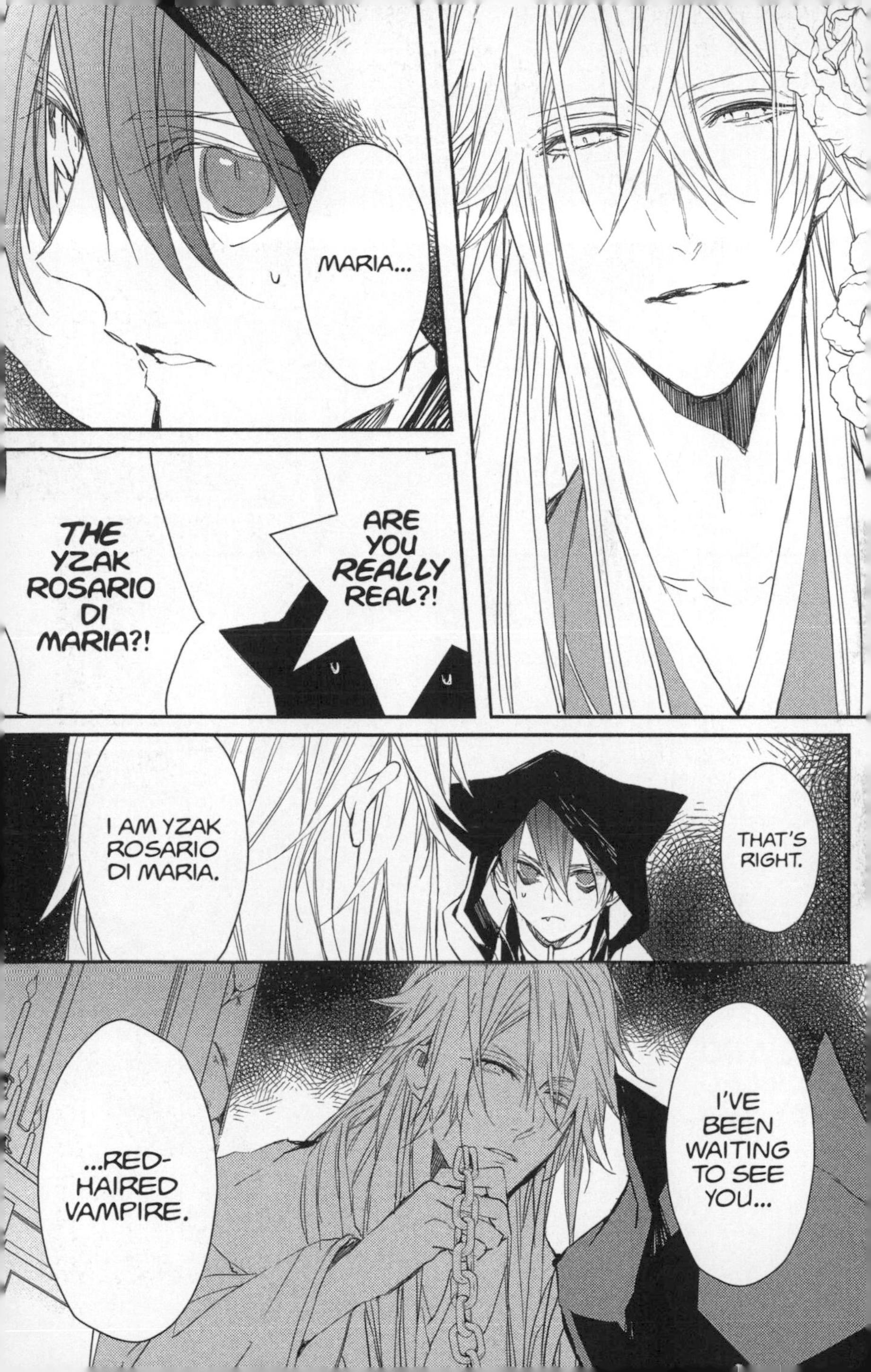
MARIA...
ARE YOU REALLY REAL?!
THE YZAK ROSARIO DI MARIA?!
THAT'S RIGHT.
I AM YZAK ROSARIO DI MARIA.
I'VE BEEN WAITING TO SEE YOU...
...RED-HAIRED VAMPIRE.

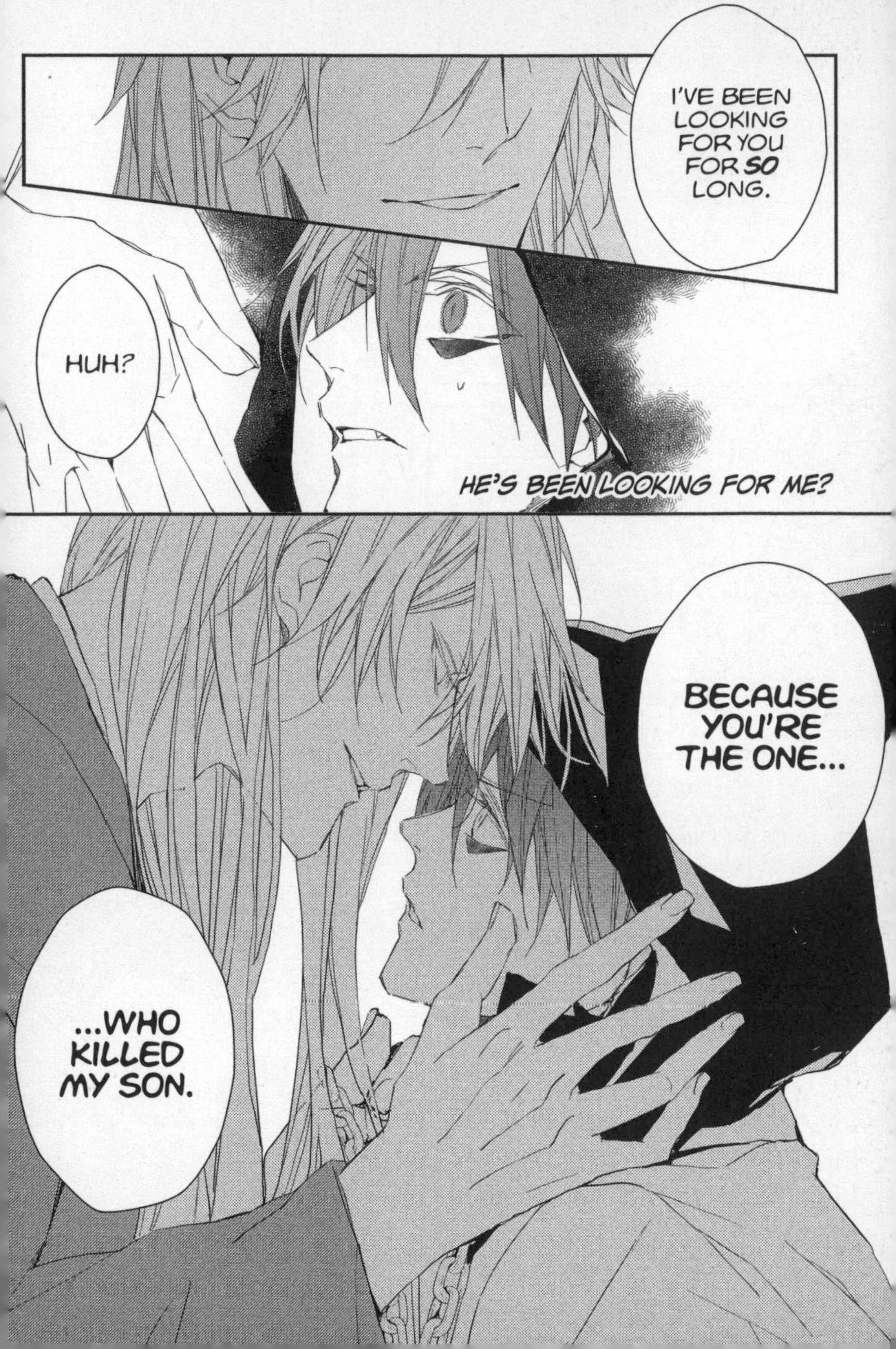
I'VE BEEN LOOKING FOR YOU FOR SO LONG.
HUH?
HE'S BEEN LOOKING FOR ME?
BECAUSE YOU'RE THE ONE...
...WHO KILLED MY SON.

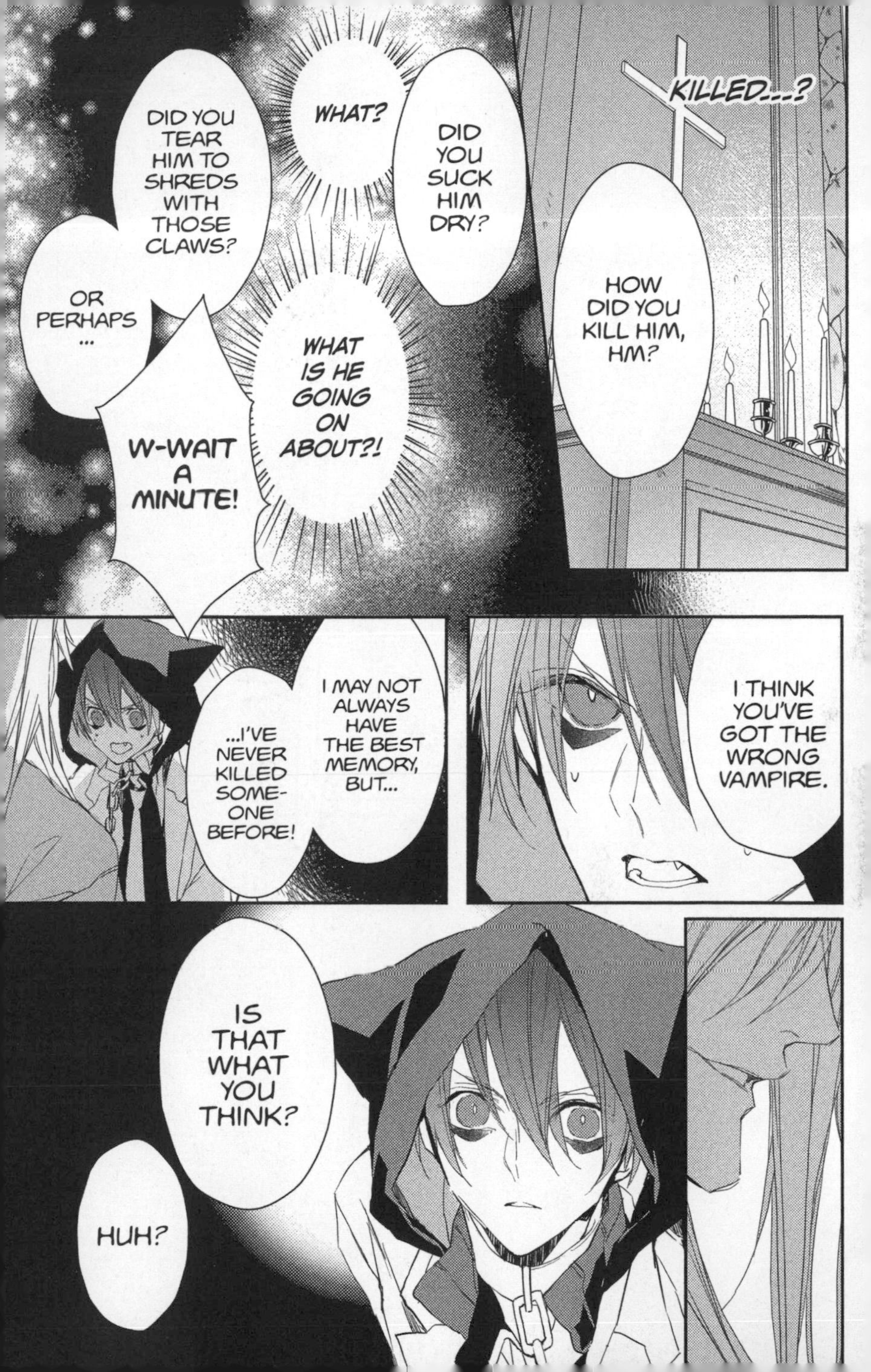
KILLED...?
HOW DID YOU KILL HIM, HM?
DID YOU SUCK HIM DRY?
WHAT?
DID YOU TEAR HIM TO SHREDS WITH THOSE CLAWS?
OR PERHAPS ...
WHAT IS HE GOING ON ABOUT?!
W-WAIT A MINUTE!
I THINK YOU'VE GOT THE WRONG VAMPIRE.
I MAY NOT ALWAYS HAVE THE BEST MEMORY, BUT...
...I'VE NEVER KILLED SOME-ONE BEFORE!
IS THAT WHAT YOU THINK?
HUH?

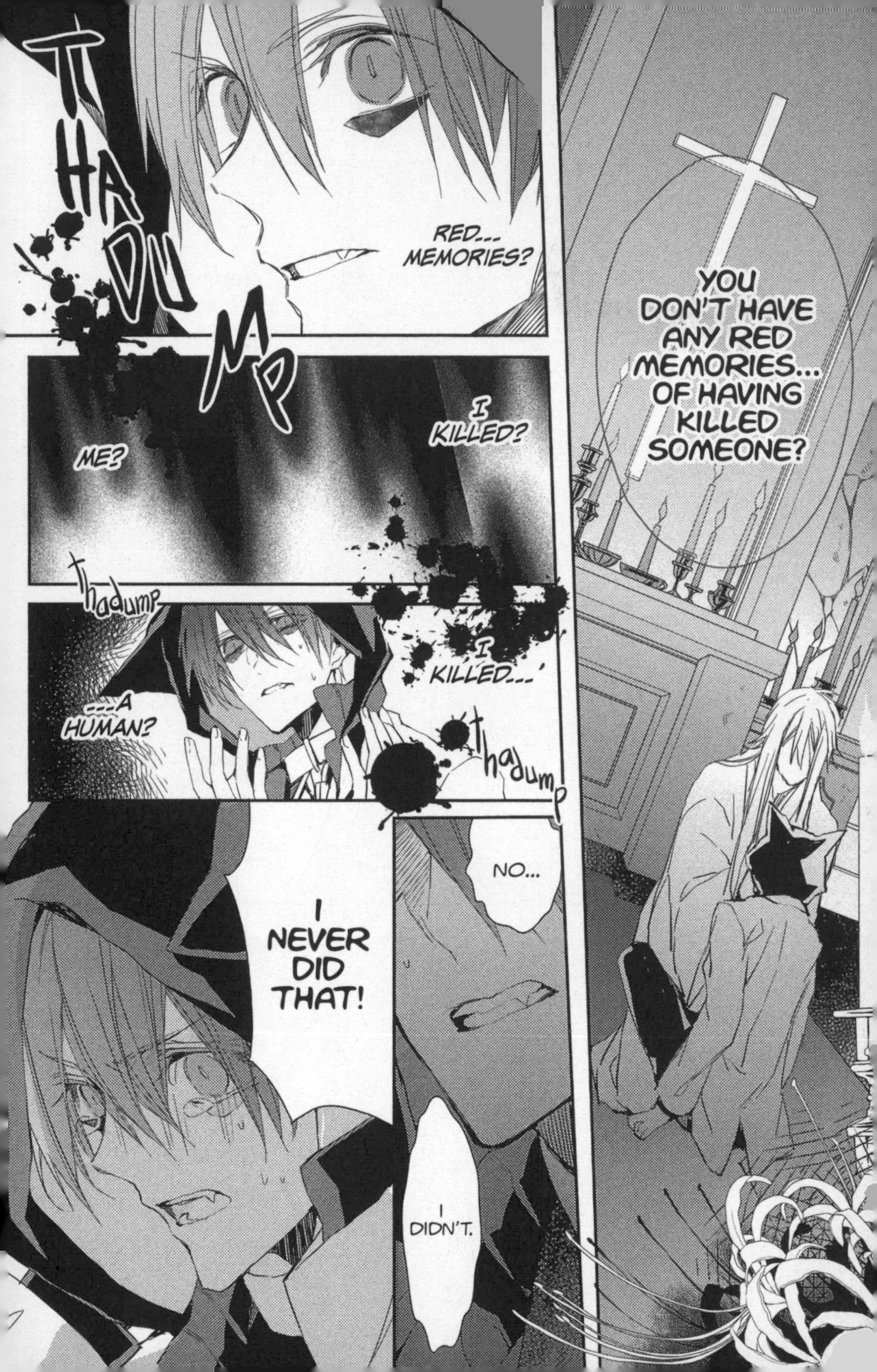
YOU DON'T HAVE ANY RED MEMORIES... OF HAVING KILLED SOMEONE?
RED... MEMORIES?
THADUMP
I KILLED?
ME?
thadump
I KILLED...
...A HUMAN?
thadump
NO...
I DIDN'T.
I NEVER DID THAT!

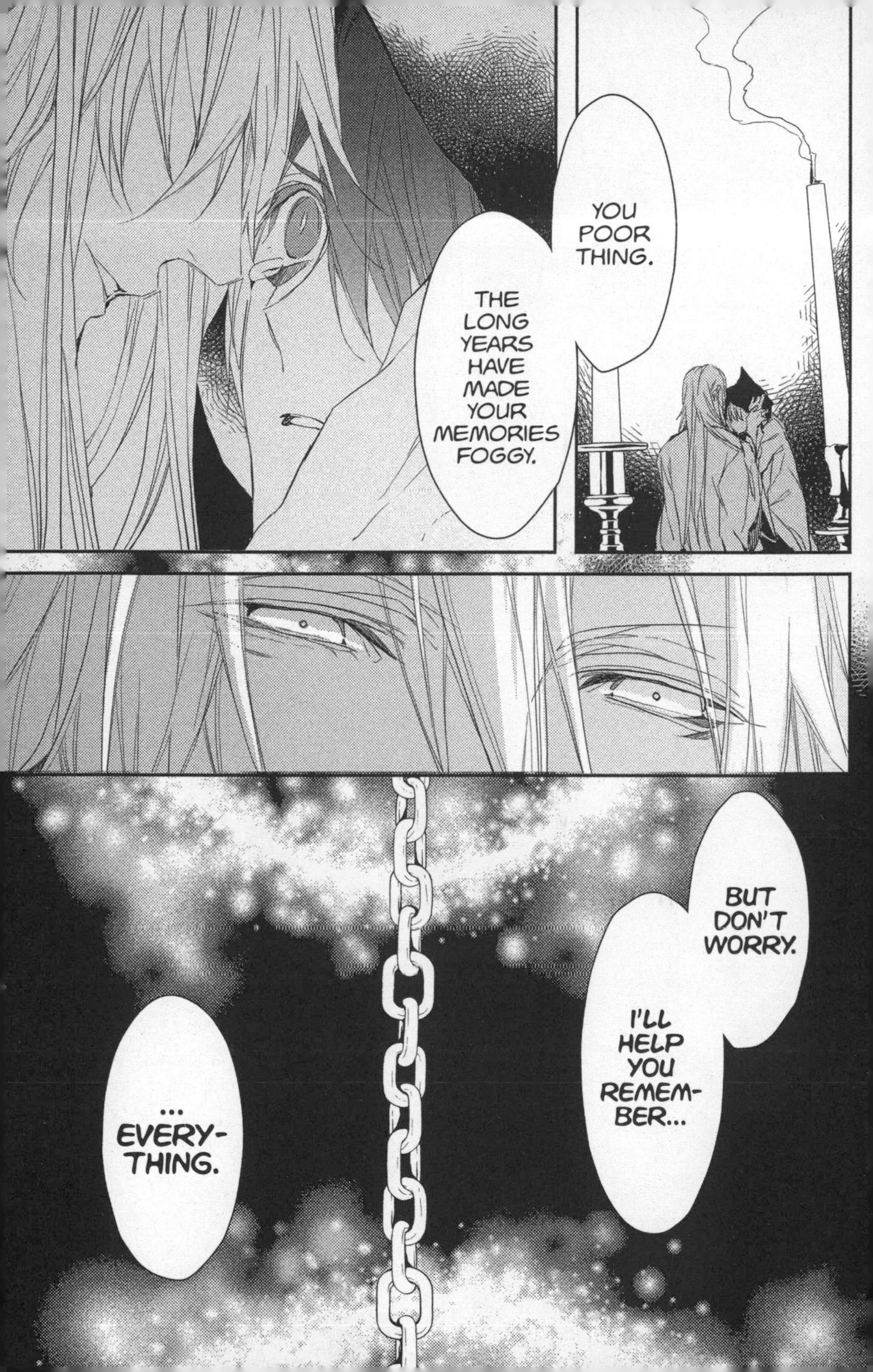
YOU POOR THING.
THE LONG YEARS HAVE MADE YOUR MEMORIES FOGGY.
BUT DON'T WORRY.
I'LL HELP YOU REMEM-BER...
... EVERY-THING.

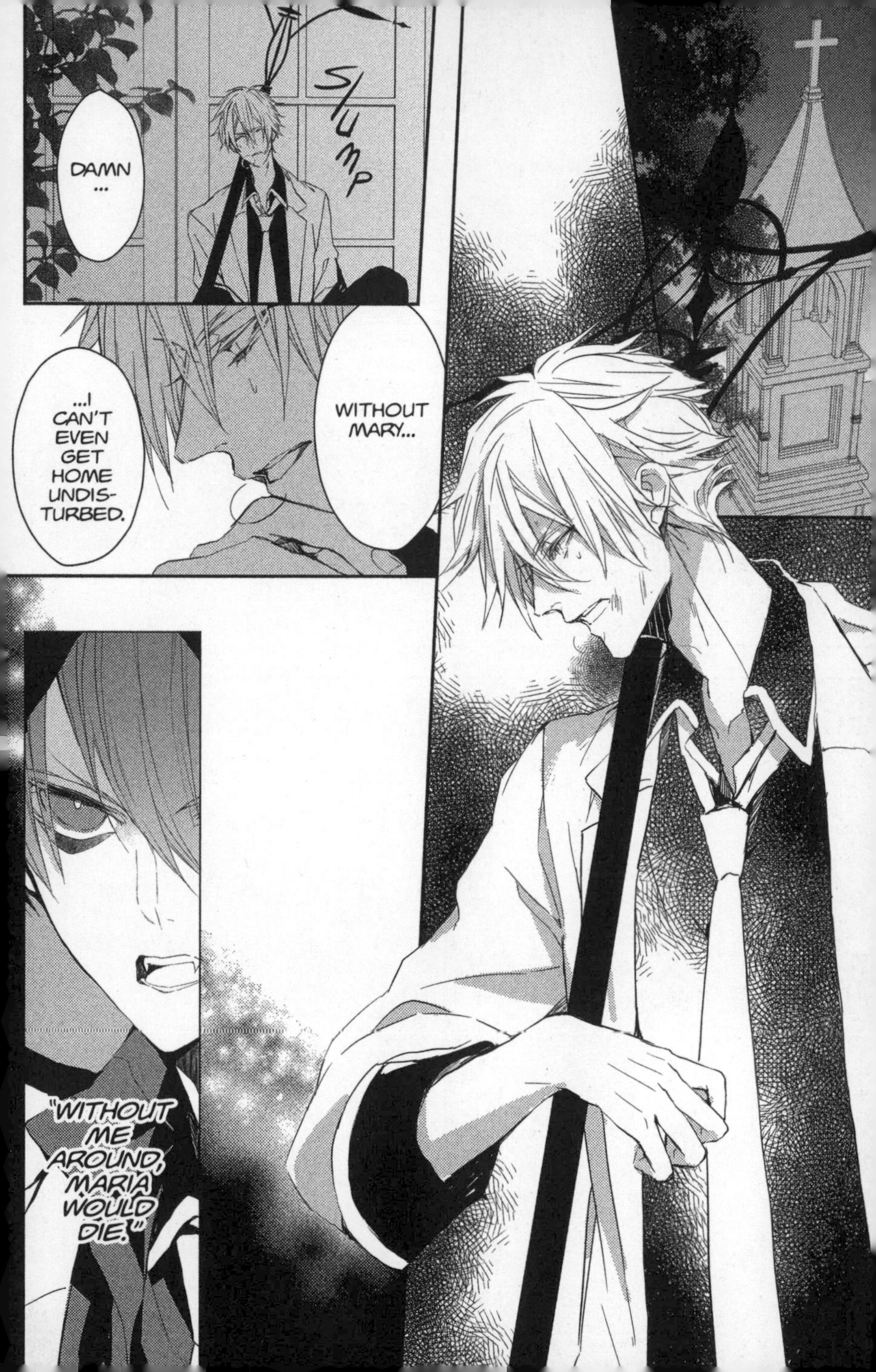
SLUMP
DAMN...
WITHOUT MARY...
...I CAN'T EVEN GET HOME UNDIS-TURBED.
"WITHOUT ME AROUND, MARIA WOULD DIE."

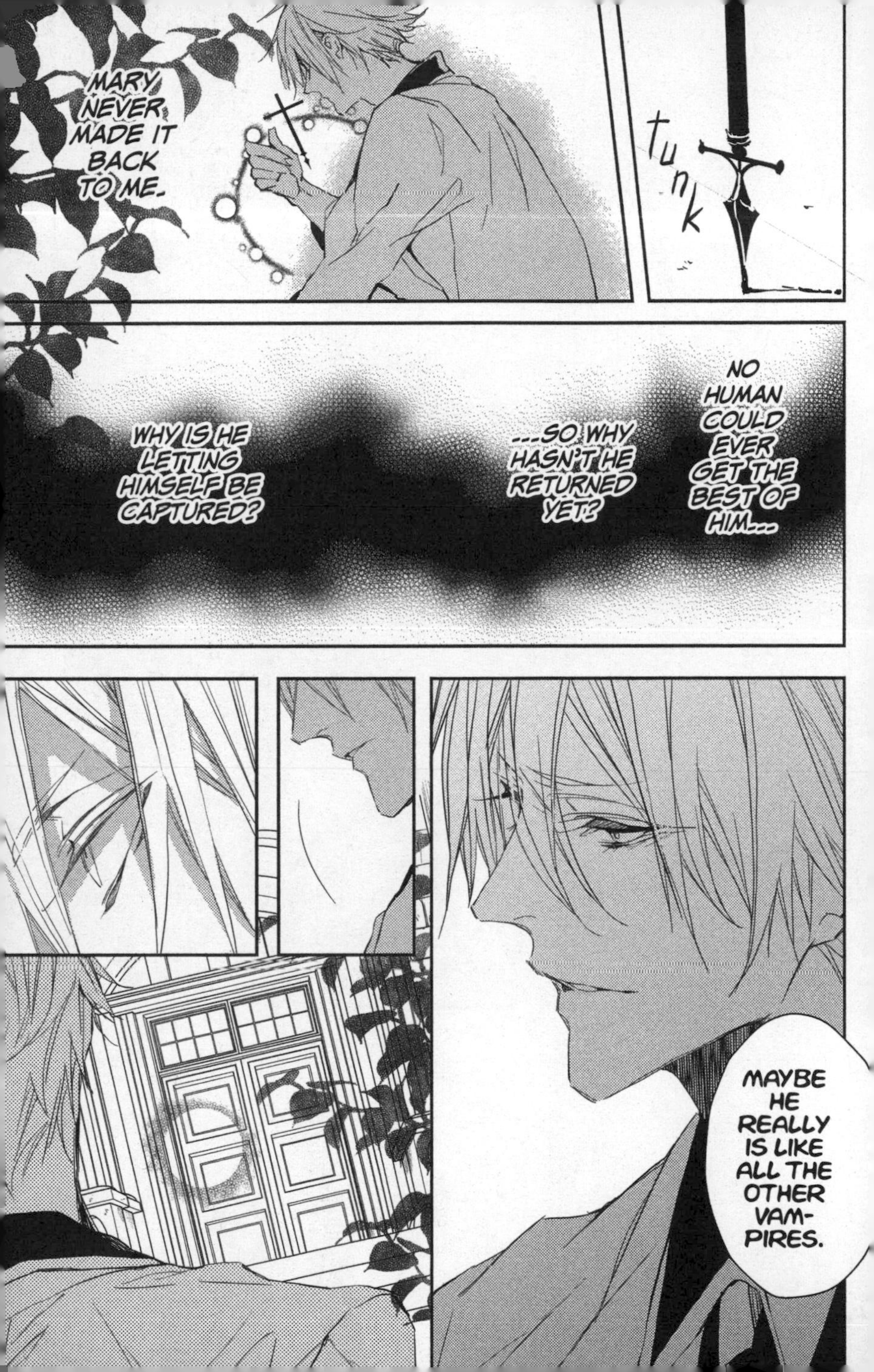
tunk
MARY NEVER MADE IT BACK TO ME.
NO HUMAN COULD EVER GET THE BEST OF HIM...
...SO WHY HASN'T HE RETURNED YET?
WHY IS HE LETTING HIMSELF BE CAPTURED?
MAYBE HE REALLY IS LIKE ALL THE OTHER VAM-PIRES.

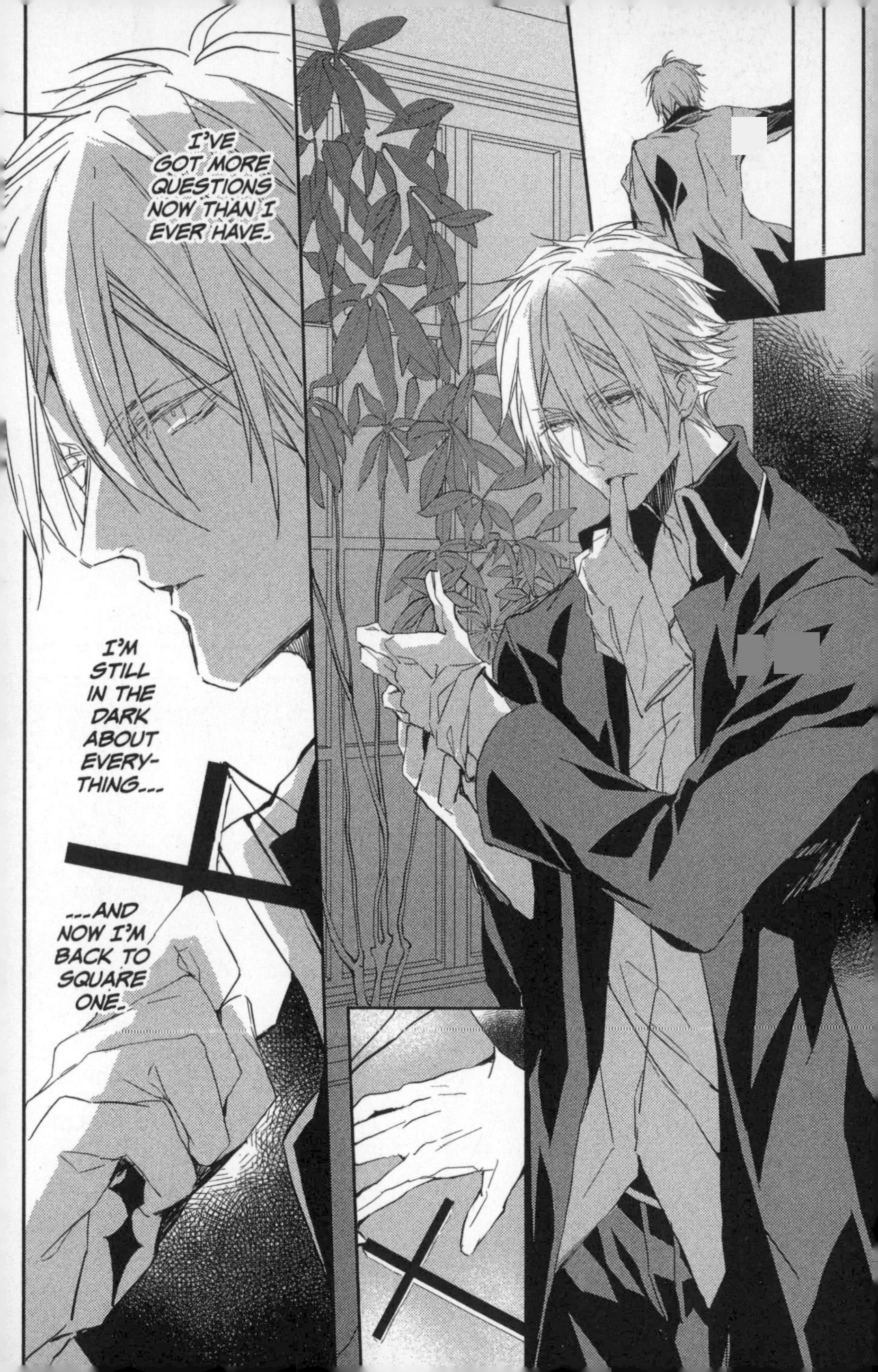
I'VE GOT MORE QUESTIONS NOW THAN I EVER HAVE.
I'M STILL IN THE DARK ABOUT EVERY-THING...
...AND NOW I'M BACK TO SQUARE ONE.

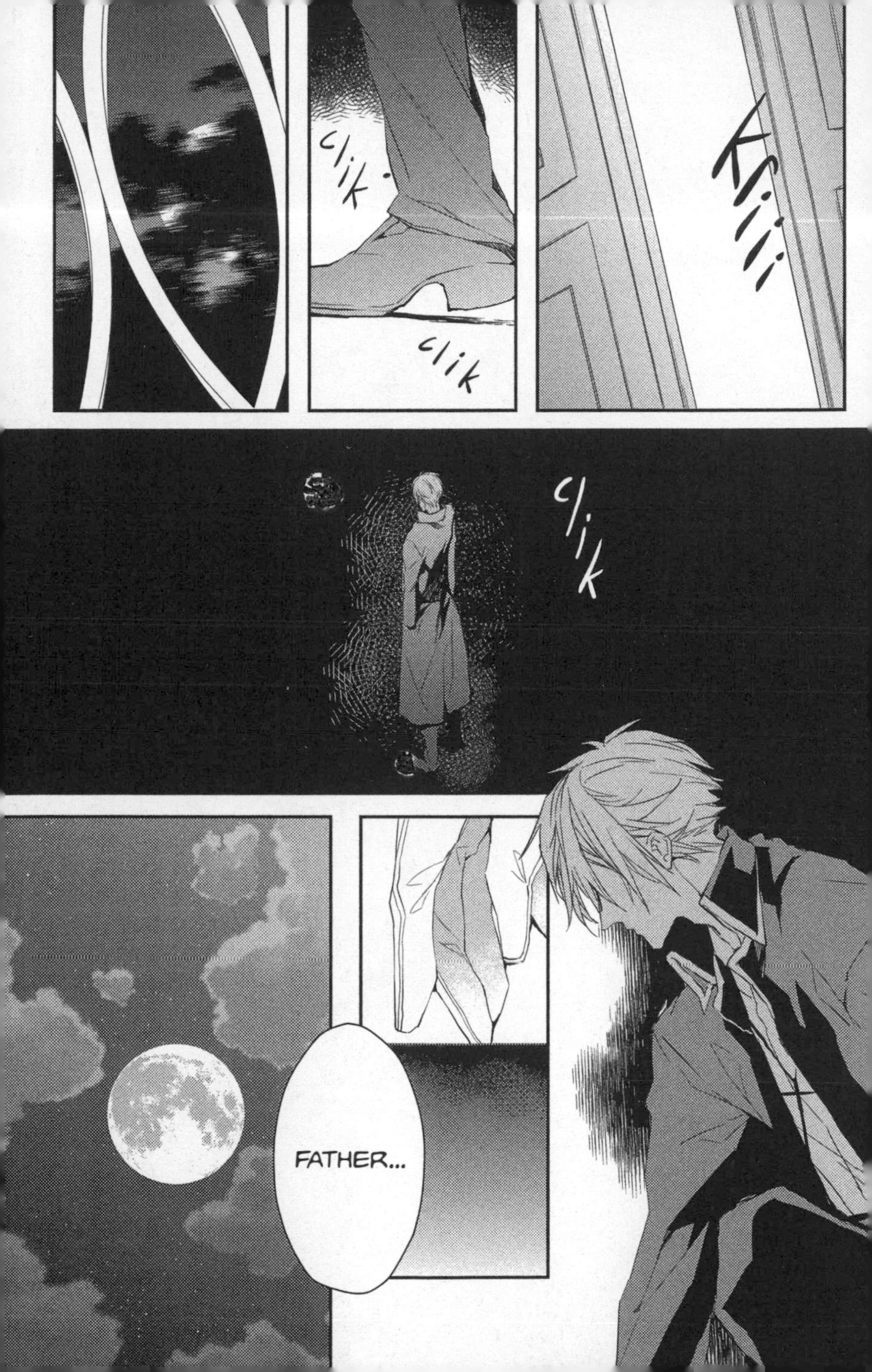
Kriiii
clik
clik
clik
FATHER...

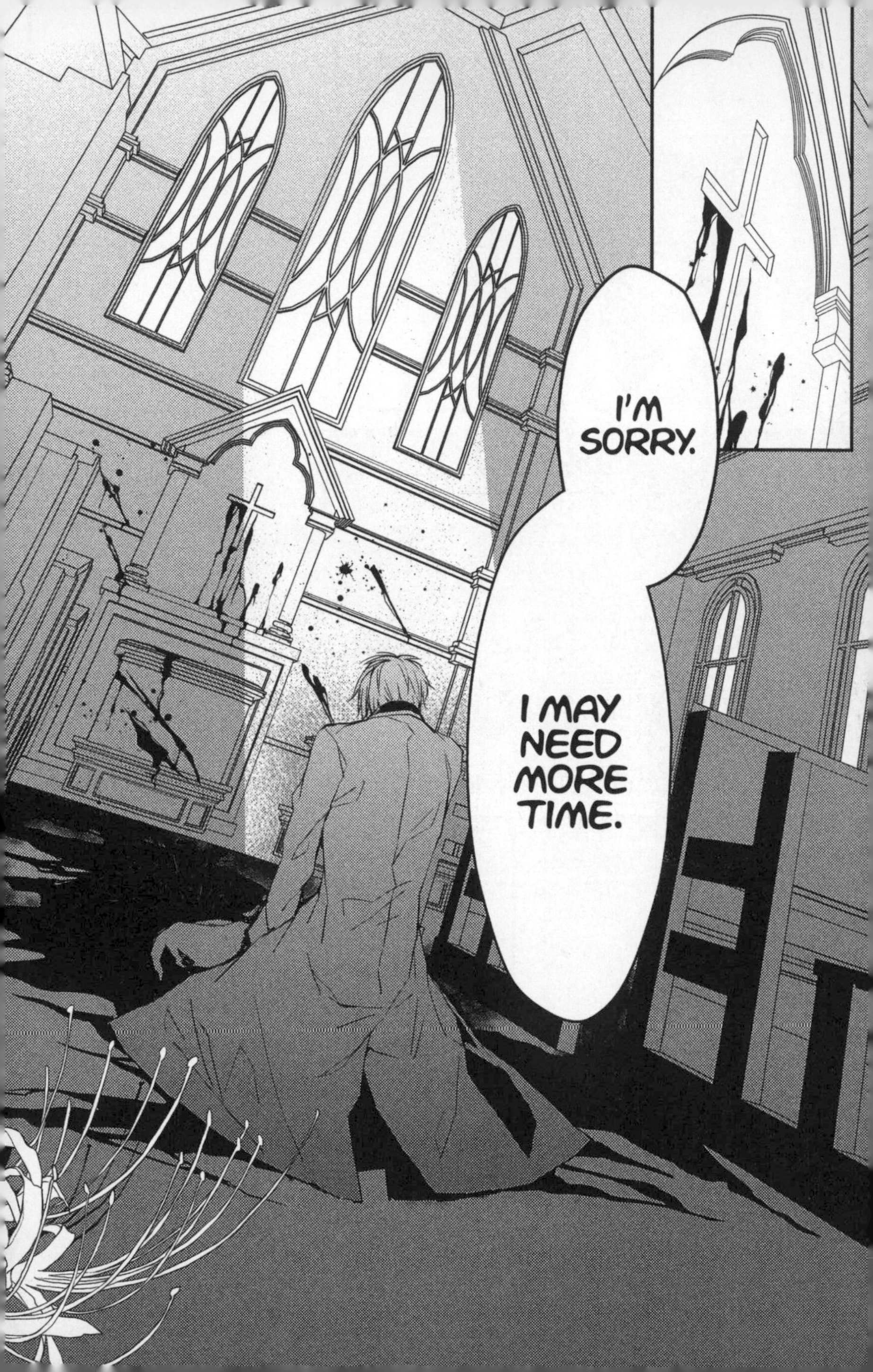
I'M SORRY.
I MAY NEED MORE TIME.

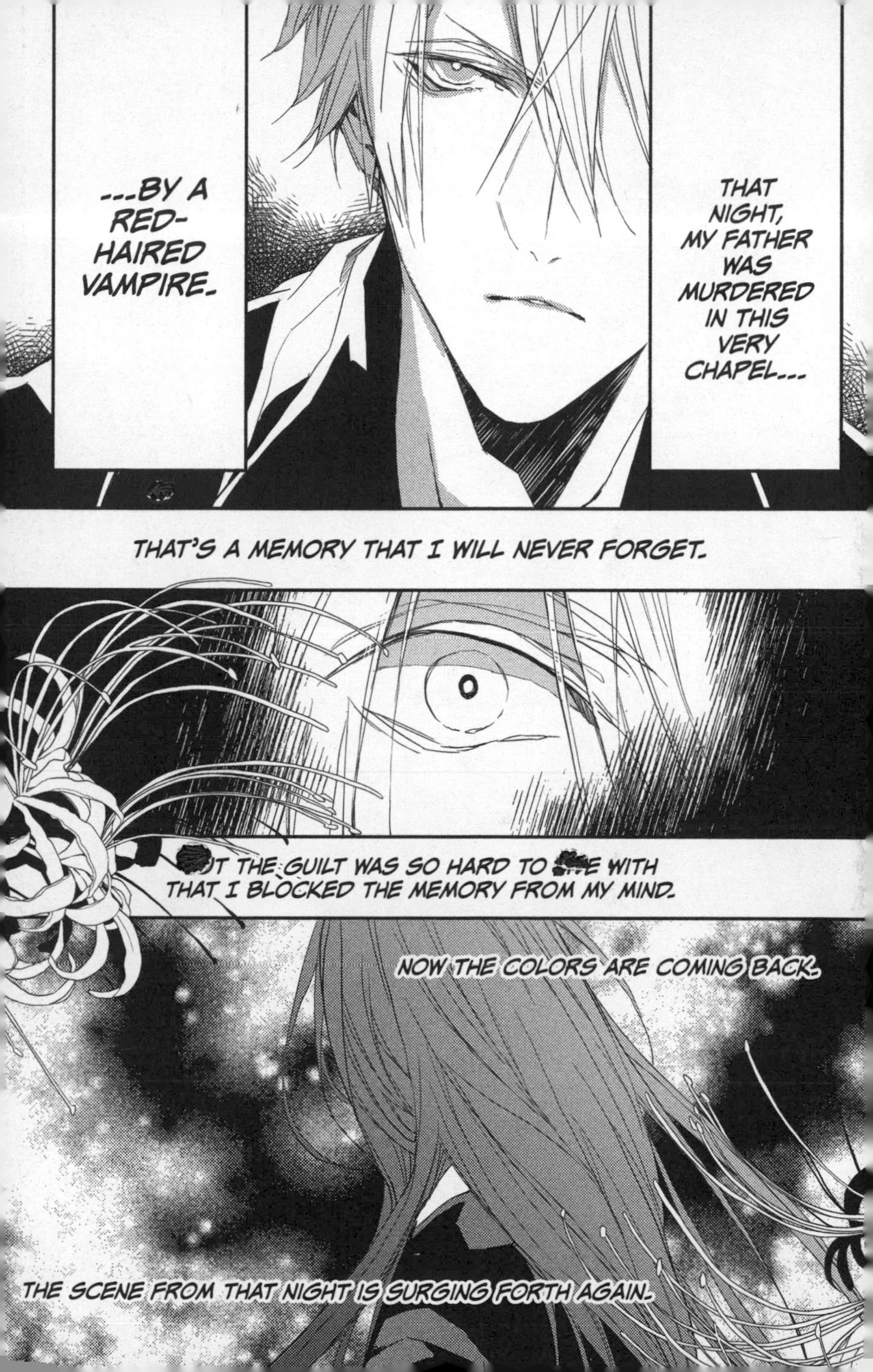
THAT NIGHT, MY FATHER WAS MURDERED IN THIS VERY CHAPEL...
---BY A RED-HAIRED VAMPIRE.
THAT'S A MEMORY THAT I WILL NEVER FORGET.
UT THE GUILT WAS SO HARD TO E WITH THAT I BLOCKED THE MEMORY FROM MY MIND.
NOW THE COLORS ARE COMING BACK.
THE SCENE FROM THAT NIGHT IS SURGING FORTH AGAIN.

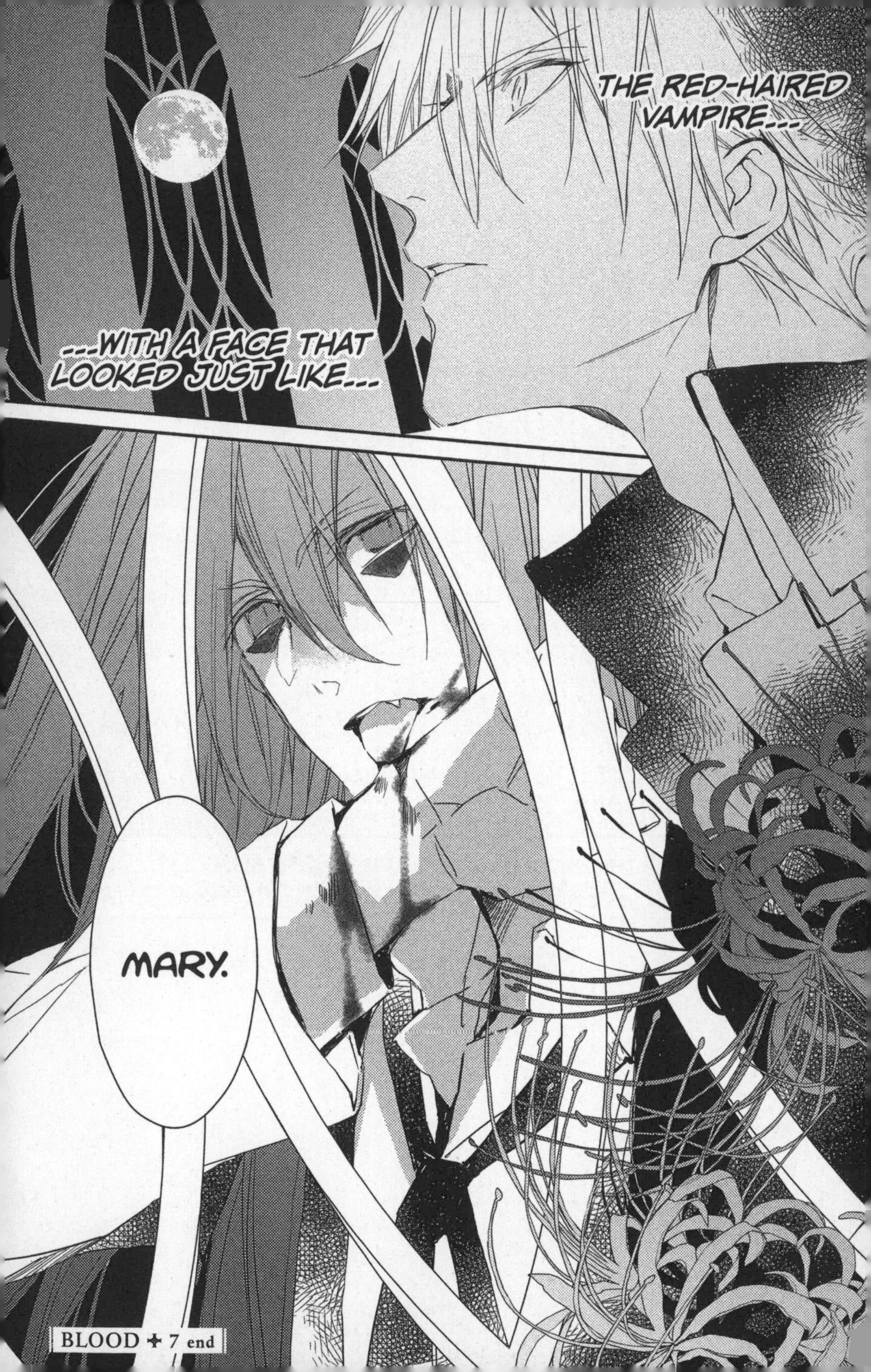
THE RED-HAIRED VAMPIRE...
...WITH A FACE THAT LOOKED JUST LIKE...
MARY.

BLOOD ✢ 7 end

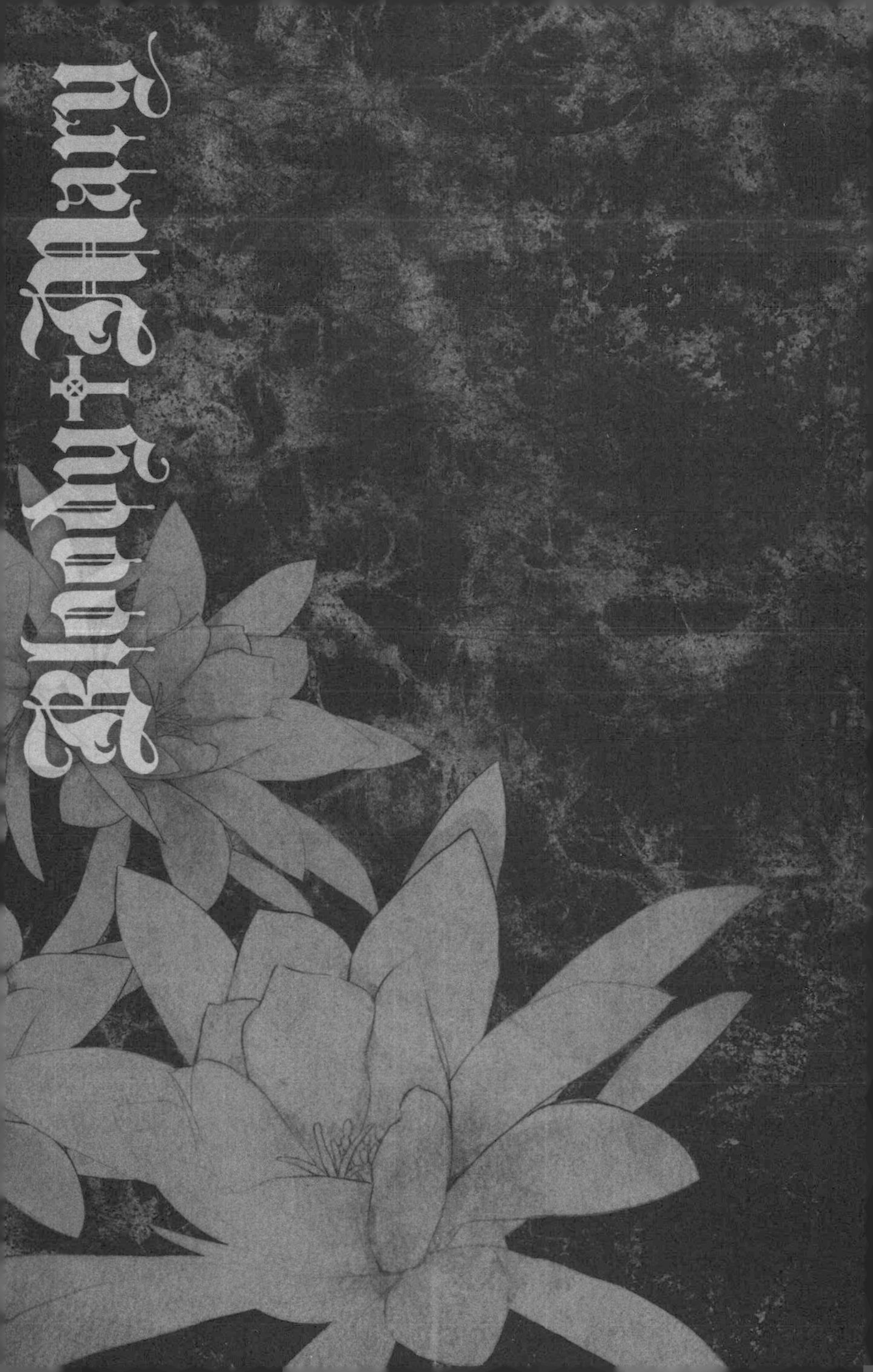
Bloody+Mary

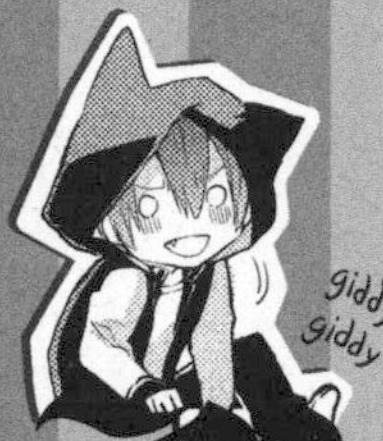

Bloody+Mary

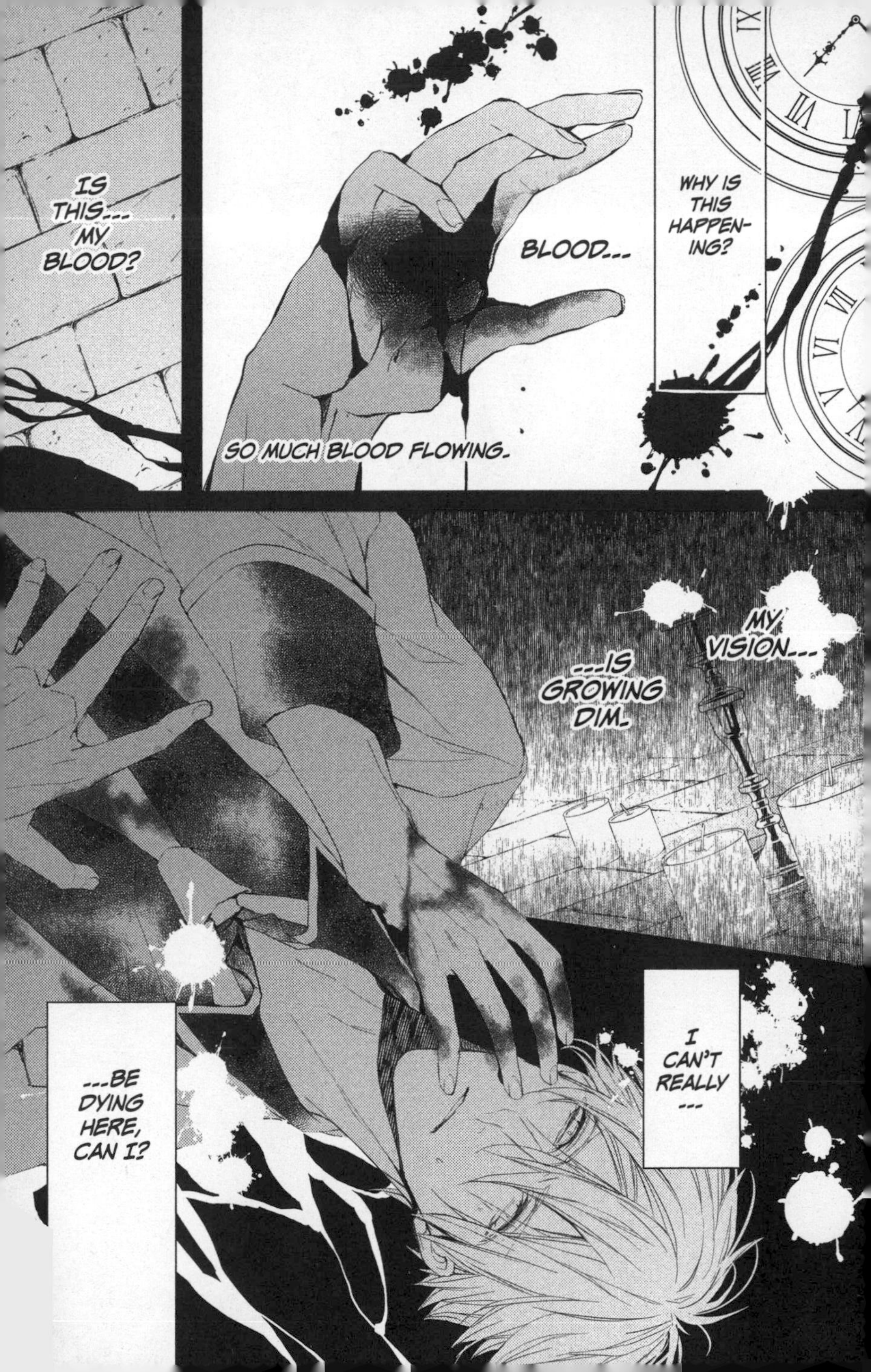
WHY IS THIS HAPPEN-ING?
BLOOD...
SO MUCH BLOOD FLOWING.
IS THIS... MY BLOOD?
MY VISION...
...IS GROWING DIM.
I CAN'T REALLY...
...BE DYING HERE, CAN I?

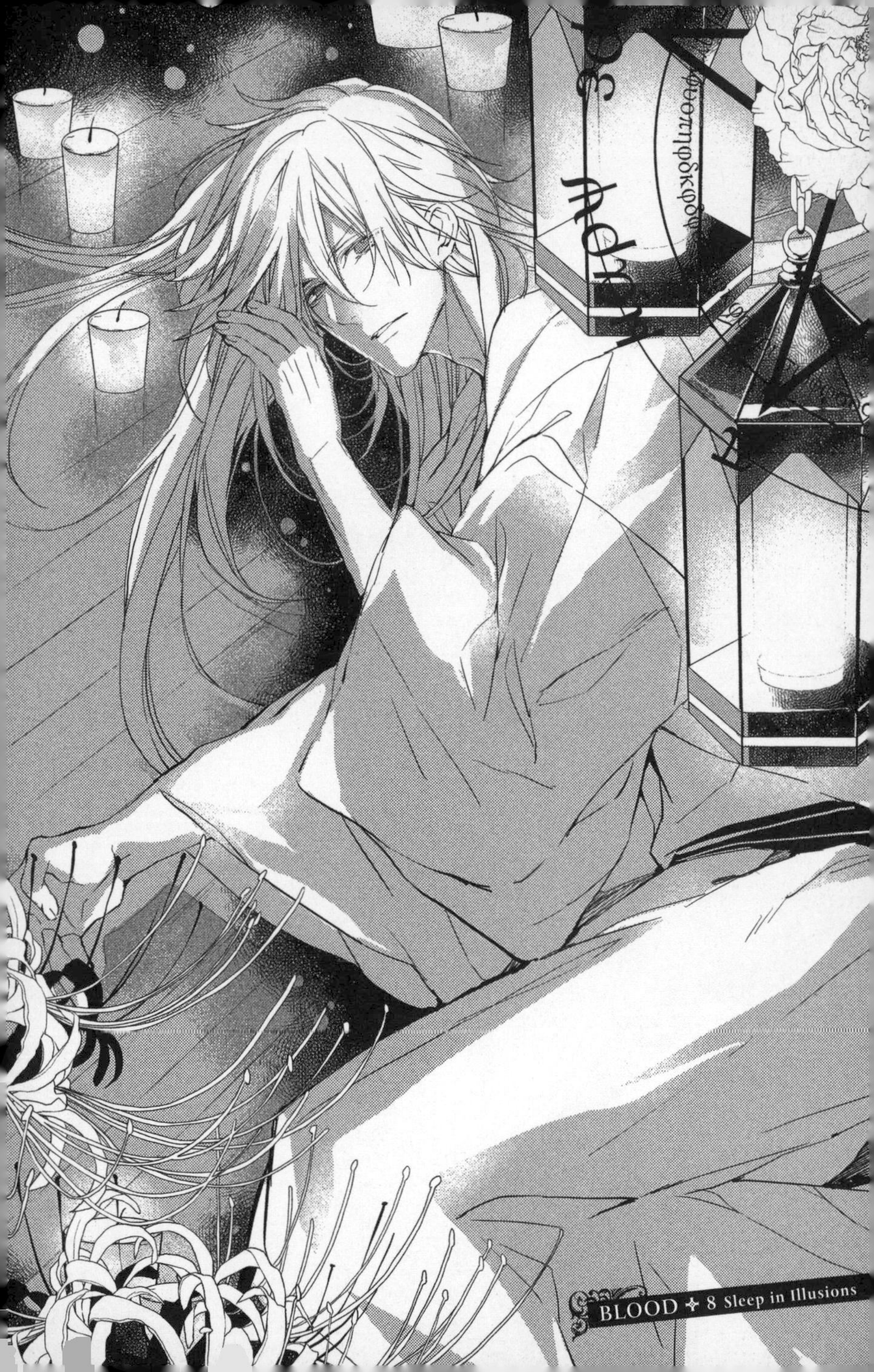
BLOOD ✦ 8 Sleep in Illusions

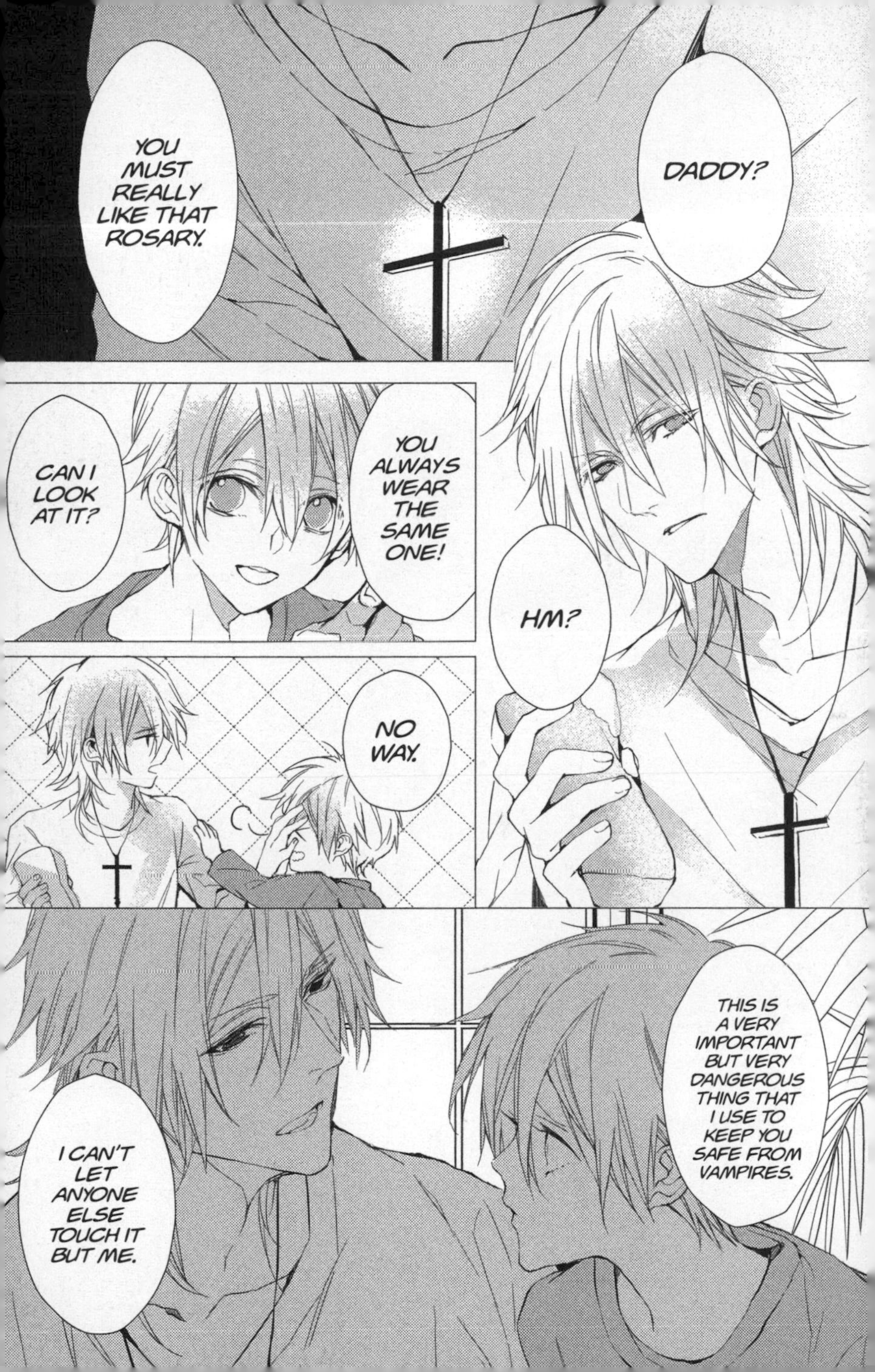
DADDY?
HM?
YOU MUST REALLY LIKE THAT ROSARY.
YOU ALWAYS WEAR THE SAME ONE!
CAN I LOOK AT IT?
NO WAY.
THIS IS A VERY IMPORTANT BUT VERY DANGEROUS THING THAT I USE TO KEEP YOU SAFE FROM VAMPIRES.
I CAN'T LET ANYONE ELSE TOUCH IT BUT ME.

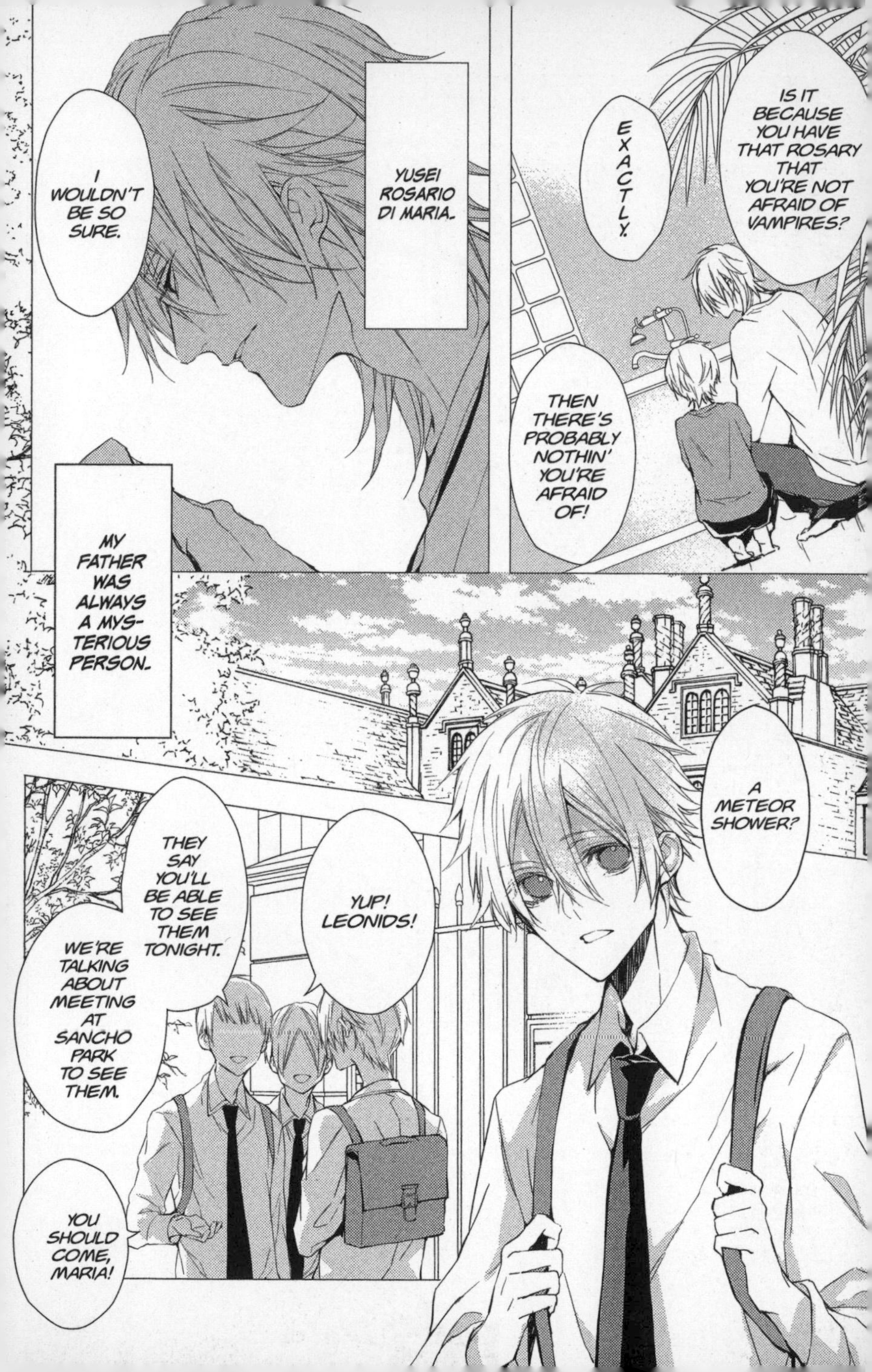
IS IT BECAUSE YOU HAVE THAT ROSARY THAT YOU'RE NOT AFRAID OF VAMPIRES?
EXACTLY.
THEN THERE'S PROBABLY NOTHIN' YOU'RE AFRAID OF!
YUSEI ROSARIO DI MARIA.
I WOULDN'T BE SO SURE.
MY FATHER WAS ALWAYS A MYS-TERIOUS PERSON.
A METEOR SHOWER?
YUP! LEONIDS!
THEY SAY YOU'LL BE ABLE TO SEE THEM TONIGHT.
WE'RE TALKING ABOUT MEETING AT SANCHO PARK TO SEE THEM.
YOU SHOULD COME, MARIA!

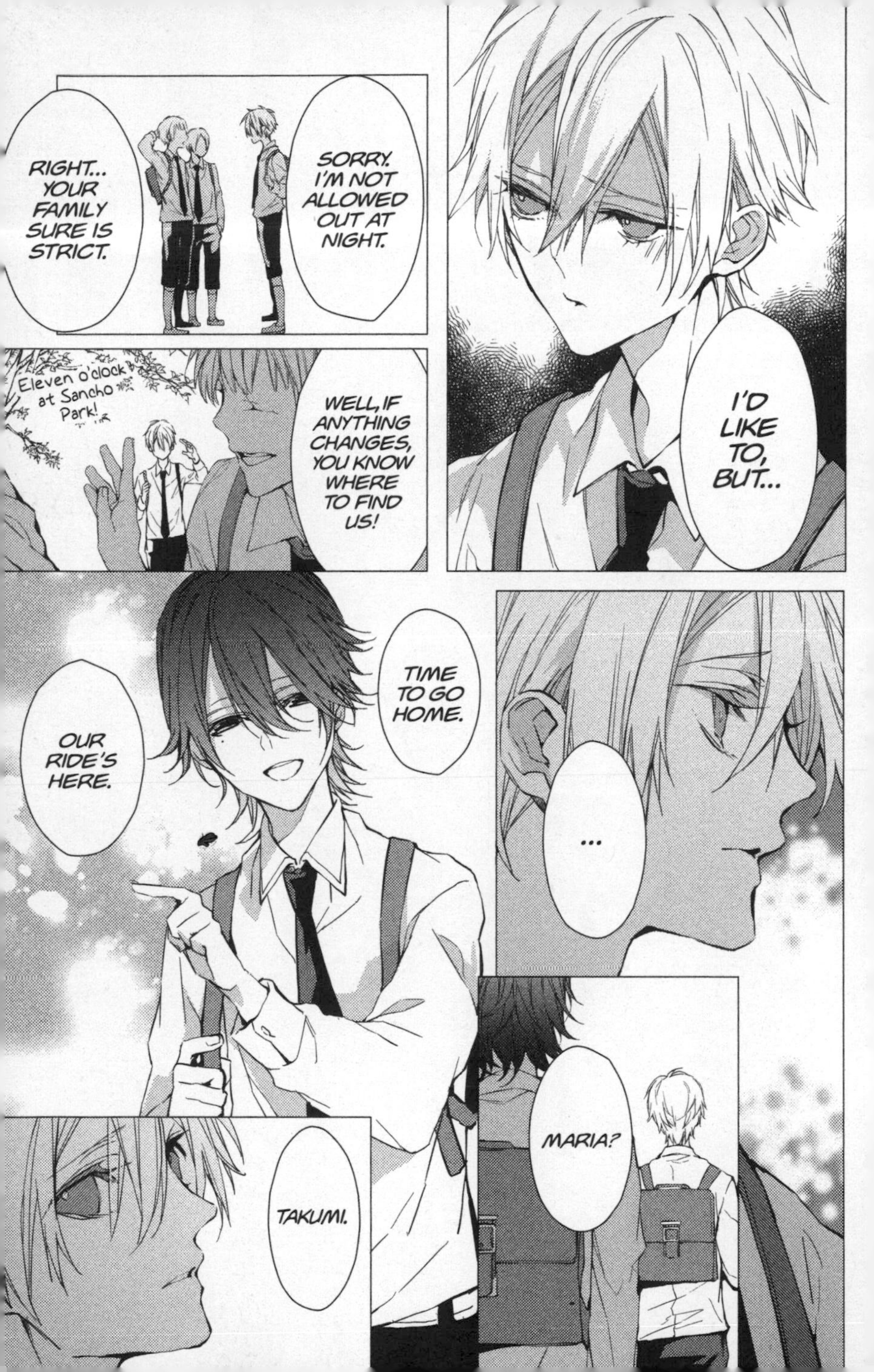
I'D LIKE TO, BUT...
SORRY. I'M NOT ALLOWED OUT AT NIGHT.
RIGHT... YOUR FAMILY SURE IS STRICT.
WELL, IF ANYTHING CHANGES, YOU KNOW WHERE TO FIND US!
Eleven o'clock at Sancho Park!
...
TIME TO GO HOME.
OUR RIDE'S HERE.
MARIA?
TAKUMI.

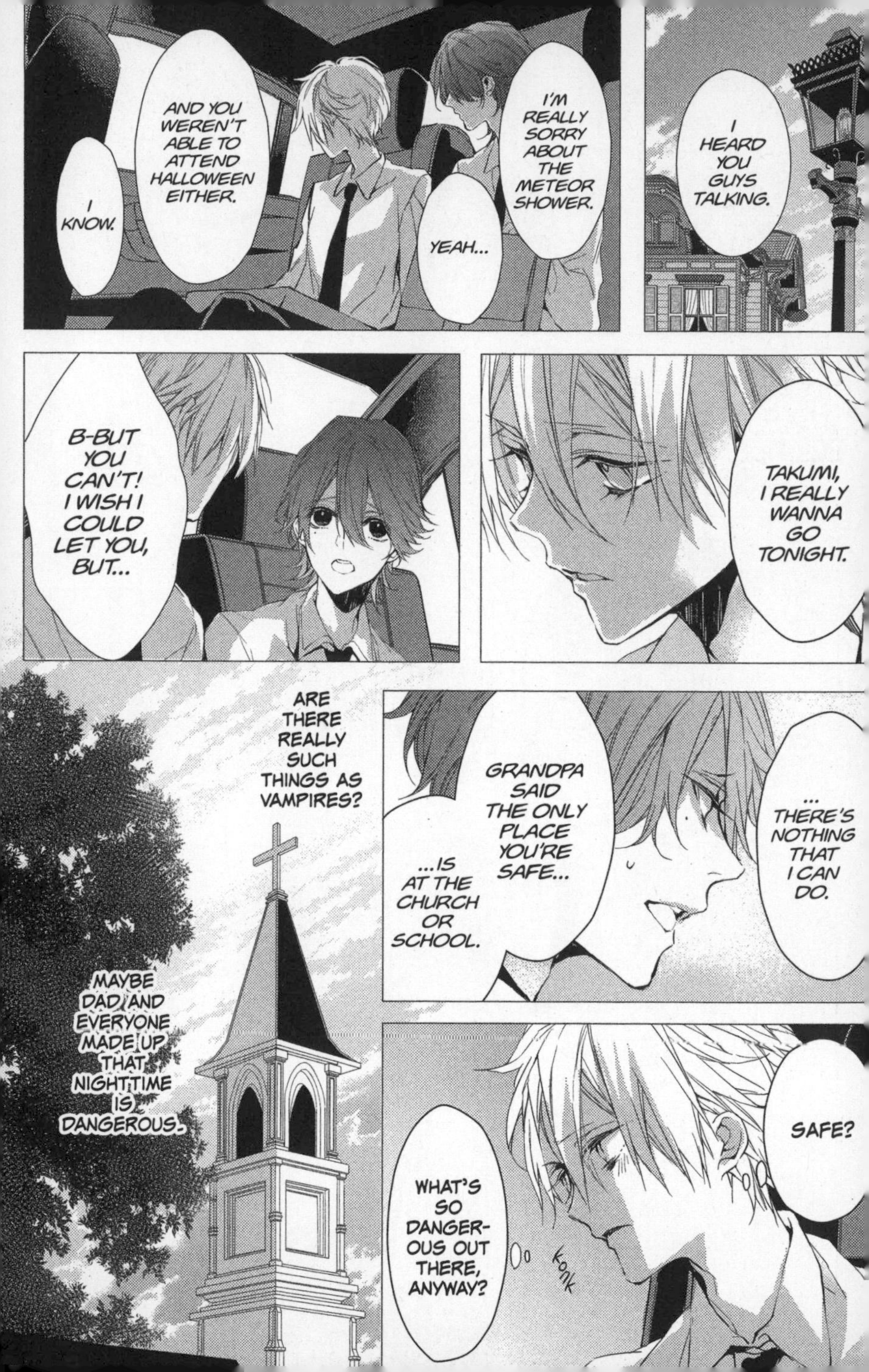
I HEARD YOU GUYS TALKING.
I'M REALLY SORRY ABOUT THE METEOR SHOWER.
YEAH...
AND YOU WEREN'T ABLE TO ATTEND HALLOWEEN EITHER.
I KNOW.
TAKUMI, I REALLY WANNA GO TONIGHT.
B-BUT YOU CAN'T! I WISH I COULD LET YOU, BUT...
...THERE'S NOTHING THAT I CAN DO.
GRANDPA SAID THE ONLY PLACE YOU'RE SAFE...
...IS AT THE CHURCH OR SCHOOL.
SAFE?
konk
WHAT'S SO DANGER-OUS OUT THERE, ANYWAY?
ARE THERE REALLY SUCH THINGS AS VAMPIRES?
MAYBE DAD AND EVERYONE MADE UP THAT NIGHTTIME IS DANGEROUS.

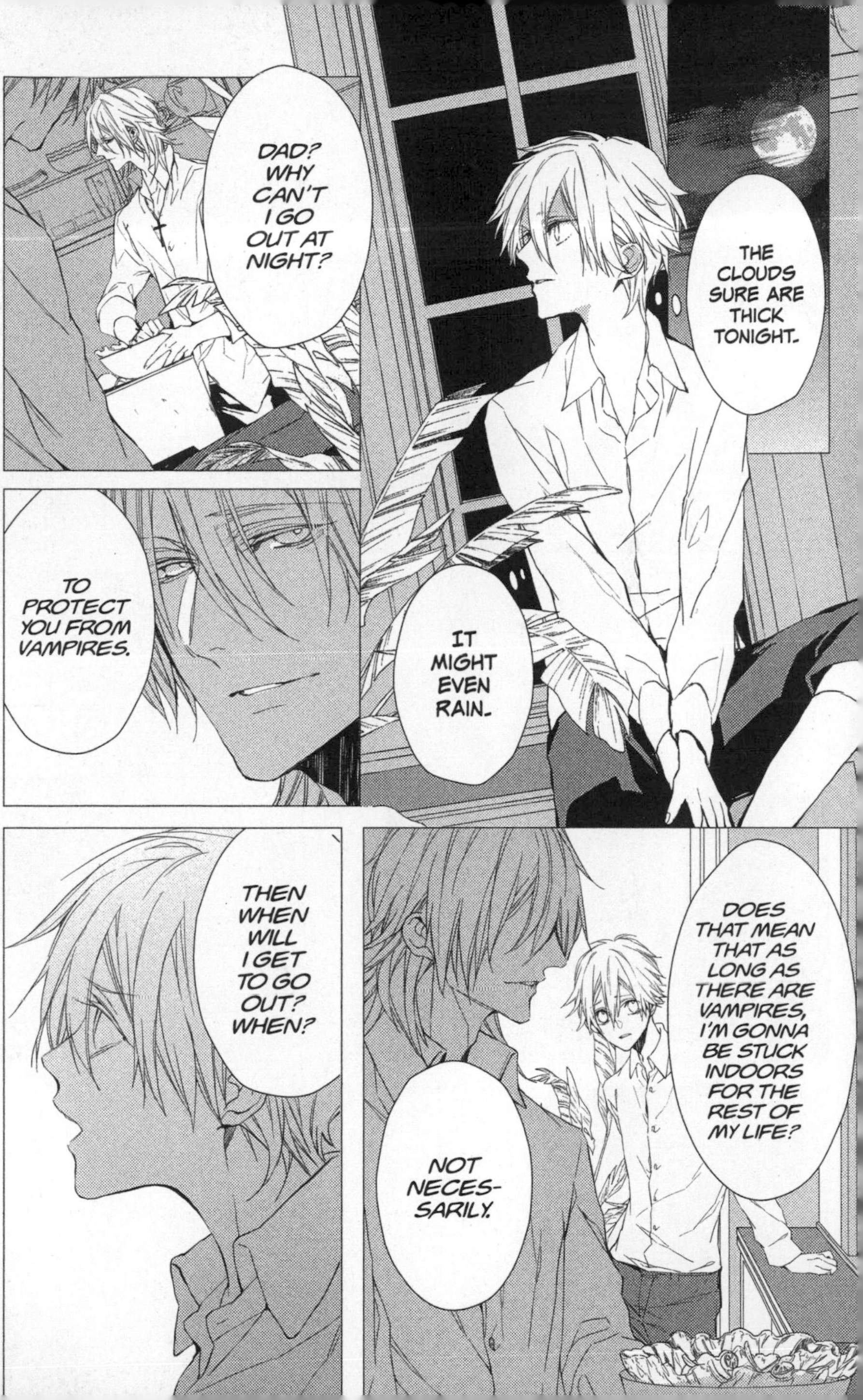
THE CLOUDS SURE ARE THICK TONIGHT.
IT MIGHT EVEN RAIN.
DAD? WHY CAN'T I GO OUT AT NIGHT?
TO PROTECT YOU FROM VAMPIRES.
DOES THAT MEAN THAT AS LONG AS THERE ARE VAMPIRES, I'M GONNA BE STUCK INDOORS FOR THE REST OF MY LIFE?
NOT NECES-SARILY.
THEN WHEN WILL I GET TO GO OUT? WHEN?

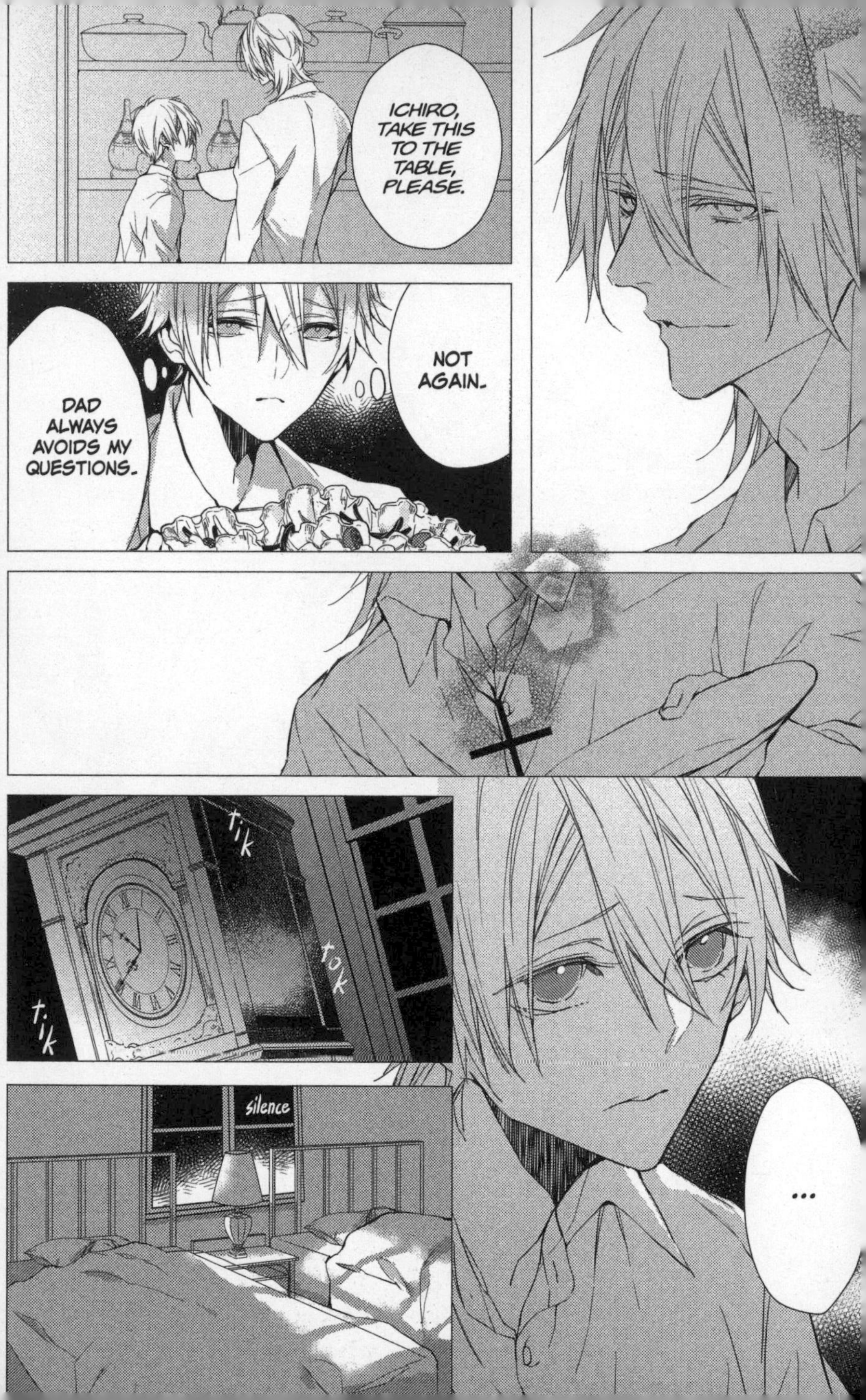
ICHIRO, TAKE THIS TO THE TABLE, PLEASE.
NOT AGAIN.
DAD ALWAYS AVOIDS MY QUESTIONS.
...
tik
tok
tik
silence

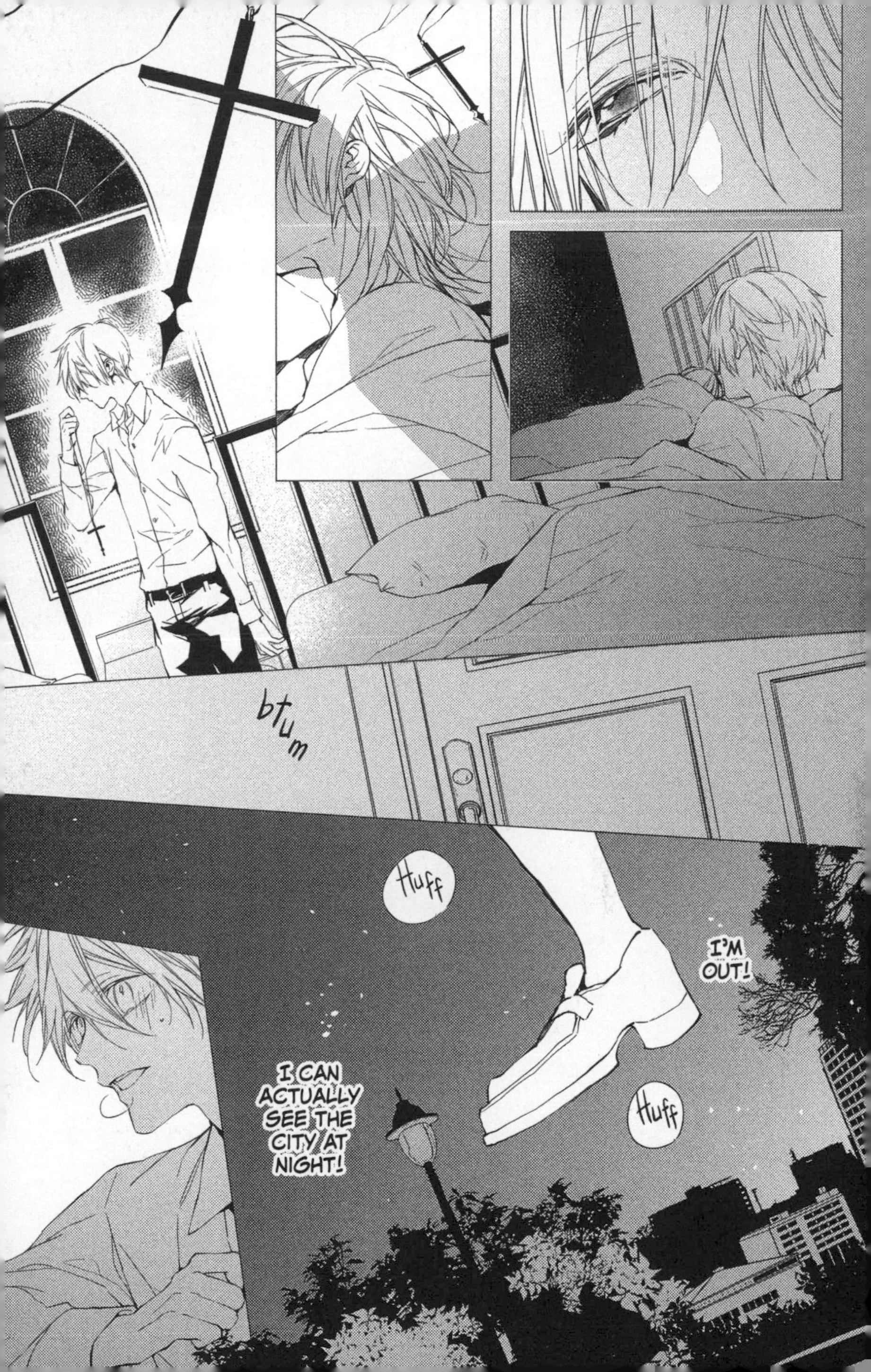
btum
Huff
I'M OUT!
Huff
I CAN ACTUALLY SEE THE CITY AT NIGHT!

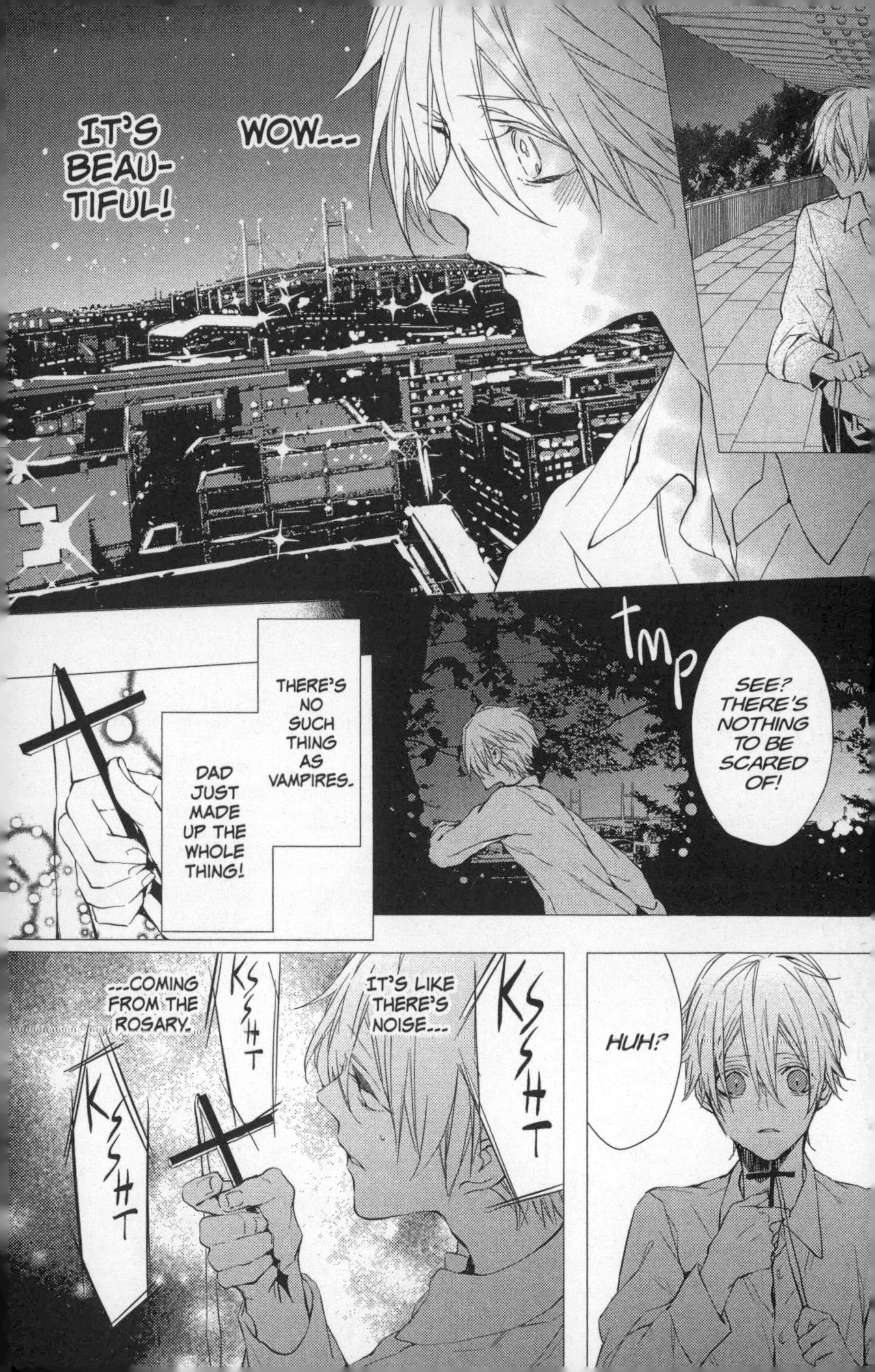
WOW...
IT'S BEAU-TIFUL!
tmp
SEE? THERE'S NOTHING TO BE SCARED OF!
THERE'S NO SUCH THING AS VAMPIRES.
DAD JUST MADE UP THE WHOLE THING!
HUH?
KSSHT
IT'S LIKE THERE'S NOISE...
...COMING FROM THE ROSARY.
KSSHT
KSSHT

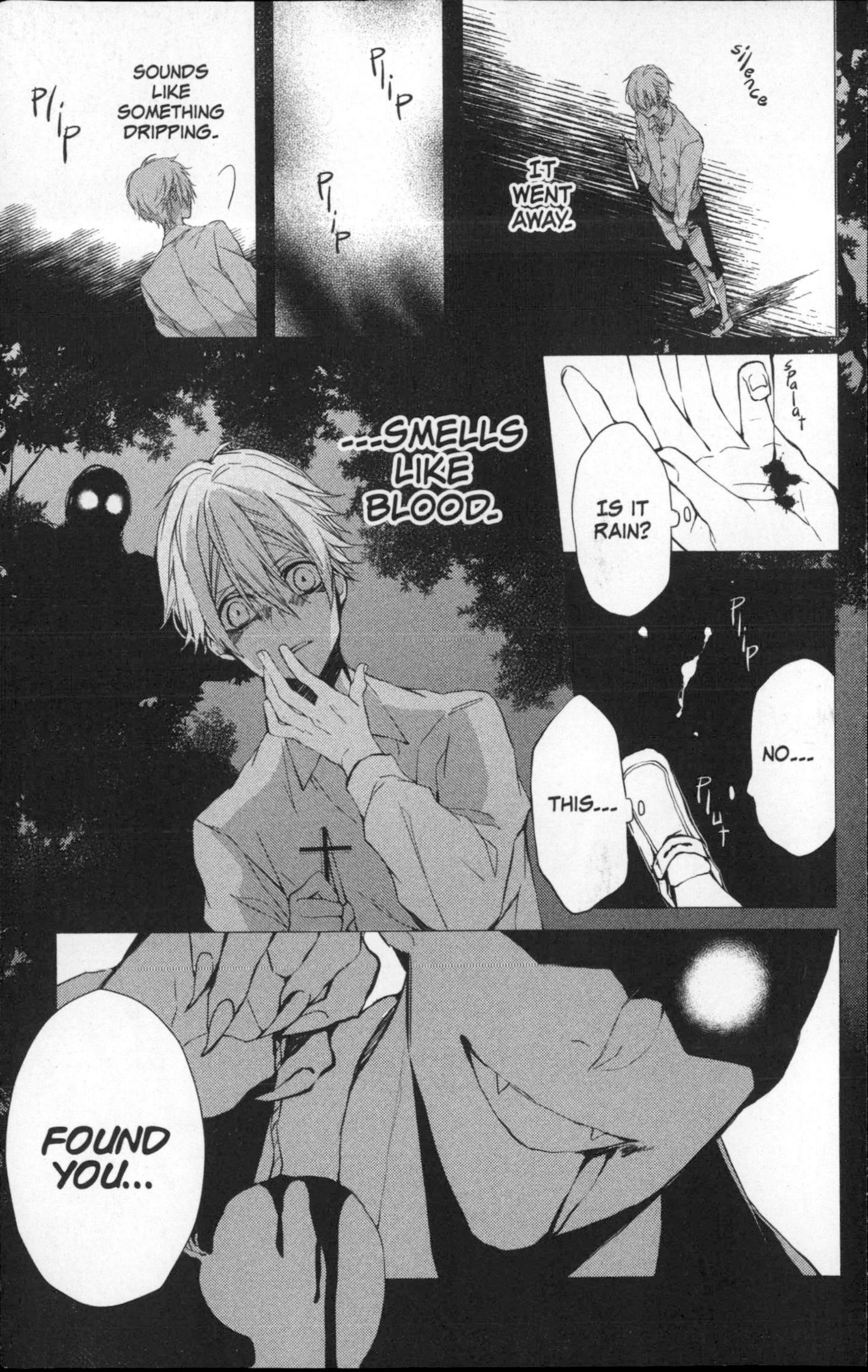
silence
IT WENT AWAY.
Plip
Plip
Plip
SOUNDS LIKE SOMETHING DRIPPING.
Splat
IS IT RAIN?
Plip
NO...
Plut
THIS...
...SMELLS LIKE BLOOD.
FOUND YOU...

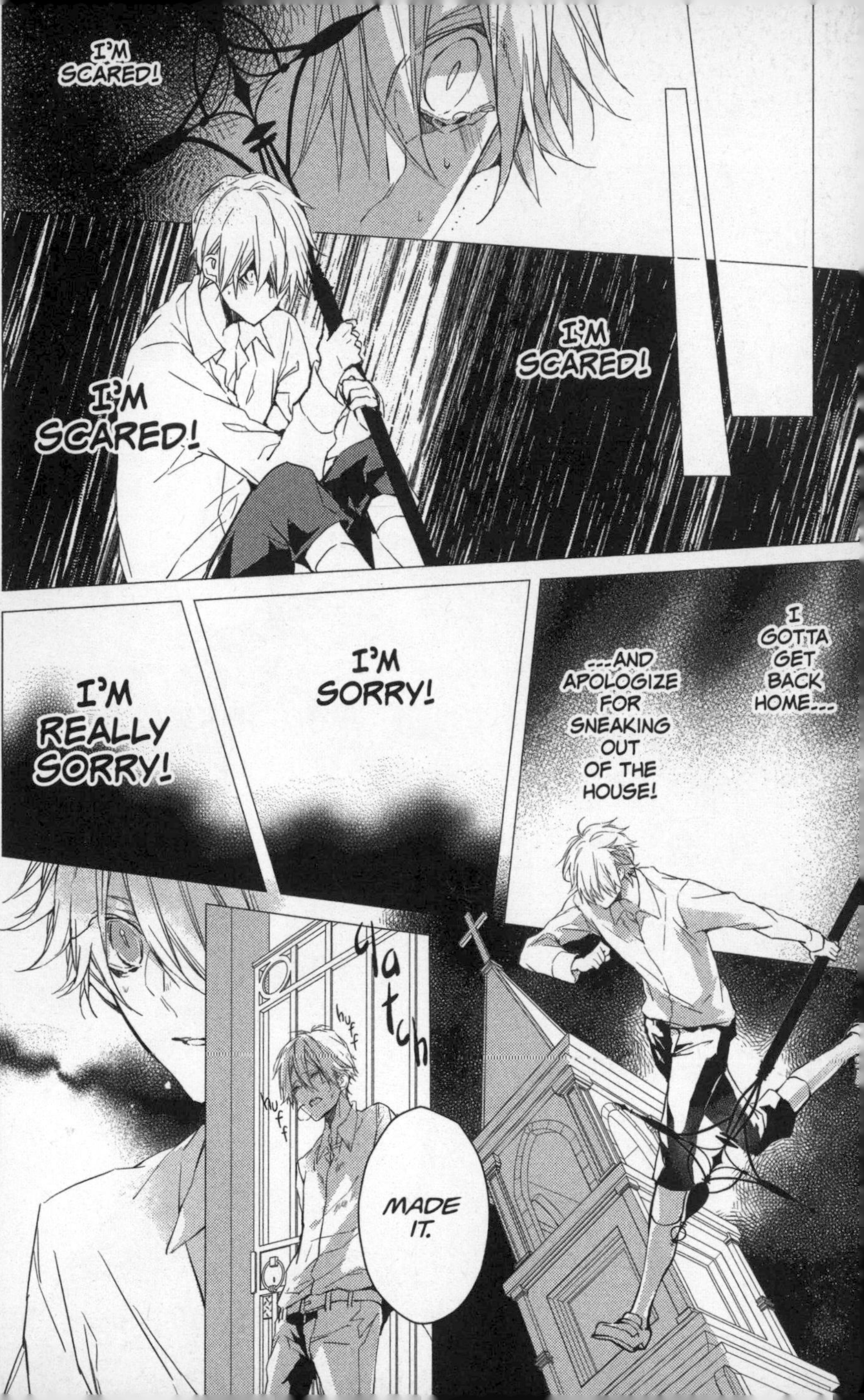
I'M SCARED!
I'M SCARED!
I'M SCARED!
I GOTTA GET BACK HOME...
...AND APOLOGIZE FOR SNEAKING OUT OF THE HOUSE!
I'M SORRY!
I'M REALLY SORRY!
clatch
huff
huff
MADE IT.

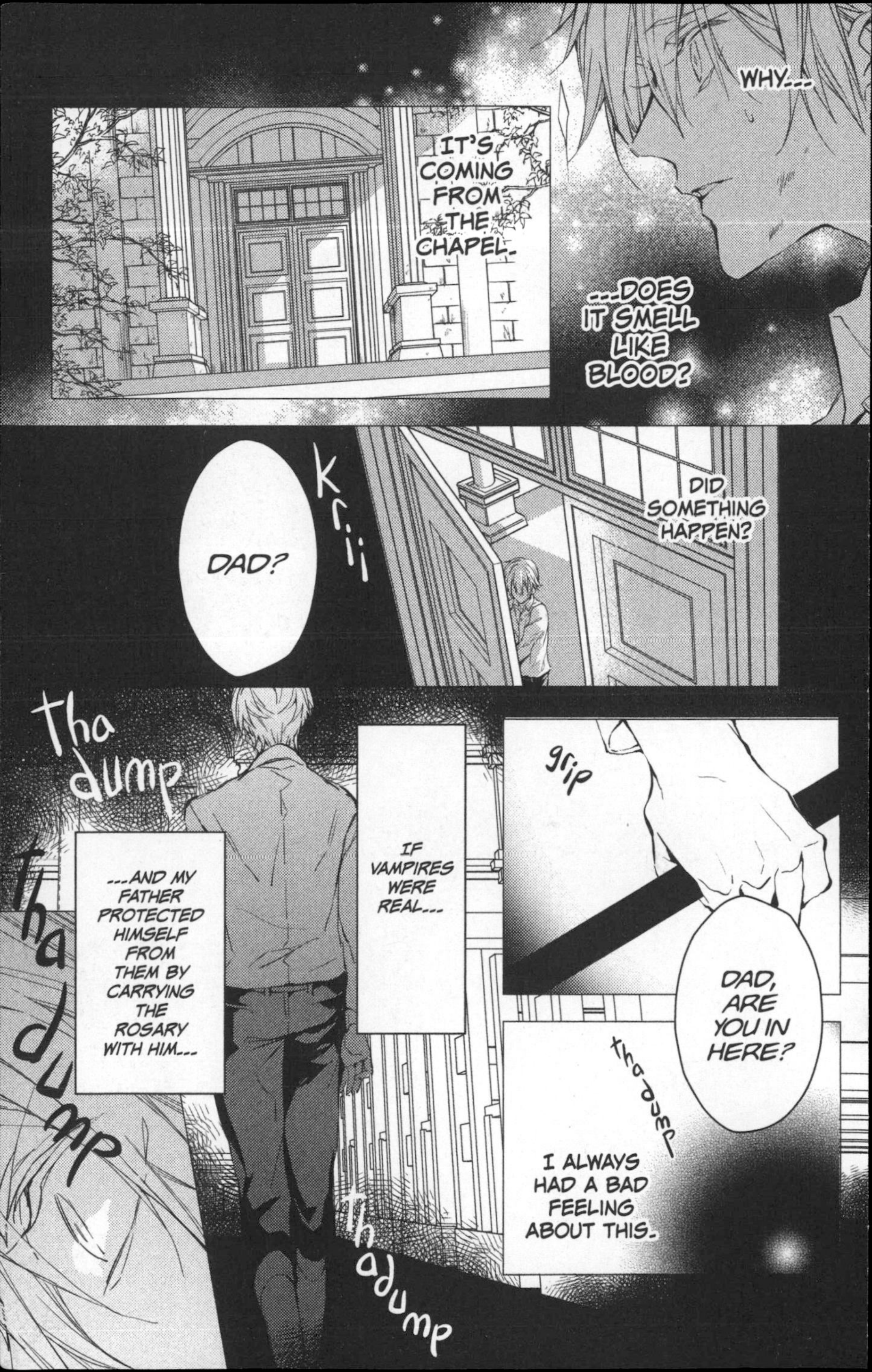
WHY...
...DOES IT SMELL LIKE BLOOD?
IT'S COMING FROM THE CHAPEL.
DID SOMETHING HAPPEN?
kriii
DAD?
grip
DAD, ARE YOU IN HERE?
thadump
I ALWAYS HAD A BAD FEELING ABOUT THIS.
IF VAMPIRES WERE REAL...
...AND MY FATHER PROTECTED HIMSELF FROM THEM BY CARRYING THE ROSARY WITH HIM...
tha dump
tha dump
thadump

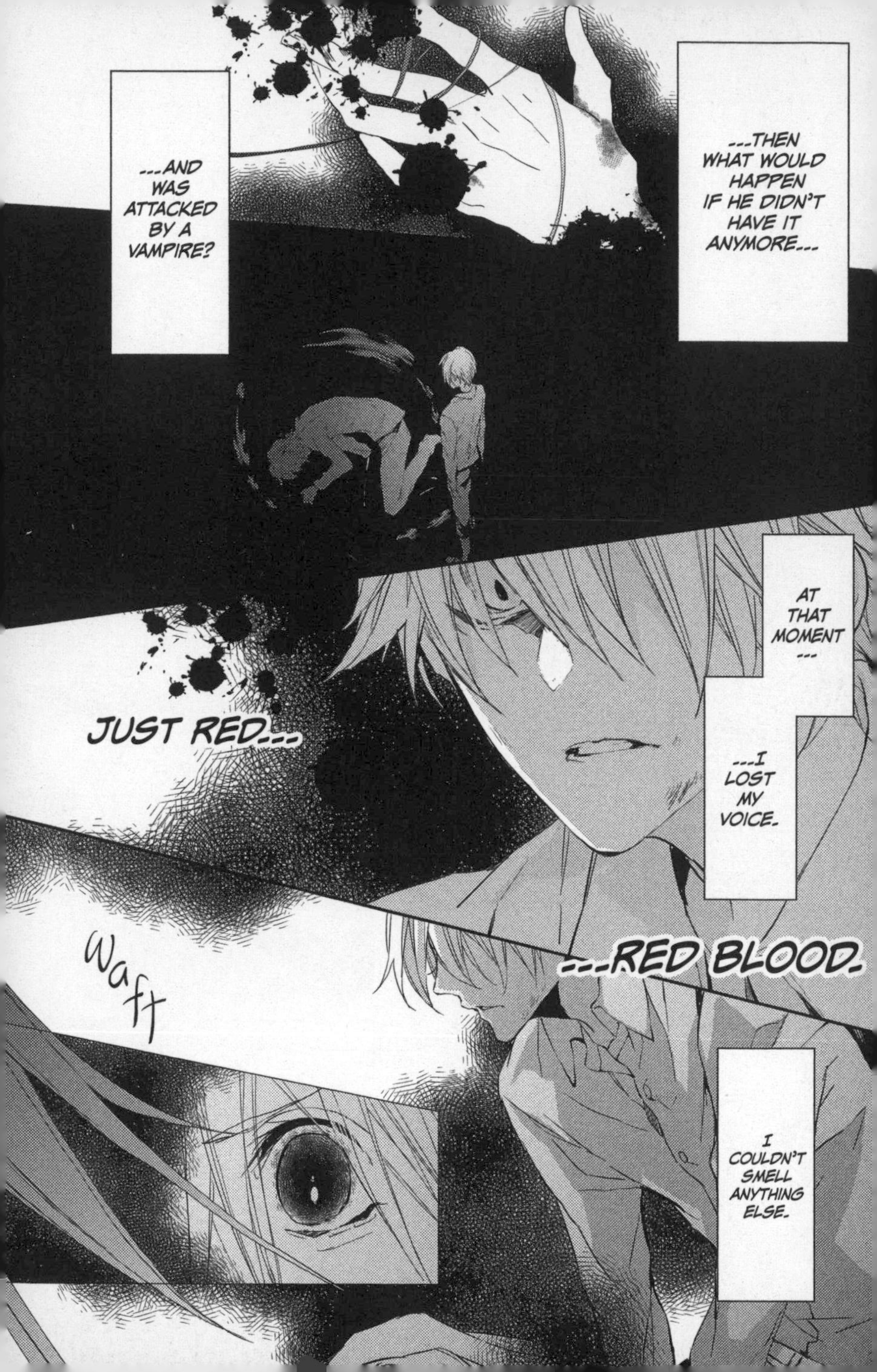
---THEN WHAT WOULD HAPPEN IF HE DIDN'T HAVE IT ANYMORE---
---AND WAS ATTACKED BY A VAMPIRE?
AT THAT MOMENT ---
---I LOST MY VOICE.
JUST RED---
---RED BLOOD.
I COULDN'T SMELL ANYTHING ELSE.
Waft

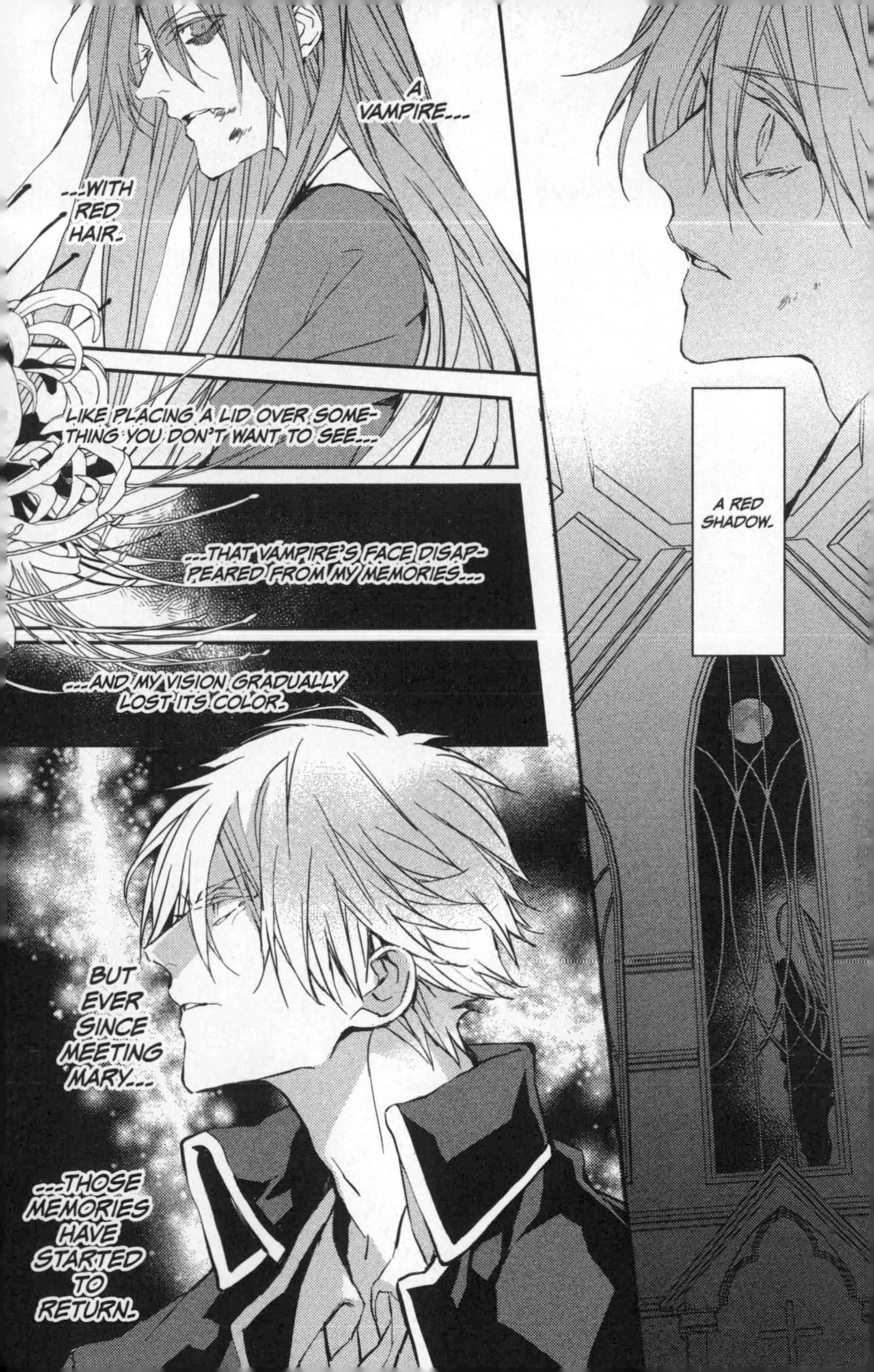
A RED SHADOW.
A VAMPIRE...
...WITH RED HAIR.
LIKE PLACING A LID OVER SOMETHING YOU DON'T WANT TO SEE...
...THAT VAMPIRE'S FACE DISAPPEARED FROM MY MEMORIES...
...AND MY VISION GRADUALLY LOST ITS COLOR.
BUT EVER SINCE MEETING MARY...
...THOSE MEMORIES HAVE STARTED TO RETURN.

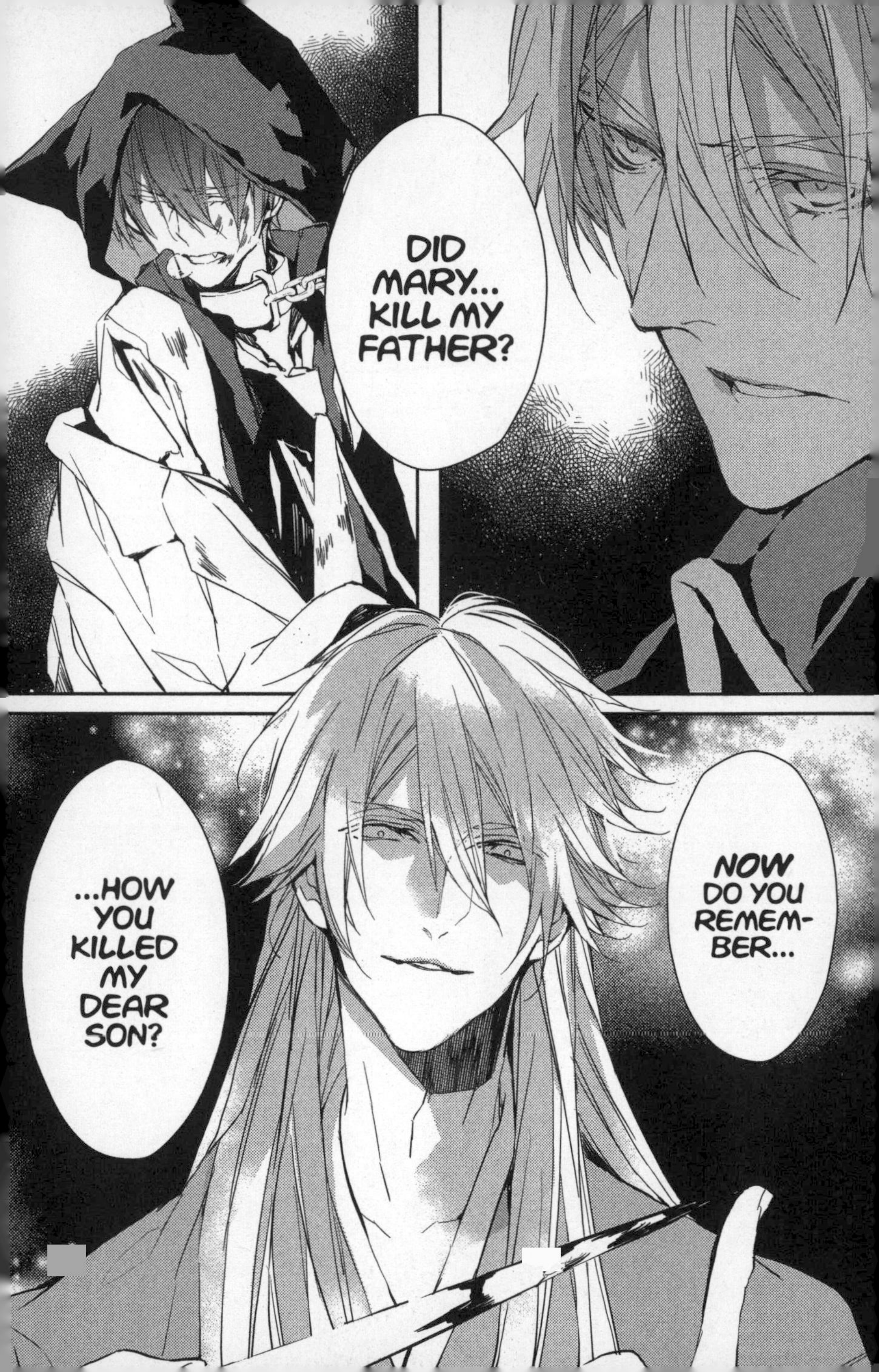
DID MARY... KILL MY FATHER?
NOW DO YOU REMEMBER...
...HOW YOU KILLED MY DEAR SON?

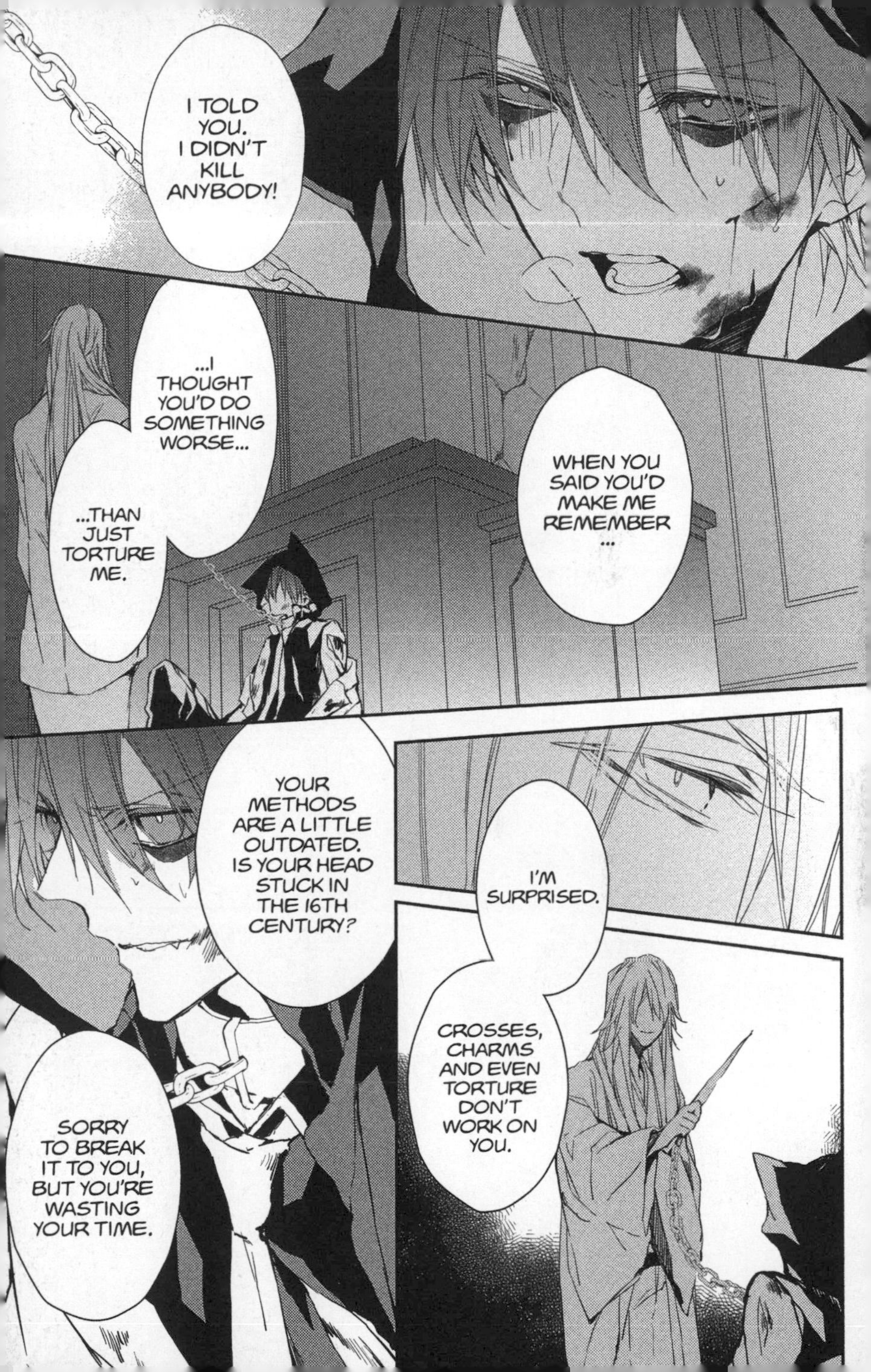
I TOLD YOU. I DIDN'T KILL ANYBODY!
WHEN YOU SAID YOU'D MAKE ME REMEMBER ...
...I THOUGHT YOU'D DO SOMETHING WORSE...
...THAN JUST TORTURE ME.
I'M SURPRISED.
CROSSES, CHARMS AND EVEN TORTURE DON'T WORK ON YOU.
YOUR METHODS ARE A LITTLE OUTDATED. IS YOUR HEAD STUCK IN THE 16TH CENTURY?
SORRY TO BREAK IT TO YOU, BUT YOU'RE WASTING YOUR TIME.

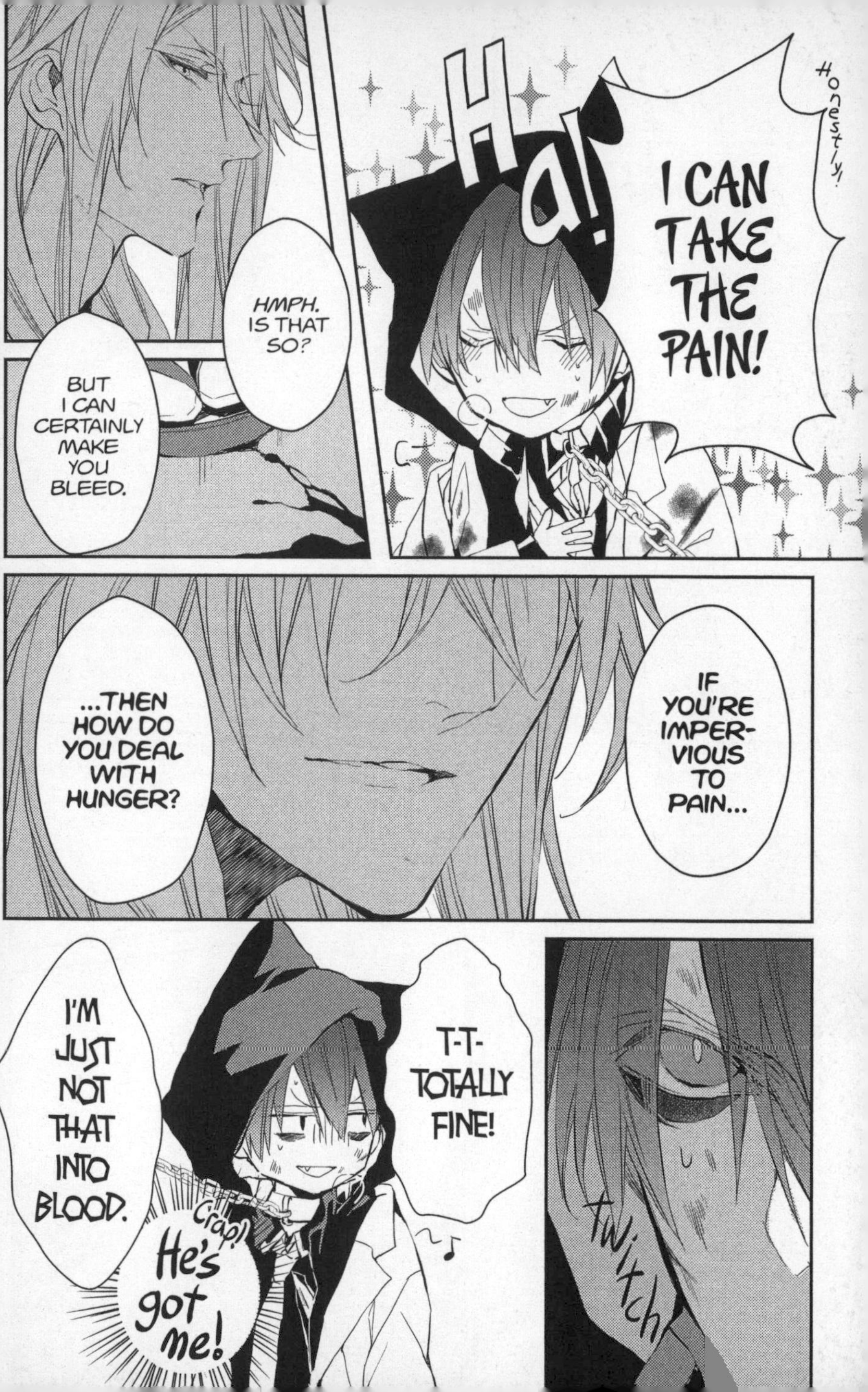
Ha!
I CAN TAKE THE PAIN!
Honestly!
HMPH. IS THAT SO?
BUT I CAN CERTAINLY MAKE YOU BLEED.
IF YOU'RE IMPERVIOUS TO PAIN...
...THEN HOW DO YOU DEAL WITH HUNGER?
Twitch
T-T-TOTALLY FINE!
I'M JUST NOT THAT INTO BLOOD.
Crap!
He's got me!

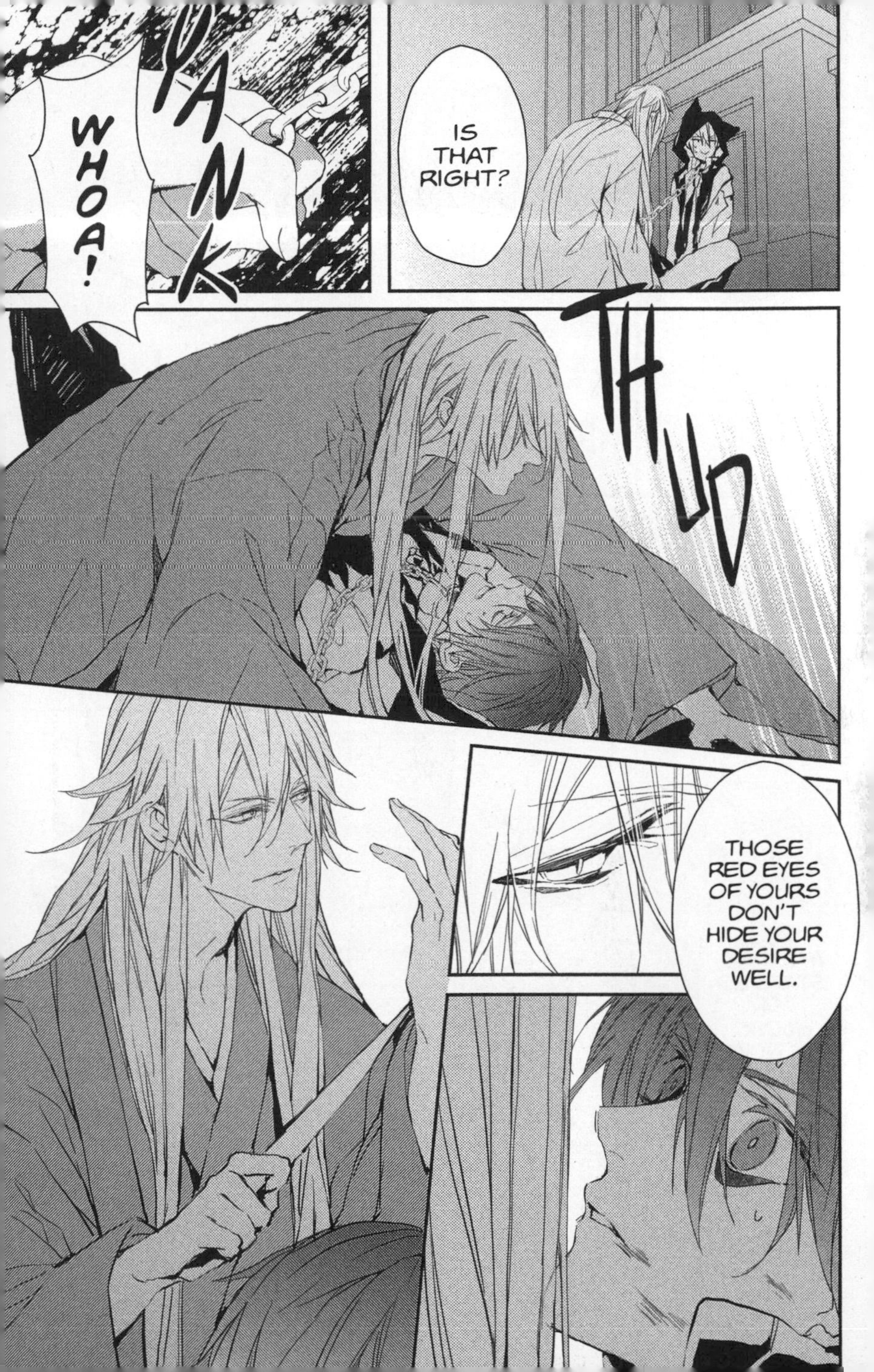
IS THAT RIGHT?
YANK
WHOA!
THUD
THOSE RED EYES OF YOURS DON'T HIDE YOUR DESIRE WELL.

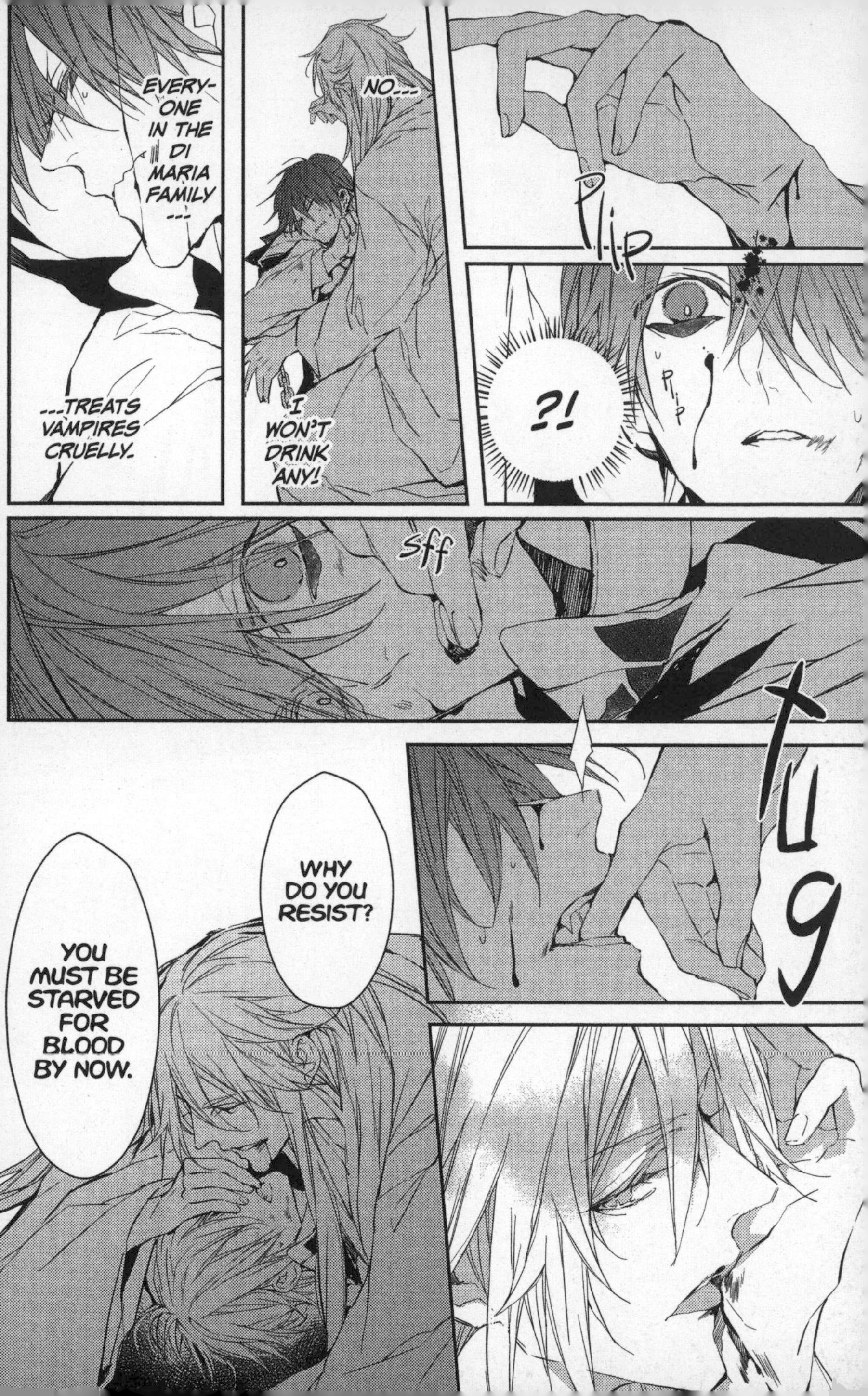

Plip
?!
Plip
NO...
I WON'T DRINK ANY!
EVERYONE IN THE DI MARIA FAMILY...
...TREATS VAMPIRES CRUELLY.
sff
tug
WHY DO YOU RESIST?
YOU MUST BE STARVED FOR BLOOD BY NOW.

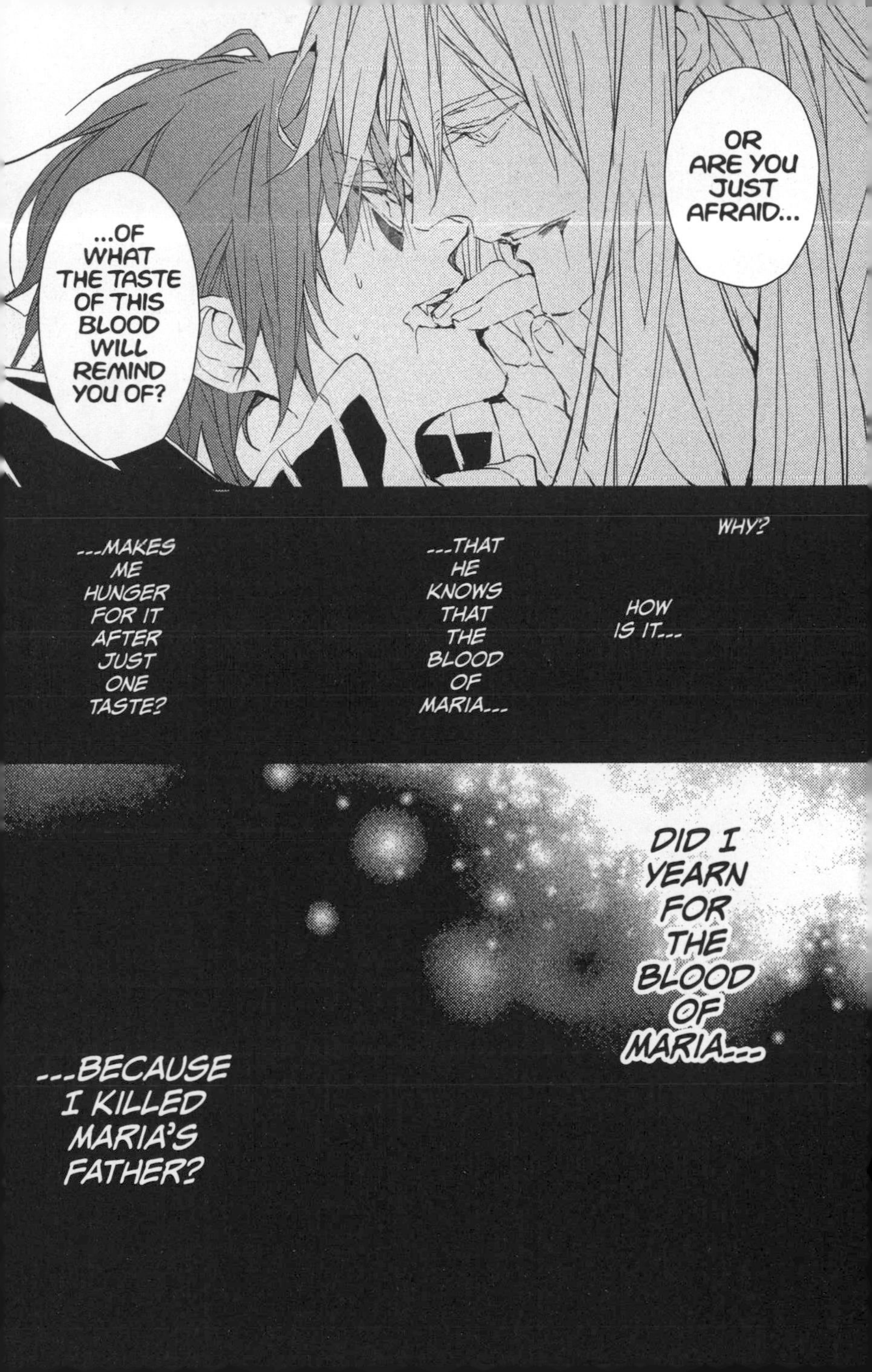
OR ARE YOU JUST AFRAID...
...OF WHAT THE TASTE OF THIS BLOOD WILL REMIND YOU OF?
WHY?
HOW IS IT...
...THAT HE KNOWS THAT THE BLOOD OF MARIA...
...MAKES ME HUNGER FOR IT AFTER JUST ONE TASTE?
DID I YEARN FOR THE BLOOD OF MARIA...
...BECAUSE I KILLED MARIA'S FATHER?

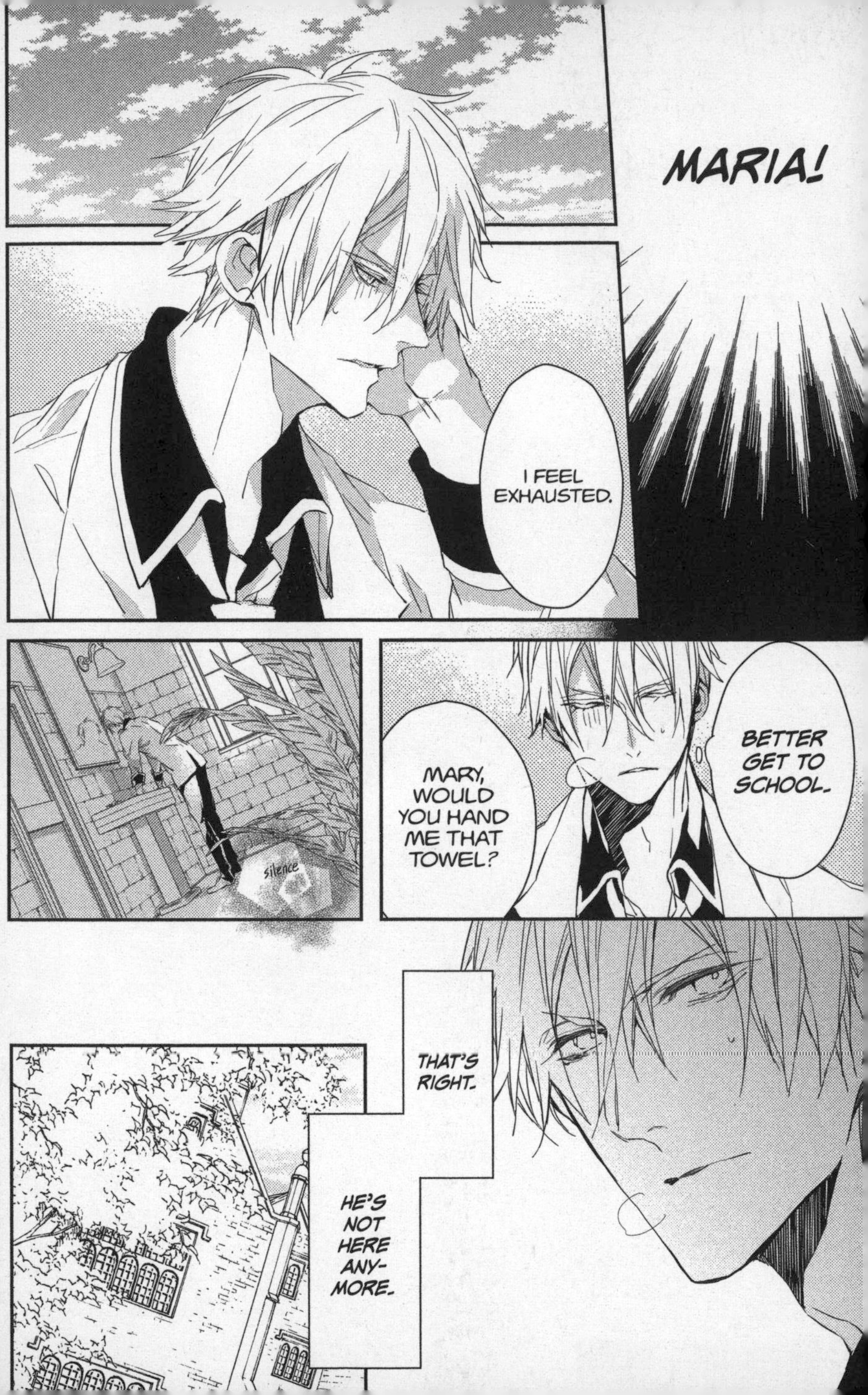
MARIA!
I FEEL EXHAUSTED.
BETTER GET TO SCHOOL.
MARY, WOULD YOU HAND ME THAT TOWEL?
silence
THAT'S RIGHT.
HE'S NOT HERE ANYMORE.

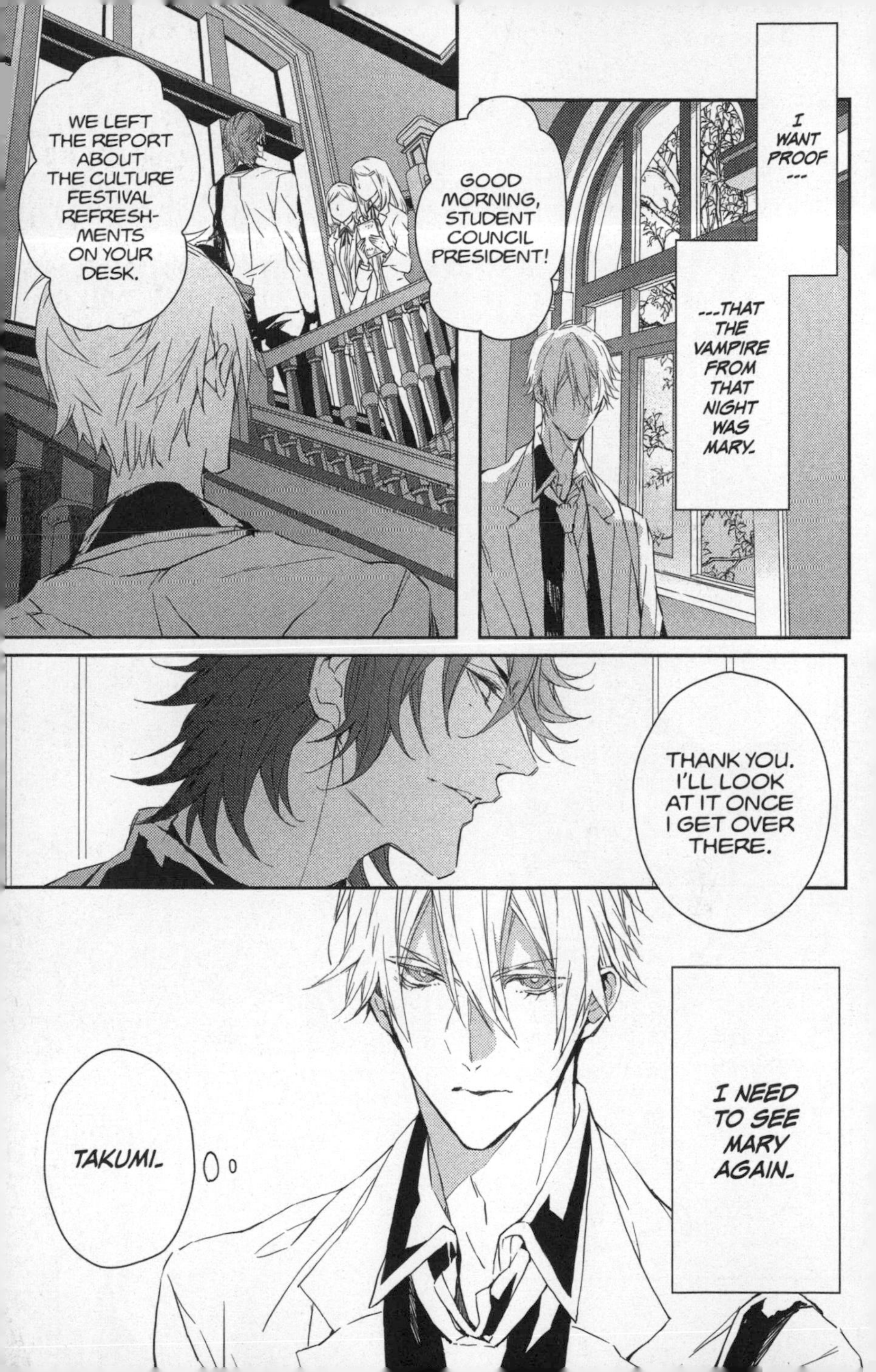
I WANT PROOF ---
---THAT THE VAMPIRE FROM THAT NIGHT WAS MARY...
GOOD MORNING, STUDENT COUNCIL PRESIDENT!
WE LEFT THE REPORT ABOUT THE CULTURE FESTIVAL REFRESH-MENTS ON YOUR DESK.
THANK YOU. I'LL LOOK AT IT ONCE I GET OVER THERE.
I NEED TO SEE MARY AGAIN...
TAKUMI...

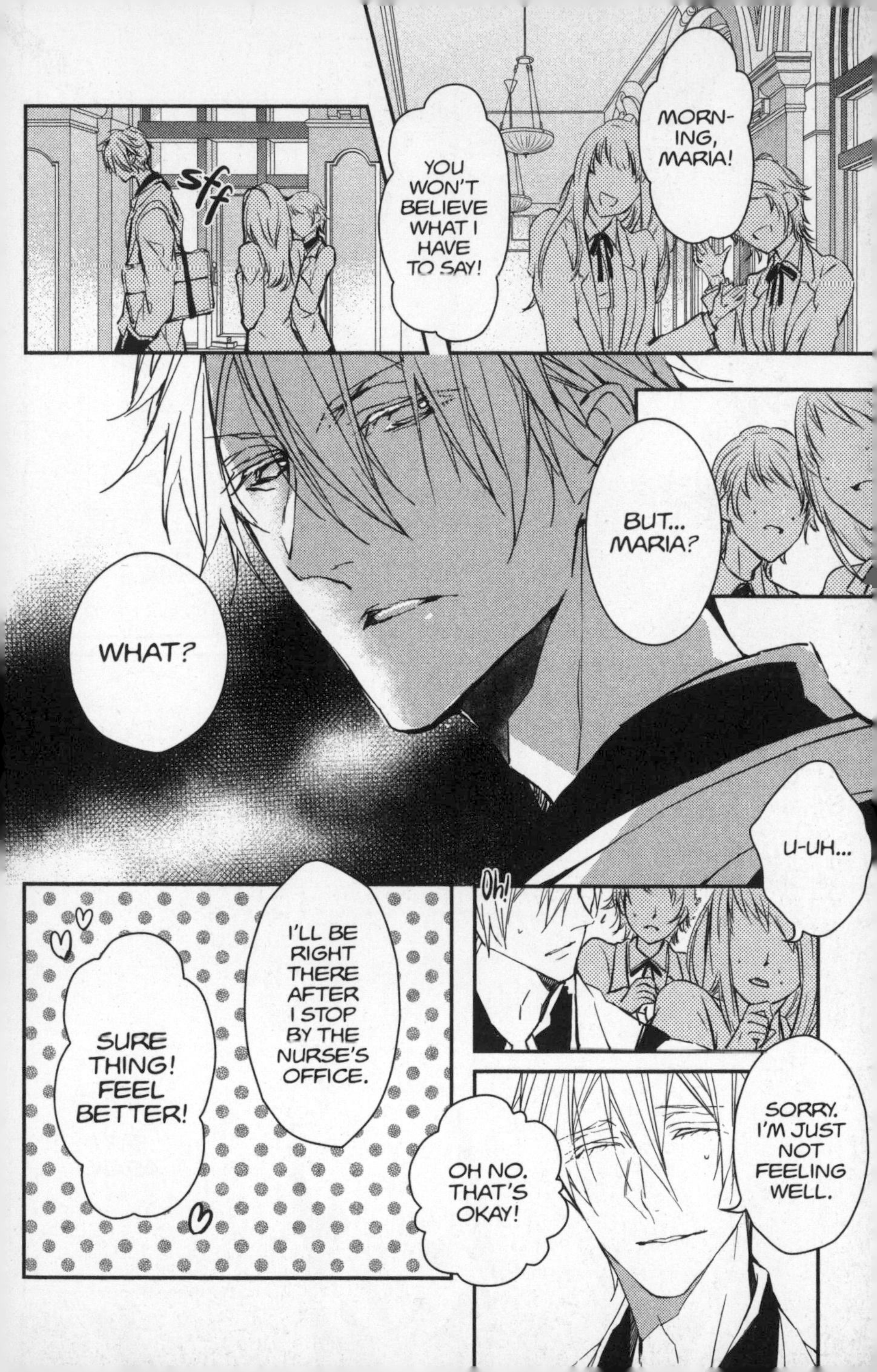
MORN-ING, MARIA!
YOU WON'T BELIEVE WHAT I HAVE TO SAY!
sff
BUT... MARIA?
WHAT?
U-UH...
Oh!
SORRY. I'M JUST NOT FEELING WELL.
OH NO. THAT'S OKAY!
I'LL BE RIGHT THERE AFTER I STOP BY THE NURSE'S OFFICE.
SURE THING! FEEL BETTER!

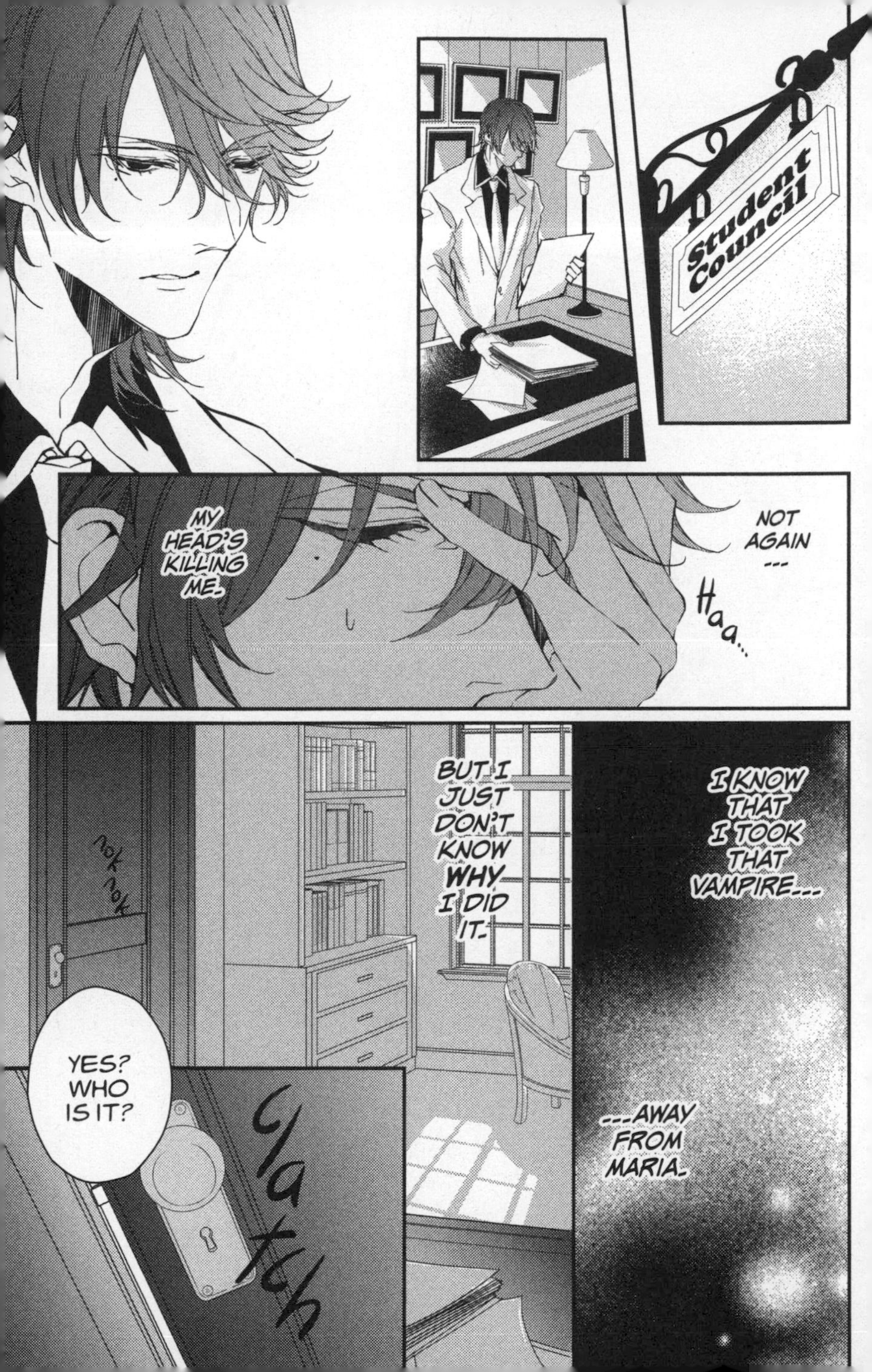
Student Council
NOT AGAIN ---
Haa...
MY HEAD'S KILLING ME.
I KNOW THAT I TOOK THAT VAMPIRE...
...AWAY FROM MARIA.
BUT I JUST DON'T KNOW WHY I DID IT.
nok nok
YES? WHO IS IT?
clatch

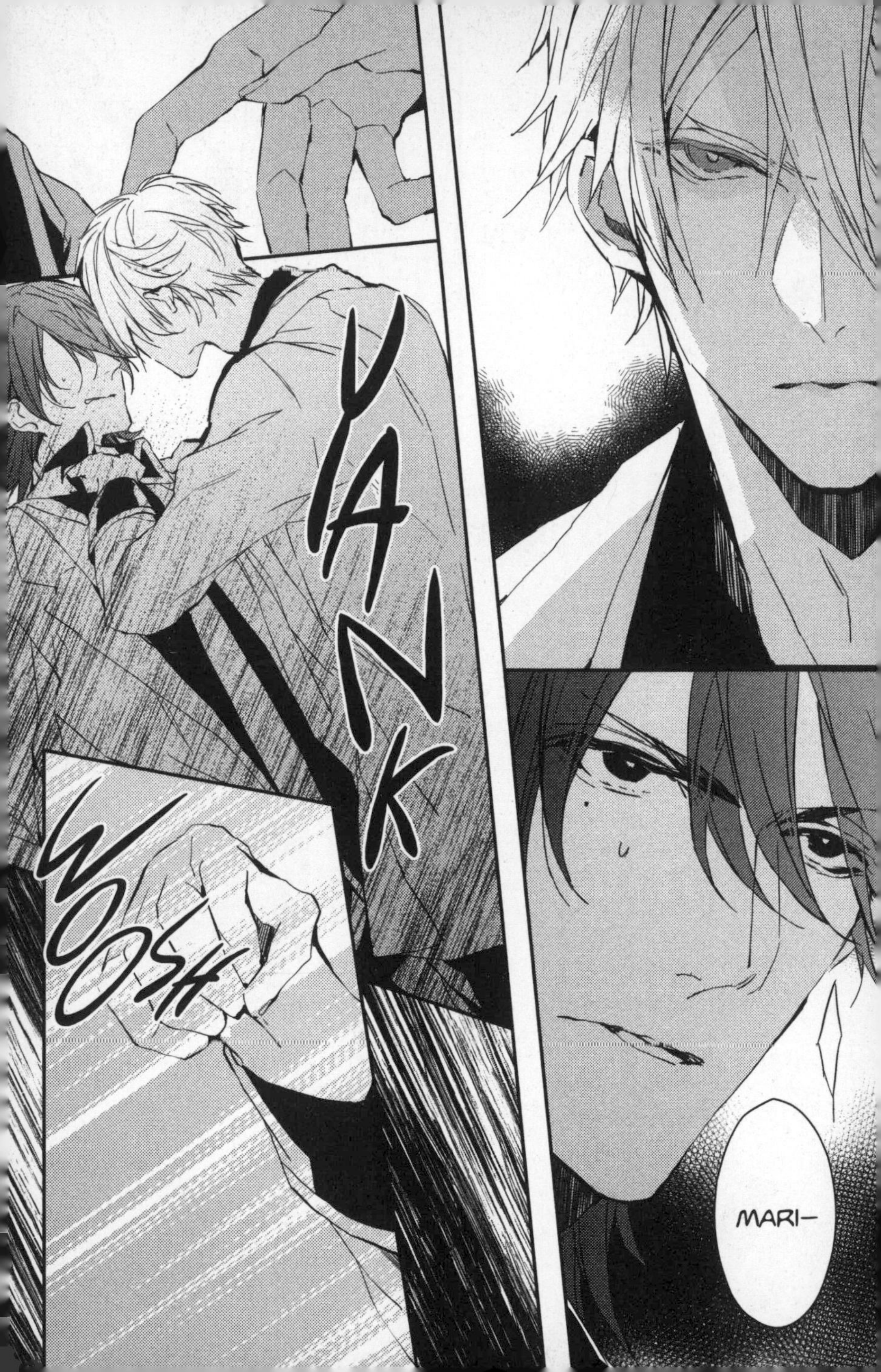
MARI—
YANK
WOOSH

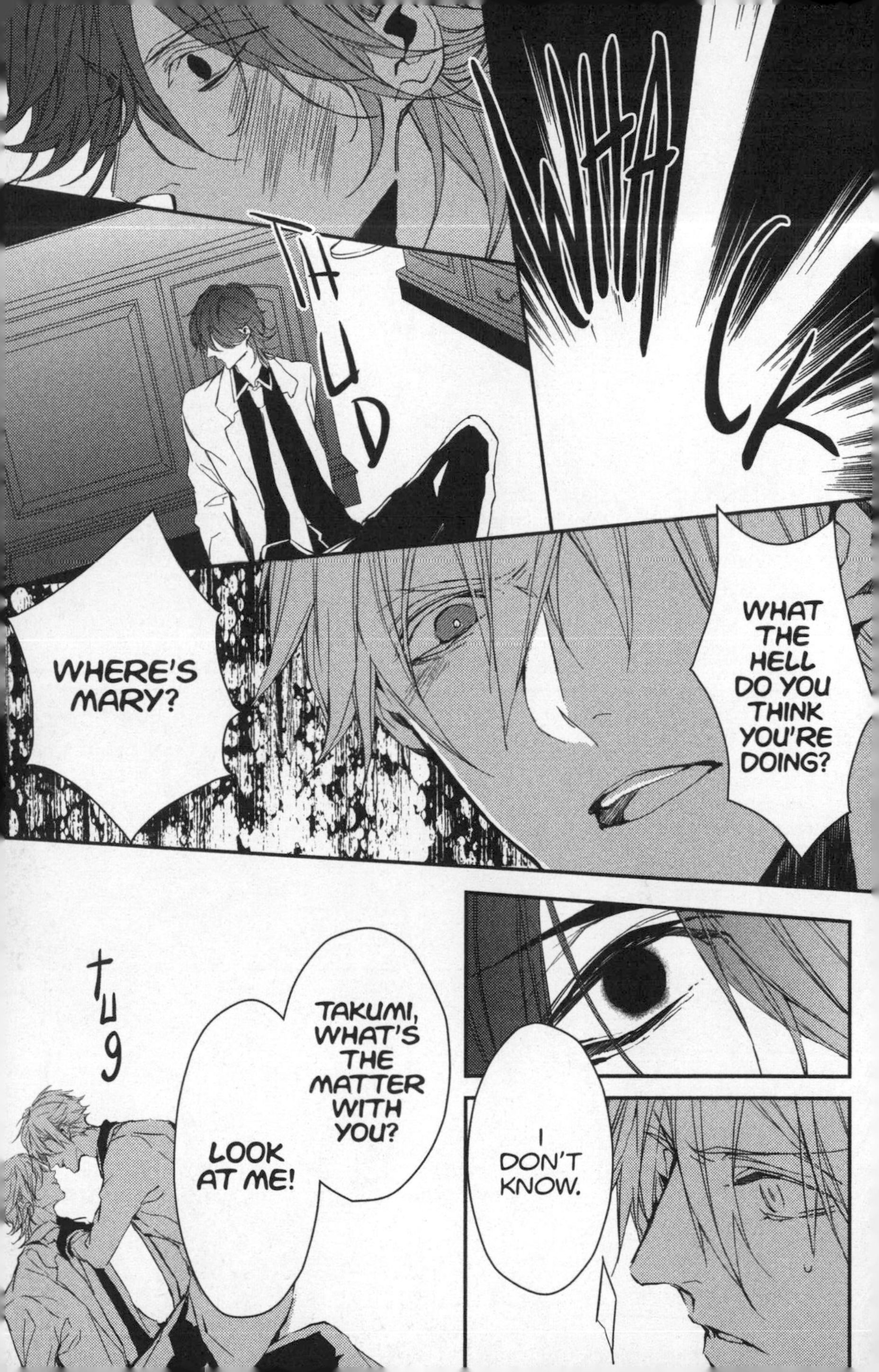
WHACK
THUD
WHAT THE HELL DO YOU THINK YOU'RE DOING?
WHERE'S MARY?
I DON'T KNOW.
TAKUMI, WHAT'S THE MATTER WITH YOU?
LOOK AT ME!
TUG

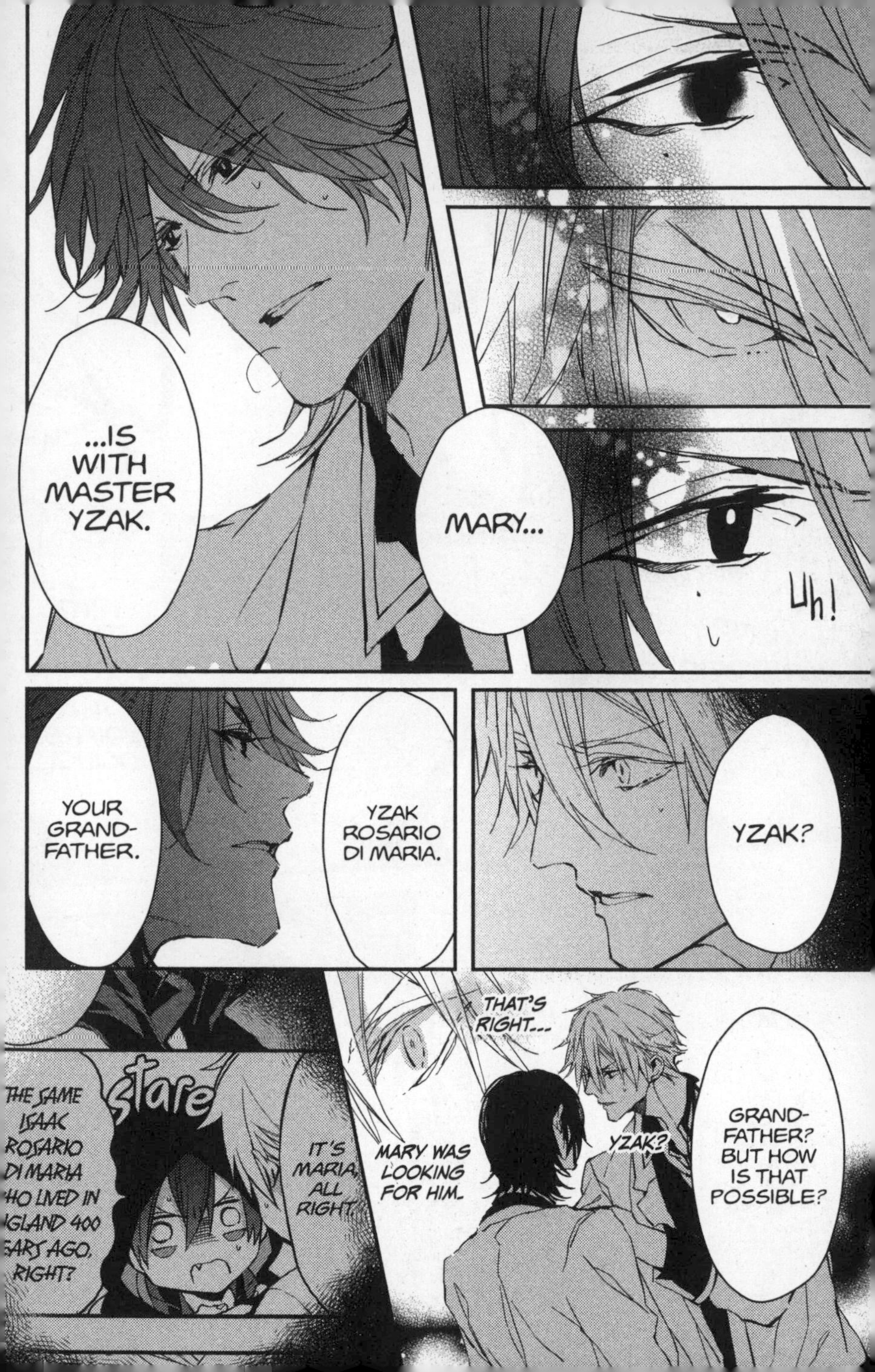
MARY...
Uh!
...IS WITH MASTER YZAK.
YZAK?
YZAK ROSARIO DI MARIA.
YOUR GRAND-FATHER.
GRAND-FATHER? BUT HOW IS THAT POSSIBLE?
THAT'S RIGHT...
YZAK?
MARY WAS LOOKING FOR HIM.
IT'S MARIA, ALL RIGHT.
stare
THE SAME ISAAC ROSARIO DI MARIA HO LIVED IN GLAND 400 EARS AGO, RIGHT?

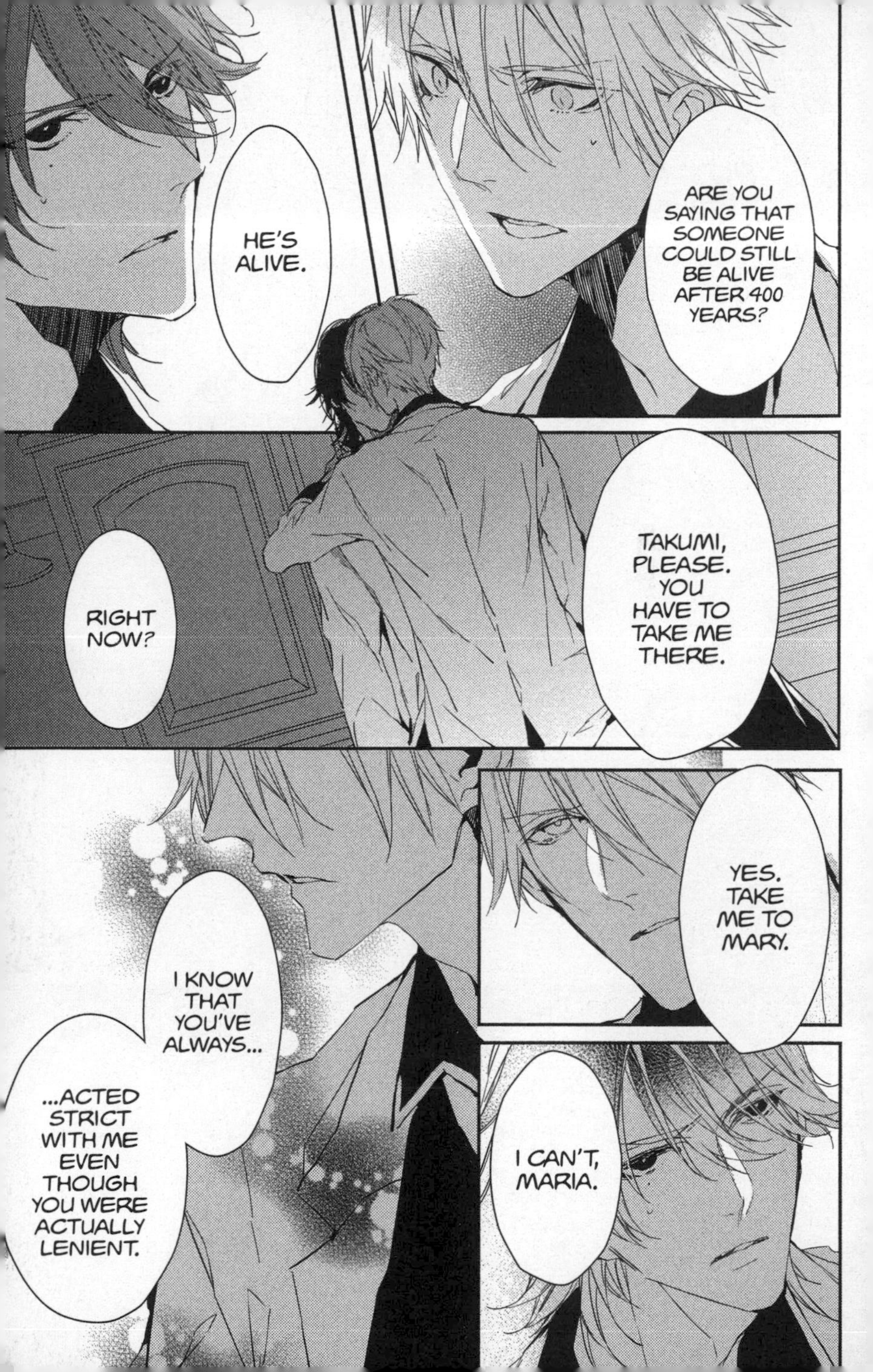
ARE YOU SAYING THAT SOMEONE COULD STILL BE ALIVE AFTER 400 YEARS?
HE'S ALIVE.
TAKUMI, PLEASE. YOU HAVE TO TAKE ME THERE.
RIGHT NOW?
YES. TAKE ME TO MARY.
I CAN'T, MARIA.
I KNOW THAT YOU'VE ALWAYS...
...ACTED STRICT WITH ME EVEN THOUGH YOU WERE ACTUALLY LENIENT.

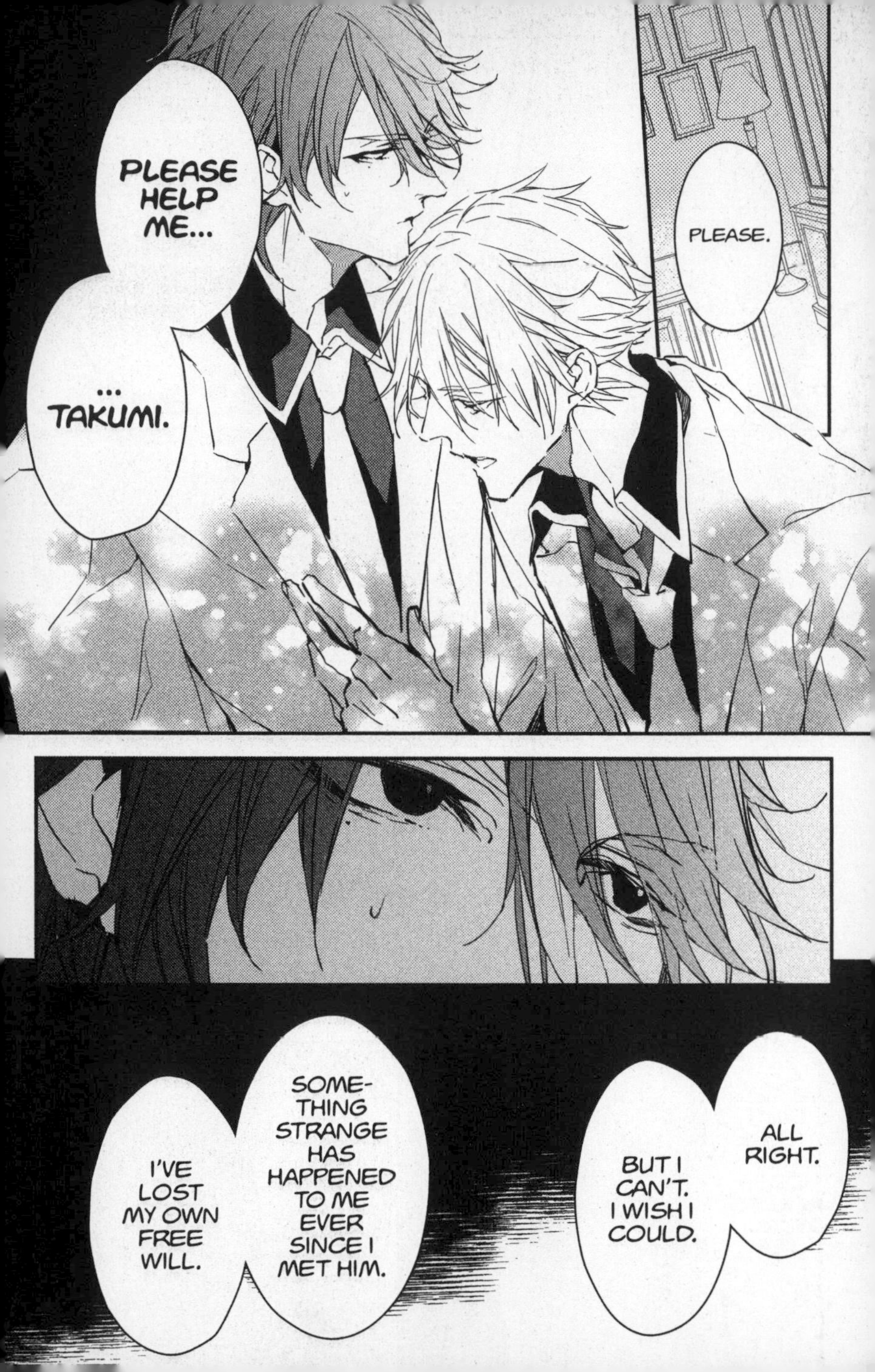
PLEASE.
PLEASE HELP ME...
... TAKUMI.
ALL RIGHT.
BUT I CAN'T. I WISH I COULD.
SOME-THING STRANGE HAS HAPPENED TO ME EVER SINCE I MET HIM.
I'VE LOST MY OWN FREE WILL.

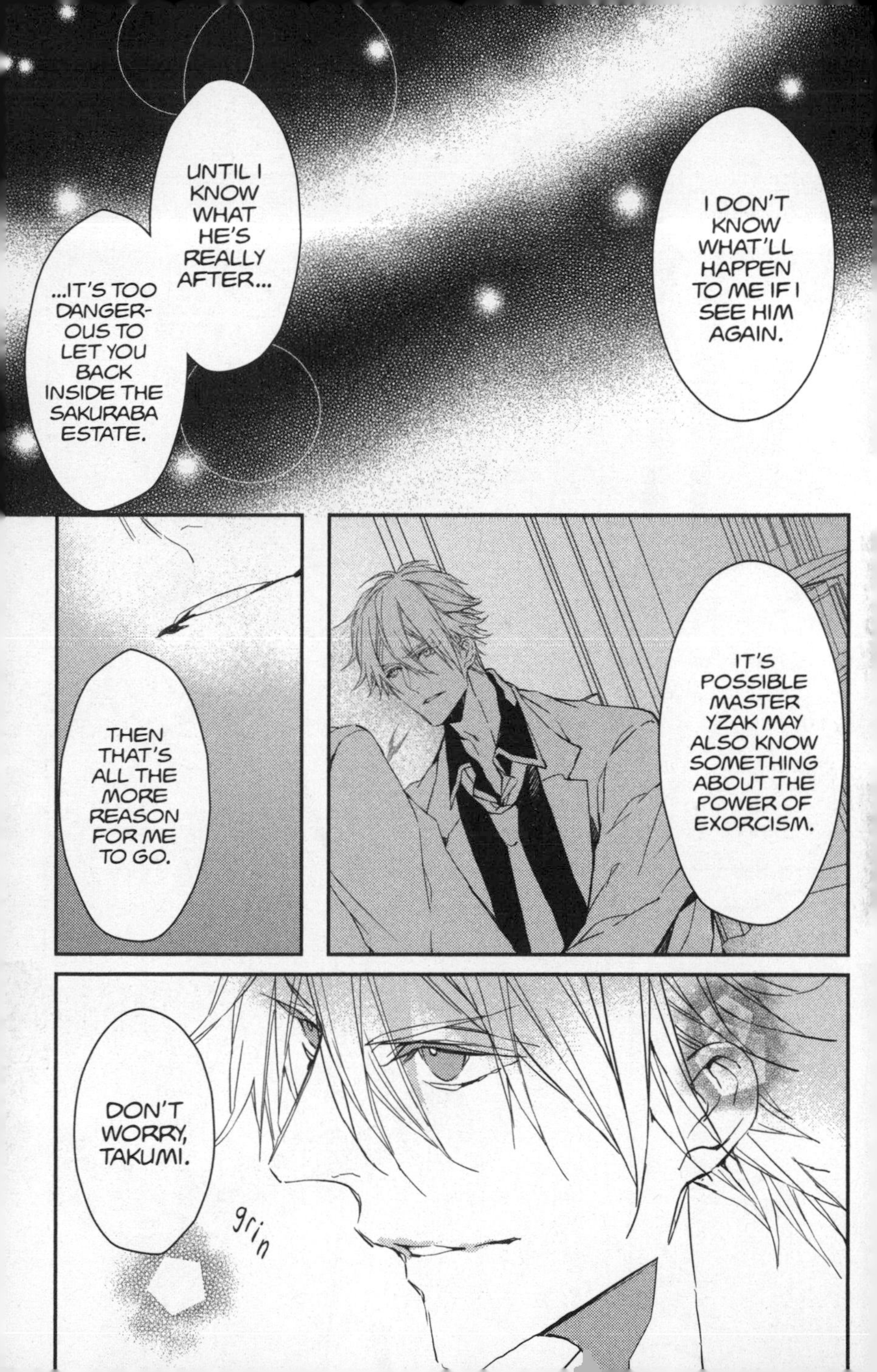
I DON'T KNOW WHAT'LL HAPPEN TO ME IF I SEE HIM AGAIN.
UNTIL I KNOW WHAT HE'S REALLY AFTER...
...IT'S TOO DANGER-OUS TO LET YOU BACK INSIDE THE SAKURABA ESTATE.
IT'S POSSIBLE MASTER YZAK MAY ALSO KNOW SOMETHING ABOUT THE POWER OF EXORCISM.
THEN THAT'S ALL THE MORE REASON FOR ME TO GO.
DON'T WORRY, TAKUMI.
grin

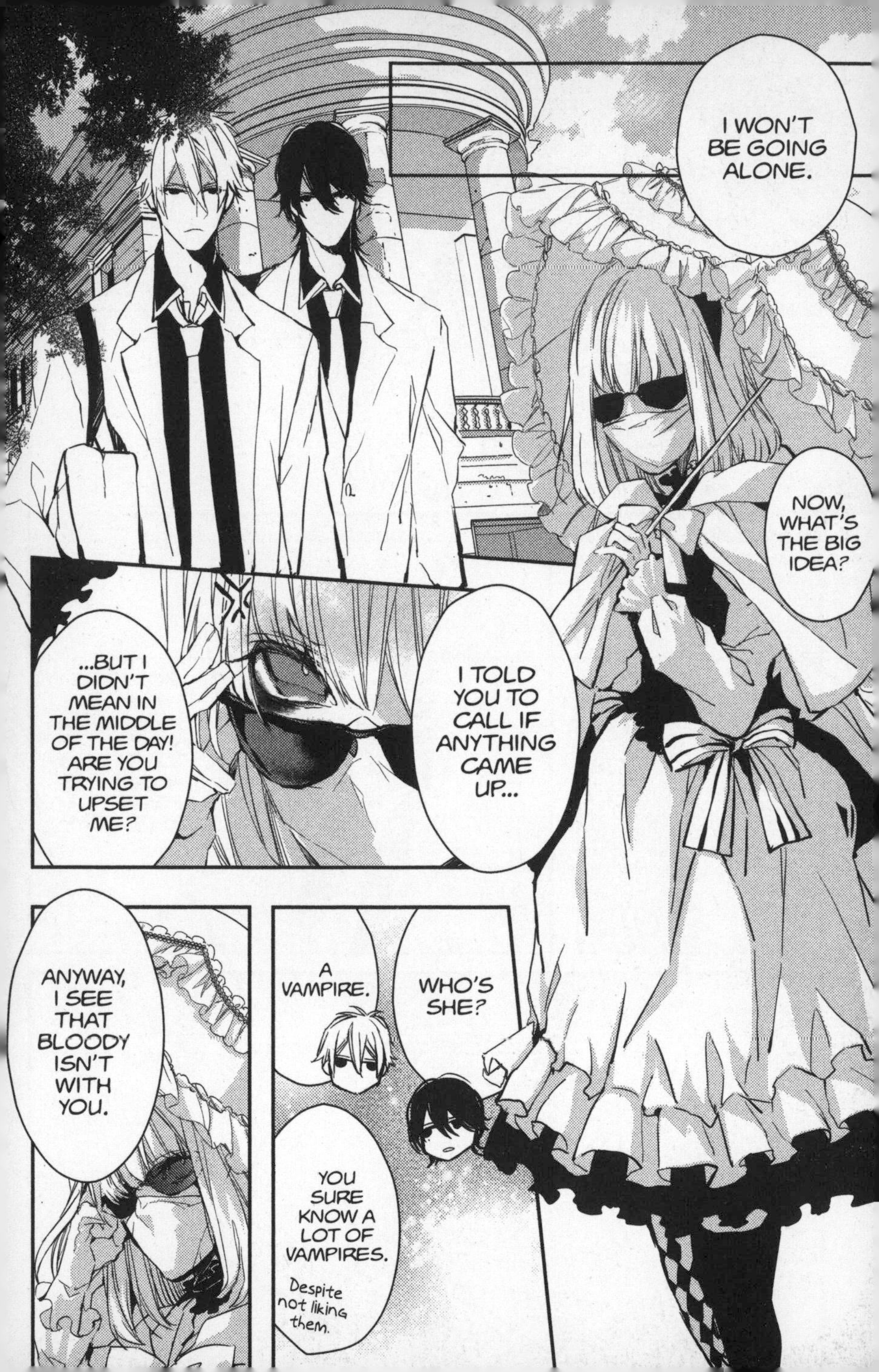
I WON'T BE GOING ALONE.
NOW, WHAT'S THE BIG IDEA?
I TOLD YOU TO CALL IF ANYTHING CAME UP...
...BUT I DIDN'T MEAN IN THE MIDDLE OF THE DAY! ARE YOU TRYING TO UPSET ME?
WHO'S SHE?
A VAMPIRE.
YOU SURE KNOW A LOT OF VAMPIRES.
Despite not liking them.
ANYWAY, I SEE THAT BLOODY ISN'T WITH YOU.

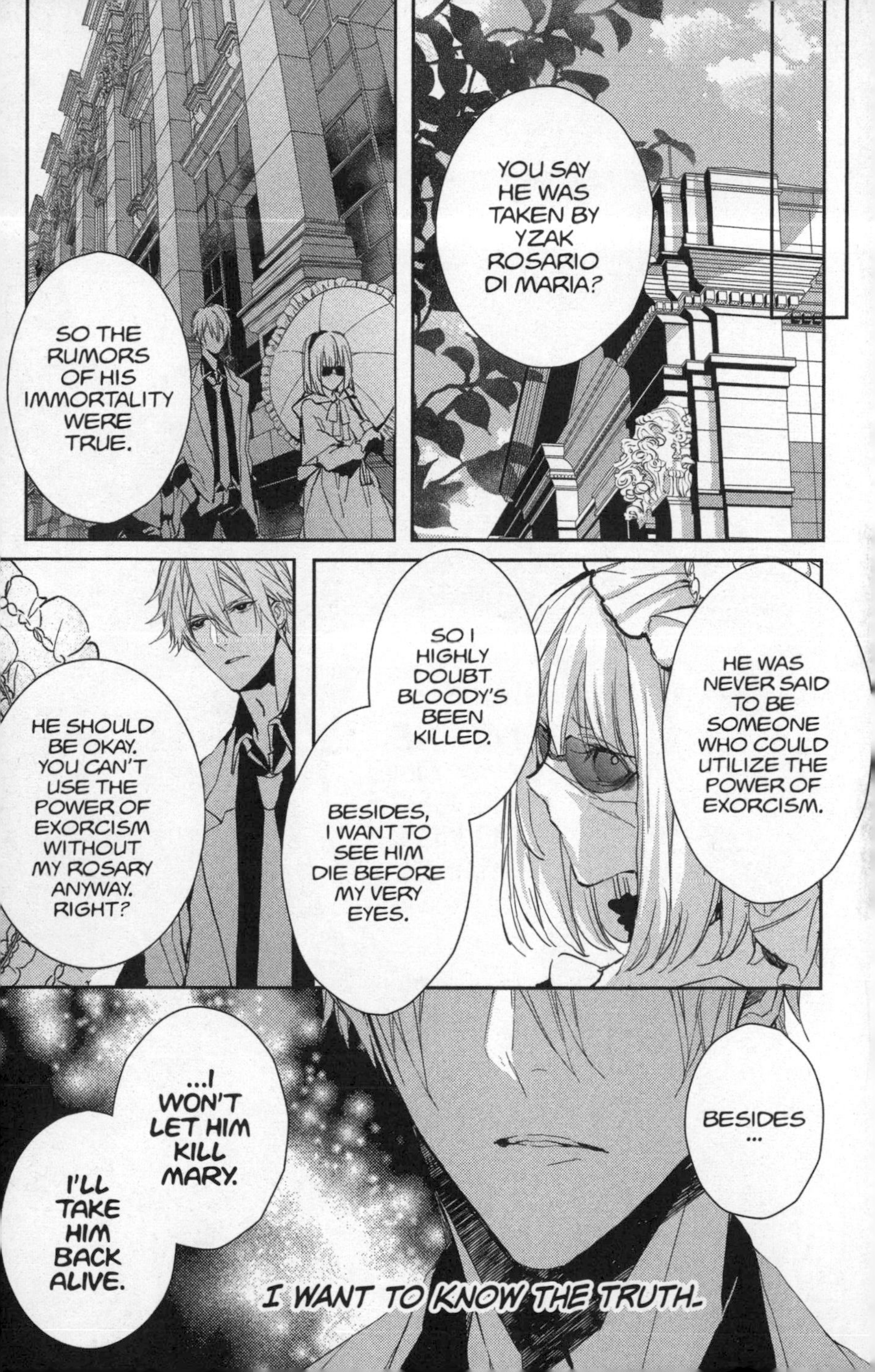
YOU SAY HE WAS TAKEN BY YZAK ROSARIO DI MARIA?
SO THE RUMORS OF HIS IMMORTALITY WERE TRUE.
HE WAS NEVER SAID TO BE SOMEONE WHO COULD UTILIZE THE POWER OF EXORCISM.
SO I HIGHLY DOUBT BLOODY'S BEEN KILLED.
BESIDES, I WANT TO SEE HIM DIE BEFORE MY VERY EYES.
HE SHOULD BE OKAY. YOU CAN'T USE THE POWER OF EXORCISM WITHOUT MY ROSARY ANYWAY. RIGHT?
BESIDES...
...I WON'T LET HIM KILL MARY.
I'LL TAKE HIM BACK ALIVE.
I WANT TO KNOW THE TRUTH.

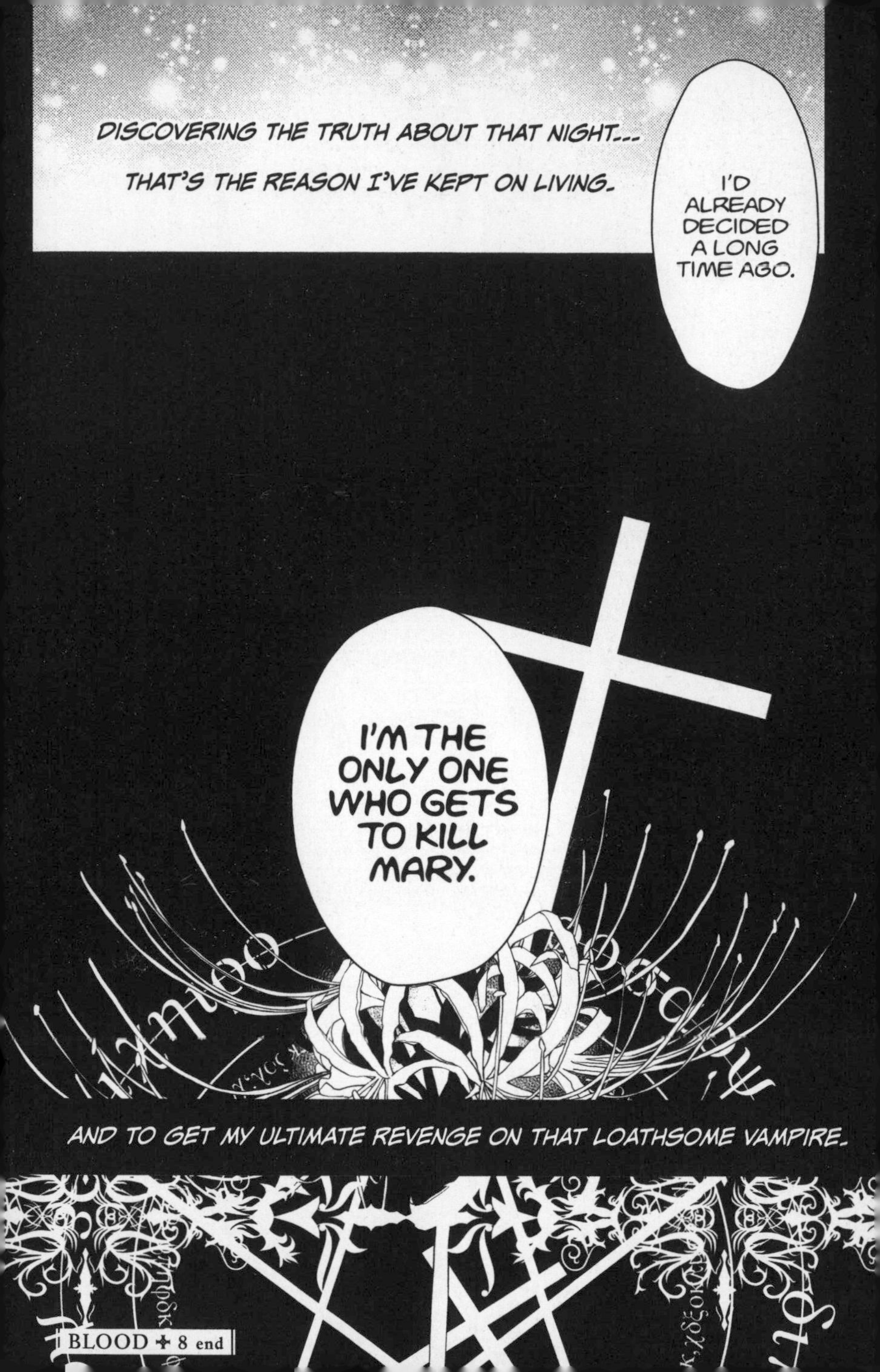
I'D ALREADY DECIDED A LONG TIME AGO.
DISCOVERING THE TRUTH ABOUT THAT NIGHT...
THAT'S THE REASON I'VE KEPT ON LIVING.
I'M THE ONLY ONE WHO GETS TO KILL MARY.
AND TO GET MY ULTIMATE REVENGE ON THAT LOATHSOME VAMPIRE.
BLOOD ✦ 8 end

Bloody+Mary

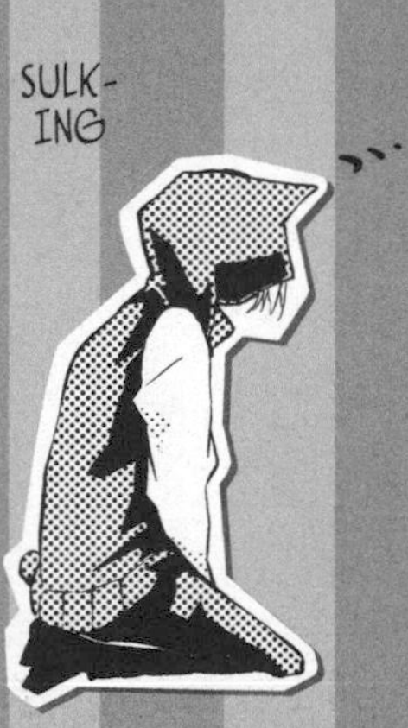
SULK-
ING

Postscript

Thank you for reading *Bloody Mary* volume 2! It's all thanks to you that I made it to the second volume. I also really appreciate all the feedback I got for volume 1. All I could see were its shortcomings, but I tried my best to make it at least somewhat entertaining.

I know it can get a little confusing with all the "Maria"s running around and how Mary isn't really "Mary," but I hope that you decide to stick around for volume 3.

HP http://sama.ciao.jp
Twitter samamiya

◁ Up next

Check out the joint manga I made with magazine *Yokohama Walker*, plus a spoof story that I got to draw as a bonus for the publisher ASUKA. My editor actually asked me if I'd draw it, but I drew this right after the chapters were first running in the magazine, so Maria looks so young! Now, I think he's too old looking...

SPECIAL THANKS

Mihoru, S-hon, H-saka, H-gawa, M-fuchi, T-sui, I-zaki, the material suppliers, Haruo, Sumida, Editor S and the designers.

Yokohama Walker
Sachiko Takatori, Haruka Kuriyama, Enterbank On, Taichi Saito (Studio Baku,) Shingo Suzuki (Meta+Maniera) and everyone else who was involved.

And thank you, the readers.

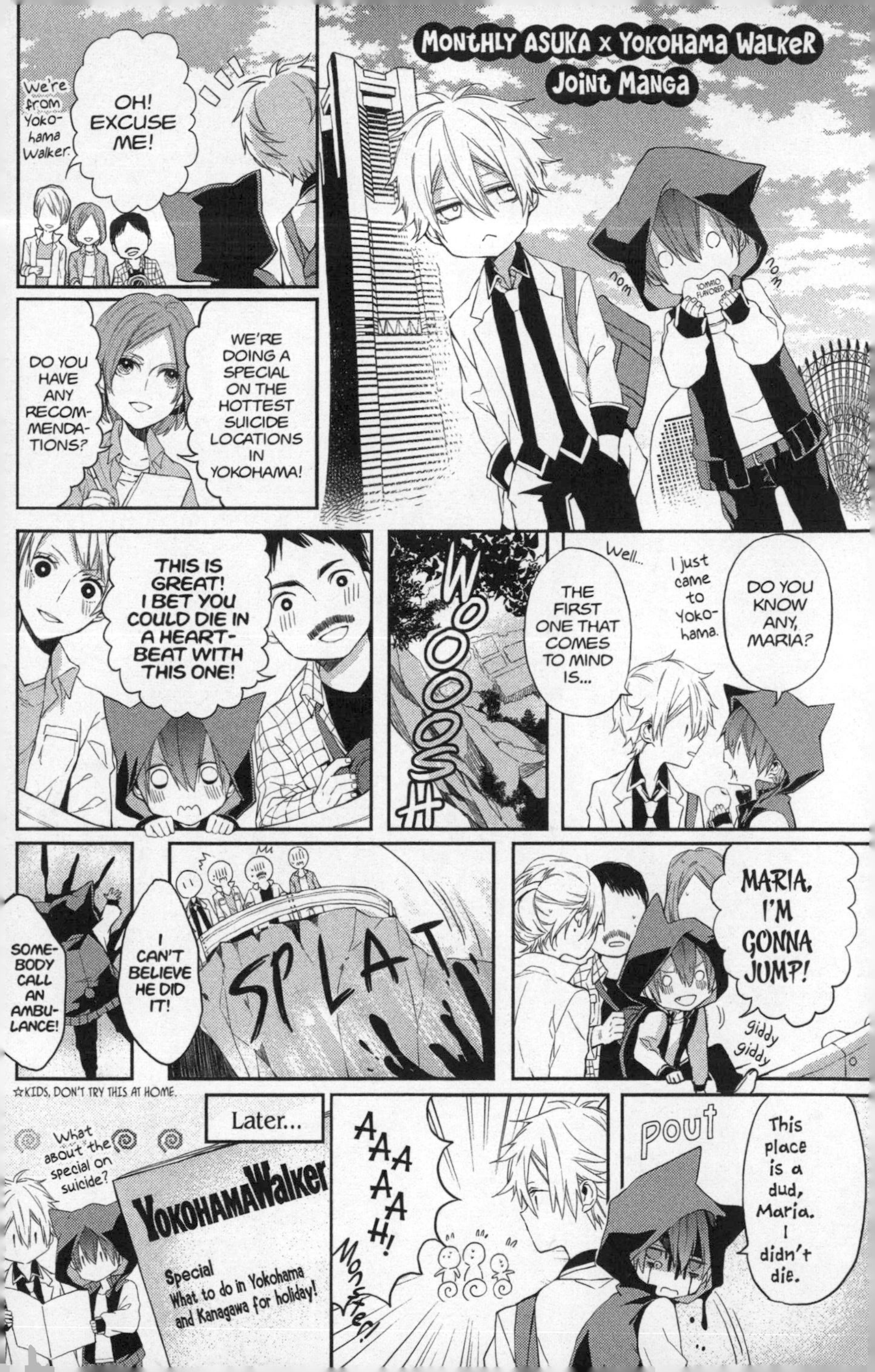

Monthly ASUKA x Yokohama Walker Joint Manga
nom nom
TOMATO FLAVORED
OH! EXCUSE ME!
We're from Yokohama Walker.
WE'RE DOING A SPECIAL ON THE HOTTEST SUICIDE LOCATIONS IN YOKOHAMA!
DO YOU HAVE ANY RECOMMENDATIONS?
DO YOU KNOW ANY, MARIA?
I just came to Yokohama.
Well...
THE FIRST ONE THAT COMES TO MIND IS...
WOOOOOSH
THIS IS GREAT! I BET YOU COULD DIE IN A HEARTBEAT WITH THIS ONE!
MARIA, I'M GONNA JUMP!
giddy giddy
SPLAT
I CAN'T BELIEVE HE DID IT!
SOMEBODY CALL AN AMBULANCE!
☆KIDS, DON'T TRY THIS AT HOME.
pout
This place is a dud, Maria. I didn't die.
AAAAAAH!
Monster!
Later...
What about the special on suicide?
YOKOHAMA Walker
Special
What to do in Yokohama and Kanagawa for holiday!

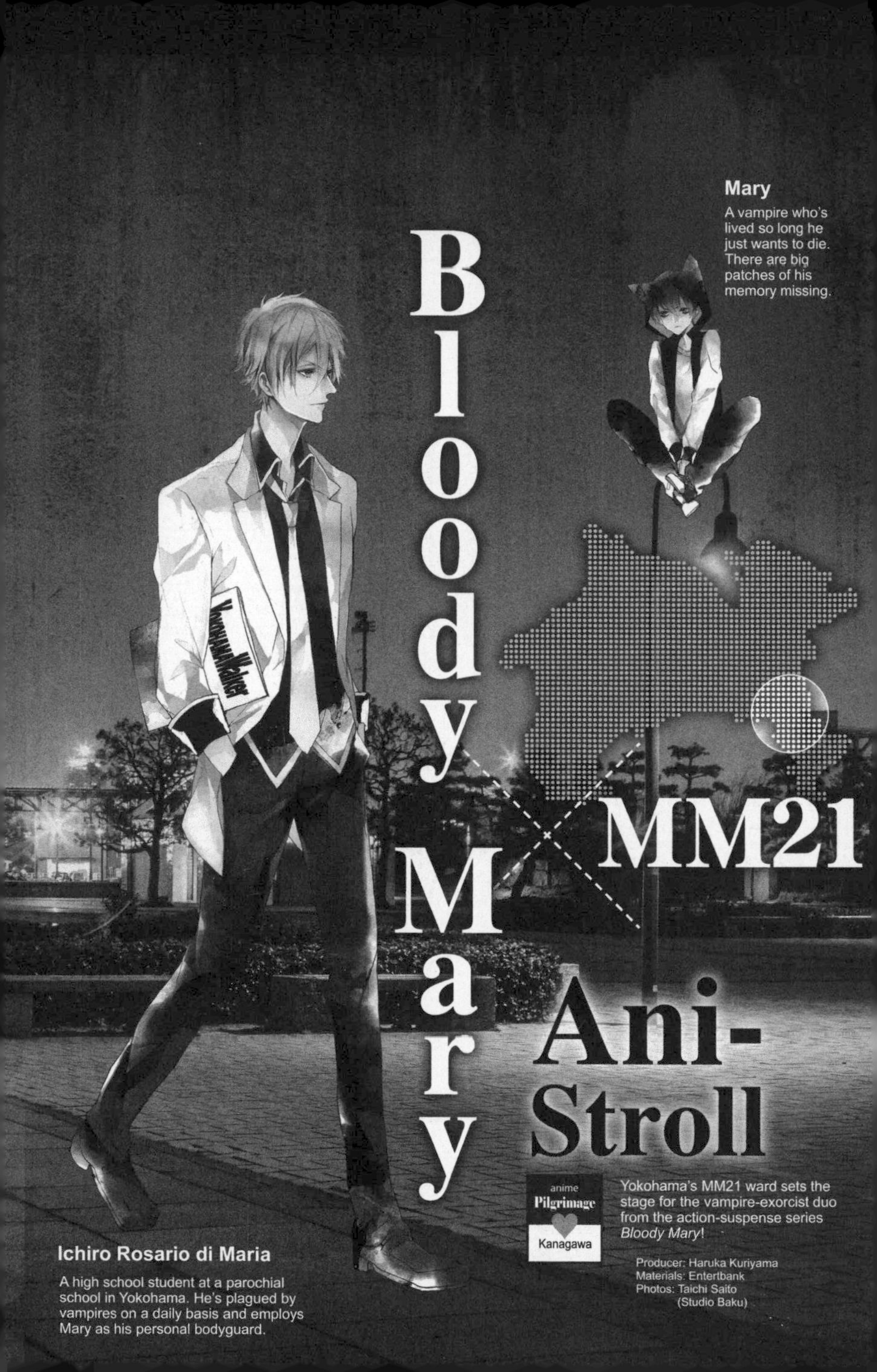
Bloody Mary × MM21 Ani-Stroll
Mary
A vampire who's lived so long he just wants to die. There are big patches of his memory missing.
Yokohama Walker
anime Pilgrimage Kanagawa
Yokohama's MM21 ward sets the stage for the vampire-exorcist duo from the action-suspense series Bloody Mary!
Producer: Haruka Kuriyama
Materials: Entertbank
Photos: Taichi Saito (Studio Baku)
Ichiro Rosario di Maria
A high school student at a parochial school in Yokohama. He's plagued by vampires on a daily basis and employs Mary as his personal bodyguard.

I made my beloved Yokohama the setting!

ASUKA

Author:
Akaza Samamiya

"I wanted to make Yokohama the setting for this story because I've lived here all my life and always wanted to use my beloved Yokohama as the backdrop to a story. I also felt that the exotic architecture and features of the city would match the gothic undertones of this vampire-exorcist story. In order to get the message across to readers, I featured key landmarks, such as Chinatown and Marine Tower. Next up in the story, we'll learn why Mary can't die, as well as why Maria is fixated on living. Get ready for some massive flashbacks!"

A Yokohama Red Brick Warehouse

In the very first scene when Maria is attacked by the vampires, this location was used as the backdrop.

B Bashamichi

A landmark known for its gas lanterns. Mary is seen sitting on top of one of those lanterns.

C Yokohama Kaikou Memorial Museum

When Mary runs away from Maria after refusing to drink his blood, the buildings of this location appear in the scene.

D Yokohama Marine Tower

When Maria meets Mary and gives Mary his name, this location is shown.

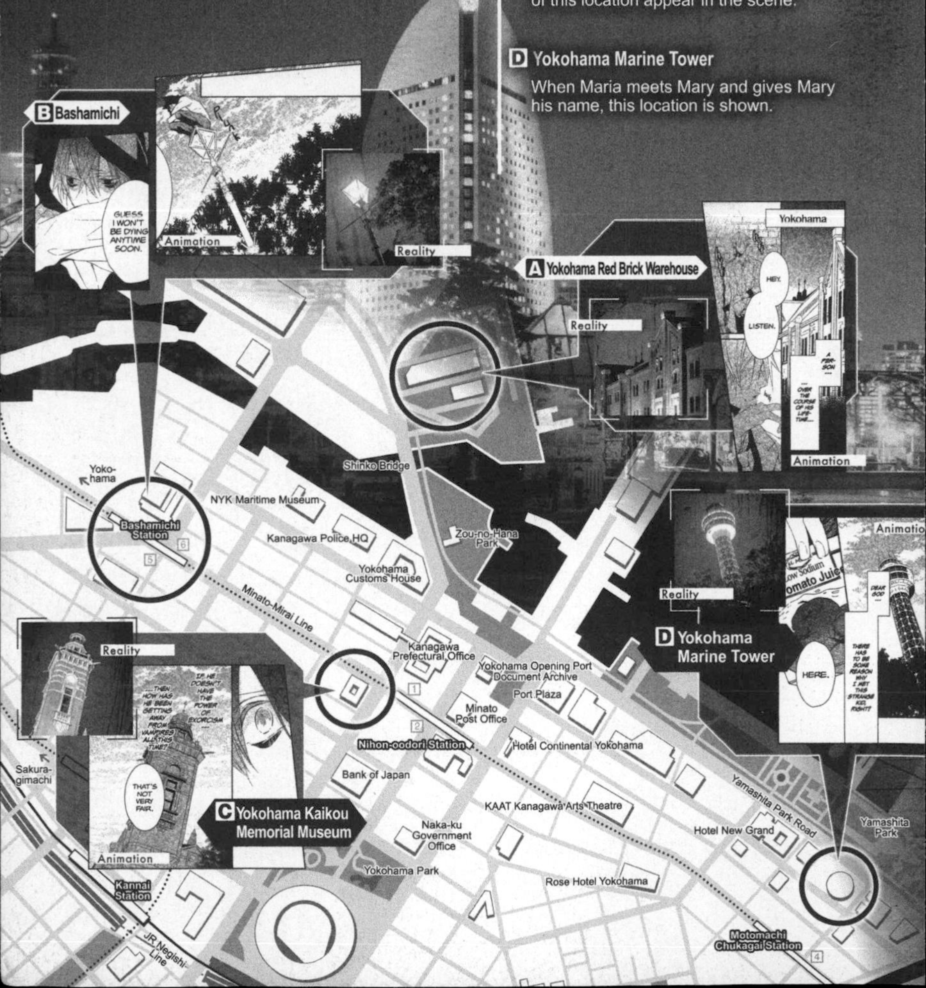

B Bashamichi
GUESS I WON'T BE DYING ANYTIME SOON.
Animation
Reality
A Yokohama Red Brick Warehouse
Yokohama
HEY.
LISTEN.
A PERSON...
...OVER THE COURSE OF HIS LIFETIME...
Reality
Animation
Yoko-hama
Bashamichi Station
NYK Maritime Museum
Shinko Bridge
Kanagawa Police HQ
Zou-no-Hana Park
Yokohama Customs House
Minato-Mirai Line
Reality
Animation
Low Sodium Tomato Juice
DEAR GOD
HERE.
THERE HAS TO BE SOME REASON WHY I MET THIS STRANGE KID, RIGHT?
D Yokohama Marine Tower
Reality
IF HE DOESN'T HAVE THE POWER OF EXORCISM...
...THEN HOW HAS HE BEEN GETTING AWAY FROM VAMPIRES ALL THIS TIME?
THAT'S NOT VERY FAIR.
Animation
C Yokohama Kaikou Memorial Museum
Kanagawa Prefectural Office
Yokohama Opening Port Document Archive
Port Plaza
Minato Post Office
Nihon-oodori Station
Hotel Continental Yokohama
Sakura-gimachi
Bank of Japan
KAAT Kanagawa Arts Theatre
Yamashita Park Road
Naka-ku Government Office
Hotel New Grand
Yamashita Park
Yokohama Park
Kannai Station
Rose Hotel Yokohama
JR Negishi Line
Motomachi Chukagai Station

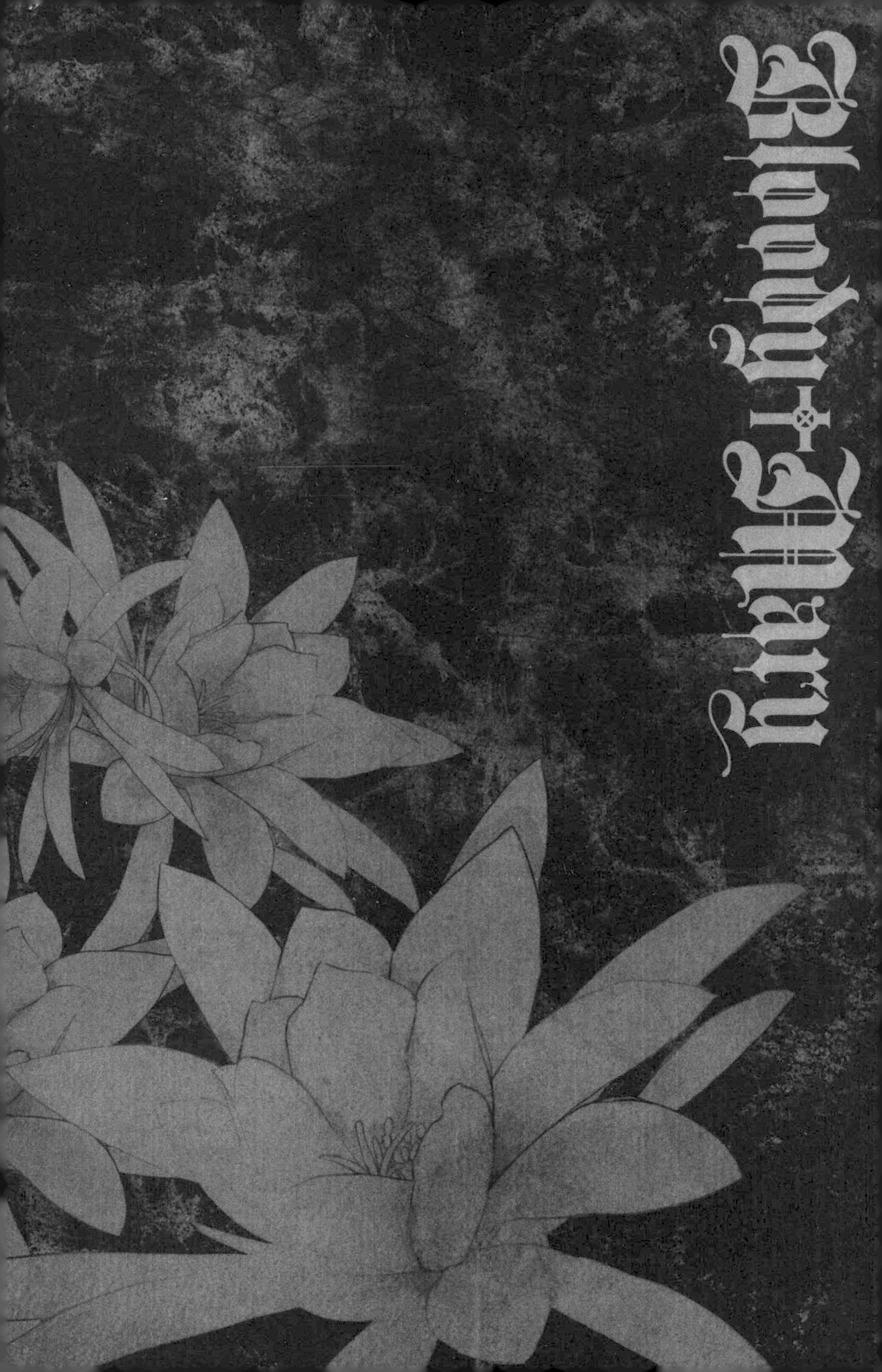
Bloody+Mary

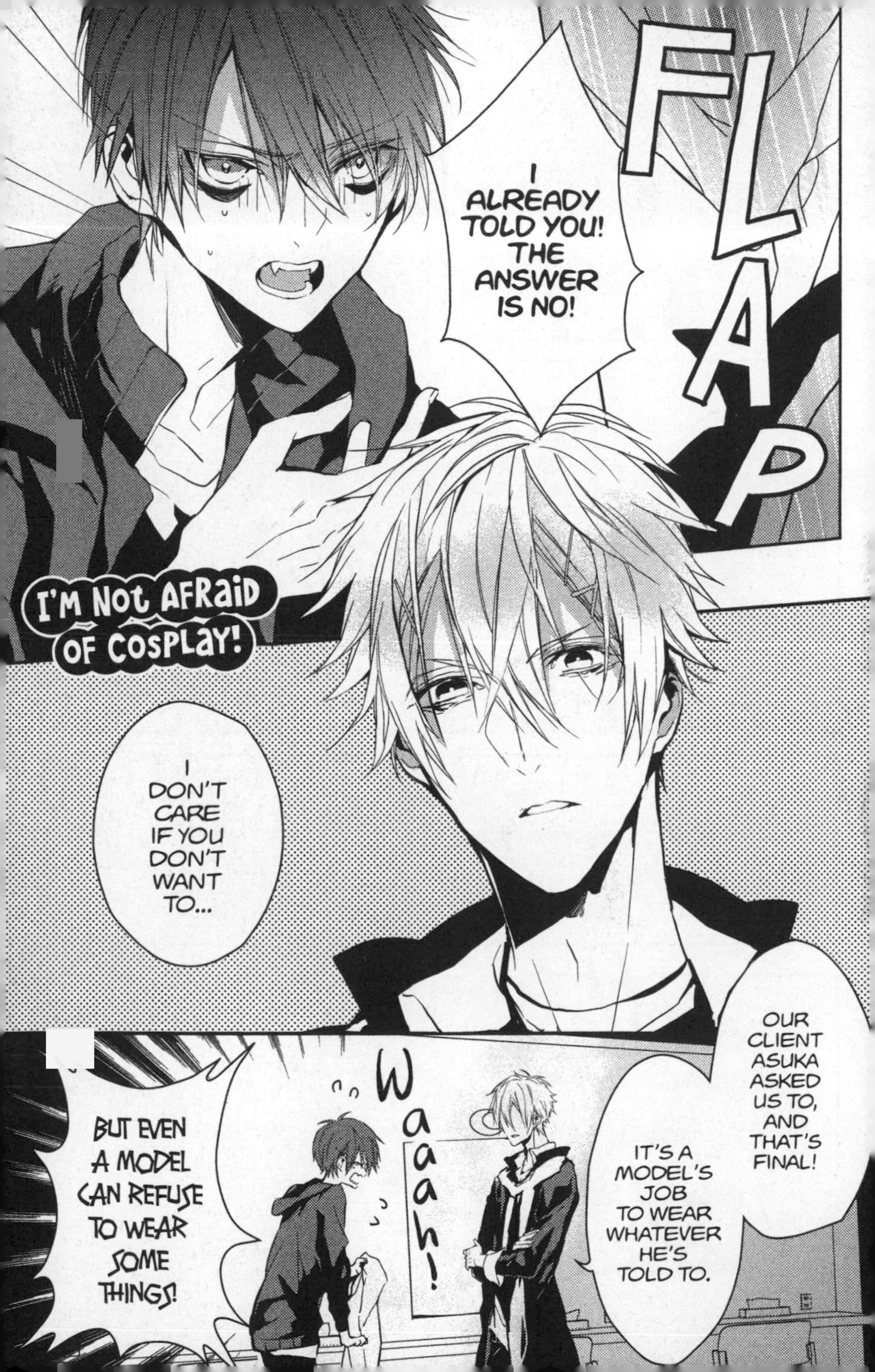
FLAP
I ALREADY TOLD YOU! THE ANSWER IS NO!
I'M Not AFRAID of COSPLAY!
I DON'T CARE IF YOU DON'T WANT TO...
OUR CLIENT ASUKA ASKED US TO, AND THAT'S FINAL!
IT'S A MODEL'S JOB TO WEAR WHATEVER HE'S TOLD TO.
Waaah!
BUT EVEN A MODEL CAN REFUSE TO WEAR SOME THINGS!

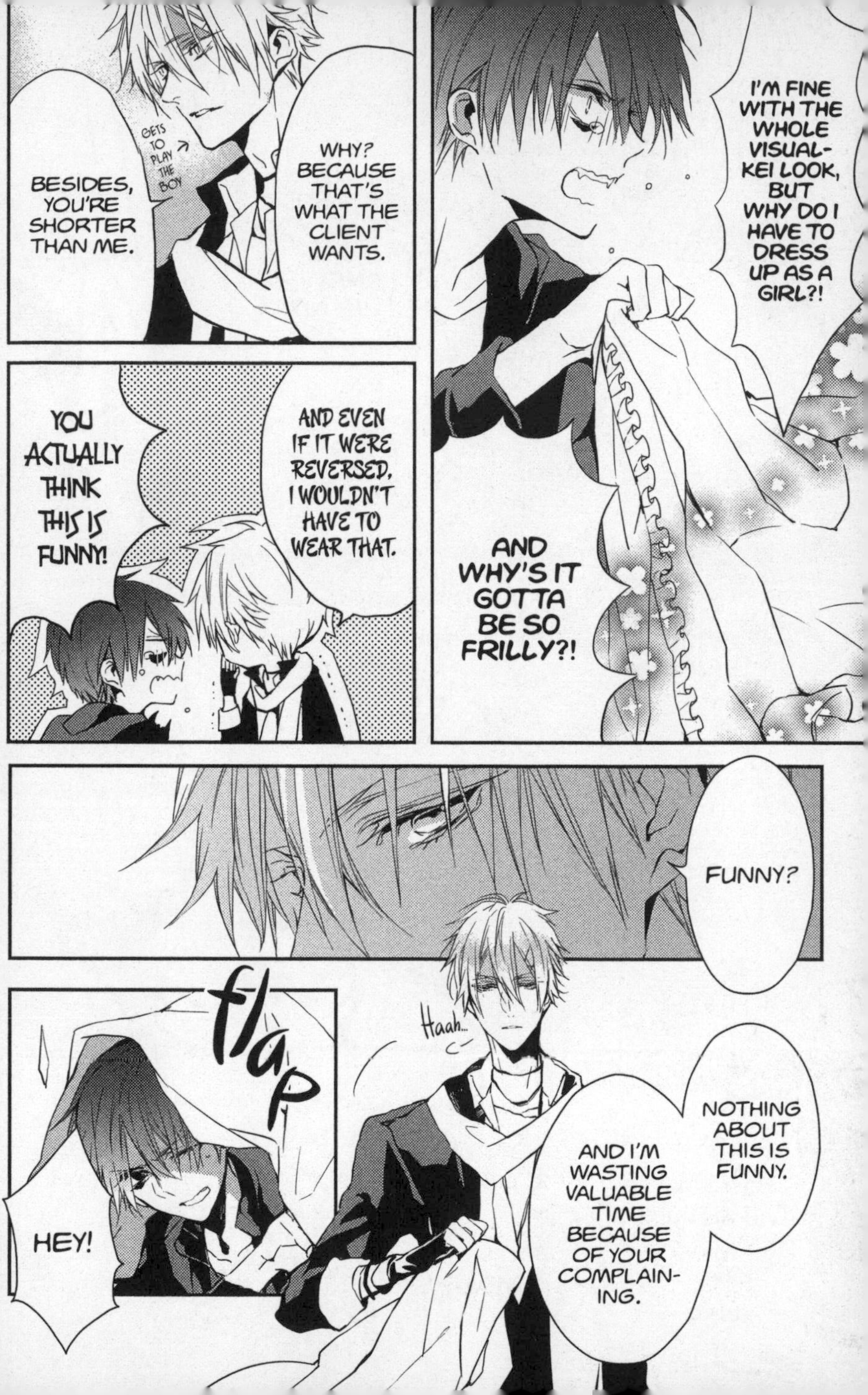
I'M FINE WITH THE WHOLE VISUAL-KEI LOOK, BUT WHY DO I HAVE TO DRESS UP AS A GIRL?!
AND WHY'S IT GOTTA BE SO FRILLY?!
WHY? BECAUSE THAT'S WHAT THE CLIENT WANTS.
GETS TO PLAY THE BOY
BESIDES, YOU'RE SHORTER THAN ME.
AND EVEN IF IT WERE REVERSED, I WOULDN'T HAVE TO WEAR THAT.
YOU ACTUALLY THINK THIS IS FUNNY!
FUNNY?
Haah...
flap
NOTHING ABOUT THIS IS FUNNY.
AND I'M WASTING VALUABLE TIME BECAUSE OF YOUR COMPLAIN-ING.
HEY!

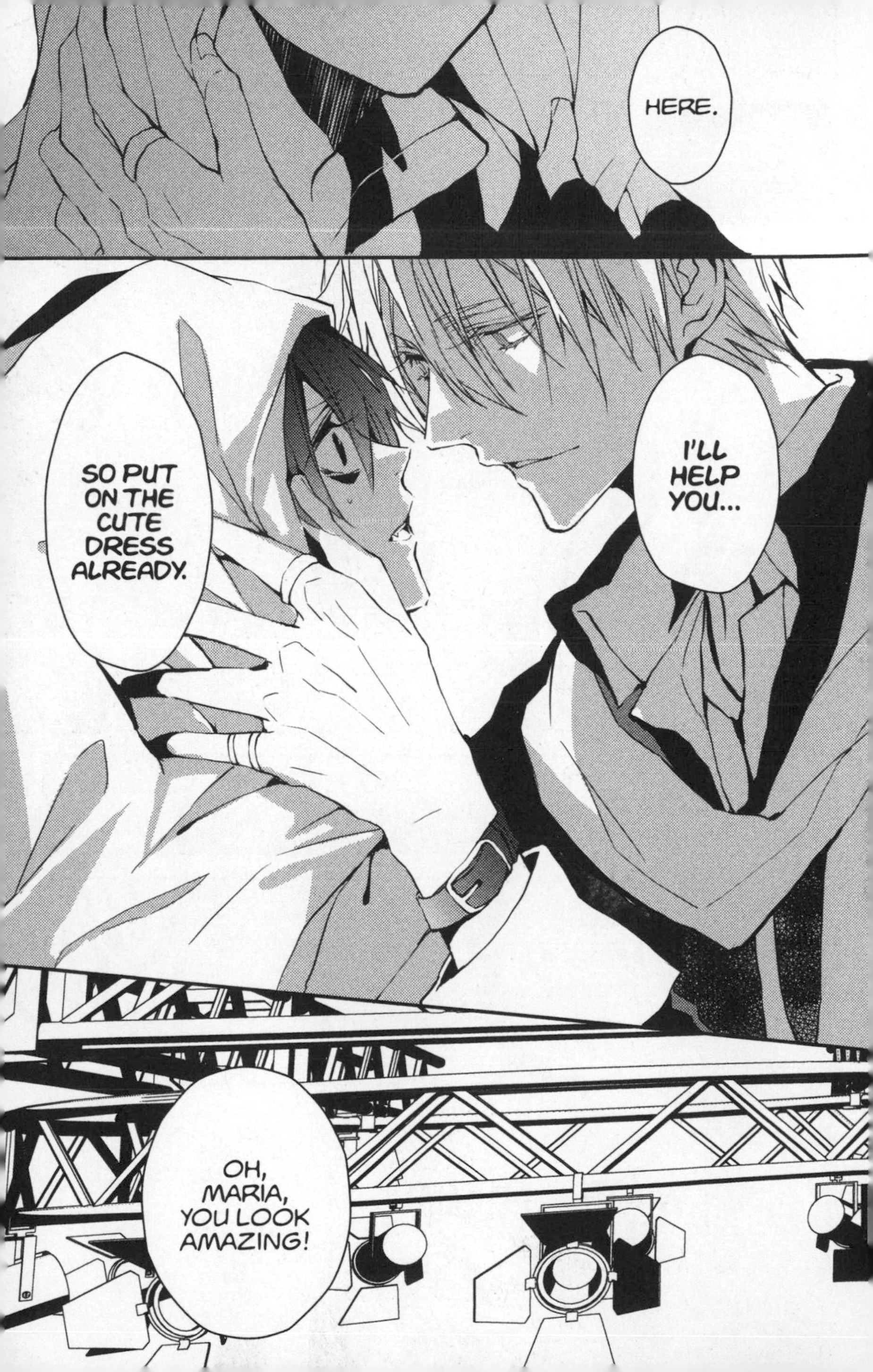
HERE.
I'LL HELP YOU...
SO PUT ON THE CUTE DRESS ALREADY.
OH, MARIA, YOU LOOK AMAZING!

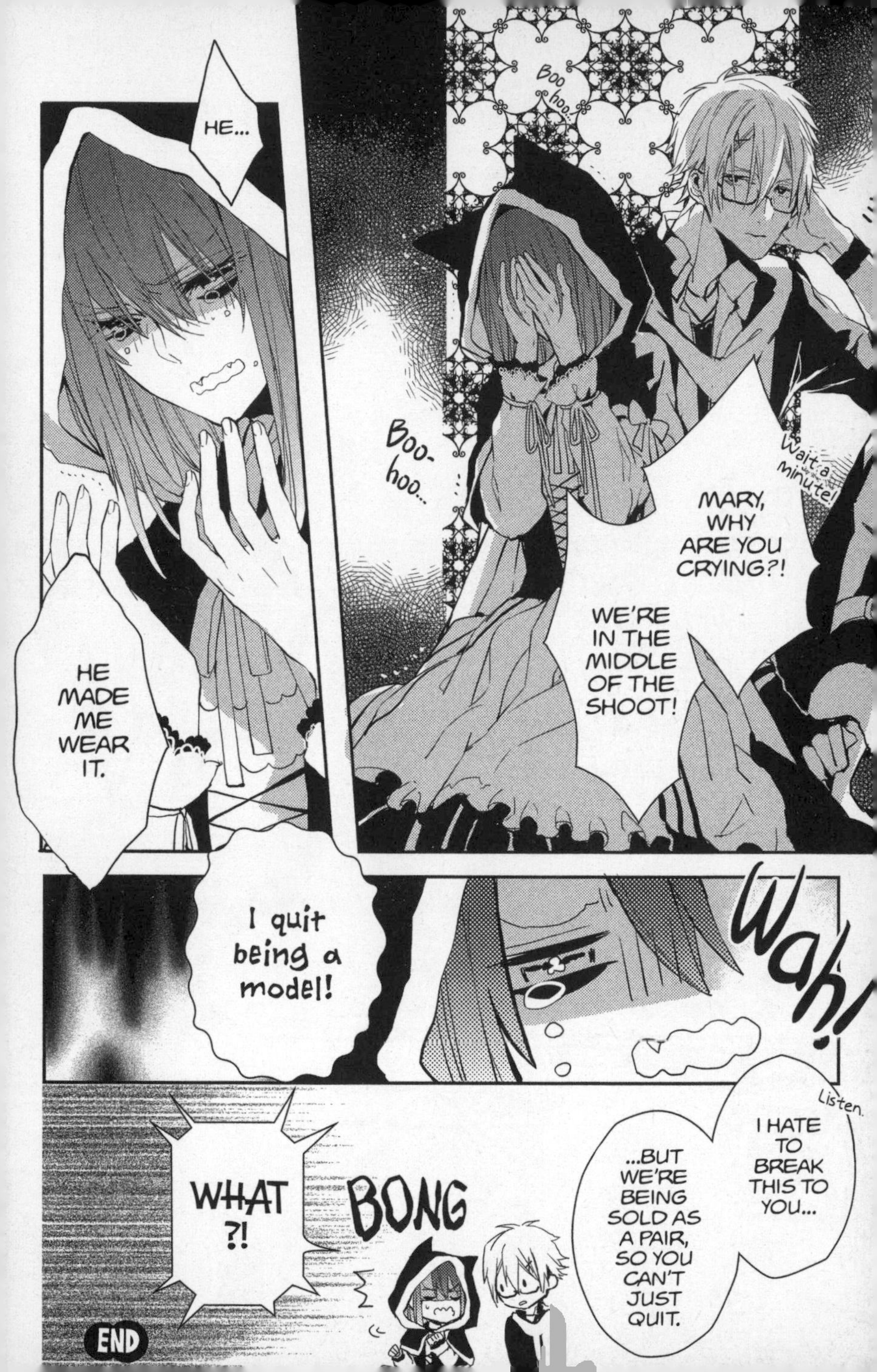
Boo hoo...
Boo-hoo...
Wait a minute!
MARY, WHY ARE YOU CRYING?!
WE'RE IN THE MIDDLE OF THE SHOOT!
HE...
HE MADE ME WEAR IT.
Wah!
I quit being a model!
Listen.
I HATE TO BREAK THIS TO YOU...
...BUT WE'RE BEING SOLD AS A PAIR, SO YOU CAN'T JUST QUIT.
BONG
WHAT?!
END

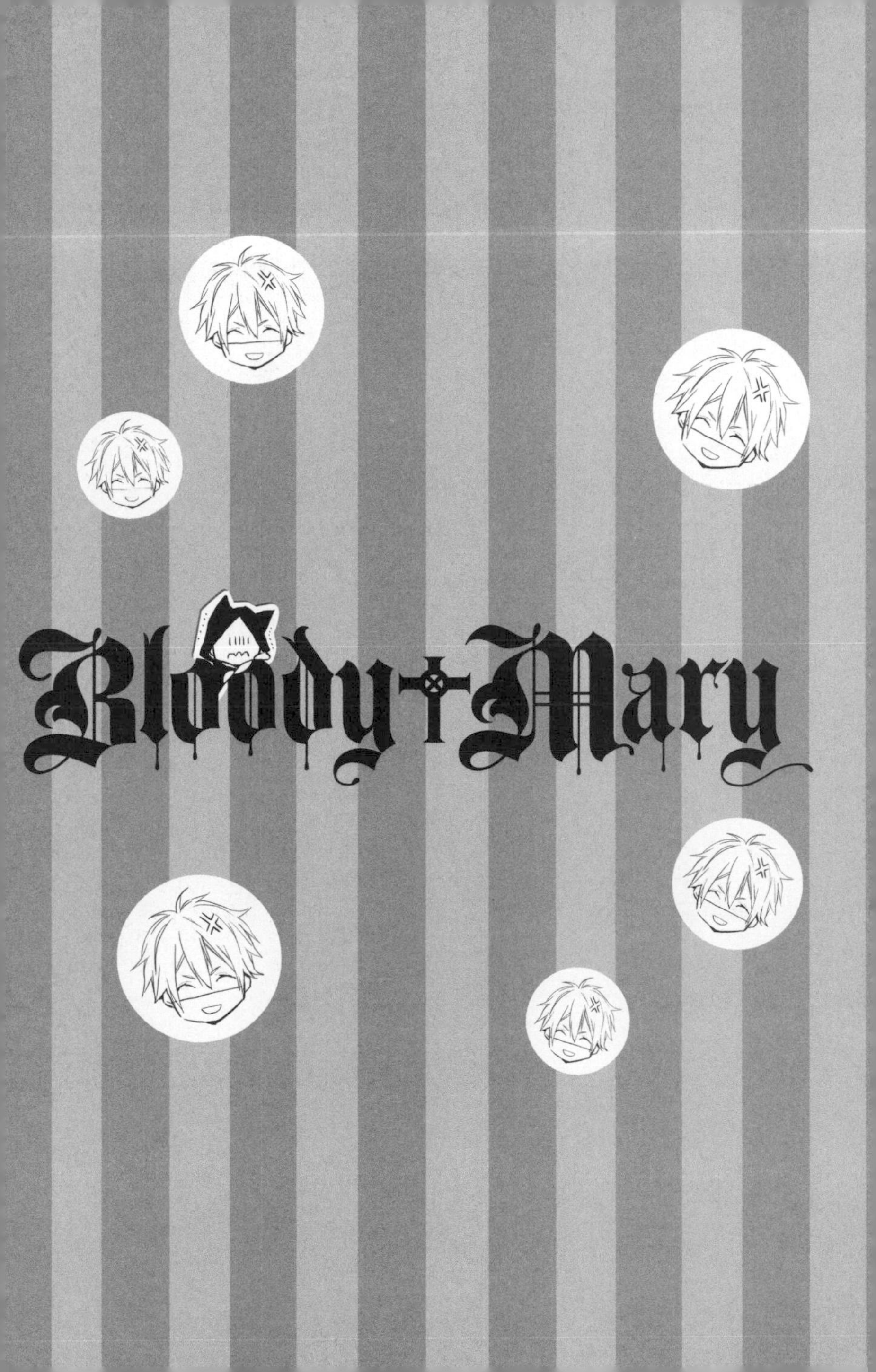
Bloody+Mary

Bloody Mary Character Designs

Bloody Mary

After it was decided that I would do a vampire story, we held a meeting in a restaurant that had a Bloody Mary on the menu. Right then and there, I decided to use that as the story title and main character's name. That's where everything started. All that was left was coming up with having an exorcist as his co-protagonist. (At first, they were both going to be vampires.)

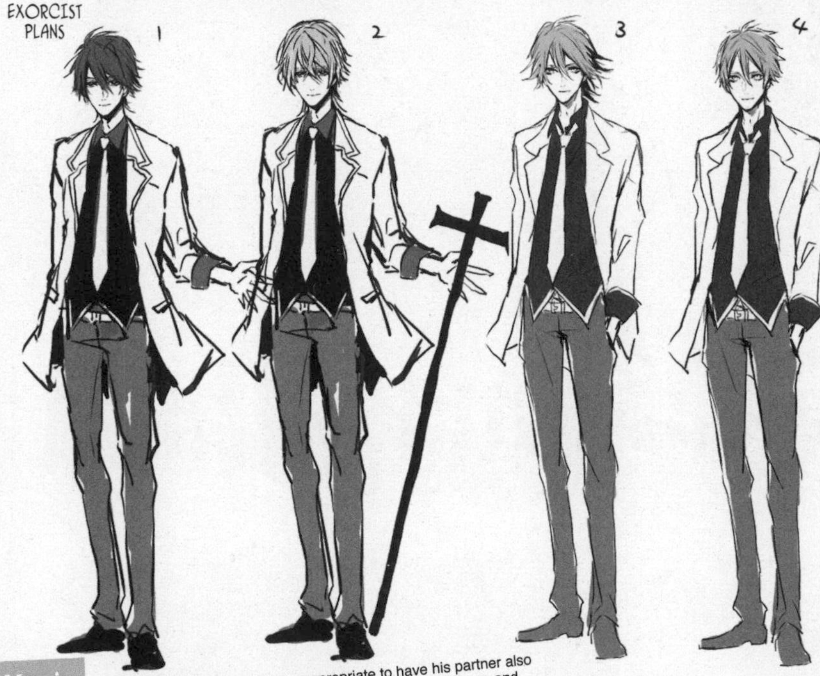
EXORCIST PLANS
1
2
3
4

Maria

Since "Mary" is a girl's name, I thought it'd be appropriate to have his partner also have a girl's name. Maria's name of "di Maria" comes from a soccer player, and "Ichiro" comes from a baseball player. Considering how physically weak he is, I doubt he'd actually enjoy either of these sports.

I was stuck on #2 for a while but eventually decided on #4. The length of his hair is somewhere between #1 and #4.

Kowtow

This was the very first thing I envisioned Mary doing. I seriously mean it when I say that I wanted the story to start with an image of him doing this.

At first, I imagined Mary spending loads on devices to commit suicide. In the actual story, Mary doesn't even use a computer.

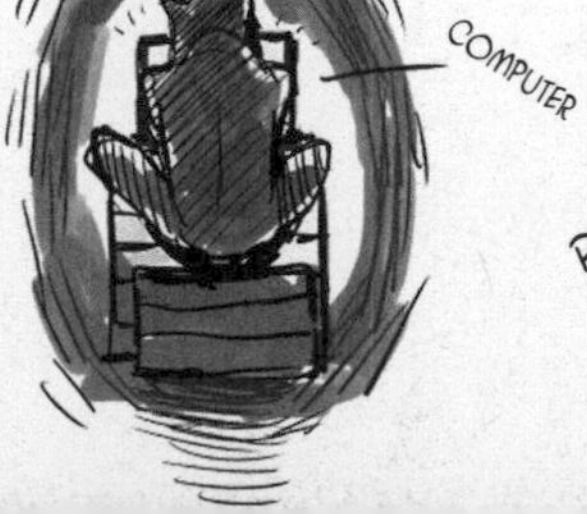
COMPUTER

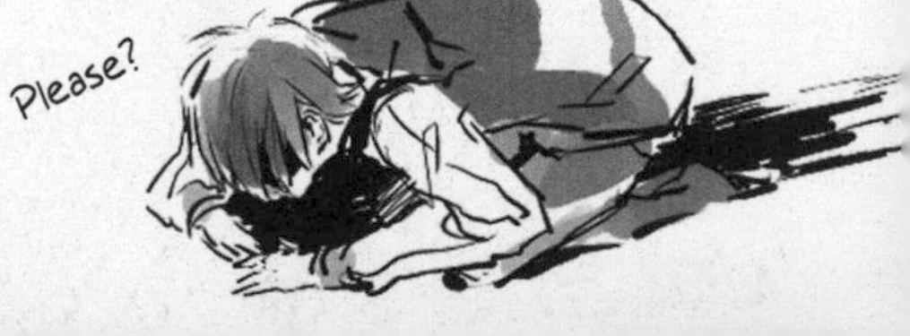
Um...
W-would you kindly kill me?
Please?

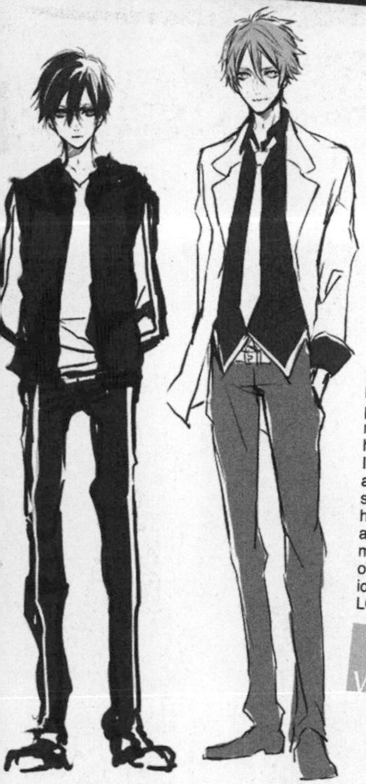

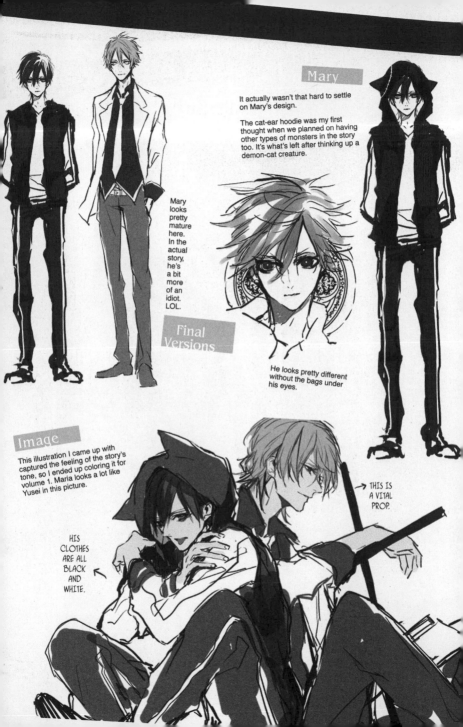

Mary

It actually wasn't that hard to settle on Mary's design.

The cat-ear hoodie was my first thought when we planned on having other types of monsters in the story too. It's what's left after thinking up a demon-cat creature.

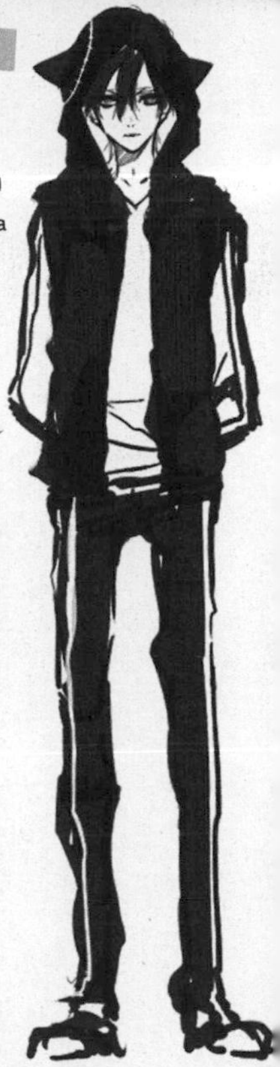

Mary looks pretty mature here. In the actual story, he's a bit more of an idiot. LOL.

Final Versions

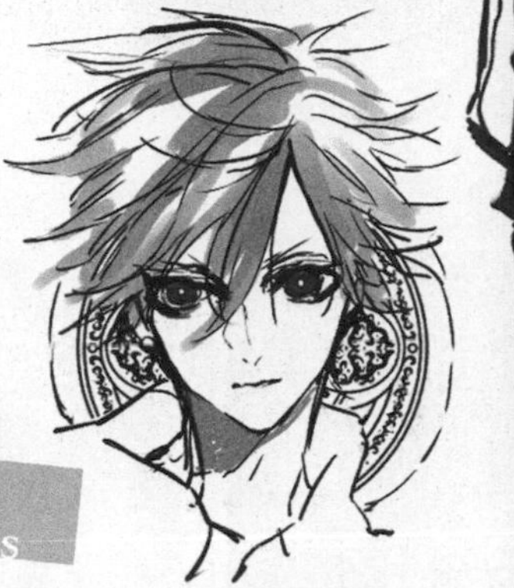

He looks pretty different without the bags under his eyes.

Image

This illustration I came up with captured the feeling of the story's tone, so I ended up coloring it for volume 1. Maria looks a lot like Yusei in this picture.

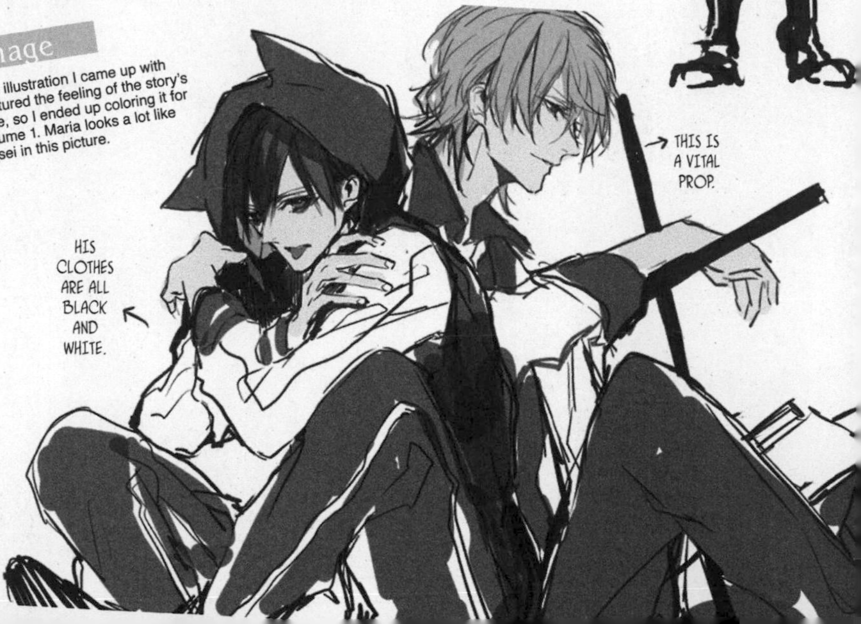
THIS IS A VITAL PROP.
HIS CLOTHES ARE ALL BLACK AND WHITE.

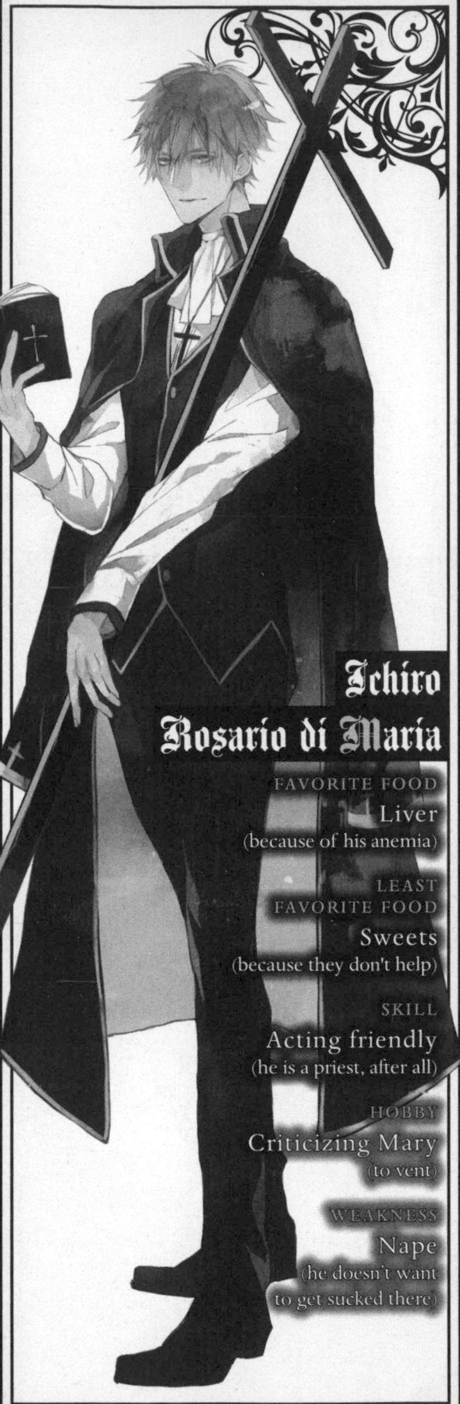
Ichiro
Rosario di Maria
FAVORITE FOOD
Liver
(because of his anemia)
LEAST FAVORITE FOOD
Sweets
(because they don't help)
SKILL
Acting friendly
(he is a priest, after all)
HOBBY
Criticizing Mary
(to vent)
WEAKNESS
Nape
(he doesn't want to get sucked there)

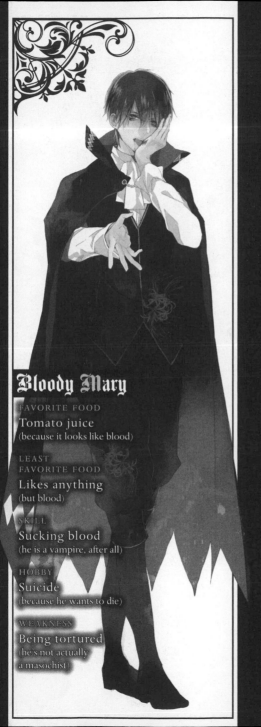

Bloody Mary

FAVORITE FOOD
Tomato juice
(because it looks like blood)

**LEAST
FAVORITE FOOD**
Likes anything
(but blood)

SKILL
Sucking blood
(he is a vampire, after all)

HOBBY
Suicide
(because he wants to die)

WEAKNESS
Being tortured
(he's not actually
a masochist)

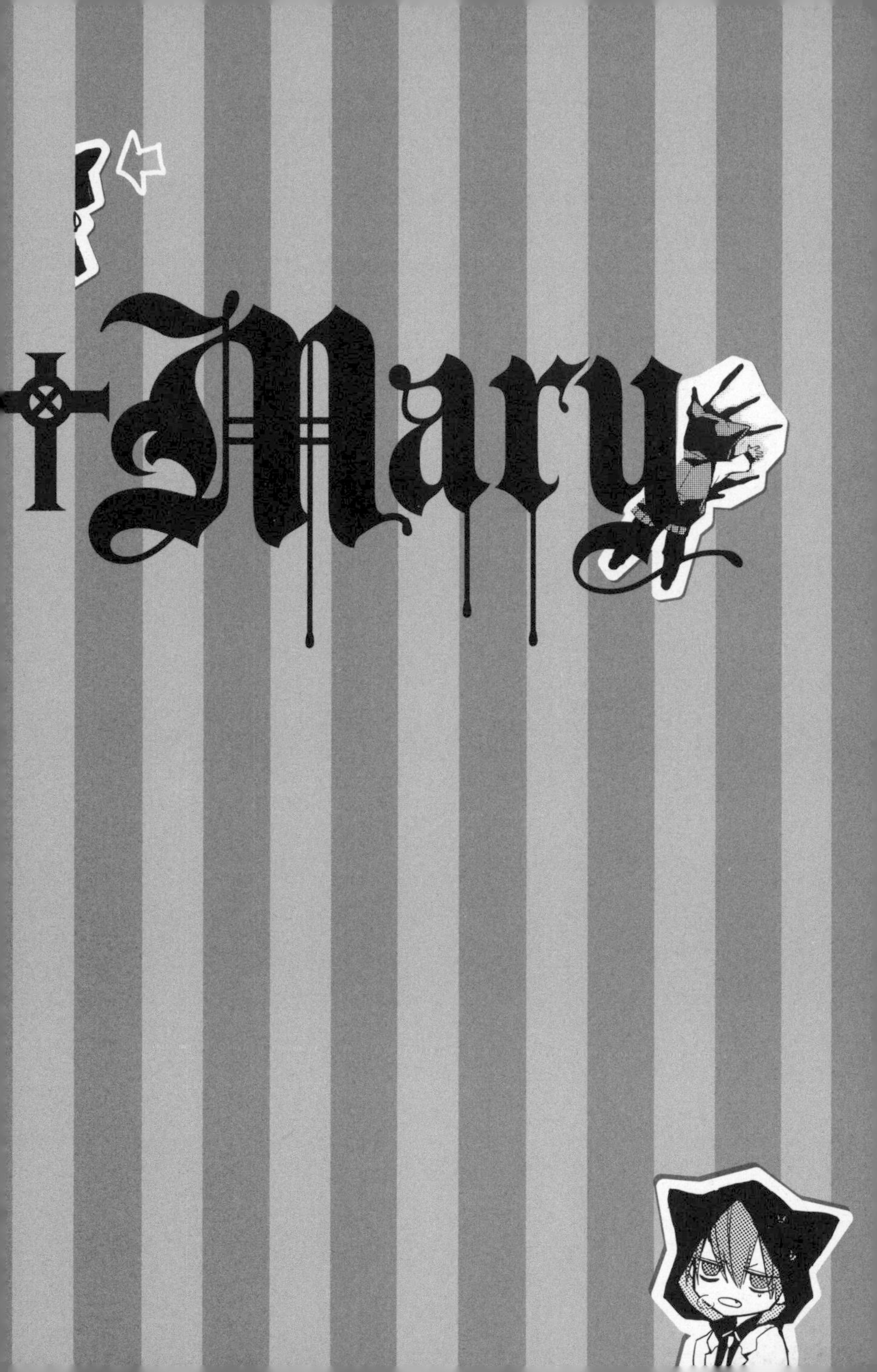
Mary

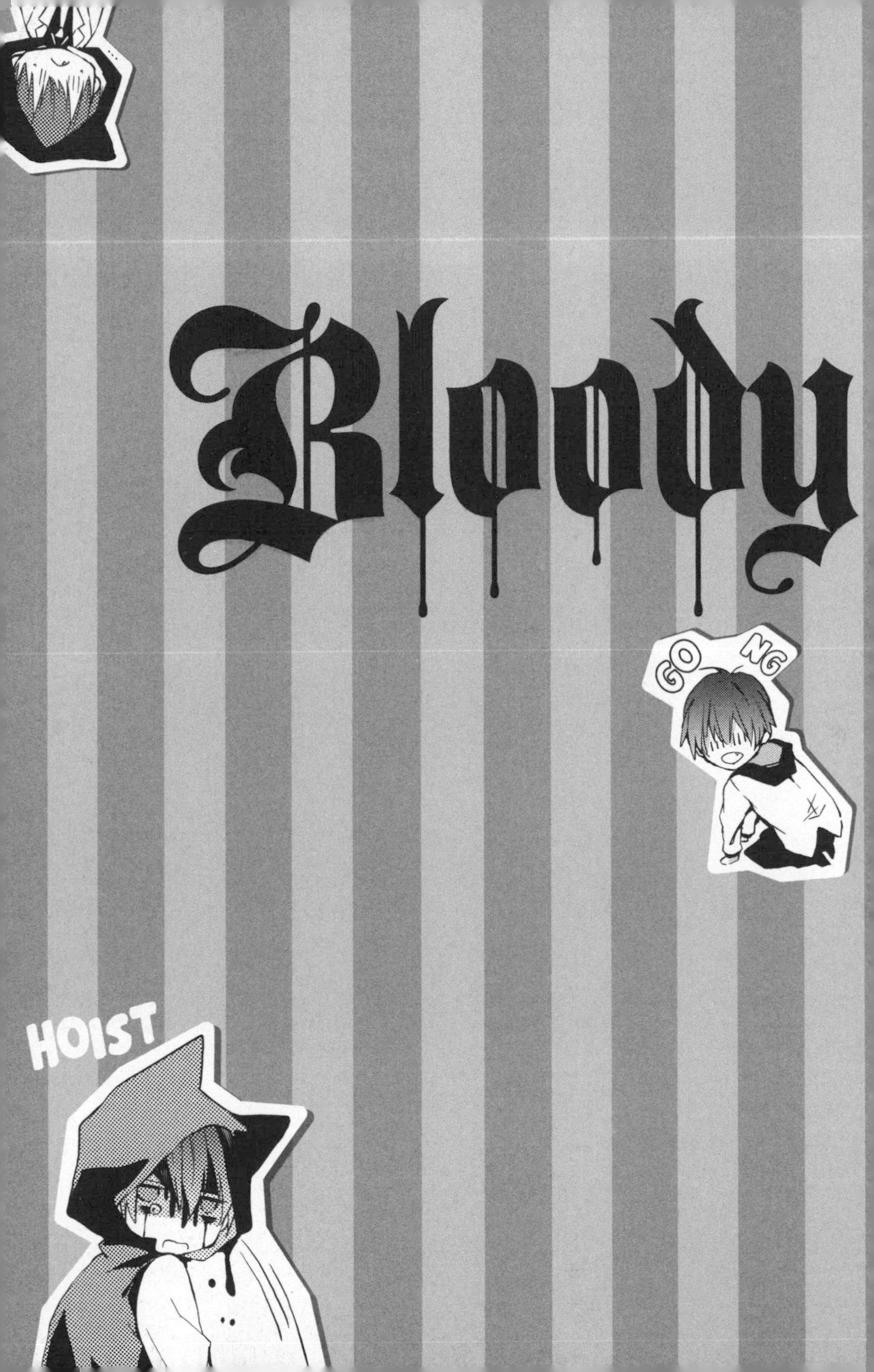
Bloody
GO NG
HOIST

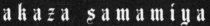

akaza samamiya

Born November 7, Cancer, blood type B.
Because I love oyster shells but
hate saltwort, I was able to safely get
volume 2 out! Thank you very much.
I hope you enjoy it!

Bloody Mary
Volume 2
Shojo Beat Edition

story and art by Akaza Samamiya

translation Katherine Schilling
touch-up art & lettering Sabrina Heep
design Fawn Lau
editor Erica Yee

BLOODY MARY Volume 2
© Akaza SAMAMIYA 2014
Edited by KADOKAWA SHOTEN
First published in Japan in 2014 by KADOKAWA
CORPORATION, Tokyo.
English translation rights arranged with KADOKAWA
CORPORATION, Tokyo.

Printed in the U.S.A.

Published by VIZ Media, LLC
P.O. Box 77010
San Francisco, CA 94107

10 9 8 7 6 5 4 3 2 1
First printing, March 2016

stop

YOU MAY BE READING THE
wrong way

IT'S TRUE: In keeping with the original Japanese comic format, this book reads from right to left—so action, sound effects and word balloons are completely reversed. This preserves the orientation of the original artwork—plus, it's fun! Check out the diagram shown here to get the hang of things, and then turn to the other side of the book to get started!

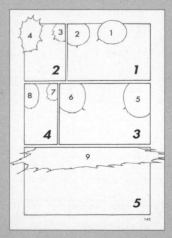